Postal Systems in the Pre-Modern Islamic V

Adam Silverstein's book offers a fascinating account
communication employed in the Near East from pre-
Mamluk period. Postal systems were set up by rulers in o
vast tracts of land. These systems, invented centuries before steam-
enabled the swift and efficient circulation of different commodities – from people
horses to exotic fruits and ice – and, of course, news and letters. As the correspondence transported often included confidential reports from a ruler's provinces, such postal systems doubled as espionage networks through which news reached the central authorities quickly enough to allow a timely reaction to events. The book sheds light not only on the role of communications technology in Islamic history, but also on how nomadic culture contributed to empire-building in the Near East, and the ways in which the nascent Islamic state distinguished itself from the Byzantine and Sasanid empires that preceded it. This is a long-awaited contribution to the history of pre-modern communications systems in the Near Eastern world.

ADAM SILVERSTEIN is Lecturer in Islamic History at the Oriental Institute, University of Oxford.

Cambridge Studies in Islamic Civilisation

Published titles in the series are listed at the back of the book

Postal Systems in the Pre-Modern Islamic World

ADAM J. SILVERSTEIN

The Oriental Institute, University of Oxford

CAMBRIDGE
UNIVERSITY PRESS

CAMBRIDGE UNIVERSITY PRESS
Cambridge, New York, Melbourne, Madrid, Cape Town, Singapore,
São Paulo, Delhi, Dubai, Tokyo, Mexico City

Cambridge University Press
The Edinburgh Building, Cambridge CB2 8RU, UK

Published in the United States of America by Cambridge University Press, New York

www.cambridge.org
Information on this title: www.cambridge.org/9780521147613

First published 2007
First paperback printing 2010

A catalogue record for this publication is available from the British Library

ISBN 978-0-521-85868-7 Hardback
ISBN 978-0-521-14761-3 Paperback

In loving memory of my grandfather,
Harold Silverstein (1915–2000),
who taught me math

Contents

Maps

Acknowledgements

This book could easily have been written without the help of the following people, but it would have been awful. It is a pleasure to thank Tarif Khalidi, who expertly supervised the doctoral thesis on which chapter 2 is based, and who instilled in me a deep appreciation of Islamic civilisation. Charles Melville and C. Edmund Bosworth examined the thesis and made several comments that improved it. I would not have found my way onto a doctoral programme of any sort, let alone one concerned with Islamic History, had it not been for the inspiring guidance of Patricia Crone, who introduced me to the subject when I was an undergraduate in Cambridge. Ever since then, she has selflessly offered me her time, help, advice, and support at numerous junctures, for which I shall always be grateful. Geoffrey Khan and Petra Sijpesteijn have generously shared their expertise in Arabic papyrology with me on a number of occasions, and both have showed me that 'humanity' and the Humanities are indeed compatible – just when I was beginning to doubt it.

A number of scholars have been kind enough to read and comment on individual chapters of this book: Patricia Crone read chapters 3 and 4; Charles Melville read chapter 4; and Robert Irwin read chapter 5. Their advice has always seemed entirely sensible even if, in my stubbornness, I have not always taken it. Chase Robinson, an ideal colleague in every way, read a draft of the entire book and improved it considerably.

I would like to thank Marigold Acland and the editors of *Cambridge Studies in Islamic Civilisation* for encouraging me to write this book, Isabelle Dambricourt and Jodie Barnes for seeing it through the process of publication. I also wish to acknowledge the generous support of the British Academy, who awarded me a three-year post-doctoral fellowship, during which period much of the research for this book was carried out.

To the extent that taking up Islamic Studies (instead of Law) was meant to be an act of teenage rebellion, my parents took it disarmingly well and have lovingly encouraged me in every way from day one. And if there is even an ounce of scholar in me, it can easily be traced to their genes. To my wife Sophie, a true woman of valour, I owe my happiness. 'Many women have excelled, but you surpass them all' (*Proverbs* 31: 29).

Abbreviations

ABD:	*Anchor Bible Dictionary* (six volumes), ed. D. N. Freedman, London, 1992
BSOAS:	*Bulletin of the School of Oriental and African Studies*
CAD (Chicago Assyrian Dictionary):	*The Assyrian Dictionary of the Oriental Institute of the University of Chicago*, Chicago, 1956–
CIS:	*Corpus Inscriptionum Semiticarum*, Paris, 1881–1930
EI2:	*The Encyclopaedia of Islam: New Edition/ Prepared by a Number of Leading Orientalists*, H. A. R. Gibb (et al.), Leiden, 1960–2003
EIr:	*Encyclopaedia Iranica*, E. Yarshater (ed.), London, 1982–
HJAS:	*Harvard Journal of Asiatic Studies*
HMEIS:	*Harvard Middle Eastern and Islamic Studies*
JAH:	*Journal of Asian History*
JAOS:	*Journal of the American Oriental Society*
JESHO:	*Journal of the Economic and Social History of the Orient*
JRAS:	*Journal of the Royal Asiatic Society*
JSAI:	*Jerusalem Studies in Arabic and Islam*
JSS:	*Journal of Semitic Studies*
ODB:	*The Oxford Dictionary of Byzantium*, Oxford, 1991
P. Oxy.	*The Oxyrhynchus Papyri*, Egypt Exploration Society in Graeco-Roman Memoirs, London, 1898–
P. Ross. Georg.	*Papyri russischer und georgischer Sammlungen*, Tiflis, 1925–35
ZDMG:	*Zeitschrift der deutschen Morgenländischen Gesellschaft*

Introduction

True to its title, this book is about postal systems in the pre-modern Islamic world. Although the terms 'postal system', 'pre-modern', and 'Islamic world' may seem self-explanatory, they deserve our attention here nonetheless, for they can be deceptively ambiguous.

Postal systems of the sort described in this book differ from modern ones in three ways. First, a modern postal system is defined by its role as an organisation that transports items for a fee. Pre-modern systems, by contrast, were defined by their method of transportation. The term 'postal' refers to the fact that people and riding-mounts were *posted* at convenient intervals along a route in order to allow couriers to rest periodically and obtain fresh mounts for the next leg of their journey.[1] Hence, whereas modern postal systems can deliver mail by aeroplane, ship, or road, pre-modern systems were – strictly speaking – exclusively road-based networks of mounted couriers.

Second, owing to the fact that pre-modern postal systems were not defined by their function, they served in a number of capacities that would not be expected of their modern counterparts. For instance, whereas in the pre-modern world privileged people such as envoys and ambassadors could be transported to their destination by post, in the modern world such practices would probably be considered a moderate form of torture rather than a privilege. Furthermore, the fact that pre-modern systems were almost always the speediest method of communication available meant that they were the most effective way of transmitting important information or intelligence reports from afar. Indeed, any history of intelligence systems almost inevitably becomes a history of postal systems, and *vice versa*.[2] Vestiges of the fact that news in Antiquity was closely associated with the method of its transmission are apparent in current newspaper titles, where the words 'Post', 'Mail', and 'Courier' are ubiquitous. Even in the Arab world, where postal

[1] On pre-modern postal systems in general, see. L. Zilliacus, *From Pillar to Post: The Troubled History of the Mail*, London, 1956.

[2] E.g. F. Dvornik, *The Origins of Intelligence Services*, New Jersey, 1974, which focuses on postal systems.

systems from the seventh century until modern times have been labelled '*al-Barīd*', newspapers have included the word *Barīd* in their title.[3]

Third, the facilities of pre-modern postal systems were reserved for the ruling authorities in a way that modern systems are not. In fact, most pre-modern systems were governmental institutions whose services were officially inaccessible to even the wealthiest of private citizens. The pre-modern world was not characterised by the literacy rates of the modern West, and the tightly knit social structure of traditional societies did not encourage the dispersal of close acquaintances that is commonplace nowadays. For these reasons, most pre-modern people would have had no need to write and send letters to distant lands (assuming they could write at all). When ordinary people – pilgrims and merchants, for instance – wanted to communicate with distant acquaintances, they would resort to relatively haphazard methods of communication such as entrusting letters to passing caravans or, in the case of wealthy individuals, to privately arranged couriers. On occasion, well-organised interest groups could even establish their own, independent postal systems, and numerous examples of such institutions are attested for medieval Europe, where universities, merchants, and even butchers developed private courier systems.[4] But the postal systems that interest us here were governmental organisations the likes of which existed in most periods and regions of the pre-modern Islamic world.

The definition of 'pre-modern' in this context is dictated by two factors. The first is the emergence of modern techniques of telecommunication, paticularly the telegraph, during the Ottoman period.[5] The telegraph was to pre-modern systems of communication what gunpowder was to ancient warfare: the beginning of a new chapter (or in this case, a new book) of history. The second is the privatisation of Near Eastern postal systems in the sixteenth century. Privatisation could entail either the devolution of control of the postal system to non-governmental bodies or the formal acceptance by the government that civilians might use the system's services for a fee.[6] These

[3] E.g. the Saudi Arabian journal *Barīd al-Ḥijāz* (1920s Jeddah, editor in chief: Muḥammad Naṣīf). Due, perhaps, to its location along the Silk Route, Kazakhstan's most popular tabloid is called *Karavan*. For the relationship between newspapers and postal systems, see M. Stephens, *A History of News: From the Drum to the Satellite*, London, 1997.

[4] On which, see *La Circulation des nouvelles au moyen âge*, (no editor), Rome, 1994; D. Gazagnadou, *La Poste à relais: la diffusion d'une technique de pouvoir à travers l'Eurasie – Chine – Islam – Europe*, Paris, 1994, pp. 83–97; and E. Ashtor, *The Levant Trade in the Later Middle Ages*, Princeton, 1983, pp. 379–81. The legacy of the enterprising Taxis family, whose postal system linked much of Europe from the fourteenth to nineteenth centuries, is apparent in the modern word 'taxi' for hired transport. On private communications networks in Islamic history, see below, pp. 116–21.

[5] See Y. Bektas, 'The Sultan's Messenger: Cultural Constructions of Ottoman Telegraphy', *Technology and Culture* 41 (2000), 669–96.

[6] On the privatisation of Near Eastern postal systems, see: W. Floor, 'The *Chapar-Khāna* System in Qajar Iran', *Iran* 39 (2001), 257–92, esp. 262–3; *Mukhtārāt min al-qawānīn al-'uthmāniyya*, Beirut, 1990, pp. 139–48, esp. p. 139, §1, where the government stresses that it retains control over the [Ottoman] '*Barīd*' despite the fact that the general population may use its services; J. Chardin, *A Journey to Persia: Jean Chardin's Portrait of a Seventeenth-Century Empire*,

factors contributed to the erosion of traditional, pre-modern postal systems and set the chronological limits adopted here accordingly. The phrase 'Islamic world' is slightly more problematic, and the regions and periods of Islamic history that are treated here are not merely those in which the general population or ruling authorities were Muslim. Rather, by necessity only those Muslim states that possessed complex postal systems (excluding e.g. Muslim Spain and Sicily) are covered, and by choice only those regions that were 'Islamic' throughout the formative and classical periods of Islamic history (excluding e.g. South-East Asia and Ottoman Europe) are considered.

The book is divided into three parts. Part I (chapter 1) deals with the postal systems employed in the pre-Islamic Near East, focusing on the East (the Persian empires from the Achaemenids to the Sasanids), the West (from the Romans to the Byzantines), and Arabia (until the Umayyad period). Part II covers the early caliphal phase of Islamic history, specifically the Umayyad (661–750) and early Abbasid period until 847 CE (chapter 2), and the Middle Abbasid period until 1258 (chapter 3), through which the postal systems of the Buyids, Seljuks, Fatimids, Samanids, Ghaznavids, international merchants, and Muslim philosophers are also encountered. Part III considers the postal systems employed in the Near East during the Mongol (chapter 4) and Mamluk (chapter 5) periods.[7]

Parts II and III are referred to as 'Conquest and centralisation – the Arabs' and 'Conquest and centralisation – the Mongols' respectively, as they represent pivotal moments in world history generally and in postal history particularly. When the Arabs and Mongols burst onto the international stage in the seventh and thirteenth centuries, they encountered settled and politically sophisticated states with deeply entrenched administrative traditions. It is well-known that both the Arabs and the Mongols came to draw heavily on the bureaucratic experience of their conquered populations. But what has hitherto eluded scholars is the fact that both conducted centralised campaigns of expansion that relied on express messengers who, moreover, employed techniques of communication that would be integrated into the caliphal and Mongol administrations within decades of their establishment.[8]

(trans. R.W. Ferrier), London, 1996, pp. 39 and 175; and C. Heywood, 'Two Firmans of Muṣṭafā II on the Reorganisation of the Ottoman Courier System (1108/1696)', *Acta Orientalia Academiae Scientiarum Hungaricae* 54iv (2001), 485–95.

7 I have chosen a chronological approach to the subject (rather than a thematic or regional one) to allow readers to focus on a particular period of Islamic history to the exclusion of others, and to highlight the elements of continuity and discontinuity between periods.

8 The emergence of a highly centralised Ottoman Empire from a *ghāzī*-movement represents a third and final phase in this process and merits scholarly attention elsewhere. On the Ottoman postal system, see C. Heywood, 'The Via Egnatia in the Ottoman Period: The *Menzilḫānes* of the *Ṣol Ḳol* in the late 17th/early 18th century', in E. Zachariadou, *The Via Egnatia under Ottoman Rule*, Crete, 1996, pp. 129–44; 'The Ottoman *Menzilhāne* and *Ulaḳ* System in Rumelī in the Eighteenth Century', in O. Okyar and H. Inalcik (eds.), *Türkiye-nin Sosyal ve Ekonomik Tarihi (1071–1920)*, Ankara, 1980, pp. 179–86; s.v. 'Ulaḳ', in *EI2* vol. X, pp. 800–1; U. Heyd, *Ottoman Documents on Palestine, 1552–1615*, Oxford, 1960, pp. 125–7; Luṭfī Pāshā, *Tewārīkh-i āl-i osmān*, Istanbul, 1341 AH, pp. 371–82; and *Das Asafname des Luṭfī Pāschā*, (ed. R. Tschudi), Berlin, 1910, pp. 10–11 (Turkish)/pp. 11–12 (trans.).

A comparison of the conquerors' techniques of communication in the pre-state phase and an analysis of the subsequent incorporation of indigenous traditions into the two empires' bureaucracies may lead us to adjust our conquest-paradigms for Near Eastern history.

For a book on an aspect of Islamic civilisation, what may seem like an inordinate amount of attention is paid to pre-Islamic institutions, for which the following explanation is offered. To most students and scholars of Islamic history, the period begins in the seventh century CE. There is, for instance, no way of expressing 'before the *hijra*' in Islamic terms. But to rulers of the Islamic world, the Near East that they were inheriting was steeped in traditions and history. In stressing the pre-Islamic heritage of a caliphal institution we are acknowledging that – as with other great civilisations in history – Islamic society did not simply emerge fully formed out of the sands and oases of seventh-century Arabia. However culturally sophisticated Arabia was at the time, one can be certain that it did not on its own equip subsequent Muslim rulers with all the necessary tools for ruling the Near East (as supporters of the *shuʿūbiyya* would point out centuries later). Thus, a detailed examination of the world into which the Arabians swept informs us of the conditions with which the conquerors had to contend and how their predecessors dealt with these conditions.

Accepting the pre-Islamic DNA of Islamic political institutions is not meant to belittle the Muslim achievement; on the contrary, it is the only way to appreciate those aspects of caliphal rule that were truly unprecedented. Whereas generations of Western scholars of Islam have pointed out the pre-Islamic provenance of various aspects of Islamic civilisation as a way of downplaying its originality and contribution to history, the approach here is to compare and contrast a caliphal institution with its antecedents as a way of highlighting those aspects of the *Barīd* that made it unique. Would the Byzantine and Sasanid postal systems have been identical to the caliphal *Barīd* had seventh-century Arabians stayed put? Or, put another way, what (if anything) makes an Islamic postal system 'Islamic'?

These and related questions are of much greater concern to modern historians than they were to pre-modern Muslim authors, and our sources provide information of direct relevance to postal history only sparingly. The *Barīd* was an administrative institution that, unlike most others, had a physical presence in all provinces of the caliphate. Postal stations, station-masters, couriers, guides, milestones, and riding-mounts were widely disseminated throughout a ruler's realms, and even those authors who had little experience of administration in the capital would have been familiar with the postal system's general infrastructure and activities. This, for an historian of the *Barīd*, is the good news. The bad news is that despite (or because of) this widespread familiarity with the system, contemporary authors almost never talked about it. Moreover, perhaps due to the clandestine nature of the *Barīd*'s role in gathering and transmitting intelligence reports, our sources do not tend to describe this aspect of its activities in detail, if at all.[9] For these and other reasons, there are no classical Arabic or Persian treatises dedicated to the postal system's history, functions, or administration;[10] the closest one gets to a *Barīd*-manual is the genre of caliphal itineraries (*masālik wa mamālik*) often written by and for postal employees.[11] These itineraries provide a gazetteer of the various provinces of the known world and the routes that linked them, but otherwise serve our needs little more than a phonebook serves the needs of an historian of telecommunications.

The shortcomings of our sources are overcome by different means in each chapter, and our historiographic approach varies as a result.[12] Our treatments of the Sasanid and 'Arabian' systems of communication are based on the many references to communications technology scattered amongst literary, documentary, and epigraphic sources in a number of languages that, despite their volume, yield only minimal evidence and tentative conclusions.[13] The Byzantine postal system, by contrast, is described in a range of primary and secondary sources that has no equivalent in Islamic letters until the Mamluk period (1250–1517). In this case, the challenge is to summarise and analyse a disparate amount of information, and relate it to the situation in the Near East on the eve of Islam. Our sources for the early caliphal period (until 847 CE) are relatively descriptive insofar as Arabic chronicles discussing the period make regular reference to the *Barīd* in action. But as most of these chronicles were only composed centuries after the events they purport to describe, it must be assumed that *topoi* and anachronisms taint literary accounts of this postal activity. A handful of *Barīd*-related documents from the period act as a corrective to the literary record and illuminate the picture considerably. The *Barīd* in the Middle Abbasid period (after 847) is repeatedly referred to in a large selection of contemporary literary and documentary sources that, taken together, allow us to arrive at a reasonably detailed understanding of the *Barīd*'s function and structure during this period. The Mamluk *Barīd* and the Mongol *Yām* are described in a wide range of contemporary accounts, many of which were written by administrators or travellers who had direct experience of the postal systems they describe.

Every effort has been made to tease pertinent information from the available evidence for each period, but it is recognised that, as we can only usefully

[9] By way of comparison, it is worth noting that in Sun Tzu's *The Art of War* (trans. S. B. Griffith, Oxford, 1963, pp. 144–9) the section on espionage is buried in the book's final chapter (chapter 13).

[10] Ibn al-Nadīm (trans. B. Dodge, *The Fihrist of al-Nadīm*, New York 1970, vol. I, pp. 228–9) mentions that Aḥmad ibn al-Ḥārith al-Kharrāz (d. 258 AH) composed a work entitled *Kitāb shiḥnat al-barīd*, although no such work survives either in modern libraries or in quotations by later authors.

[11] On this genre, see *EI2* vol. VI, p. 639, s.v. 'al-Masālik wa al-Mamālik' (Ch. Pellat).

[12] The sources for each period will be analysed in greater detail in the relevant chapters.

[13] It should also be noted that for the Sasanid and 'Arabian' postal systems there are few secondary sources of which to speak.

ask questions to which our sources provide answers, we know more about the postal systems employed in some Islamic states than we do about others. Almost inevitably, some readers will deem my use and analysis of the sources to be unduly naïve or sceptical, or otherwise misguided. My approach has been to quote the sources extensively, which should allow readers to make up their own minds on points of detail, and to take refuge in a statement of Yāqūt al-Ḥamawī's, according to whom: 'As regards the *Barīd*, there is disagreement concerning it.'[14]

[14] In W. Jwaideh, *The Introductory Chapter to Yāqūt's Muʿjam al-Buldān*, Leiden, 1959, p. 53.

PART I

The pre-Islamic background

CHAPTER 1

Pre-Islamic postal systems

In simple terms, the *Barīd* was a messenger service whose agents delivered messages between a caliph and his provinces. As a general rule, messages from the caliph contained official orders and decrees, while messages from the provinces would consist of reports on the local state of affairs. Thus, messages and messengers were central if not inherent to the functioning of the *Barīd*. Equally important is the fact that messages and messengers are central to Islamic discourse. The Arabic root *r.s.l.* ('to send') is the pivot around which Allāh's communication with man rotates. Scripture, in both its superseded and final forms, was invariably transmitted to humans through the medium of thousands of messengers (*rusul*, sing. *rasūl*) culminating in the mission (*risāla*) of Muḥammad, God's Messenger (*rasūl allāh*). It is therefore of considerable interest to this study that, in spite of the suitability of the Arabic root *r.s.l.*, the name of the messenger system employed by the caliphs was coined from a non-Arab word and that most technical terms used in the *Barīd* were also of foreign origin.

Clearly, the *Barīd* was not a characteristically 'Arabian' institution. Whether the early caliphs incorporated pre-Umayyad Arabian methods of communication into their *Barīd* is debatable and will be examined later on. What is unquestionable is that early Muslims identified their messenger system with foreign, non-Arab cultures, a fact that is spelt out by their choice of such terms as *fayj* ('courier'), *furāniq* ('courier-guide'), *askudār* ('portfolio'), *kharīṭa* (mail-bag), and even *mīl* ('[Roman] mile') and *farsakh* ('parasang') in the *Barīd* service. The pre-Islamic states with which early Muslims had continuous contact were the Byzantine and Sasanid empires, and it is to the postal systems of these states that we now turn.

The East: Iranian postal systems from the Achaemenids to the Sasanids

The Persian post-horse has nine lives. (Ella Sykes)[1]

[1] E.C. Sykes, *Through Persia on a Side-Saddle*, London, 1898, p. 309, quoted in Floor, 'The *Chapar-Khāna* System', 286 n. 115.

Introduction

Imperial communications in pre-Islamic Iran are integral to any discussion of the early history of the *Barīd* for two reasons. First, much of the caliphate comprised lands that had previously been under Sasanid rule. Thus, in order to understand the unique conditions that shaped caliphal communications in these lands it is important to understand how earlier rulers responded to the challenges that this region posed to authorities in such a vast swathe of territory. Second, pre-modern Muslim authors themselves attributed the word *barīd* and the institution that it represents to pre-Islamic Iranians. In the words of Ḥamza al-Iṣfahānī: 'Darius the son of Bahmān was the first king to establish postal stations. He set up dock-tailed mounts (at the stations) and they were called *burīda dum* ("dock-tailed"). This phrase was then arabicised and its second half was cut off, leaving the word *barīd*.'[2] Both Ṭabarī and Gardīzī also credit Darius I (r. 522–486 BCE) with this innovation,[3] while Thaʿālibī adds that Darius ordered postal mounts' tails to be docked as a distinguishing sign (*ʿalāmatan la-hā*).[4] By far the fullest account of the process through which the *Barīd* mounts came to be docked in pre-Islamic Iran is provided by Yāqūt. He writes:

> The post-horses (*khayl al-barīd*) were called by this name because messengers from certain parts of the realm of a king of the Persians were delayed on their way to him. When they finally came before the king he enquired of them as to the reason for their tardiness. The messengers complained of the governors they had passed along the way and of their failure to assist them. Whereupon the king caused the governors to be brought into his presence in order to punish them. But the governors pleaded that they had not known these men to be the king's messengers. Thereupon the king commanded that the tails and the manes of the messengers' horses be docked as a sign for those they passed, so that they would remove any obstacles which might hinder their progress. Thus, people came to say [in Persian] *burīd*, that is to say, docked. This word was later arabicised, hence the expression *khayl al-barīd* (post-horses). And God is the most knowing.[5]

From these accounts three points are clear: first, medieval Muslims held that postal systems were an Achaemenid-Persian invention;[6] second, postal mounts were distinguished from ordinary mounts by their docked tails (and manes), and this feature of the mounts was supposed to allow royal couriers to proceed unhindered from station to station; and third, this custom of

[2] *Taʾrīkh sinī mulūk al-arḍ wa al-anbiyāʾ*, Berlin, 1921–2, p. 28.
[3] Ṭabarī, *Taʾrīkh al-rusul wa al-mulūk*, Leiden, 1879–1901, vol. I, p. 692; Gardīzī, *Zayn al-akhbār*, Teheran, 1969, p. 16.
[4] This idea is expounded by other authors, including Zamakhsharī (*al-Fāʾiq fī gharīb al-ḥadīth*, Hyderabad, 1906, p. 42) and Zubaydī (*Tāj al-ʿarūs min jawāhir al-qāmūs*, Kuwait, 1970, vol. VII, p. 418).
[5] In Jwaideh, *Yāqūt's Muʿjam al-Buldān*, p. 54 (translation modified).
[6] Ibn al-Faqīh, however, believes that it was the founder of the Sasanid dynasty, Ardashīr I (r. 224–41), who first created a *Barīd* and docked the tails of postal mounts (*Kitāb al-buldān*, Leiden, 1888, p. 198).

docking the tails of postal mounts is the origin of the Arabic term *barīd*. Despite the weight of the authorities cited, we shall see that all three of these points are incorrect. But what is worth bearing in mind here is that for early Muslim writers the story of the *Barīd* begins in Ancient Iran, and we, too, shall begin there.

The Achaemenid '*Barīd*' and its legacy

There is little doubt that complex and well-organised postal systems served rulers in the Near East long before the Achaemenids came to power in the sixth century BCE.[7] However, due in part to the detailed testimony of contemporary Greek authors (and the lack of similar accounts from earlier periods), it is only from the Achaemenid period (559–330 BCE) that we have clear descriptions of such systems. Our earliest source for this institution is Xenophon, who treats the postal system in his biography of Cyrus the Great (r. 559–529 BCE). In his words:

> We have observed still another device of Cyrus to cope with the magnitude of his empire; by means of this institution he would speedily discover the condition of affairs, no matter how far distant they might be from him: he experimented to find out how great a distance a horse could cover in a day when ridden hard but so as not to break down, and then he erected post-stations at just such distances and equipped them with horses and men to take care of them; at each one of the stations he had the proper official appointed to receive the letters that were delivered and to forward them on, to take in the exhausted horses and riders and send on fresh ones. They say, moreover, that sometimes this express does not stop all night, but the night-messengers succeed the day-messengers in relays, and when that is the case, this express, some say, gets over the ground faster than the cranes. If their story is not literally true, it is at all events undeniable that this is the fastest overland travelling on earth; and it is a fine thing to have immediate intelligence of everything, in order to attend to it as quickly as possible.[8]

From this account we learn that the purpose of the postal system was to 'have immediate intelligence of everything in order to attend to it as quickly as possible'. We also learn that the system was based on relays of horses stationed at one-day intervals at stations manned by officials who would receive a letter and send it off with fresh riders on fresh horses. Despite Xenophon's well-known admiration for Cyrus and his achievements, there is little reason to

7 Cf. S. Meier, *The Messenger in the Ancient Semitic World*, Cambridge Mass., 1988; J. Kinnier Wilson, *The Nimrud Wine Lists*, London, 1972, pp. 57–60; G. H. Oller, 'Messengers and Ambassadors in Ancient West Asia', in *Civilizations of the Near East, III*, (ed. J. M. Sasson), New York, 1995, pp. 1465–73; T. Bryce, *Letters of the Great Kings of the Ancient Near East*, London, 2003, esp. pp. 60ff.; N. Na'aman, 'The Distribution of Messages in the Kingdom of Judah in Light of the Lachish Ostraca', *Vetus Testamentum* 53 (2003), 169–180; and A. Wagner (ed.), *Bote und Brief: sprachliche Systeme der Informationsübermittlung im Spannungsfeld von Mündlichkeit und Schriftlichkeit*, Frankfurt am Main, 2003.

8 Xenophon, *Cyropaedia*, (trans. W. Miller), Cambridge Mass., 1968, vol. VIII, vi: pp. 17–18.

question the veracity of this passage, and the basic outlines of the Achaemenid postal system are confirmed by Herodotus' often-quoted account:

> Now there is nothing mortal that accomplishes a course more swiftly than do these messengers, by the Persians' skilful contrivance. It is said that as many days as there are in the whole journey, so many are the men and horses that stand along the road, each horse and man at the interval of a day's journey; and these are stayed neither by snow nor rain nor heat nor darkness from accomplishing their appointed course with all speed. The first rider delivers his charge to the second, the second to the third, and thence it passes on from hand to hand, even as in the Greek torch-bearer's race in honour of Hephaestus. This riding-post is called in Persia, *angareion*.[9]

Apart from the absence of the station-master (in this account the riders interact directly), Herodotus' description demonstrates that the system was still in existence during the reign of Xerxes I (r. 486–465 BCE), and that it was called (in a Greek rendition) *angareion*.

The postal system during the reign of Xerxes I is also described in the Biblical *Book of Esther*. While the historical details of the *Book of Esther* are difficult to verify,[10] it would appear that a swift messenger system connecting all provinces of the Persian Empire was at the disposal of the ruler. In this case, the system was used not to gather information about provincial affairs but to send royal decrees throughout the realm. Thus, when Hāmān secured the King's permission to kill the Jews of the empire, 'Letters were sent by courier to all the King's provinces with orders to destroy, slay and exterminate all Jews' (*Esther* 3: 13). When, through the efforts of Mordecai and Esther, the King agreed to spare the Jews, 'Letters were sent by mounted couriers riding on horses from the royal stable. By these letters the King granted permission to the Jews in every city to unite and defend themselves ...' (8: 10); thus 'the couriers, mounted on their royal horses, were despatched post-haste at the King's urgent command; and the decree was issued also in Susa the capital' (8: 14).[11]

In this case, the Achaemenid postal system was employed to circulate royal decrees throughout the provinces of the empire, using riders 'on horses from the royal stable'. The English translation of these verses is deceptively readable and cannot be seen as loyal to the complexities of the original Hebrew text. For instance, the term *aḥashtranīm* (*Esther* 8: 10, 14) used to describe the royal mounts has conveniently been ignored in the English version. In fact, this word is a *hapax legomenon* and has generated exegetical controversy,

9 Herodotus, *Histories*, (trans. A. D. Goldey), Cambridge Mass., 1963–9, vol. VIII: p. 98.

10 Although the Masoretic Text claims to depict events at the court of Xerxes (Hebrew: Aḥašweroš), most scholars agree that the *Book of Esther* appeared in its final form only centuries later. Nonetheless, studies have shown that numerous details of the text accurately reflect an Achaemenid backdrop (e.g. S. Shaked, 'Two Judaeo-Iranian Contributions: 1. Iranian functions in the Book of Esther', *Irano-Judaica* 1 (1982), 292–303).

11 *Esther* 3: 15 is nearly identical.

Rashī[12] interpreting it to mean 'swift camels' and Ibn 'Ezrā[13] suggesting 'mules'. All agree, though, that horses were not alone in serving as postal mounts. It is also worth mentioning that the Hebrew term for 'couriers' is *raṣṣīm*, literally 'runners'. Although, as we shall see, runners operated in pre-Islamic Iran, in this case it is clear from both the context ('runners on horses') and from other Biblical instances that *raṣṣīm* is the generic term for couriers, mounted or otherwise.[14] It is also worth mentioning that in his translation of the text into Arabic, Sa'adiya Gaon (d. 942 CE) translates *raṣṣīm* as *burūd* (sing. *barīd*).[15]

Other sources for the Achaemenid postal system include the Biblical book of *Ezra*, the Persepolis Fortification Tablets (*PF*), and a number of Aramaic documents from fifth-century BCE Egypt, as well as scattered references to travel and communication in Greek sources from this period. Interesting though all this may be, the period between the Achaemenid era and the fall of the Sasanid dynasty in 651 CE spans over a millennium of history, and it would be unreasonable to assume that descriptions of the Achaemenid system could inform us about conditions under the late Sasanids in anything but the broadest of outlines. Admittedly, there is no obvious reason why the passage of time or a change in dynasty would necessitate a corresponding change in such a practical and apolitical tool of government. Moreover, it is well known that the Sasanids consciously emulated the Achaemenids in numerous ways, and the postal system may well have been one of them.[16] In fact, some scholars have gone so far as to assert that the Sasanid postal system was little more than a continuation of the Achaemenid one.[17] But there are a number of sources that treat communications technology in the Near East during the Seleucid, Parthian, and Sasanid periods; not only does the information they provide complement the Achaemenid sources, but it also reveals the various ways in which the Sasanid postal system differed from the Achaemenid one. The following analysis of pre-Islamic Iranian communications divides the material into five topics: Routes and stations, Messengers, Informants, Method of communication, and Administration.

12 Rashī, on *Esther* 8: 10. Rashī, writing in eleventh-century CE France, is widely regarded as one of the most important and reliable exegetes of Biblical and Talmudic texts.

13 Ibn 'Ezrā on *Esther* 8: 10. Ibn 'Ezrā was a leading scholar writing in eleventh-century CE Spain.

14 E.g. *2 Kings* 9: 17; *2 Samuel* 18: 19–27; and *1 Kings* 1: 42.

15 In Y. Kāfaḥ, *Ḥamesh megīlloth*, Jerusalem, 1962, p. 317, on *Esther* 8: 10. Elsewhere (*Esther* 3: 13, 15; and 8: 14), however, the Hebrew word *raṣṣīm* is translated as *fuyūj* (sing. *fayj*), a term to which we shall return below.

16 But see E. Yarshater, 'Were the Sassanians Heirs to the Achaemenids?' in *La Persia nel medioevo*, Rome, 1971, pp. 517–33, where it is argued that continuity from Achaemenid to Sasanid times has been exaggerated.

17 E.g. A. Christensen, *L'Empire des Sassanides*, Copenhagen, 1907, p. 75; *L'Iran sous les Sassanides*, Copenhagen, 1944, p. 129; Dvornik, *Origins*, p. 45; W. Floor, *EIr* s.v. 'čāpār', vol. IV, p. 764; C. E. Bosworth, *EIr* s.v. 'barīd', vol. III, p. 797; and others.

Routes and stations

Already in Assyrian times, imperial routes linked the cities and towns of the Near East with the administrative capital(s) of the state.[18] And although it is with Herodotus and the Achaemenids that the Royal Road is most frequently associated, there is much evidence to suggest that both the route(s) and the term itself predate the Persian period. Herodotus describes the 'Achaemenid' Royal Road as follows:

> Everywhere there are royal stations with excellent resting places, and the whole road runs through country which is inhabited and safe . . . [111] is the number of stages with resting-places, as one goes up from Sardis to Susa. If the Royal Road has been rightly measured [. . .] the number of kilometres from Sardis to the palace of [king Artaxerxes II] Mnemon is 2,500. So if one travels 30 kilometres each day, some 90 days are spent on the journey.[19]

The Royal Road (Greek: *hodos basilikē*) is the Persian equivalent of the Akkadian *ḫarrān šarri*[20] ('King's Highway') or *girri šarri*[21] ('King's Road'), both in its meaning and in its course – the fact that Herodotus' itinerary from Sardis to Susa takes a circuitous route through Nineveh (the Assyrian capital) being particularly telling in this regard.

Although Herodotus mentions only the route from Sardis to Susa, it is known that other 'royal roads' allowed swift and efficient courier-traffic to flow throughout the Achaemenid provinces that extended from Egypt in the west to Central Asia and India in the east. The facilities available along the 600-kilometre road that stretched from Susa to Persepolis, for instance, are known to us from frequent references to courier-traffic along this route in the *PF*[22] and from recent archaeological work in the region that has unearthed the road's twenty-two way-stations.[23] The *PF* also refer to connections between Persepolis and Bactra, Carmania, India, Arachosia and Qandahār, Aria, Sagartia, Media, Babylonia, Egypt, and Sardis,[24] while the *Book of Esther* simply mentions that couriers went out 'to all the King's provinces'

[18] On which, see: B. J. Beitzel, 'The Old Assyrian Caravan Road According to Geographical Notices Contained in the Royal Archives of Mari', in G. D. Young (ed.), *Mari at 50*, Indiana, 1990, pp. 35–57; 'Roads and Highways (pre-Roman)' in *ABD* vol. V, pp. 776–82; and E. Sachau, *Routen in Mesopotamien*, Leipzig, 1882.

[19] Herodotus, *Histories*, V: 52–3.

[20] *CAD* 'H', p. 108a. The Hebrew equivalent of this term, *drk h-mlk*, is used in *Numbers* 20: 17. In *Numbers* 21: 21–2, messengers of Israel request permission to use the facilities of the 'King's Highway' (*drk h-mlk*). On the construction of roads in Biblical times, see also *Isaiah* 40: 3f. For an early reference to Near Eastern postal systems in the Bible, see *Jeremiah* 51: 31. Pseudo-Ibn Qutayba, *Kitāb al-imāma wa al-siyāsa*, Cairo, 1904, vol. II, p. 310 refers to Hārūn al-Rashīd's road from Iraq to Mecca as *ṭarīq amīr al-mu'minīn*.

[21] *CAD* 'G', p. 90b.

[22] R. Hallock, *The Persepolis Fortification Tablets*, Chicago, 1969. The *PF* date from 509 to 494 BCE, that is to say, from the reign of Darius I.

[23] J. Wiesehöfer, *Ancient Persia from 550 BC to 650 AD*, (trans. A. Azadi), London, 1996, p. 77.

[24] P. Briant, *From Cyrus to Alexander: A History of the Persian Empire*, (trans. P. T. Daniels), Indiana, 2002, p. 357.

(*Esther* 3: 13). The itineraries of these routes were described in ancient geographical works: Ctesias, for instance, is said to have composed a detailed description of 'the relays, days elapsed, and parasangs between Ephesus and Bactra and India'[25] of the Persian Empire in the late fifth or early fourth century BCE, while Isidore of Charax's *Parthian Stations* enumerates the routes and stations of the Near East in the first century BCE.[26]

Later authors provide us with information on the road system in the Near East during the Parthian period, including important data on the speeds achieved by marching troops along the various legs of the empire's itineraries.[27] Diodorus Siculus[28] (d. 30 BCE) mentions that it took twenty-two days from Babylon to Susa (XIX.55.2), about thirty days from Susa to Persia (XIX.17.6), forty days from Susa to Ecbatana (Hamadhan) via the Royal Road across Babylonia (XIX.19.2), but only nine days via a more direct route across the Cossean mountains (XIX.19.8), a route that would have been possible for postal couriers but not, presumably, for fully equipped soldiers. From Ecbatana to Persepolis it took twenty days (XIX.46.6). These speeds are not particularly impressive: military troops could cover little more than the 30 kilometres a day expected of ordinary travellers, but from Herodotus' statement that the postal couriers could complete the ninety-day itinerary of the Royal Road in only nine days we infer that the postal system was approximately ten times faster than military travel, couriers covering up to 300 kilometres a day.

The efficiency of the postal system depended on safety along the routes and a well-organised network of relay-stations. Safe routes were associated in the Ancient Near East with a ruler's justice and power: only a negligent ruler, it was reasoned, would allow bandits and highway robbers to operate within his territory. On a practical level, ensuring that roads were safe allowed vulnerable elements of society to travel unmolested across the empire. Since Assyrian times, it was recognised that unarmed couriers were particularly vulnerable, and efforts were therefore made to ensure that major routes were guarded. A document from the reign of the Assyrian King Ashurbanipal (r. 668–626 BCE) describes the practice of posting guards along an exposed intersection of roads so that 'The Arabs would go in and out in perfect safety as in the past.'[29] In the Achaemenid period, Ezra is said to have made the

[25] Quoted in Photius, *Persica*, (trans. J. H. Freese), London, 1920, §64. Ctesias' work does not survive.

[26] W. H. Schoff, *The Parthian Stations by Isidore of Charax*, London, 1914. On the political and military character of the *Parthian Stations*, see: N. Kramer, 'Das Itinerar Stathmoi Parthikoi des Isidor von Charax: Beschreibung eines Handelsweges?', *Klio* 85 (2003), 120–30.

[27] For an overview of the imperial routes of the pre-Islamic Near East, see Briant, *Cyrus to Alexander*, pp. 357–64 and the maps on pp. 366–7.

[28] References are to the Loeb edition (*Diodorus of Sicily*, trans. R. M. Geer, Cambridge Mass., 1984).

[29] R. H. Pfeiffer, *State Letters of Assyria: A Transliteration and Translation of 355 Official Assyrian Letters dating from the Sargonid Period (722–625 BC)*, New Haven, 1935, pp. 76–7, document §90 ll. rev. 4–9.

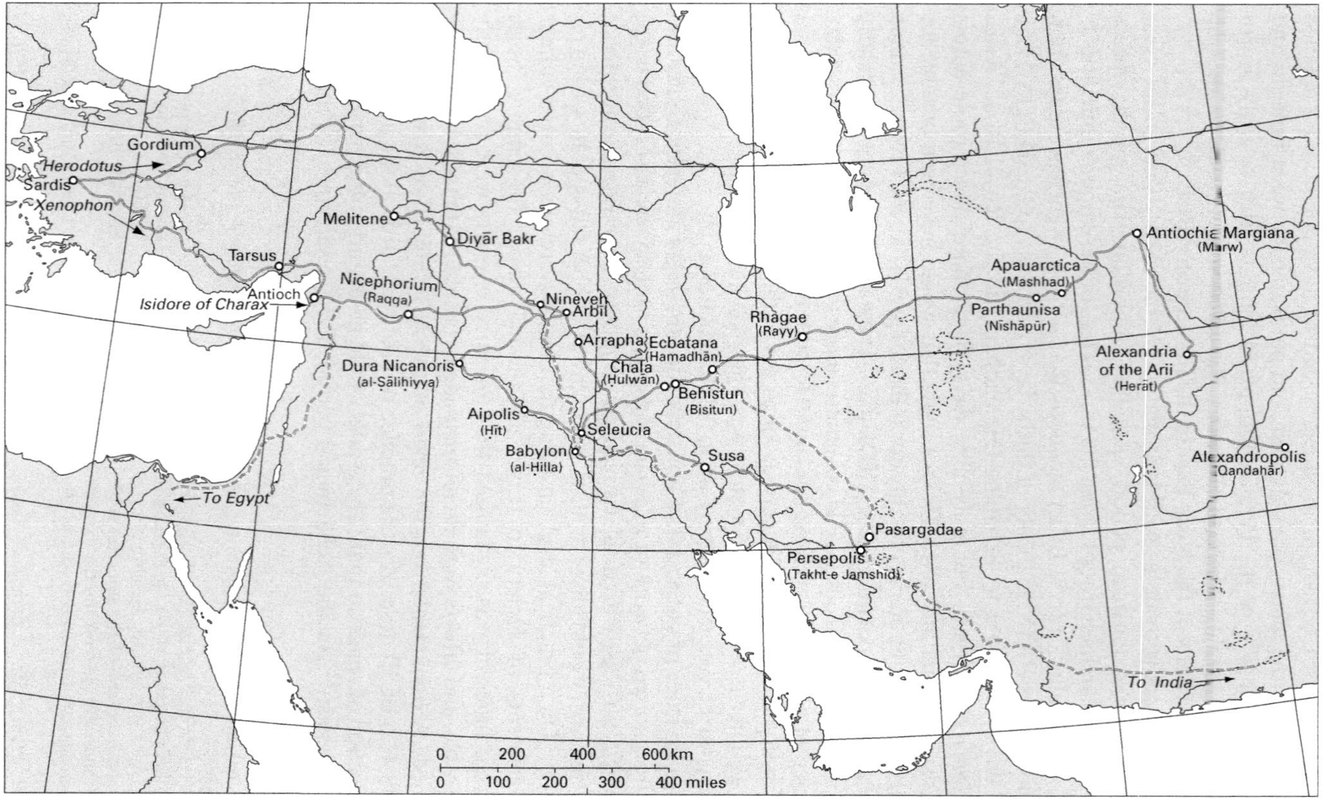

Map 1. Imperial routes in pre-Islamic Iran

journey from Persia to Jerusalem, accompanied by attendants carrying gold, silver, and other riches for the Temple. He decided against asking the king for a military escort along the route in order to demonstrate his reliance on God (rather than on the shāh) for safety on the roads.[30] What Ezra's deliberations imply is that the threat of highway robbers (*ʾwyb b-drk*, 'enemies on the road') was deemed to be real.[31]

That the roads were guarded and regularly patrolled is known to us from three anecdotes preserved by Herodotus. In one story, a message was secreted in the carcass of a hare; in the second, the message was tattooed onto the scalp of the messenger, who waited for his hair to grow back before setting out with the missive (upon arrival the recipient was instructed to shave the messenger's head); and in the third, a secret letter was inscribed on a wooden tablet and covered in a fresh coat of wax, to deceive the guards along the road (Greek: *hodophylakoi*).[32] Even if we are to reject the historicity of these stories, what can be inferred from them is that the roads were manned by officials who would examine correspondence borne by travellers. The 'satrap' (provincial governor) of each region was charged with maintaining the road network within his territory, while official travellers were provided with sealed documents that would entitle them to provisions available at the postal stations along the routes.[33]

Xenophon and Herodotus describe the way-stations (Greek: *stathmoi*) as being situated at daily intervals along the routes. At the end of a day's ride the tired courier and his mount would be relieved of their duties at a way-station, and the letter would be forwarded on its way with another courier, riding a fresh mount. The *PF* mention the travel-rations to which official messengers were entitled, and it is clear from the amounts of flour and wine specified that the stations could be no more than one day apart (as the rations were only sufficient for one day).[34] But the texts also indicate that at some points along the route special postal stations were maintained for which travel-rations were calculated in monthly quantities.[35] Thus, although Herodotus specifies that stations were established at daily intervals, these intervals were calculated according to the estimated distance achievable by ordinary travellers, whereas postal couriers passed through numerous way-stations in a single day.

30 *Ezra*, 8: 21–2, 31.

31 When, later, Neḥemiah made a similar journey he opted to travel with 'military officers and cavalry' (*Neḥemiah* 2: 9). Compare *PF* 2056, where official travellers are accompanied by a large escort.

32 Herodotus, *Histories*, I: 123–4 (hare's carcass); V: 35 (shaved head); and VII: 239 (waxed tablet).

33 See below, pp. 26–8. It is worth pointing out that contemporary sources make no reference to docked horses.

34 Hallock, *Persepolis*, p. 6.

35 E.g. *PF* 1672, ll. 5ff., where a month's worth of grain is supplied for 'express horses' (Elamite: *pirradaziš*).

From the itineraries recorded in the works of (predominantly) Greek authors, it is apparent that the distance between the stations was not uniform.[36] On average, stations were provided every 20–25 kilometres, and any variation in this distance may be attributed to topographical features of a region, the location of towns, or other considerations (such as the availability of water). Distances were usually measured in 'parasangs', a word that is found in various forms[37] and whose original meaning suggests that this distance was indicated along routes in the form of milestones.[38] By the Sasanid period, the Latin *mille* had entered the vocabulary of Babylonian Jews,[39] as had the Iranian word *awwanā*,[40] a term that is of central importance to the postal system. In describing the vows taken by Jewish ascetics, the Talmudic scholars reckoned distances either in parasangs or 'way-stations' (sing. *awwanā*),[41] just as Muslim jurists would calculate distances in terms of *burud* (sing. *barīd*),[42] that is to say, the number of postal stations passed along a route. The term *awwanā* is derived from Old Persian *ava-hāna*, which literally means '[a place for] unhitching [horses]'[43] and may have inspired the Arabic calque *ribāṭ* for a 'way-station' (literally, '[a place for un-]tying [horses])'; the term is also said to be the origin of the Arabo-Persian word *khān* ('caravanserai'), which was ubiquitous in the pre-modern Islamic world.[44] In the Sasanid period, Babylonian Jews used *awwanā* both as a measure of distance between stations and for the stations themselves.[45]

The routes of pre-Islamic Persia were also provided with way-stations or 'inns'.[46] In one episode recorded in the Babylonian Talmud, we hear of a

[36] See Briant, *Cyrus to Alexander*, pp. 358–9, where the distances between regions and the number of stations along the respective roads are tabulated.

[37] E.g. Pahlavi: *frasang*; Jewish Aramaic: *parseʾa*; Mandaic: *parsa*; and Arabic: *farsakh*.

[38] Wiesehöfer, *Ancient Persia*, p. 78.

[39] M. Jastrow, *Sefer millīm: Dictionary of the Targumim, Talmud Babli, Yerushalmi, and Midrashic Literature*, New York, 1992, p. 773b.

[40] Jastrow, *Sefer millīm*, p. 28a; and M. Sokoloff, *A Dictionary of Jewish Babylonian Aramaic of the Talmudic and Geonic Periods*, Baltimore, 2002, p. 86b. The related word *ʾdwn*, meaning 'station', occurs in the Aršam letters from fifth-century BCE Egypt (in G. R. Driver, *Aramaic Documents of the Fifth-Century BC*, Oxford, 1957, pp. 27–8, document VI, l. 5).

[41] *Nazīr* 7a. A Nazirite would take a vow of asceticism for a certain period, which can be expressed in either days or distances (i.e., the number of days it would take to cover a specific distance).

[42] Muḥammad himself is said to have measured distances in *burud* (in A. Wensinck, *Concordance et indices de la tradition musulmane*, Leiden, 1936–88, vol. I, pp. 168–9).

[43] The term *ava-hāna* is from the Indo-Iranian *sā-* ('to bind') with the pre-verb *ava-* ('away'), as in the Vedic *ava-sāna* (drawn to my attention by Almut Hintze). Compare Mandaic *auana* (in E. S. Drower and R. Macuch, *A Mandaic Dictionary*, Oxford, 1963, p. 9).

[44] On the derivation of *khān(a)* from *ava-hāna*, see E. Herzfeld, *Zoroaster and his World*, Princeton, 1947, p. 235 n. 13. But see: L. Kogan, 'Addenda et Corrigenda to the Hamito-Semitic Etymological Dictionary by V. Orel and O. Stolbova', *JSS* 47 (2002), 183–202 at 192–3, where it is argued that *khān* is from Middle Persian *kandan*, 'to dig', which is also the origin of the Arabic term *khandaq*, 'ditch'.

[45] E.g. Talmud, *Taʿanīth*, 11a, where a man 'travels from one way-station to another' (*d-qʾazīl m-awwanā l-awwanā*).

[46] These 'inns' were known in Pahlavi as *aspinj* (D. MacKenzie, *A Concise Pahlavi Dictionary*, Oxford, 1990, p. 12; and H.S. Nyberg, *A Manual of Pahlavi, Part II: Glossary*, Wiesbaden,

royal (Sasanid) messenger (*frīstaqā d-malkā*) who stopped at such an inn (*ušpīzā*) on his way to arrest a well-known Jewish scholar.[47] The pre-Islamic term for 'inn' continued to be used in Umayyad Soghdia, where the word *arspanj*, a local variation on the Pahlavi *aspinj*, denoted a 'postal station'.[48]

Messengers

The road system served to facilitate the movement of official messengers to and from the capital and provinces of the empire. Two types of messenger are discernible in the sources. The first is the official envoy who is chosen for his mission on the basis of specific attributes that qualify him as an acceptable representative of the ruler. Such envoys made the entire journey in person. The second is the simple courier, nameless and substituted by another courier upon arrival at a way-station. Both types of messenger would routinely be accompanied by an escort who would guide the traveller from one station to another. The escort was relieved of his duties at each station – even when the messenger himself was not – and would return with his (and the messenger's) tired mount to the previous station at a leisurely pace while the messenger hurried on to the next relay, accompanied by another escort. These envoys, couriers, and escorts are attested in the Near East from Neo-Assyrian times (911–612 BCE) at the very latest.

Although, in some instances, the official envoys along the roads would be foreign ambassadors,[49] more usually they would be carefully chosen members of the ruler's inner circle, despatched to accomplish a specific mission and return to the capital. Firdawsī's *ShāhNāma* (*SN*) provides us with numerous details concerning official envoys during the Sasanid period.[50] The *SN* describes Sasanid envoys as being 'shrewd', 'wise', and 'trustworthy',[51] while in four instances a scribe (*dabīr*) is chosen for an ambassadorial task.[52] Perhaps unsurprisingly, the most common adjective applied to these

1974, p. 32b); in Jewish Aramaic as *ušpīz* (Sokoloff, *Jewish Babylonian Aramaic*, pp. 98b–99a); and in Mandaic as *špinza* (Drower and Macuch, *Mandaic Dictionary*, pp. 471–2). The term survives as New Persian *sipanj*.

47 *Babā Meṣīʿā*, 86a.

48 In F. Grenet and E. de la Vaissière, 'The Last Days of Panjikent', *Silk Road Art and Archaeology* 8 (2002), 155–96, *passim*, esp. 166 and 175.

49 On foreign ambassadors using the Achaemenid road system, see Briant, *Cyrus to Alexander*, p. 368.

50 Although the value of the *SN* as an historical source is diminished by the largely unhistorical material that fills the first half of the work, it has been argued that 'the last part [of the work] is more historical and recounts poetically the reigns of the Sasanid kings' (C. Huart, *EI2*, s.v. 'Firdawsī', p. 920). According to Z. Rubin ('The Reforms of Khusrô Anūshirvān', in A. Cameron (ed.), *Studies in Late Antiquity and Early Islam III*, Princeton, 1995, pp. 225–97 at 234–5), 'a number of thorough studies of the sources of Firdawsī's *Shāhnāmeh* . . . tend to add much weight to Nöldeke's hypothesis that Firdawsī's main source was based predominantly on original Pahlavi material'. References to the *SN* are from T. Macan's edition, Calcutta, 1829; trans. A. G. Warner and E. Warner, London, 1912–25.

51 'Shrewd': *SN* pp. 1450, 1477, 1597, 2017, and 2027; 'Wise': *SN* pp. 1597, 1631, and 1777; and 'Trustworthy': *SN* pp. 1392, 1443, 1639, 1760, 1796, 1812, and 1984.

52 '*Dabīr*': *SN* pp. 1404, 1406, 1477, and 1803.

envoys is 'trustworthy' (*ustuvār* or *rāst-gū*). The trustworthiness of envoys is echoed in other Sasanid-era sources that refer to envoys as being 'the trusty ones of the king' (Syriac: *šarīre d-malkā*)[53] or 'secret-bearers' (Pahlavi: *rāzbān*).[54]

Of more relevance to this study are the simple postal couriers of whom only speed was required. The *PF* make frequent reference to 'express messengers' (Elamite: *pirradaziš*)[55] as well as ordinary messengers (Elamite: *hutlak*, literally: 'one who is despatched').[56] These are, presumably, the same 'runners on horses' (Hebrew: *raṣṣīm ba-sūsīm*) that we have encountered in the *Book of Esther*, and which Saʿadiya chose to translate as *burūd*. In his chapters on Sasanid history, Ṭabarī also refers to '*barīd*s' in describing Sasanid couriers on two occasions.[57] These instances are most probably teleological slips of the pen, however, as dozens of other references to Sasanid couriers in his *Taʾrīkh* use the term *rusul* (sing. *rasūl*). These *rusul* were very active during the Sasanid period: in his chronological survey of each shāh, Ṭabarī mentions that circular letters were despatched to all provinces upon the accession of a new ruler. Even regarding the reign of Bahrām IV (r. 388–99 CE) – about which Ṭabarī has almost nothing to say – he does not fail to mention the circular letter calling for obedience to him that the shāh distributed throughout his provinces.[58] Sending letters 'to all the king's provinces' is a familiar *topos* in Near Eastern texts, but it is a *topos* that presupposes the existence of an efficient network of couriers.[59]

Aside from the Elamite word *pirradaziš* and the anachronistic Arabic word *barīd*, Sasanid couriers were referred to using a number of terms, some of which

[53] In M. Morony, *Iraq after the Muslim Conquest*, Princeton, 1984, p. 90. This probably inspired the Arabic term *thiqāt* for a ruler's inner circle, a term that Arabic authors frequently use with reference to Sasanid messengers (e.g. Thaʿālibī, *Ghurar akhbār mulūk al-furs*, Paris, 1900, pp. 620, 628, 692, and 713; Dīnawarī, *al-Akhbār al-ṭiwāl*, Leiden, 1888–1912, pp. 73 and 89; and *Kitāb al-tāj fī akhlāq al-mulūk*, (trans. Ch. Pellat, *Le Livre de la couronne*), Paris, 1954, p. 160). On Arabic sources for the Sasanid period and the Middle Persian materials on which they are based, see Th. Nöldeke, *Geschichte der Perser und Araber zur Zeit der Sasaniden*, Leiden, 1879; and Z. Rubin, 'Ibn al-Muqaffaʿ and the Account of Sasanian History in the Arabic Codex Sprenger 30', *JSAI* 30 (2005), 52–93. On the authorship of the *Kitāb al-tāj*, see G. Schoeler, 'Verfasser und Titel des dem Ǧāḥiẓ zugeschriebenen sog. *Kitāb al-Tāǧ*', *Zeitschrift der deutschen Morgenländischen Gesellschaft* 130 (1980), 217–25.

[54] *Chronicon Paschale 284–628 AD*, (trans. M. Whitby and M. Whitby), Liverpool, 1989, p. 185 (esp. n. 488), and p. 187. And see: A. Tafazzoli, *Sasanian Society*, Cambridge Mass., 2000, p. 31.

[55] *PF* 300, 1285, 1315, 1319, 1320, 1329, and 1335. On these references and the word *pirradaziš* (*pir-ra-da-zi-iš*), see Hallock, *Persepolis*, p. 42.

[56] *PF* 1301, 1302, 1303, and 1559.

[57] Ṭabarī, *Taʾrīkh*, vol. I, p. 836, where the *burud* convey news of Shāpūr II's birth to the farthest lands; and vol. I, p. 1008, where Khusrô II sent a *barīd* to the Persians to announce the appointment of Farrukhān.

[58] Ibid., vol. I, p. 847.

[59] The *SN* also depicts Sasanid rulers sending letters (*nāma*) to all provinces (*be-har sū/gūsha*). Circular letters are sent to officials under 'Shāpūr' (*SN* p. 1444), Bahrām (p. 1489), Fīrūz (p. 1591), Khusrô I (pp. 1691, 1710), Hurmuzd (p. 1829f.), Khusrô II (pp. 1950, 1972, and 2011), and Yazdagird (p. 2077).

attest to a remarkable degree of continuity from Achaemenid to Sasanid, or from Sasanid to Islamic times. One such example is best introduced through a prophecy of Isaiah, who proclaims: 'Go, swift messengers, to a nation tall and smooth, to a people terrible from their beginning onward; a nation mighty and conquering, whose land the rivers have divided!' (*Isaiah* 18: 2). The Hebrew for 'swift messengers' is *malʾākīm qallīm*,[60] a phrase that raises two points. The first point is that the root *mlʾk* employed here highlights the philological relationship between angels and human messengers in Near Eastern history. Middle Persian *frēstag* (New Persian *fereshta*),[61] meaning 'angel', is found in the Babylonian Talmud as the *frīstaqā d-malkā* encountered above. The term literally means '[that which is] despatched', thus allowing for a certain amount of ambiguity concerning the despatching agent: when God sends a *frēstag* it is an angel; when a ruler sends a *frīstaq* it is an ordinary messenger. The Hebrew *mlʾk* used by Isaiah can therefore mean a human messenger, even though in most other cases it denotes an angel.[62] The linguistic relationship between messengers and angels (apostles) is ubiquitous in Near Eastern languages.[63]

The second point is that the Aramaic version (Targum) of *malʾākīm* as used by Isaiah translates this word as *ʾīzgad*, 'runner' or 'messenger'.[64] This term was widespread in the Near East, appearing as *ašgāndā* in Mandaic,[65] *ašgandu* in Akkadian,[66] and – interestingly – as *ʾzγnt* in Soghdian documents from the Umayyad period.[67] In the Middle Abbasid period, the Persian term *askudār*, meaning (amongst other things) 'courier', was in use, although its relationship to *ʾzgad* is tentative.[68] Another pre-Islamic term that literally means 'runner' but can denote 'courier' in a more general sense is the Pahlavi word *payg*;[69] this term survives into the Islamic period as *fayj* (pl. *fuyūj*), having already appeared in the pre-Islamic Arabic poetry of ʿAdiyy ibn Zayd,[70]

60 Compare *Job* 9: 25, where the verse 'My days are swifter than a courier' employs *qal* to denote 'swift' but *raṣ* for 'courier'.
61 MacKenzie, *Pahlavi Dictionary*, p. 34; and Nyberg, *Manual of Pahlavi*, p. 79a–b ('*frēstak*').
62 Elsewhere in the Old Testament, such angels are described as being God's messengers, mounted on horses to survey the affairs of the world (*Zechariah* 1: 8–12).
63 On which, see: W. Eilers, 'Iranisches Lehngut im arabischen Lexikon', *Indo-Iranian Journal* 5 (1962), 203–32, at 225 n. 31. To this list may be added the Arabic *rasūl* (pl. *rusul*), the Persian *paygāmbar*, and the Syriac *šlīḥā*, all of which refer both to ordinary messengers and to apostles. The English word 'angel' is derived from the Greek *angelos*, which means 'messenger'.
64 In Jastrow, *Sefer millīm*, p. 46a; and M. Sokoloff, *A Dictionary of Jewish Palestinian Aramaic of the Byzantine Period*, Baltimore, 2002, p. 43.
65 Drower and Macuch, *Mandaic Dictionary*, p. 40.
66 *CAD* 'A', vol. 2i, p. 427, where the relationship with *ašganda* is rejected; Drower and Macuch (*Mandaic Dictionary*, p. 40), however, connect the Iranian term with Sumerian *aš-gan-da*.
67 In Grenet and de la Vaissière, 'Panjikent', 159–60 (document Mug V-18, ll. 6 and 8).
68 The *Burhān-i qāṭiʿ* (ed. M. Muʿīn, Teheran, 1951–63), explains *askudār* as being derived from *az kū dārī* ('where do you have [it] from'), this being a transparently popular etymology.
69 MacKenzie, *Pahlavi Dictionary*, p. 67.
70 ʿAdiyy ibn Zayd, *Dīwān*, Baghdad, 1965, pp. 39, l. 18; 47, l. 15; 50, l. 2; and 71, l. 19. We have seen that Hebrew *raṣṣīm* can also refer to mounted couriers, despite a literal meaning of 'runners'. The Hebrew for spies, '*meraglīm*', may also have an original meaning of 'on-foot' (from Hebrew *regel*, 'foot').

and resurfaces in the Islamo-Persian courts of the Ghaznavids and Īl-khānids as *payk*.[71]

The guides who would escort couriers between stations are known to have operated in the pre-Achaemenid Near East.[72] Messengers in the ancient world would often travel with companions to ensure safety along the roads,[73] and the *PF* frequently refer to a courier's 'travel-companions'.[74] It is important to distinguish between ordinary travel-companions – who completed the journey together with the messenger – and escorts who were regularly substituted by others along the route.[75] The *PF*, for instance, make specific reference to 'elite guides' (Elamite: *barrišdama*) who escort foreigners along the roads.[76] In the Sasanid period, the Pahlavi term for such guides was *parwānag*,[77] a term that occurs repeatedly in the Babylonian Talmud as *parwwanqā*[78] and resurfaces in the Islamic period as *furāniq*.[79] In some instances, the guide himself is entrusted with delivering a letter,[80] although these cases must be seen as exceptional.

Informants

As seen, according to Xenophon, the purpose of the postal system was to 'have immediate intelligence of everything in order to attend to it as quickly as possible', and the agents responsible for gathering intelligence deserve our attention here.

71 It is interesting to note that in New Persian, the term retains the initial 'p' from Middle Persian, thus resisting the 'f' of the Arabicised *fayj*.

72 Cf. Kinnier Wilson, *Nimrud Wine Lists*, pp. 59–60, 'Escort Riders of the Corps of Eunuchs and Ghulāms', where escort-guides are referred to by the Akkadian term *raksu* (pl. *raksūti*). It seems likely that the puzzling phrase *rkby rkš* in *Esther* (8: 10, 14) refers to these guides, *contra* Herzfeld's suggestion (*Zoroaster*, p. 227f.). And see: G. A. Klingbeil, 'R-k-sh and *Esther* 8: 10, 14: A semantic note', *Zeitschrift für die alttestamentliche Wissenschaft* 107 (1995), 301–3; and D. Shapira, 'Judeo-Persian Translations of Old Persian Lexica', in L. Paul (ed.), *Persian Origins*, Wiesbaden, 2003, p. 232, where it is suggested that *rkš* in *Esther* is related to Rustam's horse 'Raxš'.

73 For examples from the Semitic world, see Meier, *Messenger*, pp. 96–128.

74 E.g. *PF* 1315 and 1319 (where the *pirradaziš* has one travel companion); 1320 (three companions); and 1329 (two companions).

75 For the function of such escorts in Qajar Iran, where they were referred to as *shāgird-i chāpār*, see Floor, 'The *Chapar-Khāna* System', 263.

76 Hallock, *Persepolis*, p. 42.

77 MacKenzie, *Pahlavi Dictionary*, p. 65; and Nyberg, *Manual of Pahlavi*, p. 152a.

78 In the Babylonian Talmud, the term is often used metaphorically: *'Avoda Zara* 28a ('the *parwwanqā* of the angel of death'); *Sanhedrīn* 38b ('the *parwwanqā* of forgiveness'); and *Sukka* 48b, where it is used in a midrashic tale about a conversation between 'joy' and 'happiness'. And see Drower and Macuch, *Mandaic Dictionary*, p. 363 (s.v. *paruanqa*), for more references to this term being used metaphorically.

79 Qudāma ibn Ja'far ([*Kitāb*] *al-Kharāj wa ṣinā'at al-kitāba*, Baghdad, 1981, p. 77) appears to retain a pre-Islamic spelling for the term *furāniq*, which he spells *frw'nq*.

80 For a *raksu* delivering the message, see Kinnier Wilson, *Nimrud Wine Lists*, p. 59. Babylonian Jews had a saying, 'The reader of the epistle must be the guide himself' (*qaryanā d-'igartā 'īhū lihwe parwwanqā*, in the Babylonian Talmud, *Sanhedrīn* 82a and 96a).

The informants and spies of pre-Islamic Persia are often associated with the phrase 'the Eyes and Ears of the King'. This phrase has generated considerable controversy amongst scholars for two reasons. First, although the terms 'Eyes' and 'Ears' are often uttered in the same breath, it would appear that these words represented distinct functionaries: the 'Eyes' are understood to have been entrusted with overseeing provincial officials, whereas the 'Ears' were spies planted amongst the general population.[81] Second, although there are numerous references to these 'Eyes and Ears' in literature dating from the Achaemenid and Seleucid periods, almost all of these references occur in Greek sources, leading Hirsch to argue that the lack of corroborative evidence from the Persian world would suggest that the Greek authors were merely recycling and perpetuating a fallacy concerning Persian administration.[82] Matters are further confused by the fact that in many instances the context in which the 'Eye' of the king is mentioned in Greek sources suggests that there was only one such individual at the court, and that he was a high-ranking official rather than a lowly spy.

Interestingly, both Hirsch and proponents of the existence of the 'Eyes and Ears' cite the same passage in Xenophon's biography of Cyrus in support of their arguments. In Xenophon's words:

> Moreover, we have discovered that [Cyrus] acquired the so-called 'king's eyes' and 'king's ears' in no other way than by bestowing presents and honours; for by rewarding liberally those who reported to him whatever it was to his interest to hear, he prompted many men to make it their business to use their eyes and ears to spy out what they could report to the king to his advantage. As a natural result of this, many 'eyes' and many 'ears' were ascribed to the king. But if anyone thinks that the king selected one man to be his 'eye', he is wrong; for one only would see and one would hear but little; and it would have amounted to ordering all the rest to pay no attention, if one only had been appointed to see and hear. Besides, if people knew that a certain man was an 'eye', they would know that they must beware of him. But such is not the case; for the king listens to anybody who may claim to have heard or seen anything worthy of attention. And thus the saying comes about, 'The king has many ears and many eyes'; and people are everywhere fearful to say anything to the discredit of the king, just as if he himself were listening; or to do anything to harm him, just as if he were present.[83]

Ostensibly, this passage suggests that the Achaemenid ruler was availed of many 'Eyes and Ears' who acted as his informants. Yet a nuanced reading of Xenophon's words can imply that he was actually attempting to correct a misconception about these functionaries, his statement that 'many "eyes" and many "ears" *were ascribed to* the king' being pivotal in this context.

[81] On this distinction, see R. Frye, *The History of Ancient Iran*, Munich, 1984, pp. 108–9.

[82] S. W. Hirsch, *The Friendship of the Barbarians: Xenophon and the Persian Empire*, London, 1985, chapter 5: 'The King's Eye'. Hirsch forcefully argues his case by adducing dozens of references to the 'eyes and ears' of the Persian king in Greek literature.

[83] Xenophon, *Cyropaedia*, VIII, ii: 10–12.

To some extent, Hirsch's case is convincing, and the assertion that 'As for Persian sources, no mention of the King's Eye has yet been found in any document from the Achaemenid, Arsacid or Sassanian periods' would appear to clinch the argument in his favour. The problem is that, tempting though they may be, arguments from the silence of non-Greek sources for pre-Islamic Iran are deceptive. The deficiencies of internal evidence for the Achaemenid, Seleucid, Parthian, and Sasanid eras are well known, and the standards of evidence that Classicists apply to Iranian history must be adjusted accordingly. And yet there is significant internal evidence to suggest that the 'Eyes and Ears of the King' did in fact exist and that they did function as informants.

In the Aramaic proverbs of Aḥīqar, this seventh-century BCE court functionary advises his nephew Nadin to refrain from uttering 'everything which comes into your mind, for there are eyes and ears everywhere'.[84] The earliest version of these proverbs comes from fifth-century BCE Elephantine, that is to say Achaemenid Egypt. Another document from Achaemenid Elephantine makes reference to a functionary called the *gwšk'*, 'ear' (comp. Armenian *gawshak*, 'informant').[85] This term has been convincingly related to the Arabic *jāsūs*, 'spy',[86] and demonstrates terminological continuity from Achaemenid to Islamic times. Moreover, the fact that the Achaemenid 'Ears' have been found in the distant province of Egypt demonstrates that these functionaries operated throughout the empire.[87]

That the 'Eyes of the King' were in existence during the Sasanid period is known to us through the *Letter of Tansar*, a document usually dated to the reign of Khusrô I (r. 531–79). In this source, the various attributes of these 'Eyes' are cited with the aim of mollifying the population's anxieties about them. Thus, one must fear accusation by the 'Eyes of the King' only if one is deserving of accusation, as these functionaries are 'trustworthy, obedient, pure, devout, learned, religious and abstinent in worldly things', people who pose no threat to loyal subjects of the king.[88] Furthermore, in discussing the

[84] In J. M. Lindenberger, *The Aramaic Proverbs of Aḥīqar*, Baltimore and London, 1983, p. 73, §146 (l. 97). In his notes on this text, Lindenberger connects this phrase with the spies of the Ancient Near East.

[85] In B. Porten, *Archives from Elephantine*, Los Angeles, 1968, p. 50. And see: R. Frye, *The Heritage of Persia*, London, 1962, p. 103; and H. H. Schaeder, *Iranica I: Das Auge des Königs*, Berlin, 1934.

[86] Eilers, 'Iranisches Lehngut', 211.

[87] Not only were 'eyes' and 'ears' ubiquitous in the Near East but there is evidence that they had an equivalent as far away as China, if the T'ang dynasty (618–907 CE) *erh mu kuan*, 'ear and eye official', is anything to go by (in A. L. Oppenheim, 'The Eyes of the Lord', *JAOS* 88 (1968), 173–9 at 174 n. 4).

[88] *The Letter of Tansar*, (trans. M. Boyce), Rome, 1968, pp. 49–51. Khusrô I is said to have described his ideal informant as being 'selfless, wealthy, experienced, upright, austere, who cares for the poor' (*SN*, pp. 1959–60).

Sasanid period the *SN* makes reference to a 'watchman' called *dīdabān*, a term that derives from the Persian word *dīda*, 'eye',[89] and which survives well into the Islamic period.[90]

Arabic sources inadvertently contribute evidence that the phrase 'Eyes and Ears' was used in the Near East with the meaning of spies. The two most common terms for 'spy' in classical Arabic sources are *ʿayn* (pl. *ʿuyūn*) and *jāsūs* (pl. *jawāsīs*). We have already seen that *jāsūs* is derived from the word 'ear' while *ʿayn* simply means 'eye'.[91] Crucially, the exact phrase '*ʿuyūn wa jawāsīs*', with the literal meaning of 'eyes and ears', occurs in Arabic sources from as early as the late Umayyad period.[92]

The *SN* uses the term *kār āgahān* to describe the provincial informants who operated in the Sasanid period.[93] According to this source, a newly appointed ruler would customarily send such informants to all provinces in order to keep the shāh informed of all events. This practice is mentioned with reference to the reigns of Ardashīr, 'Shāpūr',[94] Bahrām, Khusrô I, and Khusrô II.[95] Maintaining spies throughout the shāh's realms was associated with a ruler's 'justice': by keeping tabs on events in his provinces, a ruler was deemed to be concerned with the welfare of his subjects. In some cases, the shāh is purported to have sent agents (*kār āgahān*) to all his provinces in order to identify the needy and help them.[96] In other episodes, the ruler himself is said to have collected information, travelling to the provinces in disguise.[97]

Method of communication

Once informants gathered or chanced upon information, it was relayed to the ruling authorities in one of two ways: via human couriers – be they runners or

[89] And see: Eilers, 'Iranisches Lehngut', 219–20, where this term is vocalised '*daidubān*'.

[90] E.g. Ikhwān al-Ṣafā', *Rasā'il*, Cairo, 1928, vol. III, p. 15. It is likely, however, that the term *dīdabān* (pl. *dayādiba*) is unrelated to the 'Eyes of the King' (cf. C. E. Bosworth, *The History of al-Ṭabarī vol. XXXIII*, New York, 1991, p. 85 n. 220).

[91] The confusion arising from the use of the phrase 'the Eye of the King' to denote a high-ranking official in the Achaemenid period may also be solved by referring to early Arabic sources, where the term *'aʿyān* (sing. *ʿayn*) means 'notables' and is entirely distinct from *ʿuyūn* (sing. *ʿayn*) meaning 'spies'.

[92] *Kalīla wa Dimna*, Tunis, 1997, p. 264, where the [Indo-Iranian] king's 'Eyes and Ears' are planted everywhere; and ʿAbd al-Ḥamīd ibn Yaḥyā, *Rasā'il al-bulaghā'*, ed. M. Kurd Ali, Cairo, 1946, p. 192. According to ʿAskarī (*Dīwān al-maʿānī*, Cairo, 1933–4, p. 89), ʿAbd al-Ḥamīd's advice to the secretaries was based on pre-Islamic Iranian precedents.

[93] *SN*, pp. 1380, 1407, 1418, 1491, 1544, 1584, 1622, 1631, 1638, 1641, 1719, 1757ff., 1795, 1802, 1870, 1929, 1981, 1989, and 2017.

[94] The two Shāpūrs are conflated into one ruler by Firdawsī.

[95] Ardashīr: *SN* p. 1407; Shāpūr: p. 1444; Bahrām: p. 1491; Khusrô I: p. 1622; and Khusrô II: pp. 1870, 1929, and 1989.

[96] Ibid., p. 1407 (Ardashīr), and pp. 1549–50, and 1585 (Bahrām Gūr).

[97] Ibid., p. 1442 ('Shāpūr'), and pp. 1514–15 (Bahrām Gūr). Such references are obviously *topoi*, as this is a standard motif in world literatures (cf. S. Thompson, *Motif-Index of Traditional Folk Literature*, Bloomington, 1955, § P.14.19: 'King goes in disguise at night to observe his subjects').

messengers mounted on camels, donkeys, mules, or horses – who could deliver a message in person; or through an elaborate network of optical or aural signals that would transmit a very basic message.

The fact that the term 'runners' often refers to couriers in general does not mean that runners in the literal sense were not also operating during this period. In the *SN* runners (*navand*) are often mentioned in the context of transmitting news for the royal informants (*kār āgahān*),[98] and on one occasion they deliver circular letters throughout the empire.[99] That these runners are seen to operate alongside messengers mounted on camels and horses makes it clear that they are distinguishable from mounted couriers.

Despatching mounted couriers was the most common method of communication in this period. Horses (*tāzān* or *savārān*, 'horse-riders') appear frequently,[100] as do camels (*hayvān* or *uštar*).[101] In a Pahlavi text from the late Sasanid period, Khusrô II is said to have asked a companion, 'Which riding animal is the best?', to which the companion replied, 'All these riding animals are good: the horse (*asp*), and the mule, and the riding-camel (*uštar-i tazāg*), and the royal post-horse (*baγdēspānīk*).'[102] Such post-horses probably transported a courier in two-horse teams: the Pahlavi *bayaspānīg* ('post-horse')[103] and the related terms **dēspān* (Middle Persian), *despan* (Armenian), *dusfān* (Arabic), and *dū aspa* (New Persian) all indicate that royal carriages were originally drawn by two mounts.[104]

It is likely that mules and donkeys were also used to transport royal correspondence. Evidence for the use of donkeys in the Sasanid postal system comes from the Babylonian Talmud. In discussing the legal status of those who borrow animals from one another, the jurists debate whether a man is liable to the owner of a donkey if the animal is 'seized for the *angaria*'.[105] As we have seen, Herodotus states that the Achaemenid postal system was labelled *angareion*, and there is little doubt from other references in the Talmud that by the Sasanid period the term still retained its postal

98 Ibid., pp. 1544, 1641, 2017, and 2051. 99 Ibid., p. 1551.

100 Ibid., pp. 1380, 1388, 1471, 1489, 1514–15, 1551, 1591, 1648, 1790, 1866, 1919, and 2027.

101 Ibid., pp. 1369, 1446, 1464, 1551, 1577, 1585, 1747, 1777, 1806, and 2057. In the Targum to the *Book of Esther*, one of the terms for postal mounts is *bny h-rmkyn* (8: 10), rendered *rmkn*, 'dromedaries' (in B. Grossfeld, *The First Targum to Esther: According to MS Paris Hebrew 110 of the Bibliothèque Nationale*, New York, 1983).

102 J. M. Unvala, *The Pahlavi Text King Husrav and his Boy*, Paris, 1921, p. 36, §99.

103 MacKenzie, *Pahlavi Dictionary*, p. 18; and Nyberg, *Manual of Pahlavi*, p. 46a (where the term is vocalised '*bayāspān*').

104 Herzfeld, *Zoroaster*, p. 228. And see: Jastrow, *Sefer millīm*, p. 302b, for Jewish Aramaic **dyspq* ('a litter carried by mules'). B. Geiger ('Zum Postwesen der Perser', *Wiener Zeitschrift für die Kunde des Morgenlandes* 29 (1915), 309–14) makes a similar observation based on the terms *akbarēδ*, *dobarēδ*, and *sēbarēδ* in the *SN*, used with reference to postal mounts. However, the general absence of *barēδ* for 'postal mount' in other pre-Islamic Iranian sources suggests that this is a post-Islamic interpolation of the term *barīd*.

105 *Babā Meṣī'ā* 78a–b. This chapter is an elaboration on the Mishna of *Babā Meṣī'ā* 6: 3.

connotations.[106] In attempting to determine the legal status of the borrower, the Talmudic scholars plunge into a detailed examination of what constitutes a case of *angaria*. The bone of contention is the contradiction between the ruling of the Mishna (which exonerates the borrower) and that of the Talmud (which holds the borrower responsible). This apparent contradiction is resolved by drawing a distinction between the two types of *angaria* that were prevalent at the time: 'returning *angaria*' and 'non-returning *angaria*'. The former refers to a case in which the postal officials would confiscate a donkey for their use until the donkey became tired, when another would be requisitioned, the first donkey being returned to its previous owner (most probably by the escort). The latter concerns a situation in which the donkey is not returned to its original owner, in which case the borrower is required to compensate the owner. The *angaria* would be 'non-returning' when time was of the essence, whereas 'returning *angaria*' points to the regular contributions that ordinary people made to the postal system in their region, a point to which we shall return below.[107]

Optical signalling was used in the Near East from ancient Babylonian times,[108] and it was also used in Ptolemaic Egypt[109] and in the Achaemenid world.[110] For the Seleucid period we have the testimony of Diodorus, who describes the famous Antigonus the One-Eyed as having 'established at intervals throughout all that part of Asia of which he was master a system of fire-signals and despatch-carriers, by means of which he expected to have quick service in all his business' (XIX.57.5). From references in the *SN* it would appear that a system of smoke signals was used in the early Sasanid period,[111] though there is no evidence to suggest that this system survived the administrative reforms of Shāpūr II. In the early Sasanid period, Jews used a complex system of optical signals to inform their co-religionists in the Diaspora (specifically in Babylonia) that the new moon was sighted – a fact that would determine the precise dating of Jewish festivals. By the mid Sasanid period, however, this system had to be replaced by a network of

[106] For a nuanced discussion of the possible meanings of *angaria* in the Talmud, see S. Friedman, *Talmūd arūkh: Babā meṣīʿā VI*, Jerusalem, 1990, pp. 153–69 (in Hebrew). See also: M. Rostowzew, 'Angaria', *Klio* 6 (1906), 249–58; D. Sperber, 'Angaria in Rabbinic Literature', *L'Antiquité Classique* 38i (1969), 162–8; and B. Isaac, *The Limits of Empire*, Oxford, 1992, pp. 291–7.

[107] That ordinary people supplied the authorities with postal mounts explains why donkeys and mules were often used in the Sasanid postal system in addition to the more noble (and expensive) horses. See also Herzfeld, *Zoroaster*, pp. 228–9, for the use of mules in Iranian communications.

[108] See: C. Fries, 'Babylonische Feuerpost', *Klio* 3 (1903), 169–70; and 'Zur babylonischen Feuerpost', *Klio* 4 (1904), 117–21; and Herzfeld, *Zoroaster*, pp. 223–4.

[109] E. Van't Dack, 'Postes et télécommunications ptolémaïques', *Chronique d'Egypte* 73 (1962), 338–41.

[110] Herodotus, *Histories*, IX: 3, describes the 'chain of beacons' that relayed news of a victory over the Greeks to Xerxes.

[111] *SN* pp. 1388, 1390.

couriers who relayed news from Jerusalem to Iraq in person, since a group of Samaritan sectarians (*kūtīm*) managed to sabotage the signalling system by lighting fires on mountain-tops even before the new moon was sighted, thereby setting off the chain of beacons throughout the Diaspora on the wrong day.[112] Thus it would appear that by the end of the Sasanid period neither the official system of smoke signals nor the (private) Jewish network of beacons was in operation.

Aural signalling was practised from the Achaemenid period at the latest.[113] The Seleucids also used this system, and Diodorus explains the method through which a military order could reach troops who are thirty days away within a single day:

> Persia is cut by many narrow valleys and has many lookout posts that are high and close together, on which those of the inhabitants who had the loudest voices had been stationed. Since these posts were separated from each other by the distance at which a man's voice can be heard, those who received the order passed it on in the same way to the next and then these in turn to others until the message had been delivered at the border of the satrapy. (XIX.17.6f.)

Optical and oral signalling were probably not systems maintained continuously as a means to convey information; it would appear that such techniques were reserved for use in military contexts, as early-warning systems. Similar systems were employed by the early Abbasid caliphs and their generals during campaigns,[114] and by the Mamluk sultans.[115] The use of optical and aural signals was complementary to – rather than a substitute for – the system of runners or mounted couriers of which pre-modern postal systems were comprised. Despite the immense speed at which information could be transmitted using such signals, the content of a message would have to be extremely limited, and it is only through written correspondence that detailed reports and orders could be conveyed.

Administration

Official documents were sealed and transported in leather mail-bags from as early as the Achaemenid period. Leather mail-bags survive from as late and as

[112] An in-depth discussion of this system of beacons may be found in the Talmud, *Rosh ha-Shana* 22b–23b.

[113] E.g. Herodotus, *Histories*, IV: 141; and VII: 117. Note the use of *shofār*-trumpets for transmitting intelligence gathered by spies (*meraglīm*) in *2 Samuel* 15: 10.

[114] E.g. Ṭabarī, *Ta'rīkh*, III, pp. 1229–30, where watchmen (*dayādiba*, sing. *dīdabān*) were stationed on mountain-tops during al-Muʿtaṣim's campaign against Bābak. And see Ṭabarī, *Ta'rīkh*, III, p. 1188, for reference to watchmen stationed on mountain-tops (*kūhbāniyya*). Both *dīdabān* and *kūhbān* are terms that can be traced back to the pre-Islamic period, and it is likely that the fact that these terms and the systems to which they correspond occur in the eastern provinces of the Abbasid world is beyond coincidence. On *dīdabān*, see above above p. 23; on *kūhbān*, see Nyberg, *Manual of Pahlavi*, p. 119 s.v. 'kofīdār'.

[115] See below, pp. 176–9.

far east as fourth-century CE Soghdia and as early and far west as fifth-century BCE Egypt.[116] In the *PF*, sealed documents from the king are referred to as Elamite *halmi*[117] and are always borne by express messengers. Messengers also carried documents that identified them as being on official business, allowing them use of postal facilities along the routes. One such document has survived from Achaemenid Egypt,[118] and the existence of comparable texts from most periods and regions for which we have material evidence suggests that such 'passports' were unexceptional.

In the Achaemenid period, letters were referred to by Aramaic terms such as *'grh* (=*iggereth*),[119] a term that appears frequently in both literary and documentary sources.[120] In later periods, Iranian words such as *nāmag* and *paygām* came to replace Semitic ones.[121] The *SN* routinely refers to official missives as *nāma*, and Pahlavi papyri from the Sasanid occupation of Egypt (610–28 CE) employ the terms *nāmag* and *paygām* side by side within the same document.[122] Letters were usually written on leather or, in Egypt, on papyrus.

Travel documents were issued by local satraps, who were also responsible for the upkeep of the routes and stations in their region.[123] Although the satraps would co-ordinate the supply of mounts, fodder, and manpower for local postal stations, it was the local population that was expected to shoulder these burdens. We have seen that mounts would be 'seized by the *angaria*' in Sasanid Iraq, and from numerous references in the Talmud we know that forced labour was amongst other *angaria*-duties.[124] That the population served in and provided for the postal system is an arrangement that dates back to Achaemenid times, if not earlier,[125] and is confirmed by the testimony of Diodorus for the Seleucid period (XVIII.32.2).

[116] Fifth-century BCE Egypt: Driver, *Aramaic Documents*, p. 3; fourth-century CE Soghdia: N. Sims-Williams, 'Ancient Letters', in *EIr*, vol. II, p. 7.

[117] The term *halmi* is almost certainly a borrowing from Aramaic *kh.t.m.* (on this, see G. Cameron, *The Persepolis Treasury Tablets*, Chicago, 1948, p. 53).

[118] Driver, *Aramaic Documents*, pp. 27–8 (document VI).

[119] Probably derived from Akkadian *egirtu*, 'letter' (e.g. Pfeiffer, *State Letters*, pp. 76–7, §90, l. 18).

[120] Driver, *Aramaic Documents*, documents X, XI, and XII (twice); *Ezra* 5: 6; and so forth. And see P. E. Dion, 'Aramaic words for "Letter"', *Semeia* 22 (1981), 77–88.

[121] In *Ezra*, both *iggereth* and *ptgm* (=*paygām*) are used interchangeably (*Ezra* 4: 17; and 5: 6).

[122] D. Weber, *Corpus inscriptionum iranicarum: Part III Pahlavi Inscriptions, Ostraca, Papyri und Pergamente*, London, 1992, pp. 145–9, document §45, ll. 11, 24, 28, and 29 (*nāmag*) and l. 21 (*paygām*). According to Weber (p. 149), this is the only reference to the term *paygām* in Pahlavi papyri.

[123] Briant, *Cyrus to Alexander*, pp. 362–3, and 372. According to the *Kitāb al-aghānī* (Cairo, 1927, vol. II, p. 100), the Sasanids used to entrust control of the '*Barīd*' to the sons of the *marāziba* (sing. *marzubān*, 'frontier-officer').

[124] *Angaria* as 'forced labour': *Yomā* 35b; and *Soṭa* 10a. *Angaria* levied during wartime: *Babā Qamā* 38b. In '*Avoda Zara* 26a there is a reference to the fact that the *bay-do'ar* is manned as a corvée by the local population. Whether or not this *bay-do'ar* is a post office (from Hebrew *do'ar*, 'mail') or a courthouse (from Pahlavi *dādwar*) is open to debate. From *Shabbath* 19a it would appear that *do'ar* meant 'post'.

[125] See Jastrow, *Sefer millīm*, p. 81a for the fact that Jewish writers associated the tax called *halak* in *Ezra* 4: 13 with the *angaria*.

Regarding the postmaster himself, little is known. It may be argued on linguistic grounds that the character by the name of Ašpenaz in *Daniel* (1: 3), who was in charge of the eunuchs at the Achaemenid court, was a high-ranking postal official whose name is a corruption of the term [*rab*] *ašpinia*, suggesting that he was the director of the royal way-stations.[126] The related term *ušpīzkān* ('inn-keeper') is found in the Talmud and in other contexts.[127] Ultimately, of course, it was the shāh himself who had the final say in postal matters, and Mas'ūdī relates that late Sasanid rulers had a special signet ring reserved for the '*Barīd*'.[128] Certain Sasanid rulers are singled out as having taken particular interest in reports from the provinces. The *SN* dedicates a chapter to 'The Edicts (*tawqī'*) of [Khusrô] Anūshirvān', a chapter that relates the various instances in which Khusrô I received reports from his provincial agents and how he responded to them.[129] Similarly, Khusrô II is said to have divided his day into quarters, one of which was spent reading reports of 'world affairs',[130] and it is with regard to this shāh that Firdawsī repeats the sentence: 'He sent vigilant spies to find out the affairs of the world.'[131]

Conclusions

From the foregoing analysis of pre-Islamic Iranian postal systems three points of particular relevance to this study emerge. First, when Muslims conquered the Sasanid provinces of the Near East they were heirs to a region that was steeped in postal experience and traditions. Second, medieval Muslim authors were unapologetically conscious of the pre-Islamic Iranian provenance of the caliphal *Barīd*. Third, the fact that much of the *Barīd*'s terminology can be traced to pre-Islamic Iran attests to the considerable degree of direct continuity from pre-Islamic to caliphal times. Even within the pre-Islamic period, the resilience of postal phraseology from the Ancient Near East to Sasanid times is remarkable: by some means, terms such as *angaria*,[132] *ašganda*, and *awwanā* managed to outlast the various Semitic, Persian, and Hellenic dynasties that dominated the region, and to withstand repeated changes to the official language.

There is, however, one term of central importance to the caliphs' postal system that cannot be traced back to pre-Islamic Iran with confidence: this is the word *barīd* itself. For this term and for the postal system that spawned it, we must turn westwards, to the Roman Empire.

[126] For this possibility, see R. Coxon, 'Ashpenaz' in *ABD* vol. I pp. 490–1.

[127] Jastrow, *Sefer millīm*, p. 36a; and Sokoloff, *Jewish Babylonian Aramaic*, p. 99.

[128] Mas'ūdī, *Murūj al-dhahab wa ma'ādin al-jawhar*, Beirut, 1965, vol. I, p. 309, §626 (Khusrô I) and vol. I, p. 320, §650 (Khusrô II).

[129] *SN* pp. 1757–64. [130] Ibid., p. 1990. [131] Ibid., pp. 1870, and 1929.

[132] The term *angaria* has survived into modern times with the meaning of 'forced labour' (in Y. Sabar, *A Jewish Neo-Aramaic Dictionary*, Wiesbaden, 2002, p. 98 s.v. ''anqara').

The West: the *Cursus Publicus* from Rome to Byzantium

Introduction

Although medieval Muslim authors assumed that the *Barīd* was based on pre-Islamic Iranian precedents, modern Western scholars have argued that the Romano-Byzantine *Cursus Publicus*[133] is more likely to have been the model after which the Umayyad caliphs fashioned their own postal system.[134] The *shuʿūbiyy* undertones of medieval, philo-Iranian scholars do not, in this case, have an exact parallel in the modern preference for a Byzantine origin of the *Barīd*: despite the general tendency of Western scholars to view pre-modern empires through a Roman prism, there are in fact two compelling reasons for tracing the *Barīd* back to the Byzantine Empire. First, the term *barīd* appears to be an Arabised form of the Latin *veredus*, 'post-horse'. This alone has convinced some scholars that the caliphal postal system was based on the Byzantine one. In the words of a recent, highly regarded publication: '[The Islamic Empire's] system of post-horses and of governmental information on which its extended rule depended was called after its Roman predecessor *veredus*, *al-barīd*.'[135] Second, as the Umayyad caliphs who created the *Barīd* were based in Syria, a province conquered from the Byzantines, it is reasonable to assume that the caliphal institution was simply a continuation of the Byzantine postal system that had been in place in this region on the eve of Islam. Indeed, it is very likely that the local postal infrastructure – including way-stations, milestones, and so forth – was retained by the caliphs who, in any event, were served and advised by functionaries with direct experience of Byzantine administration in Syria and Egypt.

Neither of these arguments is entirely satisfactory: the Latin etymology of *barīd* is far from established, and the fact that much of the terminology associated with the *Barīd* is of Persian origin would suggest either that the word *barīd* is also Persian or that the institution was the hybrid product of more than one culture.[136] And although the Umayyad capital was Byzantine,

[133] Although the postal system is sometimes called *Vehiculatio*, the term *Cursus Publicus* is far more prevalent both in primary sources and modern scholarship. On these respective terms, see A. Coskun's review of A. Kolb, *Transport und Nachrichtentransfer im römischen Reich*, Berlin, 2000, in *Bryn Mawr Classical Review*, 2002.03.14 (at: http://ccat.sas.upenn.edu/bmcr/2002/2002-03-14.html).

[134] E.g. Dvornik, *Origins*, p. 199; R. Hartmann, 'Barīd' in *EI1*; C. E. Bosworth, 'Barīd' in *EIr*; D. Sourdel, 'Barīd' in *EI2*; and others.

[135] In G. Bowerstock, P. Brown, and O. Grabar (eds.), *Late Antiquity: A Guide to the Post-Classical World*, Cambridge Mass., 1999, p. vii.

[136] On the uncomfortable relationship between the etymology of *barīd* and the origins of the institution itself, see A. Silverstein, 'Etymologies and Origins: A Note of Caution', *British Journal of Middle Eastern Studies* 28i (2001), 92–4. For recent (and conflicting) discussions of the etymology of *barīd*, see M. Ullmann, *Zur Geschichte des Wortes Barīd, 'Post'*, Munich, 1997, pp. 5–14; and D. Gazagnadou, 'Note sur le mot *Barīd* (*al-barīd*)', *Luqmān* 15i (1999), 35–42, which is a repetition of *La Poste*, p. 124f.

the Byzantine capital was never Umayyad; thus, at best, the Umayyads in Syria were heirs to a provincial administration rather than to the nerve-centre of an empire.[137] Despite this, the view that the *Barīd* was squarely based on the *Cursus Publicus* has gained widespread acceptance amongst scholars.[138] All would agree that the *Cursus Publicus* had *some* sort of formative influence on the *Barīd*. What was the nature of this influence, and what, more generally, was the *Cursus Publicus*? These are the questions to which we shall turn in the following pages.

The Roman postal system

The *Cursus Publicus* was the Roman postal system, adopted with some modifications by the emperors at Constantinople in the fourth century CE. Famous for their impressive network of roads, the Romans ruled an empire so vast that the creation of a postal system was probably inevitable. However, it was only during the reign of Augustus (r. 23 BCE–14 CE), whose imperial and absolutist ambitions allowed for such a system, that a regular Roman postal service was created. According to Suetonius,

> To enable what was going on in each of the provinces to be reported and known more speedily and promptly, [Augustus] at first stationed young men at short intervals along the military roads, and afterwards post-chaises (carriages). The latter has seemed the more convenient arrangement, since the same men who bring the dispatches from any place can, if occasion demands, be questioned as well.[139]

In the preceding period, Julius Caesar is said to have 'often arrived at his destination before the messengers who had been sent ahead to announce his approach';[140] Augustus' creation of the *Cursus Publicus* was thus a timely and important innovation.

Suetonius' account alerts us to two further points. First, it would appear that initially Augustus established a system in which the messengers would be

[137] Conversely, although the Sasanid capital was inherited by the Umayyads, its location in Iraq meant that its status was relegated to that of a province.

[138] In Sauvaget's words, 'The *Barīd* is no more than, as its name suggests, a reincarnation of the Roman and Byzantine *Cursus Publicus*, re-established under new auspices by the Umayyad caliphs of the seventh century …' (Sauvaget, *La Poste aux chevaux dans l'empire des Mamelouks*, Paris, 1941, p. 1).

[139] Suetonius, *The Lives of the Caesars I: Julius. Augustus. Tiberius. Gaius. Caligula*, (trans. J.C. Rolfe), Cambridge Mass., 1998, IL: 3. Compare *Kitāb al-aghānī*, vol. II, p. 251, where Muʿāwiya interrogates a *Barīd* courier on the local conditions in the land from which he set out, implying that – unlike the Achaemenid system of relay-couriers – in both the *Cursus Publicus* and Muʿāwiya's *Barīd* the same courier made the entire journey from start to finish.

[140] The quote is from Suetonius (in Dvornik, *Origins*, p. 84). For official communications in the preceding period, see A.W. Ramsay, 'A Roman Postal Service under the Republic', *The Journal of Roman Studies* 10 (1920), 79–86; and A.C. Leighton, 'Secret Communication amongst the Greeks and Romans', *Technology and Culture* 10ii (1969), 139–54.

relieved of their letters at each relay,[141] only to replace this arrangement with a relays of mounts (or carriages), thereby allowing the same messenger to complete the entire journey. This early instance of tinkering with the original arrangement distinguished the Roman postal system from the ancient Iranian ones and also served as a sign of things to come: we shall see that the *Cursus Publicus* was regularly subjected to reforms over the following centuries. Second, what this new arrangement gained in 'convenience' (as Suetonius puts it), it lost in speed: a single messenger could not complete his mission without stopping for sleep (or food), and the Roman postal system is said to have covered only about 75 kilometres per day on average.[142]

The infrastructure of the *Cursus Publicus* consisted of relay-stations (Latin: *mutationes*) and resting-stations (*mansiones*). The stations were usually equipped with grooms, veterinarians, carpenters, accountants, and anything else deemed necessary for the system.[143] Use of these facilities was limited to those in possession of warrants or diplomas that specified the privileges of the bearer, ranging from the simple *evectiones* that authorised transportation on the mounts of the postal system, to the *tractoriae* that entitled the bearer to all necessary lodging and provisions.[144] From the third century CE, the *Cursus Publicus* was subdivided into ordinary and swift branches. The former is by far the less well understood of the two and was not available in every period and region. Called the *Cursus Clabularis*, it consisted of wagons pulled by oxen, usually in the service of the military or whenever the rapid mounts of the *Cursus Velox*, the swift branch of the postal service, were unable to bear the weight of a particular load. The *Cursus Velox* is usually what is meant by the Roman postal system. Predominantly using horses (Latin: *veredi*, sing. *veredus*), the *Cursus Velox* did not depend on the upkeep of the paved Roman roads and was concerned with the rapid conveyance of anything – messages, orders, reports, and people – across the empire. It is the *Cursus Velox*, therefore, that doubled as a system of information-gathering and, ultimately, internal surveillance.

During this period, the agents of the *Cursus Publicus* were invariably arranged according to the promotion scales of a cavalry unit in the military.

141 Some scholars detect echoes of the Achaemenid postal system (as described by Herodotus and Xenophon) in Augustus' initial arrangement and argue that it is likely to have been influenced by Persian precedents (Dvornik, *Origins*, p. 89; and O. Kurz, 'Cultural Relations between Parthia and Rome', *The Cambridge History of Iran III*, Cambridge, 1983, p. 564).

142 In cases of urgency, of course, the speeds recorded were considerably more impressive, attaining – in some instances – four times the average speed (cf. A. W. Ramsay, 'The Speed of the Roman Imperial Post', *The Journal of Roman Studies* 15 (1925), 60–74; and C. W. J. Eliot, 'New Evidence for the Speed of the Roman Imperial Post', *Phoenix* 9ii (1955), 76–80).

143 For documents from two *mansiones* of fourth-century Egypt, see *P. Oxy.* 40: 4087–8.

144 There are numerous studies of the *Cursus Publicus*, including E. J. Holmberg, *Zur Geschichte des Cursus Publicus*, Uppsala, 1933; A. H. M. Jones, *The Later Roman Empire 284–602*, Oxford, 1964, pp. 830–4; Kolb, *Transport und Nachtrichtentransfer*; A. H. Lee, *Information and Frontiers: Roman Foreign Relations in Late Antiquity*, Cambridge, 1993; and R. M. Sheldon, *Intelligence Activities in Ancient Rome*, London, 2004.

All types of courier could eventually become involved in surveillance activities, usually in policing the routes of the postal system itself. Until the late third century CE, the couriers were referred to as *frumentarii*; thereafter, Diocletian (r. 284–305 CE) reorganised these 'grain-providers' under the new name of *agentes in rebus* ('those active in affairs'). From the late fourth century we also find the term *veredarii* applied to imperial couriers, whose functions, responsibilities, and privileges appear to have been identical to those of the *agentes in rebus*, though the latter continued to function at least into the late seventh century.

Generally speaking, the Later Roman or 'Byzantine' postal system was modelled on the Roman one. The clear distinction that modern scholarship tends to make between the Roman Empire and its eastern continuation was far from clear at the time: the Byzantine population regarded themselves as *Romaioi*, 'Romans', and later Arabic authors continued to view them as the *Rūm*. Yet the creation of Constantinople in 330 CE did have tangible effects on the *Cursus Publicus*, amongst other things. The location of the new capital represented an eastward shift in Roman power and prestige, and, accordingly, the saying '*omnes viae Romam ducunt*' gradually lost its accuracy. Moreover, the official adoption of Christianity meant that clergymen, religious scholars, and, on occasion, even pilgrims could expect to benefit from the facilities of the postal system on their travels. This led to an increase in the number of postal warrants issued, as well as a commensurate increase in the burden placed on the local population who provided mounts and manpower for the system. The proliferation of postal warrants, the frustrating imposition that supporting the *Cursus Publicus* had on the populace, and the scandalous behaviour of some *frumentarii* and *agentes in rebus* who terrorised the provinces with arbitrary requisitions and with fabricated accusations of subversion, made the postal system intensely unpopular throughout the empire. In response to this, the *Cursus Publicus* was repeatedly subjected to adjustments and reforms that distinguish the Late Antique postal system from its Augustan predecessor. The following treatment of the *Cursus Publicus* in Late Antiquity covers the material under three rubrics: Routes and stations, Messengers and informants, and Administration.

Routes and stations

Although, theoretically, the postal infrastructure of the Byzantine period was simply a continuation of the earlier, Roman system of *mansiones* and *mutationes*, in practice there were two perceptible differences between the Byzantine and Roman road systems. The first difference is that in the Byzantine lands that would eventually be incorporated into the caliphate, the distinction between relay-stations and resting-stations appears to have been ill-defined: the Latin terms *mansiones* and *mutationes* are covered in Greek sources by the single term *stathmoi* (sing. *stathmos*), and by the mid sixth century descriptions of the earlier, Roman system do not reflect an awareness of the distinction between relay- and resting-stations. In his description of the pre-Justinian postal system, Procopius – a native of greater Syria – remarks that,

Within the distance included in each day's journey for an unencumbered traveller [the Roman Emperors of earlier times] established stations, sometimes eight, sometimes less, but as a general thing not less than five. And horses to the number of forty stood ready at each station. And grooms in proportion to the number of horses were detailed to all stations. And always travelling with frequent changes of the horses, which were of the most approved breeds, those to whom this duty was assigned covered, on occasion, a ten-days' journey in a single day.[145]

As the context of this passage makes clear, Procopius' intention here is to contrast the efficiency of the *Cursus Publicus* in previous times with that of Justinian's reign, and the fact that he does not mention the distinction between *mansiones* and *mutationes* would suggest that he was unacquainted with this notable aspect of the Augustan system.[146]

The second difference between the Byzantine and Roman road systems is that the former relied far less on wheeled vehicles and, by extension, paved roads than the latter did. Bulliet has shown that at some point between the fourth and sixth centuries CE, widespread domestication of the camel in the Near East led to the abandonment of wheeled transportation.[147] This affected the *Cursus Publicus* in two ways: first, the *Cursus Clabularis*, which relied on oxen drawing heavy wagons, was abolished in the eastern provinces of the empire as early as the reign of Leo (r. 457–74).[148] Thereafter, heavy transport

145 Procopius, *Anecdota*, (trans. H. B. Dewing), Cambridge Mass., 1969, XXX: 3–5.

146 It is possible that in the later Byzantine period, centuries after the rise of Islam, a dual system of relay-stations and resting-stations was reintroduced into the Byzantine world. Michael Psellus (eleventh century CE), for instance, makes reference both to *stathmoi* and *hippostaseis*, the latter being a Greek equivalent of the *mutationes* (in M. F. Hendy, *Studies in the Byzantine Monetary Economy c. 300–1450*, Cambridge, 1985, p. 609).

147 R. Bulliet, *The Camel and the Wheel*, Cambridge Mass., 1975, *passim*, esp. p. 26. The sudden disappearance of milestones from the roads of the Byzantine Near East during this period also indicates a decline in the state of imperial routes on the eve of Islam (cf. B. Isaac, 'Trade Routes to Arabia and the Roman Presence in the Desert', in T. Fahd (ed.), *L'Arabie préislamique et son environnment historique et culturel*, Leiden, 1989, pp. 241–56 at p. 248; and A. Kazhdan, 'Milestone', in *ODB*, p. 1372).

148 Leo is said to have abolished the *Cursus Clabularis* in the prefecture of Oriens in 467–8 (J. M. Carrié, 'Cursus Publicus' in G. Bowerstock, P. Brown, and O. Grabar (eds.), *Late Antiquity: A Guide to the Post-Classical World*, Cambridge Mass., 1999, p. 402). Hendy (*Studies*, pp. 294–6) has shown that until the reign of Anastasius (r. 491–518), taxes were paid in kind, and the transportation of these taxes to the battlefield was amongst the most important duties of the *Cursus Clabularis*. Thereafter, however, the commutation of the taxation to taxes in coin meant that the *Cursus Velox* could transport the revenue to the capital, thereby largely rendering the *Cursus Clabularis* obsolete. The fact that for Procopius (*Anecdota*, XXX: 2) one of the chief functions of the postal system was 'that those who conveyed the annual taxes might reach the capital safely and without either delay or risk' confirms that by the mid sixth century it was the *Cursus Velox* that transported tax revenues to the capital.

was arranged through irregular requisitions which, interestingly, are referred to as *angariae* – a term the Byzantines borrowed from their Persian rivals.[149] Second, the *Cursus Velox* no longer used the variety of carriages that had been employed in the Roman period. Procopius knows only of 'horses to the number of forty stood ready at each station', rather than the four-wheeled *rheda* or the two-wheeled *birota* (amongst other carriages) that were used frequently in the Roman *Cursus Velox*.[150]

Procopius' passage also alerts us to the complex and controversial issue of the distance between postal stations. According to him, between five and eight stations were established over the distance that an 'unencumbered traveller' could cover in a day. Assuming a daily average of 35 kilometres for such a traveller, the postal stations were available every 4 to 5 kilometres.[151] These figures do not tally with the distances between stations reported by travellers or recorded in such official road books as the *Itinerarium Antonini*, the *Itinerarium Burdigalense*, or the *Tabula Peutingeriana*.[152] There is, accordingly, considerable controversy amongst scholars concerning the precise distances between stations,[153] and it is likely that this controversy reflects infrastructural inconsistencies: distances may have been determined by the importance of the road in question or by its distance from or proximity to the capital, amongst other factors.

The financial implications of maintaining stations along imperial routes were considerable and had important (though often neglected) ramifications for the infrastructure of the road system. The fact that – as we shall see – farmers and peasants living along the imperial routes were expected to supply fodder and other provisions for the postal stations in their region means that relay-stations could not be situated at distances beyond what a peasant and his loaded donkey could cover in a day, considering that the peasant would

[149] Procopius (*Anecdota*, XXX: 15) refers to the 'great number of camels, which followed the Roman army as it moved against an enemy and carried all the provisions', demonstrating that the *Cursus Clabularis* was obviated by the domestication of the camel in the Near East.

[150] On the vehicles employed in the *Cursus Publicus*, see R. J. Forbes, *Studies in Ancient Technology II*, Leiden, 1955, p. 159.

[151] Ibn Ḥawqal (*Kitāb al-masālik wa al-mamālik*, Leiden, 1873, p. 130) suggests that in the tenth century the Byzantine '*Barīd*' stations were located at 1-parasang intervals, this being every 6 kilometres.

[152] On these sources, see Hendy, *Studies*, p. 604. It is worth mentioning that of these three itineraries, only the *Itinerarium Burdigalense* indicates *mutationes* in addition to the *mansiones* recorded in the other sources. On the composition of route books in the context of 'geographical intelligence', see Sheldon, *Intelligence*, pp. 148–50; and Dvornik, *Origins*, pp. 111ff. On the use of detailed road-maps during military campaigns, see Vegetius, *Epitoma Rei Militaris*, Stuttgart, 1885, III: 6.

[153] Dvornik (*Origins*, p. 100) suggests 60–75 kilometres between *mutationes* and 100 between *mansiones*; Gazagnadou (*La Poste*, p. 120) says that 'stations' were 30–36 kilometres apart; Casson (*Travel in the Ancient World*, New York, 1994, p. 184) has put forward 25–35 miles between *mutationes*, but less the nearer that one was to the capital; and Jones (*Later Roman Empire*, p. 831) holds that postal stations were no more than 15 (and only rarely more than 8 or 9) 'miles' apart.

then have to return within the same day. On this basis, Hendy has argued that the average distance between stations was 16 to 18 kilometres.[154]

It is difficult to ascertain to what extent either the *mansiones* or the *mutationes* were maintained in the eastern provinces of the empire on the eve of Islam. Procopius states that 'for all the rest of the East as far as Egypt [Justinian] allowed one station only for each day's journey, using not horses, however, but mules and only a few of them'. Procopius does accept, though, that 'on the route leading into Persia [Justinian] did allow the previous arrangement [of five to eight stations for each day's journey] to stand'.[155] It is unclear which 'route leading into Persia' the emperor is supposed to have spared,[156] but it is most probable that it passed through territory that would become part of the caliphal lands. Furthermore, regardless of Justinian's supposed reduction of the *Cursus Publicus* in the East, it would appear that the basic infrastructure of the system was still in place during the period immediately preceding the Islamic conquests. Thus, in the *Life of St Theodore of Sykeon* (*ca.* 550–640) we are told that Theodore's father was an imperial courier who impregnated the woman who was the station-master of the way-station where the courier lodged.[157] The same source makes direct reference both to the postal system and to the postal stations that were used during the reign of Phocas (r. 602–10).[158] The *Chronicon Paschale* (written *ca.* 630) reports that news of the Byzantine victory over the Sasanids in 628 was circulated throughout the empire and that intelligence reports were successfully transmitted even under the harshest weather conditions.[159] There is little doubt, then, that the roads and stations of the *Cursus Publicus* were in use in the eastern regions of the Byzantine Empire on the eve of Islam. But the suspension of the *Cursus Clabularis*, and the lack of wheeled vehicles in the *Cursus Velox*, meant that the Arab conquerors of the seventh century would have come into possession of a postal system that differed in significant ways from Diocletian's *Cursus Publicus*.

Messengers and informants

The infrastructure of the postal system benefited official and non-official travellers alike. While the facilities of the relay-stations were only available to those who possessed the necessary documentation, the *mansiones* were open to paying travellers of whatever nature. Moreover, with the adoption of

[154] Hendy, *Studies*, p. 606. This is not to say that stations were provisioned on a daily basis, but that delivering supplies to a station and returning had to be accomplished within a single day, suggesting that the total distance covered cannot have been more than 35 kilometres.

[155] Procopius, *Anecdota*, XXX: 10. John Lydus makes similar remarks, albeit without directly implicating the emperor (see below, p. 39).

[156] Hendy, *Studies*, p. 609.

[157] *Vie de Théodore de Sykéon*, (ed./trans. A. J. Festugière), Brussels, 1970, chapter 3.

[158] Ibid., chapter 120 (postal system); and chapter 142 (postal stations).

[159] *Chronicon Paschale*, pp. 182–3 (news of victory); and p. 186 (intelligence reports).

Christianity as the state religion in the mid fourth century, the category of 'official travellers' was often expanded to include clergymen and pilgrims.[160] Already in 383 we find pilgrims making use of the *Cursus Publicus*,[161] and in 436 Melania the Younger journeyed from Constantinople to Jerusalem equipped with warrants entitling her to horses of the system.[162] In fact, some of the most detailed descriptions of the *Cursus Publicus*'s infrastructure are provided in the travel accounts of pilgrims from this period.[163] In most cases, however, those using the facilities of the *Cursus Publicus* were the imperial couriers known as the *frumentarii* (sing. *frumentarius*, 'grain-provider') and – from the fourth century onwards – the *agentes in rebus* (sing. *agens in rebus*, 'those active in affairs'), the *veredarii* (sing. *veredarius*, 'those who ride the *veredi*, post-horses'), and the *notarii* (sing. *notarius*, 'secretary' in the original sense of the word). On occasion, the messengers would be accompanied by a groom or escort (*parhippus*), who probably served the same purpose as the Sasanid *parwānag*.[164]

Towards the end of the third century, the *frumentarii* came to be regarded by the provincial population as a plague, and Diocletian replaced them with a new corps called the *agentes in rebus*. This move may have placated the populace, but its consequences proved to be ephemeral: the *agentes in rebus* came to be as unruly and as despised as the *frumentarii* had ever been, and many contemporary observers were unable to detect any real difference between the old and new categories of couriers, beyond the shift in nomenclature.[165] With the benefit of hindsight, modern scholars have highlighted three aspects of the *agentes in rebus* that distinguished them from their predecessors.[166] First, the *frumentarii* were military personnel, whereas the *agentes in rebus* belonged to the civil service, despite the fact that they progressed through the ranks of a cavalry unit. Second, while the *frumentarii* were employed by and answerable to the Praetorian Prefect, the *agentes in rebus* were placed under the newly created *Magister Officiorum* ('Master of Offices'), a post that was to be the most influential administrative position in the Byzantine Empire until the creation of the Logothete of the Drome in the

160 Additionally, informants such as the *agentes in rebus* would now ferret out heretics within the empire, rather than persecute Christians, as the *frumentarii* had done (Sheldon, *Intelligence*, p. 254).

161 In Isaac, *Limits of Empire*, p. 205.

162 Her entourage, however, did not possess the necessary warrants and attempted to secure postal horses through bribery (Casson, *Travel*, p. 301).

163 On these sources, see Hendy, *Studies*, p. 73.

164 N. Audollent ('Les Veredarii: émmissaires impériaux sous le Bas Empire', *Mélanges d'Archéologie et d'Histoire* 9 (1889), 249–78, at 263) believes that the *parhippi* were the mounts ridden by a courier's groom, while Forbes (*Ancient Technology II*, p. 155f.) assumes that the *parhippus* was a courier's packhorse.

165 According to St Jerome, *frumentarius* was simply an antiquated word for an *agens in rebus* (in Audollent, 'Veredarii', 274).

166 The following is based on W. G. Sinnigen, 'Two Branches of the Late Roman Secret Service', *The American Journal of Philology* 80 (1959), 238–54; and Sheldon, *Intelligence*, pp. 261–3.

mid eighth century.[167] Third, the *agentes in rebus* were noticeably more numerous than the *frumentarii* had ever been: in the second century the latter are said to have numbered no more than 200 men in the entire empire,[168] whereas the *agentes in rebus* are said to have exceeded 10,000 men within a century of their establishment.[169] This figure is almost certainly an exaggeration, and a better indication of their numerical superiority is the fact that Theodosius II (r. 408–50) limited them to 1,174 and Leo to 1,248 for the East alone.[170]

Regardless of whether or not these distinctions between the two *scholae* adequately explain the nature of Diocletian's reform, two points must be stressed: first, the emperor could not rule without the service of his imperial couriers. In creating the *agentes in rebus* he felt that he was maintaining such a service while solving the problem of the *frumentarii*. Second, it is unlikely that the *frumentarii* were merely replaced by a similar corps with a different name, as there are no precedents in Roman history for changing the name of a *schola* that needed to be disciplined. The common solution in such cases was to pass laws restricting the privileges or limiting the numbers of the unruly corps. This was the course of action when the *agentes in rebus* themselves got out of hand: they were reprimanded and circumscribed by laws recorded in legal codes of the fifth and sixth centuries,[171] but they retained their name at least until the year 700.[172]

Eventually, the *agentes in rebus* evolved from mere couriers to administrators of the *Cursus Publicus*. This development was part of a larger process of bureaucratisation of the Byzantine Empire in the fifth and sixth centuries. During this period, the *notarii* gradually came to abandon their purely clerical duties and gain more meaningful influence in the imperial administration, while the *agentes in rebus* appear to have inherited the traditional functions of the *notarii*. The blurriness of the vocational divide between the two *scholae* reached a high-point in the sixth century, and in episodes from this period an imperial ambassador is referred to both as a *notarius* and an *agens in rebus* alternately.[173]

By the late sixth century, we find the *agentes in rebus* to be more active in the administrative contexts that were formerly associated with the *notarii* and less active in those duties – surveillance, assassinations, arrests, and requisitions – that originally contributed to their notoriety. This is not to

[167] The close relationship between the Master of Offices and the *agentes in rebus* can be seen in the occasional labelling of the latter as '*magistrianoi*', 'the Master's men' (in N. J. E. Austin, and B. Rankov, *Exploratio: Military and Political Intelligence in the Roman World*, New York and London, 1995, p. 219).

[168] W. G. Sinnigen, 'The Roman Secret Service', *The Classical Journal* 57ii (1971), 65–72 at 68.

[169] Jones, *Later Roman Empire*, p. 578.

[170] *Codex Theodosianus*, Berlin, 1905, 6.27.23 (Theodosian II); *Codex Iustinianus* (in P. Krueger, *Corpus Iuris Civilis II*, Berlin, 1954), 12.20.3 (Leo).

[171] For a complete survey of the numerous laws that were passed during this period regarding the *Cursus Publicus* and its functionaries, see Holmberg, *Cursus Publicus*, pp. 151–5.

[172] Sheldon, *Intelligence*, p. 263.

[173] On the relationship between the *notarii* and the *agentes in rebus* during this period, see Sinnigen, 'Late Roman Secret Service'. In Sinnigen's words, these *scholae* 'formed two interrelated branches of what may be called the Late Roman secret service'.

say that the *agentes in rebus* ceased to function as imperial couriers or informants; in reality, much of their 'informing' was carried out within the context of their administrative duties: as *curiosi*, 'snoops', they policed the routes and stations of the *Cursus Publicus*, and as *principes officii*, 'chiefs of staff', they would independently supervise the provincial administration in a manner that foreshadows the role of the *mushrif* in the Middle Abbasid period.[174] The function of the *agentes in rebus* as imperial couriers was maintained throughout their existence, although it is interesting to note the prevalence of the term *veredarii* in describing official couriers at a time when the *agentes in rebus* were becoming settled in the administration.

The term *veredarius* is attested already in the late fourth century,[175] and it is the *Book of Esther* that once again provides intriguing evidence in this context: although the *raṣṣīm* ('runners') of *Esther* 3: 13 are rendered in the Latin translation of the Bible by the term *cursores regis* ('royal runners'), the 'runners on horses' of *Esther* 8: 10 and 14 are translated by the word *veredarii*.[176] From the fifth century the term became increasingly prevalent with reference to imperial couriers (as distinct from the multi-tasking *agentes in rebus* or *notarii*), and it is significant that Procopius uses the Greek version of this word to the exclusion of all other terms in describing official couriers in his time. Two statements of his are especially telling: in one he remarks that 'they captured those who are occasionally sent to bear the royal response, **whom they call** *beredarioi*', while in the other he writes, '[Justinian] restored a bath at the lodgings of the *beredarioi*, **as they are called**'.[177] What this suggests is that a late sixth-century resident of a province that would eventually be conquered during the Islamic conquests consistently labelled imperial couriers *beredarioi*.[178] The *Chronicon Paschale*, however, refers to the bearers of official messages not as *veredarii* but as *a secretis*, this being a term that suspiciously mirrors the Sasanid *rāzbān* ('bearer of secrets') to which reference has been made.[179]

Administration

Covering, at its height, some 75,000 kilometres of roads, the imposing infrastructure of the *Cursus Publicus* was probably second only to the military in

[174] Cf. C. Kelly, *Ruling the Later Roman Empire*, Cambridge, Mass., 2004, pp. 206–7. On *ishrāf*, see below, pp. 114, 125–6.

[175] Audollent, 'Veredarii', 267.

[176] Compare Saʿadiya's use of *fuyūj* for the 'runners' of *Esther* 3: 13, and *burūd* for the mounted couriers of *Esther* 8: 10 and 14.

[177] Procopius, *History of the Wars of Justinian*, (trans. H. B. Dewing), Cambridge Mass., 1961–8, III: 12 (my emphasis); and *Buildings*, (trans. H. B. Dewing), Cambridge Mass., 1961, V: 3 (my emphasis). Dewing spells the term *veredarii*, reflecting the original Latin form of the word.

[178] The sixth-century Syriac text of Zachariah of Mitylene also refers to couriers in the service of the Byzantine and Sasanid rulers as *beredarioi* (in *The Syriac Chronicle Known as that of Zachariah of Mitylene*, (ed./trans. E. W. Brooks and F. J. Hamilton), London, 1899, p. 206 n. 6, and p. 208 n. 4).

[179] *Chronicon Paschale*, pp. 126, 185, and 187.

its command of manpower and resources. Ensuring that the system functioned smoothly and efficiently was thus a daunting undertaking that continually posed dilemmas for rulers and senior bureaucrats.

The burden of providing for the material needs of the *Cursus Publicus* usually fell upon the population in the provinces through which the imperial routes passed.[180] A number of emperors attempted to shift some of the expenses to the Treasury, but such attempts were invariably of short-lived success: although Augustus relied on the population for mounts, fodder, and manpower for the postal system, Nerva (r. 96–8) was the first to abolish this system, issuing coins that proudly proclaimed 'The obligation of caring for the post suppressed in Italy.'[181] By Hadrian's reign (r. 117–38), however, the populace was once again supporting the system financially; and despite subsequent attempts to redistribute the costs of the system,[182] by the Byzantine period the responsibility of the provincial population to provide for the *Cursus Publicus* was no longer in question.

Although this situation was ostensibly burdensome upon the empire's subjects, there were resourceful arrangements by which the costs to the local population were defrayed. Procopius tells us that in pre-Justinian times,

> The owners of the land everywhere, and particularly if their lands happened to lie in the interior, were exceedingly prosperous because of this [postal] system. For every year they sold the surplus of their crops to the Government for the maintenance of horses and grooms, and thus earned much money. And the result of all this was that while the Treasury regularly received the taxes assessed upon each man, yet those who paid the taxes received their money back again immediately, and there was the further advantage that the State business has been accomplished.[183]

Bearing in mind Procopius' well-known hostility to his patron Justinian, it would be tempting to treat this passage and the statement that Justinian discontinued these favourable arrangements[184] as exaggerated and unwarranted criticism of the emperor, were it not for the fact that John Lydus makes similar remarks (despite absolving Justinian of any direct blame for these developments).[185] The *Cursus Publicus* was thus integrated into the routine of the provincial economy in a way that alleviated some of the burden that the populace was made to bear.

While it was the people who lived in the vicinity of postal stations who were ordinarily expected to provide both material and manpower for the system, the station-masters (Latin: *mancipes*, sing. *manceps*) were often

[180] Isaac, *Limits of Empire*, p. 201. [181] In Dvornik, *Origins*, p. 95.
[182] Sheldon, *Intelligence*, pp. 146–7. [183] Procopius, *Anecdota*, XXX: 6–7.
[184] Ibid., XXX: 1, where Justinian's curtailing of the *Cursus Publicus* indicates his lack of 'consideration for the welfare of the state'.
[185] Quoted in Hendy, *Studies*, p. 295. John Lydus believes that the Praetorian Prefect in the East deemed the postal system (Greek: *dēmosioi hippoi*) to be useless, and he abolished the system without Justinian's knowledge. To Procopius, however, Justinian was personally behind this initiative. See also W. Threadgold, *Byzantium and the Army, 284–1081*, Stanford, 1995, p. 169.

low-ranking officials who would serve in this capacity for five years. The position was unpopular both on account of the exacting duties associated with registering the traffic of couriers, and for the fact that it required that officials be stationed on the road throughout their tenure. Moreover, those manning the stations often did so for no pay,[186] and documents from Egypt show that locals served in the stations as a compulsory service.[187] The station-masters were supervised by *agentes in rebus*, one or two of whom were sent to each province to oversee the administration of the postal infrastructure and to discourage corruption or other abuses of the system.[188]

Until the reign of Diocletian, the *Cursus Publicus* was controlled by the Praetorian Prefects who had been responsible for the couriers (*frumentarii*), the routes and stations, and the granting of *evectiones* to official travellers. In the fourth century, control over the couriers (*agentes in rebus*) and the distribution of *evectiones* were reassigned to the *Magister Officiorum*.[189] Accordingly, the administration of the postal system was divided between two rival officials. The Praetorian Prefects were the overseers of tax-collection in their prefectures, and the funding of the *Cursus Publicus* remained their responsibility. The Master of Offices was responsible for the internal security of the empire, and the *agentes in rebus*, as couriers and informants, were subject to him. The rivalry between these two officials is the central theme of John Lydus' *On the Magistrates* and can be seen to have reached a high-point in the second half of the sixth century.[190] Thus, the Byzantine system of communications and surveillance, whose counterpart under the caliphs would eventually be limited to a single *dīwān* of the *Barīd*, was split between rival functionaries on the eve of Islam.

Conclusions

Any comparison between the Byzantine *Cursus Publicus* and the caliphal *Barīd* must take into account three significant issues. First, the Byzantine capital at Constantinople was relatively easily accessible to boats arriving from all major ports of the empire. For this reason, the *Cursus Publicus* – despite

186 Jones, *Later Roman Empire*, p. 832; and Hendy, *Studies*, p. 604. But see J. M. Carrié, 'Cursus Publicus', in *Late Antiquity*, p. 402, where it is argued that the *manceps* was paid for his service.

187 E.g. *P. Oxy*. 6: 900 (322 CE), and *P. Oxy*. 51: 3623 (359 CE).

188 *Codex Theodosianus*, 6.29.4.

189 John Lydus, *On the Magistrates*, (ed./trans. T. F. Carney), in *Bureaucracy in Traditional Society: Roman-Byzantine Bureaucracies Viewed from Within, Volume II*, Kansas, 1971, III: 40.4–5. Officially, the granting of *evectiones* was the responsibility of the *regendarii* (sing. *regendarius*).

190 Only with the creation of the Logothete of the Drome, who replaced the Master of Offices at some point in the eighth century and who was also in charge of the postal system (now referred to by its Greek name, *Dēmosios Dromos*), was this institution reunited under a single office (see D. A. Miller, 'The Logothete of the Drome in the Middle Byzantine Period', *Byzantion* 36 (1966), 438–70).

being a land-based system in essence – could be complemented by river and sea-based travel. Documents from Egypt refer to imperial couriers travelling on the Nile,[191] and Procopius tells us that when Justinian reduced the number of postal stations in the East,

> [He] compelled all the couriers, much against their will, to proceed from Byzantium directly to Helenopolis by sea. When they make the passage, then, in small boats of the kind the folk are accustomed to use in crossing the strait, in case a storm happens to descend upon them, they come into great danger. For since the haste which is obligatory keeps urging them on, it is impossible for them to watch for the right weather and wait for the next calm.[192]

Travel by sea or river is unquestionably cheaper for the authorities than using the facilities of the *stathmoi*, but it is also less reliable (for the reasons stated by Procopius), and generally less apt for comparison with the caliphal *Barīd*, than an entirely land-based system such as that of the Sasanids.

Second, although the Sasanid postal system appears to have been running efficiently in the early seventh century, the Byzantine *Cursus Publicus* was clearly in decline on the eve of Islam. Here too, it is Procopius' testimony that is indispensable. In his words, the reduction of the *Cursus Publicus* during Justinian's reign meant that 'the things which take place in each country, being reported both with difficulty and too late to give opportunity for action and behind the course of events, cannot be dealt with at all'.[193] By contrast, Procopius notes that Khusrô I 'increased the salaries of his spies and profited by this forethought. For nothing that was happening among the Romans escaped him.'[194] Thus, although the fifty-year peace treaty of 561 between the Byzantines and Sasanids stipulated that the official envoys of each empire should be availed of full use of the respective empire's postal system,[195] it is likely that when riding through Sasanid lands the Byzantine envoys enjoyed superior facilities to those on offer in their own lands to Sasanid envoys.[196] The fact that the *Cursus Publicus* was in decline during this period also means that even if we are to assume that the early caliphs deliberately adopted the Byzantine postal system in creating their own *Barīd*, the resulting institution would have been significantly different from the Augustan or early Byzantine postal systems on which our sources are so informative. The paved roads, the numerous milestones, the countless horses stationed at relay- and resting-stations, and the entire *Cursus Clabularis* – all of these being characteristic

[191] E.g. *P. Oxy*. 33: 2675; and *P. Oxy*. 51: 3623; and R.S. Bagnall, *Egypt in Late Antiquity*, Princeton, 1993, pp. 36, 40, and 67.

[192] Procopius, *Anecdota*, XXX: 8–9. [193] Ibid., XXX: 11.

[194] Ibid., XXX: 18. Procopius' statement is confirmed by the evidence of the *SN* and other sources (see above, p. 28).

[195] Menander Protector, *The History of Menander the Guardsman*, (trans. R.C. Blockley), Liverpool, 1985, p. 212.

[196] On foreign envoys using the facilities of the *Cursus Publicus* in the West, see A. Gillet, *Envoys and Political Communication in the Late Antique West, 411–533*, Cambridge, 2003, pp. 238–43.

features of the fourth-century *Cursus Publicus* – were nowhere to be seen in the Syria and Egypt of the early seventh century.

Third, in centring their empire on the previously Byzantine province of Syria, the Umayyad caliphs were able to tap into the rich bureaucratic resources that the Byzantines (and their predecessors in the region) had bequeathed to them; it is well known that for decades after the conquest of Egypt and Syria, the functionaries and even the language of the Byzantine administration were retained by the caliphs. But neither the *Magister Officiorum* nor his trusty *agentes in rebus* would have been retained in this way. The administration of the *Cursus Publicus* was not something with which the Arabs or the populations they came to rule would have had any meaningful experience. For these reasons, statements that dismiss the caliphal *Barīd* as being 'no more than . . . a reincarnation of the Roman and Byzantine *Cursus Publicus*'[197] are misleading generalisations at best.

Communications in pre-Umayyad Arabia[198]

Introduction

On the face of it, there would appear to be little reason to turn to 'Arabia'[199] in accounting for the early history of the caliphal *Barīd.* With the exception of South Arabia, there is no evidence for the existence of complex states in the region before the rise of Islam. Thus, it would have been unnecessary for stateless Arabians to establish costly and unpopular institutions such as the Sasanid and Byzantine postal systems were.

That said, there are three reasons why methods of communication in pre-Umayyad[200] Arabia are worthy of our attention here. First, although filing documents or conducting land surveys are not skills that we can reasonably expect Arabians to have had, riding horses or camels at speed while bearing a message is something that they were certainly able to do. Moreover, we know that in the contexts of raiding and warfare Arabians during this period had gained considerable experience gathering and transmitting information

[197] See above, n. 138.

[198] The following is a synopsis of my article 'A Neglected Chapter in the History of Caliphal State-Building', *JSAI* 30 (2005), 293–317. A more detailed treatment of this topic, including full references to the primary sources, may be found there.

[199] While it is recognised that the terms 'Arabia' and 'Arabians' do not capture the cultural and topographical diversity of the Arabian Peninsula (for which, see R. Hoyland, *Arabia and the Arabs from the Bronze Age to the Coming of Islam*, New York, 2001), these terms are employed here with reference to the Arabian Peninsula and its inhabitants for the sake of convenience.

[200] As most scholars – both medieval Muslim and modern Western ones – credit Muʿāwiya or ʿAbd al-Malik with the creation of the *Barīd*, all evidence of organised communication that predates the Umayyad period may be considered together, regardless of whether it refers to the period before or after Muḥammad's emigration from Mecca in 622. Accordingly, the term 'pre-Umayyad Arabia' has been adopted here rather than the more commonplace 'pre-Islamic Arabia'.

about other tribes.[201] Second, there is evidence that in their long-standing rivalry both the Byzantines and the Sasanids employed Arabians as messengers and spies, a point to which we shall return. Thus, even if we are to assume that the early Umayyads simply perpetuated the practices of the pre-Islamic empires in creating their own system of communication, the methods of communication employed by Arabians would still be of relevance to this study. Third, it will be shown that despite having little need for such a system themselves, Arabians acquired familiarity with the Byzantine and Sasanid postal systems on the eve of Islam. When, during the early Islamic conquests, Arabians came to require a reliable system of swift communication, they were able to adopt (a rudimentary version of) the imperial systems with which they had become acquainted.

Arabian communications

By its very nature, pre-Umayyad Arabian society was very mobile. The nomadism that characterised life in much of Arabia depended on the ability of all members of society to travel, and the centrality of pilgrimage and trade to the Arabian 'economy' is another aspect of Arabian mobility.[202] But the swift transmission of messages was irregular and relatively disorganised. There are three aspects of this type of communication that are central to any discussion of the early *Barīd*. The first is the use of the term *bashīr* with reference to Arabian couriers. The second is the *risāla mughalghala* ('relayed message') that was transmitted by Arabian couriers. The third is the frequent use of two couriers to deliver a single message. Importantly, each of these aspects was associated by later writers with the early Umayyad *Barīd*.

The *bashīr*

The term *bashīr* is often taken to mean 'bearer of glad tidings', but during this period the word was not limited to bearers of good news.[203] It is important to note that there was no specific functionary called the *bashīr* in Arabia; the label was applied retroactively to someone who had delivered a message. This would also be true for the caliphal *Barīd*, a system that consisted of routes and stations to be used by authorised travellers, not of a body of professional couriers. Furthermore, the Arabian *bashīr* is seen to deliver news of victories

201 On which, see: M. Suleman, 'The Role of Intelligence in the Successful Defense of Medina in AH 5', *Islamic Quarterly* 28 (1984), 47–52; and 'Espionage in Pre-Islamic Arabia', *Islamic Quarterly* 32 (1988), 21–33.

202 Cf. S. al-Afghānī, *Aswāq al-ʿarab fī al-jāhiliyya wa al-islām*, Damascus, 1960; and N. Groom, *Frankincense and Myrrh*, London, 1981.

203 Silverstein, 'Neglected Chapter', 296. The related Hebrew root *b.sh.r.* is defined as to 'bear tidings . . . even of evil' (in F. Brown, S. R. Driver, and C. A. Briggs, *A Hebrew and English Lexicon of the Old Testament*, Oxford, 1962, p. 142).

and of the deaths of notables, these two being responsibilities that would eventually fall to messengers using the *Barīd*.[204]

More important is the fact that early Muslim writers would often use the terms *bashīr* and *barīd* interchangeably. In seventh-century poetry, some verses quoted in one collection using the term *bashīr* are elsewhere recorded as using the term *barīd* instead.[205] It may be argued that since both words follow the same *faʿīl* pattern and share two of three consonants, later writers simply confused them rather than deliberately comparing the pre-Umayyad *bashīr* with the caliphal *barīd*. But in a telling passage, Ṭabarī writes: '[Regarding the Qurʾānic verse 12: 96, that says] "then came the *bashīr*": this means the *barīd* that Joseph sent by post (*abradahu*) to Jacob',[206] thereby consciously equating the two terms. The fact that in Qajar Iran the postmaster-general was referred to as *Bashīr al-Dawla* shows that the postal connotations of the word *bashīr* persisted long into the Islamic period.[207]

Finally, from a verse in the ode of ʿAlqama ibn ʿAbda al-Faḥl (sixth century) we can infer that a *bashīr* would signal that he bears good news by waving the fringes of his robe.[208] Although this detail appears to be inconsequential, it resurfaces in the Sufyanid period, when Abū Bakra is described as having 'signalled with his cloak' (*alāḥa bi-thawbihi*) that he bears good news.[209] The practice does not appear to have survived into the Marwanid or later periods.

The *risāla mughalghala*

Following the medieval Muslim lexicographers, Lane explains this term as meaning 'A message, or letter, conveyed from town to town, or from country to country'.[210] The term appears almost always in poetry, and the contexts in which it is used point to the fact that the message is delivered speedily, usually under urgent circumstances. It occurs repeatedly in the *dīwān* of the tribe of Hudhayl, and twice in Ibn Hishām's biography of Muḥammad.[211]

As was the case with the *bashīr*, here too the term is most important to us for its association with the early *Barīd*. In one instance, Saʿīd ibn al-ʿĀṣ (sixth century) sends a *barīd* to his family telling them of his captivity, and the courier is described as delivering the message *mughalghalatan*.[212] In another instance, Farazdaq (d. 728/30) writes: 'Who will tell Ziyād about me

204 Silverstein, 'Neglected Chapter', 296. 205 Ibid., 297.

206 Ṭabarī, *Taʾrīkh*, I, p. 408. That Muslim writers believe Joseph to have had a *Barīd* system is clear from Jāḥiẓ's statement that 'Joseph was the vizier of the King of Egypt . . . and he had *burud* (sing. *barīd*), and to him the reports were brought' (*Kitāb al-ḥayawān*, Cairo, 1940, vol. IV, p. 31).

207 Floor, 'The *Chapar-Khāna* System', 260.

208 In *Fuḥūl al-ʿarab fī ʿilm al-adab: sharḥ dīwān ʿalqama*, Algiers, 1925, p. 94.

209 Ṭabarī, *Taʾrīkh*, II, p. 12.

210 E. W. Lane, *Arabic-English Lexicon*, London and Edinburgh, 1863, vol. I, p. 2279.

211 Silverstein, 'Neglected Chapter', 298ff.

212 Zubayr ibn Bakkār, *Jamharat nasab quraysh*, Beirut, 1962, p. 428.

mughalghalatan, the *Barīd* gallops on with the message'.[213] Once again, it is significant that the term *mughalghala(tan)* is almost entirely absent from accounts of later periods, and that our sources are associating the *Barīd* with a pre-Umayyad method of sending news.

Two couriers

Whether a message was sent by a *bashīr* or was relayed 'from town to town', it was often the case that two messengers were despatched with the same message. This practice was particular to 'Arabia' rather than to 'Arabians'; hence, Byzantine or Sasanid messengers travelling within the region might also travel in pairs, since the reason for doing so was directly related to the terrain and conditions of the Arabian landscape.[214] A fascinating glimpse into these conditions is provided in Musil's account of traditional Arabian society of the early twentieth century. He writes:

> I went to bid farewell to the Prince and found him in front of his tent, squatting among the camels and issuing important orders to two Bedouins who were about to set out on speedy camels to al-Ǧowf. As soon as he dismissed them they swung upon their mounts and presently disappeared beyond a slope that hedged the camp on the east. They could not trifle with time, for they had orders to reach al-Ǧowf before dawn on the morrow and to report to the Prince the following day; and al-Ǧowf was 150 kilometers distant. The Prince had despatched two couriers in order to be sure that, in the event of a mishap to one of them, his message would be delivered by the other.[215]

According to this account, the practice resulted from the lack of confidence in a single messenger's ability to complete the mission successfully.[216] Such considerations apply only in places where the terrain is exceptionally harsh or the roads are deemed insecure, both of these being conditions that characterised Arabia for millennia. In other, non-Arabian societies where routes were insecure, similar techniques were employed: from the Ancient Near East to Medieval Europe rulers are seen to despatch two messengers with a single letter to double the chances of successful delivery.[217]

213 Ṭabarī, *Ta'rīkh*, II, p. 107. Further examples of the relationship between the 'relayed message' and the early *Barīd* are provided in Silverstein, 'Neglected Chapter', 298–300.
214 Thus, Khusrô II is reported to have sent two messengers to Muḥammad in the year 6 AH (Ṭabarī, *Ta'rīkh*, I, pp. 1572–3).
215 A. Musil, *Arabia Deserta*, New York, 1927, p. 120.
216 It is interesting that in the 'Constitution of Medina', Muḥammad stipulates that 'In every foray a rider must take another behind him' (in A. Guillaume, *The Life of Muhammad*, Karachi, 1955, pp. 231–3 clause §18), although there is no reason to believe that this statement extended to couriers in this context. See also Hoyland, *Arabia*, p. 191 plate 29(d) for an Assyrian relief (*ca.* 650 BCE) that depicts two Arabians riding a single camel.
217 Ancient Near East: Meier, *Messenger*, pp. 96–128 (chapter entitled 'Safety in Numbers?'); Medieval Europe: A. C. Leighton, *Transport and Communication in Medieval Europe AD 500–1100*, Newton Abbot, 1972, pp. 19–20.

With regard to pre-Umayyad Arabia, the sources mention two *bashīr*s sent out with news,[218] two vanguard-scouts (*ṭalīʿa*, pl. *ṭalāʾiʿ*) sent to gather intelligence,[219] and two messengers (*rasūl*) sent by Musaylima to Muḥammad bearing a letter in which the former proposes that they share 'the land' between them.[220] Ibn Qutayba relates that when Muḥammad himself is said to have sent *Barīd*-couriers 'from town to town' (*min balad ilā balad*; compare the *risāla mughalghala* above), he would order them 'to find a travel-companion ... as this is something that people have done in every period [of history]'.[221] In another noteworthy episode, Balādhurī relates that Muʿāwiya – at this point the governor of Syria – sent ʿUmar news of the Muslims' victory in Caesarea with two men. Fearing that they would not be quick enough, he then sent another messenger who was instructed to travel by day and night.[222] Interestingly, although Ṭabarī's version of this episode is nearly identical, he subsequently refers to the *Barīd* as having transmitted the news to ʿUmar,[223] thereby associating the *Barīd* with the despatch of two couriers. Examples of this practice survive well into the Islamic period, as evidenced in documents from the Cairo Geniza,[224] and from references to the caliphal *Barīd* using two couriers.[225]

One of the earliest references to the despatch of two couriers within Arabia is also the most interesting for our purposes. In Abraha's Maʾrib Dam inscription (542 CE) it is written that, upon hearing that the dam had been breached, 'they sent forward two couriers to the place where the Arabs were approaching'.[226] The word for 'two couriers' is represented by the consonants *BRDNN*. The Latin translation of the inscription renders this as *veredarius*, the final 'N' indicating the dual ('two couriers'). This is important for two reasons: first, as this reference has reached us in a datable inscription, it is not open to the historiographical objections that may be levelled at the literary references to two couriers to which reference has been made. Second, the fact that these Arabian couriers are referred to as *BRDN* indicates that the (foreign) term *barīd* was introduced to this region over a century before the Umayyad period,[227] and suggests that Arabians were familiar with the postal systems of the neighbouring empires, as we shall now see.

[218] Ṭabarī, *Taʾrīkh*, I, p. 1368.

[219] Balādhurī, *Futūḥ al-buldān*, Leiden, 1866, p. 130. On the *ṭalīʿa* in pre-Umayyad Arabia, see Silverstein, 'Neglected Chapter', 295f. In the Bible, Joshua sends two spies to Jericho (*Joshua* 2: 1).

[220] Ṭabarī, *Taʾrīkh*, I, p. 1749.

[221] Ibn Qutayba, *Taʾwīl mukhtalaf al-ḥadīth*, Cairo, 1326 AH, pp. 204–5.

[222] Balādhurī, *Futūḥ*, p. 142. [223] Ṭabarī, *Taʾrīkh*, I, pp. 2397–8.

[224] In S. D. Goitein, *A Mediterranean Society. Volume I: Economic Foundations*, Berkeley, 1967, p. 284.

[225] E.g. Iṣfahānī, *Kitāb al-aghānī*, vol. VII, p. 15, and Ṭabarī, *Taʾrīkh*, II, p. 1750, where a pair of *Barīd* couriers bring news of the caliph Hishām's death.

[226] *Corpus Inscriptionum Semiticarum*, Paris, 1881–1930, IV: 541, l. 48.

[227] Other Semiticised versions of the Latin *veredarius* (or Greek *beredarion*) include the Syriac term *byldrʾ* (in C. Brocklemann, *Lexicon Syriacum*, Halle, 1928, p. 75) and the Modern Hebrew *beldar* (in E. Klein, *A Comprehensive Etymological Dictionary of the Hebrew Language for Readers of English*, Jerusalem, 1987, p. 74).

Arabians and the imperial postal systems

There are ten references to the term *barīd* in pre-Umayyad poetry that complement the epigraphic reference discussed above.[228] These references demonstrate that Arabians were exposed both to the Byzantine and Sasanid postal systems, either as users or as observers of the imperial *Barīd*s, in the pre-Umayyad period.

Some of the verses offer more persuasive evidence for Arabian familiarity with the imperial postal systems than others. For instance, there are two verses attributed to Imru' al-Qays that describe the poet as having used the *Cursus Publicus* himself, and that are replete with telltale signs of later interpolations. In the first verse, reference is made to a 'courier-guide (*furāniq*) on a robust horse with loose leg-veins and a docked tail' who recites '[We are] riding on the horses of [the tribe of] Barbar with docked tails who repeatedly [deliver] the *Barīd* every night'.[229] In the second verse, Imru' al-Qays says, 'I drank wine with the Caesar in his kingdom, he sent me off, and I rode the *Barīd*. When we gathered at a postal station (*sikka*) I hurried the courier-guide (*furāniq*) to a far distance.'[230] These verses arouse our suspicions on account of the anachronistic use of such terms as *furāniq* (a term that would be more verisimilar with reference to the Sasanid postal system) and *sikka*;[231] both of these words would come to enrich *Barīd* terminology in the mid eighth century, but there is no other evidence for their existence in this period.[232] Furthermore, the poet's insistence that the postal mounts had docked tails smacks of later interpolation, as medieval Muslim lexicographers were at pains to derive the term *barīd* from the Persian *burīda-dum* ('dock-tailed').[233] Ullmann dates these verses to no earlier than the eighth century.[234]

Most of the verses from this period appear to be more reliable than those attributed to Imruʾ al-Qays. Two such verses depict Qurashī Arabians using the Byzantine postal system. In one, ʿUthmān ibn al-Ḥuwayrith mentions that a courier (*barīd*) riding a postal mount (*barīd*) arrived from Syria with news of a death. In the other, Saʿīd ibn al-ʿĀṣ refers to a courier (*barīd*) bearing a relayed message (*mughalghala*) through which he alerts his family

[228] For a close analysis of these references, see Silverstein, 'Neglected Chapter', 306–10.

[229] In W. Ahlwardt, *The Divans of the Ancient Arabic Poets Ennabiga, ʿAntara, Tharafa, Zuhair, ʿAlqama, Imruulqais*, London, 1870, pp. 128–31.

[230] In Jāḥiẓ, *Kitāb al-qawl fī al-bighāl*, Cairo, 1955, p. 62 (§92) and p. 71 (§108).

[231] The etymology of the word *sikka* is obscure. As the meaning of the term is not related to other words derived from the root s.k.k., it is likely that the usage of *sikka* for 'station' is inspired by the Hebrew *sukka* ('booth'), although the exact relationship between the two terms is unclear. That the Feast of Tabernacles (*Sukkoth*) has 'postal' undertones is confirmed by the custom of hosting *ūšpīzīn* ('[spiritual] guests') to one's tabernacle, this being a term that is derived from the Iranian word *aspinj* ('inn', 'way-station') encountered above.

[232] Even if *sikka* is derived from the Hebrew *sukka*, the use of *ribāṭ* in the Qurʾān (8: 60) would suggest that this was the term for postal station in pre-Umayyad Arabic.

[233] See above, pp. 8–9. [234] Ullmann, *Geschichte*, p. 55.

to his captivity.[235] Neither verse specifies the type of mount ridden, but if we are to relate the Arabic term *barīd* to the Byzantine *veredus*, then we must assume that horses were used.

The other pre-Umayyad references to the term *barīd* refer neither to horses nor to Arabians as users of the Imperial postal systems. Rather, in these instances *barīd* is used metaphorically to denote the speed at which a camel[eer] (if the mount is specified) is travelling. Examples are attributed to al-Muthaqqib al-ʿAbdī (d. 578),[236] to the brothers Mutammim and Mālik ibn Nuwayra,[237] to Muzarrid ibn Ḍirār,[238] and to others.[239] The Qurʾān refers to mules, horses, and camels (16: 8), and, importantly, to 'mounts of the *ribāṭ*' (8: 60), anticipating the later development of the *ribāṭ* stations that would form an integral part of the *Barīd*'s infrastructure at a later date.

If the term *ribāṭ* is a calque on the Iranian *awwanā*, then its existence in the Qurʾān could hint at Sasanid fingerprints on seventh-century Arabian communications. Later writers certainly assumed that the Sasanid *Barīd* was used widely in pre-Umayyad Arabia, as Jāḥiẓ points out in a tantalising passage on the use of mules in the *Barīd*. In his words,

> The *burud* for the imperial letters (*kutub al-mulūk*) extended from the extremes of Ferghāna to al-Sūs al-Aqṣā. The *burud* were set up for Khursô (Kisrā), from the remotest corner of the Yemen to its capital (lit. 'gate'), in the days of Wahrīz and in the days when Masrūq the Abyssinian leader was killed … And so too were Khusrô's *burud* [sent] to al-Ḥīra – to Nuʿmān and his ancestors, and so too were his *burud* [sent] to Baḥrayn – to al-Mukaʿbar the *marzubān* of al-Zāra and to Miskāb, and to al-Mundhir ibn Sawa. And so too were his *burud* [sent] to ʿUmān – to al-Julanday ibn al-Mustakbir, since both the Arabian Desert and its settled regions were permeated by [Khursrô's] *burud*, with the exception of the regions that belonged to Syria (al-Shām)… And could Khusrô's *burud* to Wahrīz, and Badhām, and Fayrūz the Daylamite, and to al-Mukaʿbar the *marzubān* of al-Zāra in the Yemen, and to al-Nuʿmān in al-Ḥīra, have been anything other than mules? Could they have found anything more suitable than [mules]?[240]

The contribution of the Sasanid '*Barīd*' is also evident in the poetry of ʿAdī ibn Zayd (d. 600), in whose verses the term *fayj* (Pahlavi *payg*, 'courier') appears on four occasions.[241] ʿAdī's familiarity with the term may be related

[235] Zubayr ibn Bakkār, *Jamharat nasab quraysh*, p. 419 (ʿUthmān ibn al-Ḥuwayrith), and p. 428 (Saʿīd ibn al-ʿĀṣ).
[236] *Al-Mufaḍḍaliyyāt*, (ed. C. J. Lyall), Leiden, 1924, p. 105, verse 6.
[237] In Ullmann, *Geschichte*, p. 15, no. 3 (Mālik), and pp. 15–16, no. 4 (Mutammim).
[238] Ibid., p. 15, no. 2; and Lane, *Lexicon*, vol. I, p. 185.
[239] An unidentifiable poet, whose verse on the *Barīd* is quoted repeatedly in classical Arabic lexicons (e.g. Ibn Manẓūr, *Lisān al-ʿarab*, Cairo, 1883–91, vol. IV, p. 53), uses the term metaphorically with reference to a camel riding at great speed, suggesting a pre-Umayyad Arabian context to the verse.
[240] Jāḥiẓ, *Bighāl*, 71–2 (§§ 108–9). The answer to Jāḥiẓ's rhetorical question is: 'Yes, camels!'
[241] See above, n. 70.

to the fact that his father is said to have been appointed postmaster-general of the Sasanid Empire by Khusrô I.[242]

Not only were Arabians acquainted with the Byzantine and Sasanid postal systems, but on occasion they also served as messengers and spies for the two empires. Both the Ghassanids and Lakhmids, serving as client kingdoms of the Byzantines and Sasanids respectively, were used by their overlords in the context of communications and 'intelligence-gathering'. The fifty-year peace treaty of 561 includes a clause that specifically restricts the passage of travellers across imperial borders, and Shahid has shown that the main consideration behind this proviso was to prevent the other power from using the Arabs as spies.[243] Arabs were used by the empires as spies for two reasons. First, being the indigenous population in the Syrian frontier region that separated the powers, the movement of Arabs on either side of the border would not have appeared suspicious to local authorities. Such undetected movement could only be controlled by limiting the Arabs' mobility. Second, being the native inhabitants of the region, the Arabs were most familiar with the local topography and conditions. Thus, it was natural for the imperial powers to use the Arabs of this region for the purposes of communication and espionage.

Transition to a conquest state

Despite having been exposed to the workings of an imperial postal system, pre-Umayyad Arabians had little need for a complex system of communication until the early Islamic conquests. Whether any such system was adopted as early as the conquests has been debated by scholars: some have argued that express-couriers were used by the conquerors,[244] a position that is supported by the numerous references in Arabic sources to Muslim commanders communicating effortlessly with their distant troops;[245] while others have dismissed such accounts as mere *topoi*, suggesting instead that the *Barīd* dates to no earlier than *ca.* 700 CE.[246]

There is evidence that the Muslim conquerors made effective use of indigenous Arabs (and others) in the conquered territories, who served as spies and messengers in a way that resembles the two empires' use of Arabs for these purposes on the eve of Islam.[247] And with particular regard to the *Barīd*, it is in their descriptions of the conquests that early Muslim historians begin to

[242] Iṣfahānī, *Kitāb al-aghānī*, vol. II, p. 101.
[243] I. Shahid, 'The Arabs in the Peace Treaty of AD 561', *Arabica* 3 (1956), 181–213, at 196–7.
[244] D. R. Hill, 'The Role of the Camel and the Horse in the Early Arab Conquests' in V. J. Parry, and M. E. Yapp (eds.), *War, Technology, and Society in the Middle East*, London, 1975, p. 34; and F. Donner, 'The Formation of the Islamic State', *JAOS* 86 (1986), 283–96 at 286–7.
[245] For examples, see Silverstein, 'Neglected Chapter', 303f.
[246] A. Noth and L. I. Conrad, *The Early Arabic Historical Tradition: A Source-Critical Study*, (trans. M. Bonner), New Jersey, 1994, p. 76.
[247] W. Kaegi, *Byzantium and the Early Islamic Conquests*, Cambridge, 1992, pp. 16, 30, 42, 55, 70, 91, 154, 239, and 250.

refer to *Barīd* couriers (as opposed to the *bashīr*, *rasūl*, or other such terms) as delivering news to and from the battlefield.[248] Ṭabarī refers to the *Barīd* as reporting victories at Caesarea (15 AH), Nihāwand (21 AH), and Wāj al-Rūdh (22 AH), while the *Barīd* also reports the death of Abū Bakr (13 AH) and is used in an exchange of gifts between ʿUmar I's wife and the Byzantine empress.[249]

Even disregarding the early Islamic sources that describe the *Barīd* in action during this period, it is significant that comparable conquest movements developed rudimentary postal systems even before establishing a stable administrative framework into which such a system could be incorporated. The Mongols, for instance, made use of (existing) postal routes, stations, and couriers during the earliest stages of their expansion.[250] If we are to accept the Mongol conquests as a valid historical paradigm for the Islamic conquests, then we can also expect the Muslim conquerors to have availed themselves of a courier-network. In fact, in the Umayyad period, when the caliphal lands were still expanding considerably, postal routes and stations were often set up shortly after a region was conquered in order to establish a contiguous network of communication with adjoining provinces.[251] Furthermore, it was expected that news of successful conquests would be relayed to the authorities via the *Barīd*.[252]

Based on another conquest-paradigm we can assume that Muslim conquerors adopted the imperial postal infrastructures that they encountered in the 640s and 650s. There is evidence to suggest that during their occupation of seventh-century Syria and Egypt, the Sasanids retained (what was left of) the *Cursus Publicus* in the lands occupied,[253] thereby establishing a precedent for devolving control of the local postal stations to conquerors. That the

[248] It is impossible to determine precisely which aspects of the imperial systems the Arabs adopted, but the shift in terminology would suggest that it was during the conquests that a courier-network that the Arabs associated with the neighbouring empires was created.

[249] Ṭabarī, *Taʾrīkh*, I, p. 2398 (Caesarea); p. 2629 (Nihāwand); p. 2651 (Wāj al-Rūdh); p. 2096 (Abū Bakr); and p. 2823 (ʿUmar I's wife). For references to the *Barīd* in the context of Muḥammad's career, see Silverstein, 'Neglected Chapter', 305f.

[250] See below, chapter 4.

[251] Hence, Ṭabarī (*Taʾrīkh*, II, p. 1045) records that Ibn al-Ashʿath (who at this point was still loyal to the Umayyad caliphs) set up postal stations to link the conquered lands (*waḍaʿa al-burud fīmā bayn kull balad wa-balad*). The Delhi Sultan ʿAlāʾ al-Dīn Khaljī (r. 1296–1316) is also said to have established a postal system during campaigns of expansion (in S. Sabahuddin, 'The Postal System during the Muslim Rule in India', *Islamic Culture* 18iii (1944), 269–82, at 271).

[252] Note that when Asmāʾ ibn Khārija died, a poet exclaimed that 'the skies ceased to produce rain, and the *Barīd* ceased to return [from the battlefield] with [news of] booty' (in Jāḥiẓ, *Bighāl*, p. 63).

[253] C. Foss, 'The Persians in the Roman Near East (602–630 AD)', *JRAS* 13ii (2003), 149–70, at 168; and 'The *Sellarioi* and Other Officers of Persian Egypt', *Zeitschrift für Papyrologie und Epigraphik* 138 (2002), 169–72. For the Sasanid occupation of Syria and Mesopotamia, see M. G. Morony, 'Syria under the Persians 610–629', in M. A. al-Bakhīt (ed.), *Proceedings of the Second Symposium on the History of Bilād al-Shām during the Early Islamic Period*, Amman, 1987, vol. I, pp. 87–95.

Muslims benefited from this precedent is demonstrated by documents from Egypt. A number of [Greek] papyri from the first two decades of the Muslims' presence in Egypt make reference to postal stations, and to the requisition of fodder for the official stables of the Fayyum region.[254] Moreover, although literary sources indicate that the Greek term *beredarion* (pl. *beredarioi*) was in use in sixth-century Syria, this term appears to have fallen out of use in Egypt after the fourth century, if the papyrological record is anything to go by.[255] With the arrival of the Muslims in this region, however, the term resurfaces in numerous documents, and it is tempting to interpret this phenomenon as being the direct result of Arab influence.[256] The Arabs, after all, were referring to postal couriers by the term *barīd* long before they arrived in Egypt.[257] Regarding the eastern provinces of the Islamic world, we are told that postal stations were established in the *amṣār* in derelict churches,[258] while ʿUmar I ruled that old postal stations inherited from the Sasanids should be considered 'state land'.[259] It is thus in the pre-Umayyad period that Muslims began to adapt the pre-Islamic postal systems of the Near East to their needs.

But the creation of an inter-regional postal system, controlled from a bureaucratically sophisticated capital, would have to wait for the Umayyad period. And it is only after considering the postal system of the Umayyad and early Abbasid periods that we will be in a position to assess the relative contributions of Sasanid, Byzantine, and 'Arabian' communications technology to the caliphal *Barīd*.

254 *P. Ross. Georg.* III: 50 (Arsinoe, 643) refers to the delivery of a considerable amount of fodder for official mounts; and *P. Merton* II: 100 (Arsinoe, 669) is a requisition order for goods to be delivered to the local postal station (drawn to my attention by Lennart Sundelin and Petra Sijpesteijn). The fact that these documents differ very little from later ones (e.g., *P. Ross. Georg.* IV: 25, concerning a postal station in early eighth-century Aphrodito) suggests that the early Marwanid *Barīd* was not manifestly different from the postal arrangements made by the Muslim conquerors.

255 Admittedly, the serendipitous survival of papyrus documents from this period is not the steadiest ground on which to construct an argument of this sort. But the sudden appearance (and repeated use) of the term *beredarion* in the mid seventh century is striking nonetheless.

256 This is suggested in P. M. Sijpesteijn, 'The Muslim Conquest and the First Fifty Years of Muslim Rule in Egypt', in R. Bagnall (ed.), *Egypt in the Byzantine World*, Cambridge, forthcoming (drawn to my attention by Petra Sijpesteijn). A problem with this interpretation is that when the term *beredarion* appears in [the Greek side of] bi-lingual documents, it is always rendered *rasūl* in the Arabic, rather than *barīd* (cf. A. Silverstein, 'Documentary Evidence for the Early History of the *Barīd*', in P. M. Sijpesteijn and L. Sundelin (eds.), *Papyrology and the History of Early Islamic Egypt*, Leiden, 2004, 153–61, at 154).

257 As the term *beredarioi* was current in sixth-century Syria, it is also possible that this word was reintroduced to Egypt not from the South-East (Arabia) but from the North-East (Syria). In the absence of fuller sources, however, this remains conjecture.

258 Balādhurī (*Futūḥ*, p. 286) mentions that the *Barīd* station in Kufa had previously been a church.

259 In A. Ben-Shemesh, *Taxation in Islam III*, London, 1969, p. 75.

PART II

Conquest and centralisation – the Arabs

CHAPTER 2

al-Barīd: the early Islamic postal system

Introduction

By the mid ninth century the *Barīd* consisted of a well-coordinated network of routes, stations, postal chiefs, and a postmaster-general, all of which were paid for by the caliph's resources. Between the adoption of a rudimentary courier-service during the conquests and the high-point of the postal system's organisation in the ninth century, the *Barīd* underwent a developmental process the major stages of which will be described and analysed below.

In some ways ʿUmarī (1301–49) has facilitated our task by describing the evolution of the *Barīd* in a straightforward, sequential account. In his words:

> The first person to establish the *Barīd* in Islam was Muʿāwiya ibn Abī Sufyān ... He established the *Barīd* to expedite the arrival of intelligence (*akhbār*) to him from his outlying provinces. He therefore ordered that Persian *dihqān*s and people of the Byzantine provinces be brought before him, and he explained to them what it is that he wanted, and they established the *burud*, using mules with pack-saddles as the means of transportation. Some, however, say that this happened during the reign of ʿAbd al-Malik ibn Marwān, when he rid himself of the Kharijites ... [The caliph] al-Walīd ibn ʿAbd al-Malik used [the *Barīd*] to transport mosaics – which is gilded tesserae – from Constantinople to Damascus ... The *Barīd* remained in existence and in constant use until the time came for the collapse of the Marwanid state, and the unravelling of Marwanid power. The Marwanids were cut off from [all the land] between Iraq and Khurasan, since the notables turned to the Shiʿism that upheld the Abbasid state. This continued until the end of Marwān ibn Muḥammad's reign – he was the last of the Umayyad caliphs. Then al-Saffāḥ ruled, then al-Manṣūr, and then al-Mahdī, but no saddle was strapped and no mount was bridled for the *Barīd*. But then al-Mahdī sent his son Hārūn al-Rashīd to campaign against the Byzantines, and [al-Mahdī] wanted to obtain immediate knowledge of [his son's] affairs, so he established *burud* between him and his son's camp, which would bring information about [his son] to him, and which would show him an updated picture of his affairs. When Hārūn al-Rashīd returned, al-Mahdī discontinued these *burud* and the situation continued in this way throughout his reign and the reign of Musā al-Hādī after him. But when Hārūn al-Rashīd became caliph, he remembered his father's excellent initiative in setting up *burud* between the two of them, and Yaḥyā ibn Khālid [al-Barmakī] said to him: 'Were

the caliph to order the establishment of the *Barīd* as it used to be this would be beneficial to his rule.' So [Hārūn] ordered him to do so and Yaḥyā established and organised [the *Barīd*] in the manner that it functioned during the days of the Umayyads, and he stationed mules at the stations ...[1]

Although this account has been quoted repeatedly by medieval and modern scholars alike,[2] most of what it says is contradicted by the surviving literary, documentary, and material evidence. We have already established that pre-Umayyad Arabians were familiar with the imperial postal systems of the Near East, which they began to appropriate during the conquests, and it is therefore unlikely that Muʿāwiya (or ʿAbd al-Malik) would have had to summon former Persian or Byzantine officials to explain to him what a *Barīd* was. That Walīd I is said to have used the *Barīd* to transport mosaics sounds suspiciously stereotypical of this caliph's later reputation as a keen patron of building projects and does not tally with the evidence that suggests that the *Barīd* was strictly a *Cursus Velox* rather than a *Cursus Clabularis* throughout Islamic history. Moreover, the argument that the Abbasids did not have a regular postal system before Hārūn al-Rashīd's reign is untenable in view of the many references – in relatively early literary sources as well as contemporary documentary ones – to the *Barīd* in action during the first four decades of Abbasid rule. For these reasons, ʿUmarī's account of the *Barīd*'s development is unsatisfactory, and the early history of the *Barīd* will be reassessed in what follows.

The Sufyanid *Barīd*

Although many scholars agree that Muʿāwiya played an important role in the creation of the *Barīd*, it is difficult to know precisely what his contribution was. Writers such as ʿAskarī and Ibn al-Ṭiqṭaqā are happy to attribute to him the creation of the *Barīd*,[3] but there are three reasons to suppose that the *Barīd* during the Sufyanid period would have been operating on a limited scale compared with that of later periods. First, much of what would become the caliphal domain was yet to be conquered during this period. Large parts of Eastern Iran, Central Asia, Spain, and North-West Africa (amongst other regions) would only be integrated into the caliph's realms in the eighth century or later. Second, although both contemporary Christian sources and later Abbasid ones generally remember Muʿāwiya in a (rather exceptionally) positive light, there is little mention of his administrative or leadership

[1] ʿUmarī, *al-Taʿrīf bi al-muṣṭalaḥ al-sharīf*, Cairo, 1894, pp. 184–6.

[2] Medieval scholars: Qalqashandī, *Ṣubḥ al-aʿshāʾ fī ṣināʿat al-inshāʾ*, Cairo, 1918–22, vol. I, pp. 114–28, and vol. XIV, pp. 367ff.; and Anṣarī, *Tafrīj al-kurūb fī tadbīr al-ḥurūb*, (ed./trans. G.T. Scanlon as *A Muslim Manual of War*, Cairo, 1961), pp. 14ff. Modern scholars: R. Hartmann, *EI1*, s.v. 'Barīd'; D. Sourdel, *EI2*, s.v. 'Barīd'; Saʿdawi, N., *Niẓām al-barīd fī al-dawla al-islāmiyya*, Cairo, 1953, passim; Dvornik, *Origins*, p. 226; and others.

[3] ʿAskarī, *Kitāb al-awāʾil*, Beirut, 1997, p. 162; and Ibn al-Ṭiqṭaqā, *Fakhrī fī al-ādāb al-sulṭāniyya wa al-duwal al-islāmiyya*, Paris, 1895, p. 148.

abilities; while other caliphs such as ʿAbd al-Malik, Hishām, al-Manṣūr, and Hārūn al-Rashīd are depicted in the sources as being shrewd and innovative leaders, Muʿāwiya is remembered largely for his *ḥilm*, a term that evokes images of an exemplary tribal shaykh, not of an imperial ruler. Indeed, we often hear of Muʿāwiya obtaining information about rebellious groups from the delegations (*wufūd*) of tribal leaders travelling to his court rather than from intelligence reports relayed to him through an imperial postal system. Third, compared to later Muslim leaders, the Sufyanids appear to have ruled a very loosely knit polity, and governors such as Ziyād ibn Abīhi are often regarded as the last link in the chain of command in their region.

It is also interesting to note that there are traces of pre-Umayyad Arabian methods of communication in sources that discuss the Sufyanid period. We have seen that the Arabian *bashīr*'s practice of waving his cloak as a sign that he bears glad tidings continued into the early Umayyad period, as did the *risāla mughalghala*. Furthermore, the Arabian custom of sending two couriers with a single message appears to have survived the transfer of the capital from Medina to Damascus.[4] But to view the Sufyanid caliphs as unsophisticated rulers whose administrative capabilities consisted of little more than modified *jāhiliyy* practices would be taking things too far. After all, Muʿāwiya – who is said to have been one of Muḥammad's secretaries[5] – had decades of experience governing Syria, and there are a number of references to the Sufyanid *Barīd* that indicate that a communications network was in operation during this period.

Muʿāwiya's *Barīd* exhibits characteristics of an institution that in many ways was still rough around the edges. In one episode we are told that 'Whenever Muʿāwiya's *ʿāmil* in Medina wanted to send a courier (*arāda an yubrida barīdan*) to Muʿāwiya, he would order the herald (*munādī*) to tell anyone who had a need to write to the caliph. Zirr ibn Ḥubaysh or Ayman ibn Khuraym wrote an eloquent letter (*kitāb laṭīf*)[6] and threw it among the letters, and in it was a poem ....'[7] What this account tells us is that '*Barīd*' couriers connected the capital with Medina, that messages were in writing, and that the local governor was in charge of the couriers operating within his region; all three of these points would continue to hold true for the Marwanid period, indicating that some aspects of the *Barīd* were already in place during Muʿāwiya's reign. But this account also suggests that there was no fixed

4 E.g., Ṭabarī, *Ta'rīkh*, II, p. 62, where two men are sent out on horseback to obtain strategic information. Interestingly, the two couriers are used for a mission that does not involve travel within the Arabian Peninsula, suggesting that the practice was a remnant of Arabian culture rather than a practical response to the Peninsula's topography.

5 Jahshiyārī, *Kitāb al-wuzarā' wa al-kuttāb*, Cairo, 1938, p. 12.

6 In the Fatimid period, the phrase *kutub liṭāf* referred to 'secret decrees' (cf. *EI2*, s.v. 'dīwān' ii. Egypt (2) 'The Fāṭimid Period'), and it is possible that *kitāb laṭīf* here has a similar meaning. However, the fact that this letter included poetry suggests that 'an eloquent letter' is a more suitable translation.

7 Ṭabarī, *Ta'rīkh*, II, p. 213.

routine for the system: when an *ʿāmil* decides to correspond with the caliph, he has this announced publicly to allow others the chance to send off their own letters. Anyone, it would seem, could then throw a letter onto the pile, and even 'eloquent letters' with poems could be relayed by the *Barīd* to Damascus.[8]

The geographical extent of the *Barīd*'s activity during this period exceeded the Ḥijāz.[9] We hear of Ayman ibn Khuraym (d. 685), who was with ʿAbd al-ʿAzīz ibn Marwān in Egypt, riding the *Barīd* to Bishr ibn Marwān in Iraq.[10] There is also an interesting reference to the *Barīd* travelling from Byzantium to ʿAmr ibn al-ʿĀṣ and then to Muʿāwiya: Abū al-ʿIyāl, who was in captivity in Byzantium, wrote the following letter (in rhyming verse) to the caliph: 'From Abū al-ʿIyāl al-Hudhalī. Hear my words and do not misunderstand [the message] that I send! Send Muʿāwiya ibn Sakhr (i.e. the caliph Muʿāwiya ibn Abī Sufyān) a sign from me, with which "the express *Barīd*" (*al-barīd al-aʿjal*) will rush forward, and will bring a parchment (*ṣaḥīfa*) from me to ʿAmr [ibn al-ʿĀṣ], in it a minutely written letter will shine forth.'[11] Taken together, literary sources describe the Sufyanid *Barīd* as connecting Syria with Egypt, Iraq, the Ḥijāz, and even Byzantium.

The *Barīd* played a number of roles during this period. Aside from the suspicious account of people sending apparently random letters to Muʿāwiya from Medina, and apart from the plea of a Muslim captive in Byzantium, one finds mention of the *Barīd* bringing information to the caliph[12] and of the *Barīd* bearing news of the caliph's death. The *Barīd* is said to have reported Muʿāwiya's death to 'the people of Mecca' and to the heir apparent, Yazīd. In the former case, Balādhurī quotes ʿAmr ibn Masʿūd al-Jumaḥī as saying, 'We were in Mecca when suddenly the *Barīd* passed by announcing the death of Muʿāwiya. So we got up and went to tell Ibn al-ʿAbbās . . ."O Ibn al-ʿAbbās! The *Barīd* has arrived with news of Muʿāwiya's death!".'[13] In the latter case, upon receiving news of his father's death, Yazīd is reported to have said (in rhyming verse), 'The *Barīd* has brought a parchment, the rider gallops with it, so the heart was apprehensive of the parchment and alarmed.'[14]

8 Although this episode is recorded in a relatively late text, the existence of such 'early' characteristics of the *Barīd* lends credibility to the account. It will be seen that in later periods correspondence was despatched according to a regular timetable.

9 The *Barīd* reached Medina (e.g. *Kitāb al-aghānī*, vol. II, p. 251), as well as Mecca (e.g. Balādhurī, *Ansāb al-ashrāf*, ed. M. Schloessinger, Jerusalem, 1938, vol. IVb, p. 3, where the *Barīd* brings news of Muʿāwiya's death to the Meccans).

10 In Jāḥiẓ, *Bighāl*, p. 63.

11 *Hudsailian Poems*, vol. I, p. 145 (no. 75). The phrase *al-barīd al-aʿjal* is not entirely clear, though it may simply be an Arabic rendering of the Latin *Cursus Velox*.

12 Masʿūdī (*Murūj*, vol. III, p. 189, §1774) relates that 'When Ziyād [ibn Abīhi and his nine companions bearing the rebel Ḥujr ibn ʿAdiyy al-Kindī] reached Marj ʿAdhrāʾ, 12 miles from Damascus, the *Barīd* brought news of their approach to Muʿāwiya.'

13 Balādhurī, *Ansāb al-ashrāf*, vol. IVb, p. 3.

14 Ṭabarī, *Taʾrīkh*, II, p. 203; and Balādhurī, *Ansāb al-ashrāf*, ed. M. Schloessinger, Jerusalem, 1971, vol. IVa, p. 131.

During Yazīd's reign (680–3), shortly after the death of Ḥusayn at Qarbala', the *Barīd* in Iraq is said to have relayed correspondence between the caliph and 'Ubaydallāh ibn Ziyād, concerning the treatment of Ḥusayn's imprisoned supporters. According to Ṭabarī's sources, a letter attached to a stone was thrown into the prison, on which was written: 'On such and such a day, the *Barīd* was sent to Yazīd ibn Mu'āwiya for his instructions with regard to you. [The courier] will take so many days to go and he will return on such and such a day . . ..'[15] That the *Barīd* had a predictable schedule would suggest either that the institution had improved by the end of the Sufyanid period or that it was better organised in Iraq than it was in the West.

It is, of course, possible (if not probable) that these accounts tell us less about the Sufyanid *Barīd* than they do about the assumptions and prejudices of the ninth-century scholars who transmitted them. Abbasid authors were writing at a time when the *Barīd* played a prominent role in the Near East and – having accepted that Mu'āwiya created such a system – scholars may have unthinkingly assumed that the nascent *Barīd* resembled the Abbasid institution with which they were familiar. Therefore, in many cases our literary sources refer to a *Barīd* that was not actually operating in a given context. Conversely, there are also cases in which the *Barīd* was probably used despite there being no direct reference to it. Three examples will suffice to illustrate this point. In the first instance, when Ziyād transported the rebel Ḥujr ibn 'Adiyy and his accomplices to Mu'āwiya, the prisoners are said to have been sent 'in chains', riding camels.[16] There is good reason to believe that these men were sent via the *Barīd*: only a few years later, the caliph Yazīd is said to have used the *Barīd* to transport another rebel (Ibn al-Zubyar) in chains,[17] and this practice continued well into the Marwanid period.[18] The second instance concerns 'Ubaydallāh ibn Ziyād's *mawlā* 'Ḥumrān', who is described as "Ubaydallāh's messenger to [the caliphs] Mu'āwiya and Yazīd'.[19] In a particularly *Barīd*-like episode, Ḥumrān was sent from Iraq to Syria, bearing strategic information, only to return with the news of the caliph Yazīd's death. It is very likely that the governor of Iraq's personal messenger to the caliphs would have used the *Barīd*'s services to communicate speedily news of the caliph's death.[20] And yet, as the sources do not explicitly mention the *Barīd*, its use in this case can only be inferred. In the third example, Marwān, who was in Medina, sent a messenger to the caliph Yazīd, demanding that

[15] Ṭabarī, *Ta'rīkh*, II, p. 380. [16] Balādhurī, *Ansāb al-ashrāf*, vol. IVa, p. 223.

[17] Ṭabarī, *Ta'rīkh*, II, p. 397; and Balādhurī, *Ansāb al-ashrāf*, vol. IVb, p. 17.

[18] Balādhurī, *Kitāb jumal min ansāb al-ashrāf*, ed. S. Zakkār, Beirut, 1996, vol. VIII, pp. 293–4, where a rebel in chains is sent to 'Umar II from Khurasan via the *Barīd*.

[19] Ṭabarī, *Ta'rīkh*, II, p. 436.

[20] That news of Yazīd's death led to an uprising in Khurasan (Ṭabarī, *Ta'rīkh*, II, p. 490) illustrates the importance of ensuring that such news reached local governors before merchants or other travellers disseminated it.

that messenger make the entire journey – there and back – in twenty-four days.[21] The distance between Damascus and Medina, the speed necessary to complete the mission within the required time-frame,[22] and the fact that we are dealing with communication between the governor of Medina and the caliph would all suggest that the *Barīd* was used by the envoy. Here too, the absence of any reference to the postal system is curious.

Documentary sources are not susceptible to the shortcomings associated with the literary materials quoted above, and papyri from Nessana offer us a rare glimpse into the administration of the road system in southern Palestine in pre-Marwanid times. Three Nessana documents that resemble Byzantine *evectiones* deserve our attention here. The first two letters, tentatively dated to March 684 and December 683 respectively, are from the provincial governor Abū Rashīd to 'George', the administrator of Nessana, ordering him to furnish the bearers with guides for their travels. In the first letter, Abū Rashīd writes: 'When Abū al-Mughīra, *mawlā* of ʿUrwa ibn Abī Sufyān, comes to you, be kind enough to furnish him a man from Nessana bound to guide him on the trip to the Holy Mount. Also furnish the man's pay.' In the second letter, which is addressed more generally to 'the people of Nessana', Abū Rashīd writes: 'When my wife Ubayya comes to you, furnish her a man bound to direct her on the road to Mt. Sinai. Also furnish the man's pay.'[23] If nothing else, these texts indicate that decades after the Muslim conquests 'pilgrimage' was still deemed an acceptable use of the official road system, just as the facilities of the *Cursus Publicus* were enjoyed by pilgrims in the Byzantine period.

The third document, which dates from *ca.* 685, is considerably more interesting for our purposes, as it deals directly with the administration of the local road network. In this letter George is told: '[M]ake sure that you have ready two camels and two labourers who are to perform compulsory service [on the road] from Caesarea to Scythopolis. Keep in mind also that he wants good camels, and workmen who have pack-saddles and straps . . . Peace be with you!'[24] Bearing in mind that it is approximately 80 kilometres from Nessana to Gaza and another 130 kilometres from Gaza to Caesarea, we may infer that the men being sent on this mission were professional camel drivers,

[21] Ṭabarī, *Ta'rīkh*, II, p. 406.

[22] The distance between Damascus and Medina is over 1,000 kilometres as the crow flies. The fact that the desert routes do not follow a perfectly straight line means that the actual distance that a messenger must travel is closer to 1,500 kilometres. Covering such a distance within twelve days would be particularly difficult, especially considering the topographical conditions of the route, unless the fresh mounts, food, lodgings, and other provisions associated with pre-modern postal systems were available to the messenger.

[23] C.J. Kraemer, *Excavations at Nessana III: Administrative Documents*, Princeton, 1950, pp. 205–6 (no. 72); and pp. 207–8 (no. 73).

[24] Ibid., pp. 209–10 (no. 74). That camels were the mount of choice in Nessana is known to us from other fragments (e.g. no. 35, where a levy of sixty-five camels is imposed on the village).

as the entire journey would entail traversing a distance of 420 kilometres,[25] and the terrain on the route from Nessana to Caesarea explains why camels (rather than horses, donkeys, or mules) are specified. The fact that *two* men are requested to carry out an indeterminable function on the roads is tantalising, as it brings to mind pre-Umayyad Arabian practices. But the general impression that these documents give us is that even at the very end of the Sufyanid period the road system in greater Syria hardly seemed different from that which was in operation for centuries before the Muslim conquests: Greek *evectiones* were still being distributed to pilgrims in characteristically Byzantine fashion, and local governors could still press workmen into service on the routes. It would seem that the Near East would have to wait for the Marwanid period to experience the full impact of the caliphal *Barīd*.

The *Barīd* in the Marwanid and early Abbasid periods

It is at the very beginning of the Marwanid period – as early as the short reign of Marwān ibn al-Ḥakam (684–5) – that material evidence for the caliphal *Barīd* begins to emerge, and it is from the reigns of his successors ʿAbd al-Malik (r. 685/692–705) and al-Walīd I (r. 705–15) that literary sources, documentary evidence, and the archaeological record converge to show that a sophisticated and centrally organised postal system served to link the caliphs' sprawling realms. Whether or not this evidence indicates that an Islamic state was in existence no *earlier* or no *later* than the Marwanid period,[26] there is little doubt that the basic infrastructure of the caliphal *Barīd* would be maintained (with few and minor exceptions) into the ninth century, regardless of political developments. Thus, Masʿūdī's statement that in 132 AH (749–50 CE) the *Barīd* 'began to transport letters for the Abbasids'[27] strongly implies that the masters of the postal system changed with the rise of the Abbasids, not the system itself. And although, as we shall see, various caliphs during this period would tinker with the routes, functions, or administration of the *Barīd*, it would appear that the Middle Abbasid postal system was based on an institution that had achieved a stable form by the early Marwanid period, the 'routes and stations', 'mounts and messengers', 'administration', and 'functions' of which will now be analysed.

[25] As argued by Kraemer (ibid., p. 209).
[26] The former option is argued in C. F. Robinson, *ʿAbd al-Malik*, Oxford, 2005; the latter option is argued in Donner, 'Formation'.
[27] Masʿūdī, *Murūj*, vol. IV, p. 97, §2312. Although much of ʿUmarī's account of the *Barīd*'s early development is being challenged in this chapter, his statement that the Abbasid *Barīd* was established during Hārūn al-Rashīd's reign 'in the manner that it functioned in the days of the Umayyads' (*Taʿrīf*, p. 186) is worth mentioning here.

Routes and stations

There is evidence to suggest that the general infrastructure of the *Barīd* and the caliphal route system that supported it were improved from the earliest years of the Marwanid period. Elad has shown that already during the reign of Marwān ibn al-Ḥakam, milestones were placed along the road between Mecca and ʿArafa,[28] while a number of milestones on the route from Syria to Palestine that date from ʿAbd al-Malik's reign have been discovered and their contents published.[29] This evidence is deceptively important: not only do milestones help travellers along the roads calculate and undertake their journeys, but they also attest to a deliberate imperial programme while serving as effective propaganda for a proud (or embattled) caliph. The statement and splendour of grand mosques, such as the ones in Jerusalem and Damascus, could only be appreciated by those who visited them, but milestones (like coins) are by their very nature diffused widely throughout the caliphate, and a traveller could not fail to appreciate the caliph's role in creating stability in his realms. From the perspective of this study, it is also noteworthy that the early Marwanid milestones, being square and less than a metre tall, did *not* resemble the taller and rounded milestones that had been used in Roman Syria.[30] Thus, even those elements of the postal infrastructures that are assumed to have been 'lifted' from the pre-Islamic empires acquired a distinctly caliphal form in some way.[31]

ʿAbd al-Malik's military reforms also had perceptible effects on the caliphal road system. With the creation of a 'Syrian' army, the relationship between the caliph and his provinces changed. The caliph's ability to send troops from Damascus to the East (in most cases) demanded that two conditions be satisfied. First, it was important that direct and adequately provisioned routes across the caliphate would be able to support the deployment of troops when needed. Second, reports concerning the need for military assistance or backup would have to arrive in Damascus and be answered swiftly enough to deal with a situation before the original message became obsolete due to changing circumstances on the battlefield. According to Jahshiyārī, the Sasanids had a military secretary who would accompany troops to battle and write back to the capital with 'pleas and warnings' on a regular basis.[32] This conforms to the more general trend of centralisation that is associated with

[28] A. Elad, 'The Southern Golan in the Early Muslim Period: The Significance of Two Newly Discovered Milestones of ʿAbd al-Malik', *Der Islam* 76 (1999), 33–88 at 42.

[29] E.g. A. Grohmann, *Arabische Paläographie*, Vienna, 1967–71, vol. II, pp. 82ff.; M. Sharon, 'An Arabic Inscription from the Time of Abd al-Malik', *BSOAS* 29 (1966), 369–72; and Elad, 'Southern Golan'.

[30] For pre-Islamic milestones, see A. Kazhdan, 'Milestones' in *ODB*, p. 1372; for an analysis of the Marwanid milestones, see Robinson, *ʿAbd al-Malik*, pp. 113ff.

[31] ʿAbd al-Malik's reform of the coinage is another example of this, the motivations behind which are more readily obvious than the squaring and shortening of Marwanid milestones.

[32] Jahshiyārī, *Wuzarāʾ*, p. 5.

ʿAbd al-Malik's reign,[33] the results of which were accelerated under his successor al-Walīd I (r. 705–15), who is said to have been the first caliph to establish a system of beacons (*waḍaʿa al-manār*) and to build reservoirs near the way-stations of the Syria–Mecca route.[34] Similarly, ʿUmar II (r. 717–20) is said to have instructed his governor in Khurasan as follows: 'Establish inns (*khānāt*) in your lands so that whenever a Muslim passes by, you will put him up for a day and a night and take care of his animals.'[35]

By the reign of Hishām (r. 724–43), milestones and postal stations appear to have been available along imperial routes. In one account, having passed by a milestone (*mīl*) on a journey, Hishām is said to have asked: 'Who here can tell us how far this milestone is from the next *Barīd* [station]?'[36] The existence of manned postal stations on the roads during this period is confirmed by other accounts: in one case we hear of one 'Ḥarrān ibn Karīma, a *mawlā* of one of the Arabs in the postal station (*sikkat al-barīd*)';[37] elsewhere it is related that a group of rebels entered the *Barīd* station and posted guards at its door.[38] It would also seem that by Hishām's reign certain routes were associated with the *Barīd*: Ṭabarī relates an incident whereby a delegation sent by Naṣr ibn Sayyār took the '*Barīd* Road' (*ṭarīq al-barīd*) on their journey from Khurasan to Mosul, using byways thereafter en route to Bayhaq.[39]

It was only under the early Abbasids, however, that the *Barīd* covered all parts of the caliphate. Under al-Mahdī (r. 775–85) the postal network was extended considerably, both westwards (from Egypt to North Africa and Spain) and within Arabia. The *Barīd*'s operations in the West are referred to in two instances. In the first account, al-Mahdī sent an angry letter to the Umayyads of Spain, using the *Barīd* to convey the correspondence.[40] As no itinerary is specified, it can only be assumed that the coastal route from Alexandria through Barqa and Qayrawān was provided with postal mounts. In the second account, the Shiʿite Idrīs, having fled the battle of Fakhkh,

[33] Robinson, *Abd al-Malik*, pp. 66–80.

[34] Beacons: Ṭabarī, *Taʾrīkh*, II, p. 1271; Reservoirs: Ibn al-Faqīh, *Buldān*, p. 106. According to Muqaddasī (*Aḥsan al-taqāsīm fī maʿrifat al-aqālīm*, Leiden, 1879, p. 250), the Syria–Mecca route was the *Barīd* route during the Umayyad period, but with the removal of the capital to Iraq, the route was used only by pilgrims.

[35] Ṭabarī, *Taʾrīkh*, II, 1364. Saʿdawi's assertion that the construction of *khāns* along the Khurasan Road was 'a contribution to the *Barīd*' (*Niẓām al-barīd*, p. 54) appears to be incorrect; even if we are to take this report at face value, the caliph ordered that facilities be made available for all [Muslim] travellers.

[36] Jāḥiẓ, *Kitāb al-bayān wa al-tabyīn*, Cairo, 1947, vol. II, p. 343; Ṣūlī, *Adab al-kuttāb*, Cairo, 1341 AH, p. 65. This anecdote is related by Tawḥīdī (*al-Baṣāʾir wa al-dhakhāʾir*, Damascus, 1964, vol. II, p. 250) with reference to the reign of Sulaymān I (r. 715–17). The attribution to Sulaymān may be based on a mistaken association of the subject of this anecdote with the Biblical King Solomon, who in Muslim tradition is recorded as having asked a strikingly similar question on one of his travels (in Ṭabarī, *Taʾrīkh*, I, p. 577).

[37] Ṭabarī, *Taʾrīkh*, II, p. 1709.

[38] Balādhurī, *Ansāb al-ashrāf*, ed. Kh. Athamina, Jerusalem, 1993, vol. VIb, p. 106.

[39] Ṭabarī, *Taʾrīkh*, II, p. 1720. [40] Ibid., III, p. 529.

arrived in Egypt, where the local *Ṣāḥib al-Barīd* (himself a Shiʿite) allowed Idrīs to use the mounts of the *Barīd* to continue his journey to Ifriqiyya.[41]

Although these are the first references to the *Barīd*'s activities in the West, it is possible that the lack of earlier references is merely an illusion of the sources: ninth-century historical works are disproportionally generous with the amount of detail they provide concerning the central and eastern lands of the Muslim world, and the *Barīd* may well have been functioning in North Africa during the Marwanid period, if not earlier. Conversely, al-Mahdī's role in expanding the geographical range of the *Barīd* within Arabia is described in unambiguous terms by Ṭabarī, according to whom, in 779–80 CE, 'al-Mahdī ordered the establishment of the *Barīd* between the City of the Prophet, and Mecca, and Yemen, by mule and camel, and the *Barīd* had not been established there before'.[42] It is significant that this order came after the Ḥijāz had proven to be an ineffective region from which to launch a rebellion, as the ill-fated experiences of the Arabia-based rebels of al-Manṣūr's reign showed.[43] Thus, the *Barīd*'s routes were being improved and extended as a matter of course, rather than in response to a particular circumstance.

Postal routes would also, on occasion, be shifted or even established from scratch to deal with political or military exigencies. As seen, al-Mahdī is said to have established '*burud*' on a temporary basis between himself and his son Hārūn while the latter was campaigning against the Byzantines, in order to obtain 'immediate knowledge' of his son's affairs. Even before Hārūn's reign it would appear that *Barīd* routes reached deep into Byzantine territory, as the following anecdote demonstrates:

> Ismaʿīl ibn Abī Ḥākim said: 'I was with ʿUmar ibn ʿAbd al-ʿAzīz when suddenly the *Barīd* arrived from Constantinople and [the courier] said to him: "I was doing my rounds in Constantinople when I heard a man singing beautifully, with a sorrowful voice . . . I heard singing the likes of which I had never heard before . . . I approached the sound and when I got near, there he was in a room, so I dismounted from my she-mule and tied her down and went up to the doorway of his room . . . When he finished singing, he cried and cried and then he resumed singing. This happened repeatedly. I said to him: 'Hello!' He sat up and said: 'Hello.' I said: 'Rejoice, for God has released you from captivity! For I am the *Barīd* of the caliph ʿUmar ibn ʿAbd al-ʿAzīz [sent] to this tyrant to release you from captivity.' "[44]

In other instances, political conditions dictated that additional postal routes be established in order to facilitate communications during a

[41] Ibid., III, p. 561. One of al-Mahdī's *mawālī* then murdered Idrīs and was appointed 'Chief of the *Barīd* and Intelligence in Egypt' (*ʿalā barīdi miṣra wa akhbārihi*) by the governor of Egypt, the future caliph Hārūn al-Rashīd.

[42] Ibid., III, p. 517.

[43] In the words of Lassner (*The Shaping of Abbasid Rule*, Princeton, 1980, p. 71), 'No ruler situated in Mecca or Medina could be regarded as a serious threat to the regime because no significant challenge could be launched from so politically emasculated a province.'

[44] *Kitāb al-aghānī*, vol. VI, p. 117.

campaign. Under al-Muʿtaṣim the *Barīd* routes were adjusted to allow the caliph and his generals to attend to the specific challenges posed by the unruly *Zuṭṭ*, who terrorised the roads in southern Iraq, and by the Khurramī rebel Bābak. In the former case, it is reported that al-Muʿtaṣim arranged to have information sent to him from ʿUjayf ibn ʿAnbasa, his representative in the region, on a daily basis. For this purpose '[al-Muʿtaṣim] organised between al-Baṭā'iḥ (the marshland of southern Iraq) and Baghdad a troop of horse, lean (*muḍammara*) and shorn of tails (*maḥlūbat al-adhnāb*)',[45] which enabled news to reach him on the same day.[46] In dealing with Bābak, the caliph resorted to innovative methods of communication that demonstrate the malleability of the *Barīd* network during this period. According to Ṭabarī,

> [B]ecause of his concern over the matter of Bābak and over getting news about him, and because of the bad state of the road on account of snow and other things, al-Muʿtaṣim stationed lean horses (*khayl muḍammara*) along the road from Samarra to the pass leading to Ḥulwān. At the start of each parasang was specially stationed a horse with a rapid rider (*mujrī*), who would gallop with the news, so that he might relay it personally to another man [similarly stationed], placing it in the latter's hand directly from his own. In the stretch from beyond Ḥulwān to Azerbayjān they had stationed mounts from al-Marj; these were ridden for a day or two and then would be exchanged for new mounts that were then dispatched onward, and slaves from the personnel at al-Marj would travel on their backs, each mount being stationed at the beginning of each [new] parasang. [al-Muʿtaṣim] posted for them watchmen (*dayādiba*) on the mountaintops by night and day and ordered them to cry out when news came to them (i.e. of the approach of one of the relays). When the person who was near the shouting heard the noise, he got himself ready, but his opposite number that had shouted was not to go to him until the other was waiting for him on the road; then he would take the mail-bag (*kharīṭa*). In this way, the mail-bag used to reach Samarra from al-Afshīn's army camp in four days or less.[47]

This passage is important for a number of reasons, the full significance of which will become apparent below. With particular regard to the *Barīd*'s infrastructure, the passage exemplifies the flexible nature of a postal system that had yet to achieve uniformity throughout the caliphate. Even within this single episode, the postal network relied on varying techniques of communication: from Samarra to Ḥulwān mounts were exchanged at one-parasang intervals, while from Ḥulwān to Azerbayjān mounts could be ridden for

[45] Balādhurī, *Futūḥ*, p. 375.

[46] Ṭabarī (*Ta'rīkh*, III, p. 1167), however, simply states that the caliph 'stationed horses at each of the *Barīd* stations' (*rattaba al-khayl fī kull sikka min sikak al-barīd*), without explaining in what way this arrangement differed from ordinary *Barīd* practices.

[47] Ṭabarī, *Ta'rīkh*, III, pp. 1229–30 (translation modified). A similar version of this account is preserved in Ibn Taghribirdī, *al-Nujūm al-ẓāhira*, Cairo, 1929–38, vol. II, pp. 237–8, where it is mentioned that news arrived in four days from a distance that would ordinarily take one month to traverse.

'a day or two' before being rested.[48] Importantly, the lines of communication could be drawn, it would seem, on the basis of tactical requirements, and the caliph's generals do not appear to have been constrained by pre-determined routes in attending to rebels and other enemies.

During the reign of al-Wāthiq, however, the flexibility that characterised the *Barīd* during the first two centuries of Islam was lost with the composition of Ibn Khurradādhbih's *Kitāb al-masālik wa al-mamālik*, the first version of which was presented to the caliph in 846.[49] In commissioning a work that describes the routes and stations of the caliphate, al-Wāthiq was accepting that the *Barīd* was an institution no longer in its developmental stages. Ibn Khurradādhbih's work may be seen as a caliphal equivalent of such works as the *Peutingerian Table* or the *Parthian Stations*, and the composition of such works cannot be considered by a ruler whose empire is still being built or whose borders have yet to be fixed. Rather, these works set out to delineate in a practical manner the various regions of the known world and the major routes that link them, as a summary of the *status quo* (regardless of the theoretical aspirations of world domination that a culture may maintain). Thus, Ibn Khurradādhbih's work declared the *Barīd*'s infrastructure in particular and the borders of *Dār al-Islām* in general to be firmly established. After describing the routes and stations of the caliphate, Ibn Khurradādhbih states: 'The Stations of the *Barīd* in the Empire: There are 930 stations (*sikak*). The expenditure for the mounts and their prices, as well as the salaries of the express-couriers (*banādira*, sing. *bundār*)[50] and courier-guides (*furāniqīn*, sing. *furāniq*) amounts to 159,100 dinars.'[51]

Ibn Khurradādhbih's work would serve as the basis for other route-books that would emerge in the late ninth and early tenth centuries, many of which would describe in great detail the state of caliphal roads and the provisions available thereon.[52] But for the Marwanid and early Abbasid period we have

48 See below (pp. 94–7) for the fact that postal stations were usually situated at 2- or 4-parasang intervals.

49 The standard edition is edited by M. J. de Goeje as Ibn Khurradādhbih, Abū al-Qāsim, *Kitāb al-masālik wa al-mamālik*, Leiden, 1889; confusingly, de Goeje compiled his edition on the basis of both the 846 and the 885 versions of the work.

50 On purely linguistic grounds, it may be argued that the term *bundār* is an Arabised version of *veredarius*. However, as the term occurs with this meaning in other sources (in A. Silverstein, 'A New Source on the Early History of the *Barīd*', *al-Abḥāth* 50–1 (2002–3), 121–34 at 132 n. 1), all of which emanate from and refer to the eastern lands of the caliphate, this etymological explanation seems unlikely.

51 Ibn Khurradādhbih, *Masālik*, p. 153. The fact that fewer than 850 stations are enumerated in Ibn Khurradādhbih's detailed lists of routes and their stations is besides the point, and probably says more about the state of de Goeje's edition of the text than it does about the state of the caliphal *Barīd*.

52 It is curious that from the mid ninth century – around the time when route-books began to be compiled – milestones disappear from the archaeological record of the Near East, the milestones from *Darb Zubayda* being the latest to have survived (on these, see S. A. al-Rashid, *Darb Zubaydah: The Pilgrim Road from Kufa to Mecca*, Riyad, 1980). It is possible that the availability of route-books rendered milestones obsolete, but this is mere conjecture.

only passing references to postal routes in literary sources, and there can be little doubt that the postal system and its facilities were frequently beset by inefficiencies and disturbances. Already in the Sufyanid period, we hear that Ziyād ibn Abīhi was forced to send administrative documents to the caliph Muʿāwiya 'concealed with a messenger',[53] suggesting that although the *Barīd* was already in existence, the caliph and his governor in Iraq could not expect the routes to be safe. Towards the end of the Umayyad period things were no better: in one instance a messenger of the caliph al-Walīd II (r. 743–4) is said to have been kidnapped and interrogated by rebels,[54] and in another case rebels travelling along the roads presented themselves as 'messengers from al-Walīd' and seized both the treasure of the *bayt al-māl* and the local postal chief (*ṣāḥib al-barīd*).[55]

That the Abbasid revolutionaries were able to stage a well-coordinated yet clandestine movement across the formidable terrain of the eastern caliphal lands suggests that the roads were not guarded or patrolled effectively under the late Umayyads. In the early Abbasid period, al-Manṣūr reportedly posted spies and observers along the routes,[56] mindful, perhaps, of the Umayyads' failures in this regard.[57] Subsequent Abbasid caliphs continued al-Manṣūr's initiative: before he became caliph, al-Amīn (r. 809–13) is said to have had informants in Ṭūs with whom he would correspond on the subject of his father's condition; in order to avoid detection by Hārūn's scouts along the roads, correspondence would be transported in a hollowed-out wooden chest.[58] Control of the roads from Baghdad to Khurasan was a sticking point in the rivalry between al-Amīn and his brother al-Maʾmūn (r. 813–33). Although his brother was caliph, al-Maʾmūn had the upper hand in this respect from the outset: all messengers from Iraq would be accompanied in Khurasan by al-Maʾmūn's agents, who prevented the envoys from mingling with local inhabitants. Lookout posts were established along the roads, and only travellers bearing warrants would be allowed to proceed, after being searched thoroughly. This highly developed system was in operation in lands from Rayy eastwards.[59] Al-Amīn, for his part, also introduced such controls,[60] but his attempts were considerably less successful than those of his brother, and in one case al-Maʾmūn's agents bypassed al-Amīn's travel regulations by using a woman to transmit concealed messages to a local *ṣāḥib al-barīd* ('postal chief').[61]

[53] Ṭabarī, *Taʾrīkh*, II, p. 26. [54] Ibid., II, p. 1804. [55] Ibid., II, p. 1790.
[56] Ibid., III, pp. 179, and 283–4.
[57] According to Ṭabarī (*Taʾrīkh*, III, p. 414), 'al-Manṣūr captured one of the great men of the Banū Umayya and said: "What happened to the Banū Umayya that their affairs fell into disorder?" He said: "Neglecting information" (*taḍyīʿ al-akhbār*).' On the perceived relationship between the fall of the Umayyads and the decline of their *Barīd*, see below pp. 86–7.
[58] Ibid., III, p. 765. [59] Ibid., III, p. 783.
[60] It is worth pointing out that when al-Amīn established surveillance along the roads, it was his *ṣāḥib al-ḥaras* who was involved in the project, not a *Barīd* official (in Ṭabarī, *Taʾrīkh*, III, p. 817).
[61] Ibid., III, p. 793.

Moreover, al-Ma'mūn, through his general Ṭāhir, was able to infiltrate his brother's territories with spies and scouts, who would spread rumours amongst the caliph's army in order to undermine morale.[62]

When the caliphal routes were secured and the relay-stations were well-provisioned, immense speeds could be achieved by travellers using the *Barīd*.[63] Although 'Umarī states that al-Walīd used the *Barīd* to transport mosaics for his building projects, the evidence suggests that throughout Islamic history the postal system was a *Cursus Velox*. As was the case in the pre-Umayyad period, the term *barīd* continued to be used in poetry to denote speed: in the words of an early Marwanid poet, 'The riders drive their camels at the greatest speed, just as the *Barīd* does, and they do not ride at a trot.'[64] Similarly, a courier bearing news of Qutayba ibn Muslim's death (during al-Walīd I's reign) is said to have been 'so fast that he disappeared in the blink of an eye'.[65] The maximum speeds recorded for *Barīd* travel in this period are impressive: during Hishām's reign, riders on *jammāzāt* (swift she-camels)[66] are said to have covered 85 *farsakh*s (*ca.* 510 kilometres) in 24 hours,[67] thereby clocking one of the fastest speeds in postal history.[68] Under al-Ma'mūn, a mail-bag (*kharīṭa*) from Ṭāhir to al-Faḍl ibn Sahl was transported from Rayy to Marw – a distance of 1,270 kilometres – in three days.[69] During al-Mu'taṣim's reign, medical plants in lead bowls were sent from Syria to the caliph in Samarrā within six days.[70] The only caliph to ride the intensely uncomfortable *Barīd* was al-Hādī, who, having received news (via the *Barīd*) of al-Mahdī's death, travelled by post from Jurjān to Baghdad, covering a distance of almost 2,000 kilometres in just under two weeks.[71] By *Barīd* standards this speed is not particularly remarkable,[72] but it would have been exceptionally fast for a high-ranking official and his entourage.

62 Ibid., III, pp. 840 and 852.

63 For a discussion of the speeds achievable using the *Barīd*, see below: Appendix: Distances and Speeds of the *Barīd*.

64 *Hudsailian Poems*, vol. I p. 200 ll. 29–30. The poet was Umayya ibn al-'Ā'idh. Farazdaq also makes reference to the *Barīd*'s speed in his poetry (in Ullmann, *Geschichte*, p. 51, no. 169).

65 Ṭabarī, *Ta'rīkh*, II, p. 1302.

66 On which, see below pp. 111–13.

67 Ibn Rusta, *Kitāb al-a'lāq al-nafīsa*, Leiden, 1891, p. 180. According to Ṭabarī (*Ta'rīkh*, II, p. 1657), the distance covered was only 80 *farsakh*s (480 kilometres).

68 By way of comparison, the average speed achieved by the postal system in Qajar Iran was 120–60 kilometres a day (in Floor, 'The *Chapar-Khāna* System', 261).

69 Jahshiyārī, *Wuzarā'*, p. 294; and Ṭabarī, *Ta'rīkh*, III, p. 803.

70 Hilāl al-Ṣābi', *Rusūm dār al-khilāfa*, (ed. M. Awwad), Baghdad, 1964, p. 19.

71 Jahshiyārī, *Wuzarā'*, p. 167; Ṭabarī, *Ta'rīkh*, III, p. 547; Tha'ālibī, *Laṭā'if al-ma'ārif*, (trans. C. E. Bosworth, *The Book of Curious and Entertaining Information*), Edinburgh, 1968, pp. 104–5.

72 Travelling with his attendants, the Īl-khān Öljeitü managed to cover only *ca.* 40 kilometres a day (in C. P. Melville, 'The Itineraries of Sultan Öljeitü, 1304–16', *Iran* 28 (1990), 55–70, esp. 60).

Mounts and messengers

The users of the *Barīd* during this period and the means by which they travelled varied, based on a number of considerations. Before turning to these, it is important to stress that unlike the *Cursus Publicus* – with its *agentes in rebus*, *notarii*, and *veredarii* – the caliphal *Barīd* was not served by a special *schola* of couriers. Instead, sources refer to people being sent 'via the *Barīd*' or 'on the mounts of the *Barīd*'. Two types of traveller are known to have made regular use of the postal facilities: simple couriers, usually *mawālī*, eunuchs or other socially inferior functionaries; and dignitaries, such as governors travelling to their new posts, or other officials.[73]

The couriers despatched were often *mawālī*. In some ways, it seems that the responsibilities associated with the *agentes in rebus* under the Byzantines were assumed by a governor's *mawālī* in the Umayyad period. The fact that 'governors would employ them as messengers, spies, executioners, and other agents of various kinds'[74] would suggest that *mawālī* were 'the governor's men' just as the *agentes in rebus* were 'the Master [of Offices]'s men' (*magistrianoi*) in Constantinople. This practice continued into the early Abbasid period: according to one report, al-Manṣūr interrogated a high-ranking member of the Umayyad family about the administrative practices of the late Umayyads, saying: '"Among what people did [the Umayyads] find most loyalty?" And [the Umayyad] replied, "Their *mawālī*." Al-Manṣūr wanted to ask for help from members of his family in gathering information, but then he said "It would diminish their status", and he sought help from his *mawālī*.'[75] Although it may not have taken place as recorded, this exchange reflects al-Manṣūr's preference to rely on *mawālī* for his *Barīd*-affairs; indeed, the only two postal chiefs (*aṣḥāb al-barīd*) mentioned as having served him were al-Manṣūr's *mawālī* 'Ṭarīf' and 'Maṭar', who controlled the *Barīd* in Egypt, Syria, and the Ḥijāz.[76] And when al-Manṣūr died during a pilgrimage to Mecca, it was his *mawlā* 'Manāra' who brought the news back to Baghdad, travelling by the *Barīd*.[77] With the gradual erosion of the *mawlā* status, the early Abbasids drew upon other (invariably subservient) groups such as eunuchs (Hārūn al-Rashīd) or slave-soldiers (al-Muʿtaṣim) to meet their *Barīd*-needs.[78]

[73] E.g. Qurra ibn Sharīk, who travelled to his post in Egypt via the *Barīd*, accompanied by four companions (Kindī, *Wulā miṣr*, Beirut, 1959, p. 83). And see below, n. 171.

[74] P. Crone, *EI2*, s.v. 'mawlā', vol. VI, p. 877a. [75] Ṭabarī, *Taʾrīkh*, III, p. 414.

[76] Jahshiyārī, *Wuzarāʾ*, pp. 100–1.

[77] Although it is not specified that the *Barīd* was used in this case, the occasion, the distance involved, and the speed at which the message was delivered all suggest that Manāra travelled by post (as argued in D. Ayalon, *Eunuchs, Caliphs, and Sultans: A Study in Power Relationships*, Jerusalem, 1999, p. 99 n. 15).

[78] Hārūn's reliance on eunuchs in the *Barīd* is discussed in Ayalon, *Eunuchs*, pp. 96–103. Jahshiyārī (*Nuṣūṣ ḍāʾiʿa min kitāb al-wuzarāʾ wa al-kuttāb*, (ed. M. Awwad), Beirut, 1965, p. 85) mentions that al-Muʿtamid's *ṣāḥib al-barīd* in Egypt was one 'Ḥusayn the eunuch (*al-khādim*)'.

There are two reasons why serving as a courier or postal chief was reserved for socially weaker elements of society. First, as al-Manṣūr stated, gathering intelligence was an activity that was considered to be degrading. Second, travelling on the mounts of the *Barīd* was known to be an uncomfortable experience, and there is even record of a man who was heard complaining to the caliph ʿUmar II of being sore from riding the *Barīd*.[79] Accordingly, the thought that notables would perform functions associated with the *Barīd* provoked astonishment: when Muḥammad ibn al-Ashʿath brought a letter to al-Muhallab, the latter exclaimed, 'Does someone like you, Muḥammad, come as a *Barīd*?', to which Ibn al-Ashʿath replied, 'By God, I am nobody's *Barīd* except that our slaves and *mawālī* have taken our wives, children, and families from us by force!'[80] It is perhaps for this reason that al-Hādī's use of the *Barīd* was deemed unusual enough to be included in Thaʿālibī's *Book of Curious and Entertaining Information.*[81]

Couriers on the routes were easily distinguishable from other travellers. On those rare occasions when 'runners' are mentioned, they are described as 'carrying a stick with a leather bag',[82] bringing to mind the leather mail-bags used in pre-Islamic Iran.[83] Most often, couriers were mounted on 'postal mounts': literary sources from this period refer to *dawābb al-barīd*, as do a number of Arabic documents from mid-eighth-century Egypt and Central Asia.[84] Whether these *dawābb* were horses, donkeys, mules, or camels is usually unspecified, though it is likely that local conditions generally dictated the type of mount used. What is sometimes mentioned in literary sources is the way in which the *dawābb* were modified, to distinguish them from ordinary mounts. Arabic sources for the pre-Islamic Iranian '*Barīd*' suggest that postal mounts had docked tails as an outward sign (*ʿalāmatan lahā*) of their postal status,[85] and in the Islamic period there are references both to dock-tailed and to 'lean' (*muḍammara* or *ḍāmira*) *Barīd* mounts. Although many Arabic sources insist that tail-docking was introduced as a means of

[79] Ibn Mājah, *Sunan*, Cairo, 1952, vol. II, p. 1438. [80] Ṭabarī, *Taʾrīkh*, II, p. 719.

[81] Compare the statement of Sir F. J. Goldsmid (*Eastern Persia: An Account of the Journeys for the Persian Boundary Commission 1870–71–72*, London, 1876, vol. I, p. 163), according to whom 'riding post for any distance in Persia is beyond measure fatiguing'.

[82] Cf. Ṭabarī, *Taʾrīkh*, II, p. 1302, where a messenger (on foot) with a stick and a leather bag who bears news of Qutayba ibn Muslim's death is said to 'resemble the couriers' (*yashbahu al-fuyūj*).

[83] It may be significant that this runner was setting out from eastern lands, perhaps reflecting Sasanid influence on the method of communication.

[84] The Egyptian fragments, which date from the years 745–52, are published with translation (English) in D. S. Margoliouth, *Catalogue of Arabic Papyri in the John Rylands Library*, Manchester, 1933, pp. 28–31; and republished with translation (French) and commentary in Y. Raghib, 'Lettres de service au maître de poste d'Ašmūn', *Archéologie Islamique* 3 (1992), 5–16. The Central Asian fragments include a Soghdian document from 717–18 (published in I. Krachkovsky, *Izbranniye Sočineniya* (= *Selected Works*), Moscow, 1955, vol. I, p. 184 (in Russian)), and a Bactrian document from the 760s (in G. Khan, *Arabic Documents from Early Islamic Khurasan*, London, 2006, document 6, ll. 7 and 11–12).

[85] See above, pp. 8–9.

distinguishing postal mounts from ordinary ones (thereby discouraging would-be highway robbers from attacking couriers), it would appear that this modification was expected to make the mounts more efficient.[86] The practice is said to have been adopted from Turkic soldiers, as Balādhurī writes:

In the country of al-Qīqān al-Muhallab met with eighteen Turkish knights, riding horses with docked tails. They attacked him but were all killed. Al-Muhallab said, 'How much more expeditious in manoeuvring these barbarians were than we!' In consequence, he had the tails of his own horses docked, being the first Muslim to do such a thing.[87]

Using 'lean' mounts was another widespread method of making *Barīd* mounts 'aerodynamic'. When Hishām received news of Yazīd II's death, his *kātib* immediately took excellent horses and made them *ḍāmira*, so that the news would travel as quickly as possible.[88] Similarly, in his account of al-Muʿtaṣim's campaign against Bābak, Ṭabarī reports that the caliph established 'lean horses' (*khayl muḍammara*) along the roads.[89] Ibn al-Ṭiqṭaqā actually defines *Barīd* mounts as being lean. In his words, '[the term] "*al-Barīd*" means that lean horses (*khayl muḍammara*) were stationed at a number of places'.[90] The process by which mounts became 'lean' is described in a number of sources. In the simplest of terms, a horse was fattened and then, over a period of forty days, was fed barely enough fodder to sustain it, in order to reduce the horse's flabbiness and make it firm in flesh.[91] Such mounts were used extensively in races and military campaigns.[92]

The practice of physically modifying postal mounts with the aim of enhancing their speed was common throughout Near Eastern history, and using anatomically superior mounts was therefore not unique to the *Barīd*: the Achaemenid postal system described in *Esther* (8: 10, 14) used horses 'from the royal stables' which were – according to an Aramaic translation of *Esther* composed in the late Sasanid period – 'lacking spleens and having carved hooves'.[93] The idea that postal mounts or runners had their spleens removed and their soles carved was held by Sasanid Jews,[94] and Pliny speaks of the

86 For an analysis of the references to tail-docking in the *Barīd*, see A. Silverstein, 'On Some Aspects of the Abbasid *Barīd*', in J. E. Montgomery (ed.), *Abbasid Studies: Occasional Papers of the School of ʿAbbasid Studies*, Leuven, 2004, 23–32.

87 Balādhurī, *Futūḥ*, p. 432. It is a curious fact that the name 'al-Muhallab' means 'docked'.

88 Jahshiyārī, *Wuzarāʾ*, p. 66. 89 As seen above, p. 63. 90 Ibn al-Ṭiqṭaqā, *Fakhrī*, p. 148.

91 For a summary of the various accounts of *taḍmīr*, see Lane, *Lexicon*, p. 1803a (s.v. *ḍammara*).

92 According to Maqrīzī (*Kitāb al-mawāʿiẓ wa al-iʿtibār fī dhikr al-khiṭaṭ wa al-āthār*, (ed. A. F. Sayyid), London, 2002–4, vol. III, p. 729), lean horses were used in racing as late as the fifteenth century.

93 In B. Grossfeld, *The First Targum to Esther: According to MS Paris Hebrew 110 of the Bibliothèque Nationale*, New York, 1983.

94 According to some Talmudic scholars, Adonijah's couriers (in *1 Kings* 1: 5) were without spleens and had carved soles (*Sanhedrīn*, 21b).

spleen as an organ that hinders swift runners.[95] It is unlikely, on medical grounds, that couriers or postal mounts had their spleens removed, but the point remains that inhabitants of the ancient Near East believed that those serving in *Barīd*-like institutions were anatomically superior to ordinary runners or riding animals. Tail-docking and *tadmīr*, on the other hand, most probably *were* practised in the Islamic period.[96]

In a tantalising anecdote that sheds light on the physical appearance of *Barīd* couriers, Jarīrī (d. 1000 CE) relates that Ibrāhīm ibn ʿAbdallāh, the brother of al-Nafs al-Zakiyya, escaped from the clutches of al-Manṣūr by means of a cunning ruse.[97] Having been cornered by al-Manṣūr's agents in Mosul, Ibrāhīm and a companion bought two mules and docked their tails 'as is done with *Barīd* mules' and bridled the mules 'as it is customary to do with *Barīd* mounts'. When the city gates were locked for the evening, Ibrāhīm rode one of the mules while his companion rode the other one and pretended to be the *furāniq*; the companion began 'to yell as a *furāniq* does when he is bearing a mail-bag' and Ibrāhīm followed closely behind him. The gates were opened for these fraudulent *Barīd* couriers and they managed to escape. Upon hearing what happened, al-Manṣūr was overcome with a mixture of astonishment and grief.[98]

Both in his function and his title, the *furāniq* of this and other episodes was the caliphal equivalent of the Sasanid *parwānag*. The *furāniq* would guide a courier or envoy along the road, often carrying the letter or mail-bag, and would ensure that tired mounts were returned at a leisurely pace to the relay-stations from which they came. Although the term *furāniq* suspiciously occurs in Imruʾ al-Qays' poetry on two occasions,[99] it is only from the late Umayyad period that papyri from Egypt refer to this functionary: in six documents that span the late Umayyad and early Abbasid periods, the governor of Egypt orders the *ṣāḥib al-barīd* of Ushmūn to furnish the bearer of the letter with 'two *Barīd* mounts, one of which being a mount for the *furāniq*'.[100] It is significant that this manifestly Sasanid contribution to the *Barīd* is in evidence before the Abbasid period and in a province that had not been part of the Sasanid Empire.

[95] Pliny, *Natural History*, Cambridge Mass., 1938–62, vol. XXVI, p. 83, and vol. XI, p. 80. Caelius Aurelianus, however, argues that removing the spleen was only a theoretical recommendation since he had never heard of its actually being carried out (in J. Preuss, *Biblical and Talmudic Medicine*, London, 1993, p. 216).

[96] It should be stressed, however, that these practices were not exclusive to the *Barīd*. On this point, see Silverstein, 'Abbasid *Barīd*', 27 n. 21, and 30–1.

[97] Jarīrī, *al-Jalīs al-ṣāliḥ al-kāfī*, Beirut, 1987, vol. III, p. 6 (drawn to my attention by Geert Jan van Gelder).

[98] Compare Dio Cassius, *Roman History*, (trans. E. Cary), Cambridge Mass., 1914–27, vol. IX, pp. 429–30 (79.39.2–3), where the defeated Emperor Macrinus (r. 217–18) disguised himself as a *frumentarius* when fleeing from his enemies.

[99] In Silverstein, 'Neglected Chapter', 307.

[100] '*fa-aḥmil . . . ʿalā dābbatayn min dawābb al-barīd iḥdāhumā dābbat al-furāniq*' in Margoliouth, *Catalogue*, pp. 28–31.

Administration

The administration of the *Barīd* during this period is described in a number of Arabic documents from the eighth century CE which are of fundamental importance for two reasons. First, they shed light on the funding and management of the *Barīd* during a period that is not otherwise well-served by Arabic sources: literary accounts have relatively little to say about the early *Barīd*, and the few facts that they do provide were in any case susceptible to anachronisms. Second, Arabic documents allow us to compare the *Barīd*'s administrative arrangements with those of the Byzantine and Sasanid postal systems, insofar as the latter institutions are reflected in pre-Islamic documents. It is, of course, possible to evaluate the contribution of the *Cursus Publicus* to the *Barīd* on the basis of literary sources for each system, but since the contexts of these sources are not comparable, any conclusions drawn on their basis must be viewed as tentative. The documentary evidence, on the other hand, presents the respective postal systems from a similar, bureaucratic perspective and can lend decisive weight to our conclusions. In general, literary references to the caliphal *Barīd* that conform to the the documentary record can complement it, while conflicting references may be discarded with confidence.[101]

Documents from both the West (Egypt) and the East (Soghdia and Balkh) attest to the existence of regional postal chiefs, *aṣḥāb al-barīd* (sing. *ṣāḥib al-barīd*) from the reign of al-Walīd I (r. 705–15) and thereafter. It is possible that postal chiefs such as those described in these documents were active in the Sufyanid period, and it is probable that they operated by ʿAbd al-Malik's reign; the fact that, according to early Muslim authors,[102] al-Walīd I was the first caliph to use papyri-rolls (*ṭawāmīr*, sing. *ṭūmār*, from Greek: *tomarion*, 'one sixth of a papyrus roll') may account for the lack of documentary support for pre-Walīd postal chiefs.[103] A papyrus fragment written by al-Walīd's governor of Egypt, Qurra ibn Sharīk (in office 709–14), describes the role that the postal chief played in this period. The document states:

In the name of God, the Compassionate, the Merciful. From Qurra ibn Sharīk to Basīl, the administrator of Ishqaw. [I praise] Allāh, besides whom there is no god. To the matter at hand: al-Qāsim ibn Sayyār, the postal chief (*ṣāḥib al-barīd*), has

[101] On this topic, see Silverstein, 'Documentary Evidence'.

[102] Jahshiyārī, *Wuzarāʾ*, p. 47, where it is also stated that al-Walīd was the first caliph to insist that a particular, 'administrative' format for correspondence be adopted throughout caliphal lands.

[103] M. A. ʿAbd al-Laṭīf (*Mudun wa qurā miṣr fī nuṣūṣ baʿḍ al-bardiyyāt al-ʿarabiyya fī al-ʿaṣr al-umawī*, unpublished MA thesis, University of Helwan, 2001) argues that the Arabic document *PSR Heid. Inv. Arab. 550* refers to the caliph ʿAbd al-Malik's correspondence with the postal chiefs of Ushmūn. It would appear, however, that the ʿAbd al-Malik of this text is ʿAbd al-Malik ibn Yazīd, the governor of Egypt from 133 to 136 AH, who interacts with the *ṣāḥib barīd ushmūn* in documents from the John Rylands Library (in Margoliouth, *Catalogue*, p. 28, doc. IV, l. 2).

mentioned to me that you have fined some villages in your region on account of the poll-tax (*jizya*) that is due from them. When this, my letter, comes to you do not bother any of them in any way until I have spoken to you about them, God willing . . .[104]

From this document we learn that postal chiefs went by the title '*ṣāḥib al-barīd*' and reported to regional governors on the activities of local administrators.[105] The former point is especially important in light of the fact that in contemporary Greek documents the same al-Qāsim ibn Sayyār is mentioned without a title that would indicate his status.[106] Under the Byzantines, reports such as this one would have been written by *notarii* or *agentes in rebus*, who were based in Constantinople despite spending extended periods patrolling imperial routes, whereas provincial stations would be administered by a *manceps*. With this in mind, it could be argued that in both his title and his role, the *ṣāḥib al-barīd* here was not merely an Arabised Byzantine functionary.[107]

The six Ushmūn papyri that straddle the late Umayyad and early Abbasid periods portray the local *ṣāḥib al-barīd* in a different light: in these texts the governor of Egypt orders the local postal chief to supply a specific person with postal mounts and a *furāniq*, reflecting responsibilities that are more congruous with the functions of pre-Islamic postal chiefs. Documents from Marwanid Soghdia mention local postal chiefs despatching reports,[108] while use of the *Barīd*'s facilities in this region is requested directly from the local governor (*amīr*) rather than from a *ṣāḥib al-barīd*.[109]

The role of regional postal chiefs in composing and transmitting intelligence reports to the central authorities is outlined in detail for the reign of al-Manṣūr. According to Ṭabarī,

Ibrāhīm ibn Mūsā ibn ʿĪsā ibn Mūsā reported that the *Barīd* officials in all outlying regions (*wulāt al-barīd fī al-āfāq kullihā*) would write daily to al-Manṣūr, during his reign, [reports on] the price of wheat, grains, condiments, and other foods, and [on] any judgments passed by the *Qāḍī* in their district, and [on] the governor's actions, and the income of the *Bayt al-Māl*, and any occurrence. After the evening prayer, [the postal official] would write to him with details of that which happened during that day, and after the morning prayer they would write to him regarding that which happened

[104] In A. Grohmann, *Papyri in the Egyptian Library*, Cairo, 1934–8, no. 153 (translation modified).

[105] On the *ṣāḥib al-barīd* in these documents, see: A. Dietrich, *Arabische Briefe aus der Papyrus-Sammlung der Hamburger Staats- und Universitäts-Bibliothek*, Hamburg, 1955, p. 55; and C.H. Becker, 'Arabische Papyri des Afroditofundes', *Zeitschrift für Assyriologie und verwandte Gebiete* 20 (1906), 68–104, at 96.

[106] *P. Lond. IV*: document no. 1347 (edited in H.I. Bell, *Greek Documents in the British Library IV*, London, 1910, pp. 20ff.).

[107] Furthermore, if only on the basis of his name, it would appear that this postal chief was not a *mawlā* but an Arab.

[108] Grenet and de la Vaissière, 'Panjikent', 163–4, 166, and 171–2. As these documents are not in Arabic, the term *ṣāḥib al-barīd* does not occur (the Iranian *arspan arspanj* is used instead).

[109] Krachkovsky, *Selected Works*, vol. I, p. 184. It is possible that, upon agreeing to supply postal mounts, the *amīr* would then involve an unmentioned *ṣāḥib al-barīd*.

overnight. When their letters would arrive, [al-Manṣūr] would examine their contents and if the prices remained unchanged, he would refrain from action, but if any detail changed he would write to the governor and local tax official and ask about the cause for the change in price ...[110]

Although this aspect of a postal chief's vocation is attested as early as the reign of al-Walīd I, the relationship between the *Barīd*'s officials and provincial reporting would retain a certain measure of flexibility for decades to come. For instance, the misbehaviour of Ḥijāz-based officials was reported to al-Manṣūr not by the local *ṣāḥib al-barīd* but by the *ṣāḥib al-shurṭa*.[111] And shortly thereafter, the caliph al-Mahdī is said to have ordered Ya'qūb ibn Da'ūd 'to send trusted agents (*umanā'*) to all the regions and ... no letter was allowed to be sent on behalf of al-Mahdī to a governor until Ya'qūb ibn Da'ūd had written to his trusted agent to send it'.[112] Thus, even for strictly 'postal' affairs, the expected *aṣḥāb al-barīd* are not mentioned. By Hārūn al-Rashīd's reign, the function of *ṣāḥib al-barīd* can be seen to have achieved more prominence: the role of provincial postal chief was repeatedly awarded as a prize to favoured (or disgruntled) administrators,[113] and in two instances it would appear that a *ṣāḥib al-barīd* even had the local coinage minted in his name.[114]

One development associated with the early Abbasid period is the existence of a postal chief in the capital, in addition to the provincial *aṣḥāb al-barīd*. The caliph al-Mahdī is said to have sent a mail-bag (*kharīṭa*) to the Umayyads of Spain via his *ṣāḥib al-barīd*,[115] while Hārūn al-Rashīd had a postal chief in Baghdad by the name of Sallām.[116] Moreover, under Hārūn, Yaḥyā ibn Ja'far the Barmakid was referred to as the administrator of the *Barīd* in 'the outlying regions' (*āfāq*) of the caliphate,[117] suggesting for the first time that there was a single official who co-ordinated the activities of the regional postal chiefs. But while Hārūn's bureaucracy had *dīwāns* of *al-shuraṭ*, *al-ḥaras*, *al-kharāj*, *al-rasā'il*, and *al-muṣallā*,[118] there is no mention of a

[110] Ṭabarī, *Ta'rīkh*, III, p. 435. Ṭabarī (ibid., III, p. 398) also tells us that after evening prayers al-Manṣūr would peruse 'the letters that had arrived from the frontiers, the borders, and the outlying districts'.

[111] Ibid., III, p. 377. [112] Ibid., III, p. 486.

[113] Jahshiyārī, *Wuzarā'*, pp. 249–51, where al-Faḍl ibn al-Rabī' is offered control of the *Barīd* in Mosul and Diyār Rabī'a, and is eventually rewarded with the *Barīd* of these regions in addition to Diyār Bakr, to the fury of Yaḥyā ibn Khālid the Barmakid, who had reserved the administration of the *Barīd* in these regions for his son al-Faḍl ibn Yaḥyā. Eventually, al-Faḍl ibn al-Rabī' declined the caliph's offer.

[114] The postal chiefs were Ḥammawayhi, who served as *ṣāḥib al-barīd* in Khurasan 807–9, and Nuṣayr al-Waṣīf, who was *ṣāḥib al-barīd* in 785–6 (in N. D. Nicol, 'Early Abbasid Administration in the Central and Eastern Provinces, 132–218 AH/750–833 AD', unpublished PhD dissertation, University of Washington, 1979, p. 249 n. 81).

[115] Ṭabarī, *Ta'rīkh*, III, p. 529. [116] Ibid., III, p. 764. [117] Jahshiyārī, *Wuzarā'*, p. 204.

[118] Ṭabarī, *Ta'rīkh*, III, p. 795.

Dīwān al-Barīd,[119] and Yaḥyā ibn Jaʿfar's position appears to have been tailored to him. When the Barmakids eventually fell from grace and control of the *Barīd* was transferred to eunuchs, the system declined rapidly: according to Jahshiyārī, when Hārūn died there were 'four thousand' unopened mail bags discarded in the central *Dīwān*.[120]

In fact, there is no evidence for the existence of a *Dīwān al-Barīd* at all until the reign of al-Mutawakkil (r. 847–61). This lack of evidence is especially glaring in those primary sources that carefully list the various *Dīwāns* and their administrators in summarising each caliph's reign.[121] The lack of a *Dīwān al-Barīd* during this period may be down to an accident of history: that it was Muʿāwiya and not ʿAlī who won the first civil war, and that, consequently, it was Syria and not Iraq that provided the metropolis of the first Islamic Empire, had repercussions for the entire Umayyad bureaucratic machine in general, and for the *Barīd* in particular. Syria, for all its unparalleled antiquity and strategic importance in the ancient rivalry between Rome and Persia, was never an imperial capital. When Muʿāwiya drew upon the administrative traditions of the local, Byzantine bureaucrats – both as governor of Syria and later as Umayyad caliph – he was retaining the bureaus of a province, not those of an imperial capital. Documents had to be drafted, copied, sealed, and filed in provinces, and taxes had to be collected and registered. Hence, we find *dīwāns* of *al-rasāʾil*, *al-khātam*, and *al-kharāj* very early on in caliphal history. But while the Umayyads inherited local tax-collectors and scribes, they did not inherit the Magister Officiorum, and centralised control of the *Barīd* would only be introduced in the mid ninth century.

Who, then, controlled the *Barīd* during this period? Although an eighth-century signet ring inscribed with the word '*Barīd*' has been discovered, it is difficult to know who possessed it.[122] While the caliph himself undoubtedly had the final say in all matters, the existing evidence suggests that the *Barīd* was controlled on a regional basis by provincial governors. Especially in the early Umayyad period, when powerful governors such as Ziyād ibn Abīhi and

[119] For al-Hādī's reign, only the bureaus of *zimām al-azimma*, *al-kharāj*, *al-ḥaras*, *al-jund*, *al-shuraṭ*, and *al-khātam* are mentioned (ibid., III, p. 548), and for Hishām's reign, only bureaus of *shurṭa*, *ḥaras*, *rasāʾil*, *khātam*, *kharāj*, and *jund* are enumerated by al-Madāʾinī (in Balādhurī, *Ansāb al-ashrāf*, vol. VIb, p. 4).

[120] Jahshiyārī, *Wuzarāʾ*, p. 265. The number 'four thousand' should be taken as formulaic.

[121] The fact that there is not even passing reference to a *Dīwān al-Barīd* in the thorough studies of either D. W. Biddle ('The Development of the Bureaucracy of the Islamic Empire during the Late Umayyad and Early Abbasid Period', unpublished PhD dissertation, University of Texas at Austin, 1970) or S. A. al-ʿAlī ('*Muwaẓẓafū bilād al-shām fī al-ʿaṣr al-umawī*', *al-Abḥāth* 19 (1966), 44–79) is particularly telling.

[122] The ring, which has been dated to the eighth century on the basis of its Kufic script, is discussed in A. A. Ivanov, 'Seal of the Eighth Century Secret Service', in *Sphragistica and History of Culture: Volume of Articles Dedicated to the Jubilee of V. S. Shandrovskaya*, St Petersburg, 2004, pp. 142–6 (drawn to my attention by Yusuf Raghib). I would like to thank Firuza Abdullaeva for translating the Russian text.

al-Ḥajjāj ibn Yūsuf ensured stability in the eastern provinces of the caliphate, governors are said to have been involved in major administrative developments in the capital. Ziyād, for instance, is said to have been 'the first to consolidate Muʿāwiya's government'[123] and to have copied the Sasanid system of composing, copying, and sealing documents when he was appointed governor of Iraq.[124] Similarly, although the Arabisation of the caliphal administration is often associated with the caliph ʿAbd al-Malik, it was actually al-Ḥajjāj who is credited with this initiative in Arabic sources.[125] And it is al-Ḥajjāj (rather than ʿAbd al-Malik) who came to develop a reputation for acquiring news of all events.[126]

Governors during this period are associated with both the 'reporting' and the 'postal' aspects of the *Barīd*. Regarding the former, we hear of Ziyād, al-Ḥajjāj, al-Muhallab, and Qutayba ibn Muslim composing intelligence reports during the Umayyad period,[127] whereas there is no evidence for *aṣḥāb al-barīd* gathering or transmitting news in the East until the reign of al-Manṣūr.[128] The 'postal' aspects of the *Barīd* also appear to have been within the remit of provincial governors. As early as Muʿāwiya's reign, the caliph's *ʿāmil* in Medina was in charge of the *Barīd* there,[129] and similar arrangements persisted into the Marwanid and early Abbasid periods. In one episode, al-Ḥajjāj offered Layla al-Akhyaliyya permission to travel to Khurasan via the *Barīd*,[130] and in another he communicated with Qutayba ibn Muslim and with local *amīr*s along the Khurasan Road using *Barīd* couriers, in order to track down some Muhallabid rebels who had escaped from prison.[131] On account of the vast distances involved and the timely nature of the events, it would have been impractical for governors in such cases to apply to the caliph for permission to use the *Barīd*. Perhaps more importantly, there is clear documentary evidence indicating that authorisation to use the *Barīd*'s facilities was routinely sought from provincial governors: in 717–18, Dīwāstī requested permission to use 'mounts of the *Barīd*' from the *amīr*, al-Jarrāḥ ibn ʿAbdallāh,[132] and in late Umayyad/early Abbasid Ushmūn, it is the governor of Egypt who orders the local *ṣāḥib al-barīd* to provide postal mounts for specified individuals.[133]

Governors were also charged with ensuring that *Barīd* stations in their region were adequately supplied. Unlike in the pre-Islamic period, however, both the documentary and the literary evidence suggest that only *Barīd* mounts were offered to couriers, who would have to arrange other provisions

123 *kāna ziyād awwal man shadda amr al-sulṭān wa akkada al-mulk li-muʿāwiya*, in Ṭabarī, *Taʾrīkh*, II, p. 77.
124 Balādhurī, *Futūḥ*, p. 464. 125 E.g. ibid., p. 300. 126 Ṭabarī, *Taʾrīkh*, II, p. 988.
127 Ibid., II, p. 136 (Ziyād), pp. 942–3, and 1262 (al-Ḥajjāj), p. 1042 (al-Muhallab), and p. 1284 (Qutayba).
128 As discussed above (pp. 72–3), based on Ṭabarī, *Taʾrīkh*, III, p. 435. 129 Ibid., II, p. 213.
130 Ḥusrī, *Zahr al-ādāb wa thimār al-albāb*, Cairo, 1969–70, vol. IV, p. 77.
131 Ṭabarī, *Taʾrīkh*, II, p. 1211. 132 In Krachkovsky, *Selected Works*, vol. I, p. 184.
133 In Margoliouth, *Catalogue*, pp. 28ff.

independently.[134] The papyri discussed above stipulate that the bearer be entitled only to *Barīd* mounts (for himself and for a *furāniq*-guide), while food, lodgings, and other provisions are not mentioned. Literary accounts specify that individuals 'sent via the *Barīd*' were given a sum of money for their journeys. In one case, Yazīd ibn Muhallab sent a report on the situation in Iraq to the caliph Sulaymān I (r. 715–17), despatching Ibn al-Aḥtam with the letter and giving him 30,000 dirhams to cover travel expenses along the route, in addition to use of *Barīd* mounts.[135] In another episode, the much-maligned caliph Yazīd II (r. 720–4) is said to have written to the governor of Mecca, saying, 'When my letter reaches you, give so and so, the son of Abū Lahab [a poet admired by Yazīd] one thousand dinars to cover the expenses of his journey and allow him to use whatever mounts of the *Barīd* he desires.'[136] This shows that use of the *Barīd* only entailed obtaining fresh mounts at stations and confirms that it was the local governor who was in charge of the *Barīd*'s facilities in his region. As late as the reign of al-Wāthiq, we hear of a man being sent on the *Barīd* from Baghdad to Basra being given 500 dinars for his travel expenses.[137]

The *Barīd*'s funding arrangements underwent significant changes during the first two centuries of Islamic history. For much of this period, the Byzantine and Sasanid practice of funding and providing for their postal systems through a combination of taxation, requisitions, and corvées was maintained by the caliphs. Although such a system may appear inequitable to modern readers, it should be remembered that forced labour and the haphazard commandeering of mounts and other assets by officials was commonplace in the ancient world.[138] Documents refer to forced labour, requisitions, and special taxes to fund the *Barīd* during the Sufyanid,[139] Marwanid,[140] and early Abbasid periods. The early Abbasid document, which dates from *ca.* 150 AH (767–8 CE), is a quittance from the Khurasanī governor's financial administrator (*'āmil*) to a local notable who is acknowledged as having paid that which he owes 'with regard to the expenses of the postal mounts . . . and

[134] According to Floor ('The *Chapar-Khāna* System', 264–5), in Qajar Iran 'Post-houses . . . had not much to offer to the traveller, apart from a roof over his head and relay horses.'

[135] Ṭabarī, *Ta'rīkh*, II, p. 1309; it took Ibn al-Aḥtam seven days to reach Damascus from Iraq.

[136] Mas'ūdī, *Murūj*, vol. IV, p. 32, §2201.

[137] Bayhaqī, *Kitāb al-maḥāsin wa al-masāwī*, Cairo, 1906, vol. II, p. 75.

[138] For instance, when in 555 CE a 450-kilometre stretch of the Great Wall of China was being constructed, the Northern Qi dynasty conscripted more than 1.8 million peasants to undertake the necessary work under abysmal conditions. On corvées and requisitions in medieval Islamic history, see. S. D. Goitein, *A Mediterranean Society, Volume II: The Community*, Berkeley, 1971, pp. 393–4. The fact that most pre-modern postal systems were supplied and served by the local population is discussed in K. Wittfogel, *Oriental Despotism: A Comparative Study of Total Power*, New Haven, 1957, pp. 54–9.

[139] Kraemer, *Excavations at Nessana III*, pp. 209–10, where two labourers are conscripted to perform 'compulsory service' on the roads.

[140] *P. Ross. Georg.* IV: 25 (early eighth century), where the postal station at Munachte is funded by the local population.

the travel provisions for the postal couriers and [other] envoys, and their lodgings, that is administered together with the *kharāj* of the year 147 [AH]'.[141] Unsurprisingly, amongst his other exemplary acts, the caliph ʿUmar II is said to have temporarily exonerated the population of Iraq from paying 'fees for couriers' (*ujūr al-fuyūj*).[142] Another suspicious anecdote explains how ʿUmar II supposedly made up for the financial deficit that resulted from his postal reforms: according to the legend, two baskets of dates were sent to the caliph from Jordan; when ʿUmar heard that these dates were brought to him via the *Barīd*, he protested that he 'is not more worthy of using the *Barīd*'s mounts than ordinary Muslims' and ordered that the dates be sold and the money spent on fodder for the postal mounts.[143] Even if we are to take these vignettes to be little more than formulaic references to ʿUmar II's reputation for 'justice', they still reflect on the perceived 'injustices' that prevailed in this period.

Towards the end of the Umayyad period, caliphs began to assume financial responsibility for the expenses incurred by the *Barīd*, perhaps because the system was beginning to decline. Hishām is said to have spent four million dirhams a year on the *Barīd* facilities in the Sawād region of Iraq,[144] and by al-Wāthiq's reign the postal mounts and the salaries of express-couriers (*banādira*) and *furāniq*-guides were funded by the Treasury.[145] That only 159,100 dinars were reserved for this purpose may suggest that some of the financial burden was still being shouldered by the general population.[146] By the Middle Abbasid period, however, the newly created *Dīwān al-Barīd* would come to absorb all the expenditure associated with the *Barīd*, and in a tantalising passage al-Jāḥiẓ inadvertently contributes to the impression that, in his day, the *Barīd*'s mounts were provided by the state rather than by the general public:

When the Byzantine Emperor, the son of Augusta ('*ibn ghasṭa*'),[147] boasted of his majesty, he said to a [Muslim] envoy: 'Do you [Muslims] have anything through which to challenge me?' The envoy replied, 'Yes, our ruler has designated 40,000 mules for

[141] '*nafaqāt dawābb al-barīd ... wa jawā'iz al-burud wa al-rusul wa nazlihim*' (In Khan, *Arabic Documents*, document 6, ll. 7–9 and 11–15).

[142] Ṭabarī, *Ta'rīkh*, II, pp. 1366–7. According to Subkī (*Kitāb muʿīd al-niʿam wa mubīd al-niqam*, London, 1908, p. 33), ʿUmar II was so pious that he 'used to send a *Barīd* courier to pay visits [on his behalf] to the grave of Muḥammad'.

[143] Muḥammad ibn ʿAbd al-Ḥakam, *Sīrat ʿumar ibn ʿabd al-ʿazīz*, ed. A. Ubayd, Damascus, 1964, pp. 54–5 (drawn to my attention by Lennart Sundelin).

[144] W. H. Wahba, *al-Mawardi: The Ordinances of Government*, Beirut and London, 1996, p. 192.

[145] Ibn Khurradādhbih, *Masālik*, p. 153.

[146] According to Alois Sprenger (*Die Post- und Reiserouten des Orients*, Leipzig, 1864, p. 4), the fact that such a low sum was reserved for the *Barīd*'s expenses suggests that couriers were forced to take bribes to supplement their salaries, since – in his words – 'the Oriental mentality is to both give and receive bribes'. For a discussion of Ibn Khurradādhbih's *Barīd* budget, see Saʿdawi, *Niẓām al-barīd*, pp. 80–1.

[147] The '*ibn ghasṭa*' (the son of 'Augusta', the Empress Irene) referred to here is the Emperor Constantine VI, who ruled Byzantium during Hārūn al-Rashīd's reign.

the conveyance of letters and news from the centre of his kingdom to the outlying provinces of his realms.' This shut him up.

Jāḥiẓ then says, 'This refers to the *Barīd*'s mules', and adds sourly that '[The envoy] said this, even though the situation is quite different, for [the Muslim authorities] did not [even] know how to transport mail-bags by waterways or with runners.'[148] Jāḥiẓ was clearly unimpressed with the state of the *Barīd* in the early ninth century, but he nonetheless took it for granted that an enormous number of postal mules were 'designated' (*mawqūfa*) by the caliph for the system.

Functions

As is to be expected, the *Barīd* during this period transported urgent letters and news, dignitaries, and valuable items. But there are also cases in which the system was used to transport non-essential items and people, just as there are cases in which the *Barīd* functioned in altogether unexpected capacities.

The *Barīd* conveyed news of caliphs' deaths in order to ensure that this sensitive information, together with the trappings of rulership, reached the heir apparent as quickly and securely as possible. The deaths of caliphs including Muʿāwiya,[149] Yazīd II,[150] Hishām, al-Walīd II,[151] al-Mahdī,[152] and al-Wāthiq[153] are said to have been reported by couriers using the *Barīd*, as were the deaths of other important people.[154] The episode in which Hishām's death was reported by the *Barīd* is repeated (with minor variations) in a number of sources. According to one version, on the day Hishām died, al-Walīd II wrote to one of his secretaries inviting him to go riding together. The secretary reports that,

[al-Walīd II] rode 2 miles, stopped on a hill, and started complaining about Hishām. Suddenly, he saw an approaching cloud of dust and he heard the clanking of the

[148] Jāḥiẓ, *Bighāl*, p. 59, §85. As Jāḥiẓ's statement implies, using runners or 'waterways' to transport correspondence was considerably simpler than using a network of mounted couriers.

[149] See above, p. 56.

[150] Ṭabarī, *Ta'rīkh*, II, p. 1467, where it is reported that the caliphal seal (*khātam*) and staff (*'aṣā*) were brought to Hishām via the *Barīd*. According to Jahshiyārī (*Wuzarā'*, p. 66), when Hishām received a letter with news of Yazīd II's death, his *kātib* took excellent horses and made them lean (*ḍāmira*).

[151] Ṭabarī, *Ta'rīkh*, II, p. 1854, where a succession of *burud* reported that al-Walīd II had been murdered.

[152] According to Ṭabarī (ibid., III, p. 545), Nuṣayr al-Waṣīf was sent to al-Hādī with the news of al-Mahdī's death, since 'Nuṣayr is in charge of the *Barīd*; hence no one will regard his departure with any suspicion, since he is the head of the *Barīd* for this district (*nāḥiya*)'.

[153] Ṣafadī, *Kitāb al-wāfī bi al-wafāyāt*, Wiesbaden, 1931–, vol. X, p. 187.

[154] According to Balādhurī (*Ansāb al-ashrāf*, ed. A. A. Duri, Wiesbaden, 1978, vol. III, p. 226), news of Abū Muslim's death was sent via the *Barīd*. Qutayba ibn Muslim's death was also said to have been reported by official couriers, though the *Barīd* is not mentioned specifically (Ṭabarī, *Ta'rīkh*, II, p. 1302).

Barīd – and he asked for God's refuge from the evil of Hishām – and said: 'This *Barīd* has either arrived with [news of] an unexpected death or with immediate kingship.' I said to him: 'May God bring no bad upon you, but rather may He make you happy and preserve you', when suddenly two men on the *Barīd* appeared, approaching us, one of whom was a *mawlā* of Abū Sufyān ibn Ḥarb's clan.[155]

The two men then informed al-Walīd that Hishām had died. According to Ṭabarī's version,

Al-Walīd stopped at a sandy hill and began complaining about Hishām. Then suddenly he saw a cloud of dust and he exclaimed: 'These are messengers from Hishām. Let us pray to God that they bring good news.' Then two men on *Barīd* mounts hove into sight; one of them was a *mawlā* of Abū Muḥammad al-Sufyānī and the other was Jardaba. When they came nearer they went toward al-Walīd, dismounted, ran up to him, and greeted him as caliph ... So al-Walīd asked: 'Who sent your letter?' Jardaba replied: 'Your *mawlā* Sālim ibn ʿAbd al-Raḥmān, the master of the chancellery.'[156]

Other sources report that upon receiving this news, al-Walīd composed the following lines of poetry: 'My day was progressing well, and the high-quality wine was tasty, when suddenly I received news of the death of Hishām [lit. 'He who is at Ruṣāfa']; the *Barīd* came to us proclaiming Hishām's death, and brought us the caliphal seal (*khātam al-khilāfa*).'[157] Al-Walīd is also said to have composed poetry concerning the arrival of two *Barīd* couriers with news of Maslama ibn ʿAbd al-Malik's death.[158] It is important to point out that these episodes specifically mention that *two* men on *Barīd* mounts delivered the news of a death, indicating that the pre-Umayyad Arabian practice of despatching two couriers with the same piece of news was retained late into the Umayyad period. Other sources indicate that this practice continued into Abbasid times.[159]

The *Barīd* also sent the caliph news of uprisings in the provinces[160] or of the activities of unscrupulous officials. During al-Manṣūr's reign, the *ṣāḥib al-barīd* in Ḥaḍramawt informed the caliph that the local governor was distracted by frivolities,[161] and the *ṣāḥib al-barīd* in Rayy informed the caliph

[155] *Kitāb al-aghānī*, vol. VII, p. 15. [156] Ṭabarī, *Taʾrīkh*, II, p. 1750.

[157] *Kitāb al-aghānī*, vol. VII, p. 16. Later in the text (ibid., vol. VII, p. 17), another version of this poem is recorded as follows: 'My night was long and I stayed up pouring wine, when the *Barīd* suddenly arrived with news of Hishām's decline.'

[158] 'Two *Barīd*s came to us from Wāsiṭ, trotting with unambiguous letters (*bi al-kutub al-muʿjama*)', ibid., vol. VII, p. 6.

[159] E.g. Ṭabarī, *Taʾrīkh*, III, p. 154, where two men referred to as *rusul amīr al-muʾminīn* were sent on a mission; ibid., III, p. 173, where al-Manṣūr despatches two messengers together; and ibid., III, p. 286, where a head is sent to Khurasan with two messengers. The fact that in one instance Balādhurī (*Ansāb al-ashrāf*, vol. III, p. 226) specifies that al-Manṣūr sent 'a lone messenger' (*rasūlan mufradan*) bearing a letter may suggest that this was not the usual practice.

[160] E.g. Ṭabarī, *Taʾrīkh*, III, p. 281, on Muḥammad's uprising in the Ḥijāz. And see below p. 118, on the role of the *Barīd* in transmitting news of Ṭāhir's rebellion during the reign of al-Maʾmūn.

[161] Ibid., III, p. 399.

that the local governor (the future caliph al-Mahdī) had spent an inappropriate sum of money on a poet.[162] Even governors, it would seem, were subjected to the scrutiny of the provincial postal chiefs. That the *Barīd* was the mechanism for reporting on disloyalty of whatever nature meant that rebels often targeted the postal systems, employees, and infrastructure in mounting their offensive against the ruling authorities. During Hishām's reign, it is reported that supporters of the rebel al-Ḥārith ibn Surayj escaped from prison, 'riding their mounts and driving off the mounts of the *Barīd*',[163] and when Bahlūl the Kharijite rebelled, he gathered forty supporters at Mosul who agreed to tell passers-by that they had been sent to Hishām to take up administrative posts. 'Thus, they did not pass an official but they informed him of that arrangement and took mounts of the *Barīd*.'[164] In another instance, Iyās ibn Mu'āwiya stated: 'I was with Ibn Hubayra on a Friday after the call to prayer, and a *ghulām* of his came running towards us, saying "A group of people have entered the *Barīd* [station] and stationed at its entrance someone to guard it." '[165] Later in the Umayyad period, rebels who presented themselves as being 'messengers from [the caliph] al-Walīd [II]' seized the treasures of the *bayt al-māl* and kidnapped the local postal chief.[166] During the reign of al-Mu'taṣim, the *ṣāḥib al-barīd* in Azerbayjān, a Shi'ite by the name of 'Abdallāh ibn 'Abd al-Raḥmān, wrote to the caliph concerning Mankajūr's illicit treasures; upon hearing this, Mankajūr attempted to have the postal chief killed.[167] Finally, when Ṭāhir openly rebelled against al-Ma'mūn by omitting the caliph's name from the *khuṭba*, the local *ṣāḥib al-barīd* composed a report on him and summarily prepared himself for death, as he expected Ṭāhir to kill him.[168]

There are three reasons why rebels targeted the *Barīd*'s employees, facilities, and general infrastructure. First, 'driving off postal mounts' may have been considered a form of booty in an activist's campaign against the ruler, just as seizing the treasures of the *bayt al-māl* was. Second, due to the *Barīd*'s role in informing the caliph of provincial rebellions, disrupting the postal network was an obvious method of depriving the authorities of the strategic information needed to deal with the rebellion. Third, it could be argued that the *Barīd* came to symbolise caliphal authority in distant provinces in a way that served the caliph's propaganda needs on the one hand and exposed the *Barīd* to attacks by the caliph's enemies on the other. As a propaganda tool, the existence of guarded roads with milestones and manned postal stations made the *Barīd* a constant and uniquely ubiquitous reminder to the general

[162] Ibid., III, p. 406. [163] Ibid., II, p. 1566. [164] Ibid., II, pp. 1622–3.
[165] Balādhurī, *Ansāb al-ashrāf*, vol. VIb, p. 106. [166] Ṭabarī, *Ta'rīkh*, II, p. 1790.
[167] Ibid., III, p. 1301. In Ya'qūbī's version of this episode (*Ta'rīkh*, II, p. 580), it was the *ṣāḥib al-barīd* in Armenia, one Manṣūr ibn 'Īsā al-Sabī'ī, who informed the caliph of Mankajūr's crimes.
[168] *Kitāb al-aghānī*, vol. XV, p. 237; and Ṭabarī, *Ta'rīkh*, III, p. 1064. On this episode, see below p. 118.

population of a ruler's power, prestige, and concern for the welfare of the state. As a target for rebels, the *Barīd* was an accessible and relatively vulnerable symbol of the ruler's local presence, the disruption of which could provide mounts for the rebels and deprive the authorities of a means to suppress the rebellion, while making an explicitly mutinous political statement. It is for this reason that, whereas buildings that housed administrative archives were used as hiding-places by rebels,[169] postal stations were publicly attacked by them.

More often than not, the *Barīd* managed to withstand the challenges posed by rebels and succeeded in transporting a variety of people on postal mounts, including rebels themselves.[170] The security associated with use of the *Barīd*'s facilities meant that, aside from politically sensitive rebels, high-ranking administrators would use the *Barīd* to travel to their new posts,[171] large sums of money would be transported on postal mounts,[172] and favoured individuals – including poets, scribes, and doctors – would be allowed to use the system in travelling to the capital.[173] The speed with which the *Barīd* was associated made it the caliphs' preferred method of transporting perishables – usually exotic fruits – from a distance, as using any other means of transportation could not ensure that the items would still be fresh upon arrival.[174] ʿUmar II may have rejected the baskets of dates sent to him via the *Barīd*, but al-Maʾmūn had few qualms about using the system for related

[169] On which, see. M. Bravmann, 'The State Archives in the Early Islamic Era', *Arabica* 15 (1969), 87–9.

[170] Examples of rebels being sent (usually 'in chains') via the *Barīd* include: Ṭabarī, *Taʾrīkh*, II, p. 397; ibid., II, p. 1980; Balādhurī, *Ansāb al-ashrāf*, vol. IVb, p. 17; and Masʿūdī, *Murūj*, vol. III, p. 347, §2080.

[171] Qurra ibn Sharīk rode four *Barīd* mounts – one of which was the *furāniq*'s mount – to his post in Egypt (Kindī, *Wulā miṣr*, p. 83); Ḥabīb ibn Muhallab was sent to be the temporary governor of Khurasan, and his entourage rode *Barīd* mounts to the East (Ṭabarī, *Taʾrīkh*, II, p. 1035); and when al-Manṣūr died, the new governor of Khurasan 'rode four mounts of the *Barīd*' to his new post (Balādhurī, *Ansāb al-ashrāf*, vol. III, p. 227).

[172] When, during the reign of al-Manṣūr, the governor of Balqāʾ was dismissed, his considerable treasures were brought to the caliph via the *Barīd* (Ṭabarī, *Taʾrīkh*, III, p. 416). Earlier, during Yazīd II's reign, ʿUmar ibn Hubayra was sent on five postal mounts to dismiss governors in 'the East'; when he was accosted by [the recently deposed governor] Maslama along the road, Ibn Hubayra insisted that he was sent on postal mounts in order to collect the Muhallabids' wealth (ibid., II, p. 1433), implying that transporting wealth was a convincing reason for riding postal mounts.

[173] Poets sent via the *Barīd*: Masʿūdī, *Murūj*, vol. IV, p. 32, §2201; Bayhaqī, *Kitāb al-maḥāsin wa al-masāwī*, ed. M. A. F. Ibrahim, Cairo, 1991, p. 354; and Ṭabarī, *Taʾrīkh*, II, 1743, where a sealed papyrus scroll (*ṭūmār*) containing lampooning verses of poetry is sent with a messenger riding *Barīd* mounts. Scribes: Jahshiyārī, *Wuzarāʾ*, p. 41; and Ṭabarī, *Taʾrīkh*, II, p. 1131. Doctor: Nawawī, *Tahdhīb al-asmāʾ*, Göttingen, 1842–7, p. 397.

[174] Ibn Baṭṭūṭa (below, pp. 163–4) and Marco Polo (below, p. 163) describe the Delhi and Mongol postal systems transporting fruits for the ruler, and the Mughal Sultan Jahāngir (r. 1605–27) is said to have had grapes, pomegranates, pears, apples, melons, and pineapples delivered to him by his postal system (in Sabahuddin, 'Postal System', 278). During the Eastern Han Dynasty (25–220 CE), the Chinese Emperor had tropical fruits sent to the capital by post (in J. Needham, *Science and Civilisation in China, vol. IV*, Cambridge, 1971, p. 36).

purposes: according to a number of sources, when the caliph was campaigning in Byzantine lands, he was suddenly overcome with a craving for some myrobalan fruit (*āzāz* or *āzād*). The fruit was immediately brought before him from far-away Kabul, to everyone's amazement.[175] As reported, the story appears to be apocryphal. It would not have been possible for fruits from Kabul to have reached the caliph in Byzantine lands within the week, let alone within the hour. The fruits may have been brought from a nearby location, but it is more likely that this is simply an exaggerated – if not entirely fabricated – postal myth, circulated with the intention of highlighting the legendary efficiency of the *Barīd*.

As the *Barīd* was first adopted and employed by the early Muslims during their campaigns of expansion, it is not surprising that the system continued to be used in military contexts throughout this period. As we have seen, ʿAbd al-Malik's military reforms were accompanied by (and related to) attention to the caliphal routes in general and to the *Barīd* in particular. During ʿAbd al-Malik's reign, the *Barīd* continued to be employed in military contexts. In one instance, the governor of Iṣfahān wrote to al-Ḥajjāj requesting extra troops for a military campaign; al-Ḥajjāj then sent 'men on postal mounts (*dawābb al-barīd*) in groups of ten, fifteen, or twenty, until he sent [the governor] some five hundred altogether'.[176] On another occasion, during al-Ḥajjāj's campaign against Muḥammad ibn al-Ashʿath, it is reported that Syrian horsemen were reaching al-Ḥajjāj daily from ʿAbd al-Malik 'borne on postal mounts (*ʿalā al-burud*) in groups of one hundred, fifty, ten, and less', while al-Ḥajjāj sent regular reports on the situation to the caliph.[177] During Hishām's reign, when the Byzantines invaded Malaṭiya in 740–1, the town's inhabitants despatched a messenger 'who rode a mount of the *Barīd*' to Hishām, informing him of the situation and asking him for assistance. The caliph then sent the messenger back, accompanied by horses to support the military effort.[178] Mounts and soldiers were sent via the *Barīd* under al-Manṣūr,[179] and news from the battlefield was sent to al-Maʾmūn via the *Barīd*.[180] Al-Muʿtaṣim went so far as to introduce a functionary called *ṣāḥib khabar al-ʿaskar* ('chief of military intelligence'),[181] and the postal innovations introduced by this caliph during his campaign against Bābak and the *Zuṭṭ* are also of relevance in this context.[182] These references show that the

[175] Balādhurī, *Futūḥ*, pp. 402 and 430; Ṭabarī, *Taʾrīkh*, III, p. 1135; and others. That Kabul was famous for this fruit is known from other sources (e.g. Ibn Khurradādhbih, *Masālik*, p. 38; and Muqaddasī, *Aḥsan al-taqāsīm*, p. 304).

[176] Ṭabarī, *Taʾrīkh*, II, p. 994. [177] Ibid., II, p. 1060. [178] Balādhurī, *Futūḥ*, p. 186.

[179] According to Iṣfahānī (*Maqātil al-ṭālibiyyin*, Najaf, 1964, p. 344), under al-Manṣūr, Ibrāhīm ibn ʿAbdallāh's revolt in the Ḥijāz was suppressed by sending troops from Khurasan to Arabia via the *Barīd* (*ʿalā mā yaḥmiluhu al-barīd*). Ṭabarī (*Taʾrīkh*, III, p. 292) offers a similar report, although in his account contingents from the Syrian army were to be sent daily on *Barīd* mounts in groups of ten.

[180] Ṭabarī, *Taʾrīkh*, III, pp. 1086–7. [181] Ibid., III, pp. 1260, 1293, and 1296.

[182] See above, pp. 63–4.

Barīd served two functions in campaigns, one as a means for gathering and transmitting news from the front line, the other as a method of despatching mounts and people to the battlefield.

There are also cases in which the *Barīd* was put to use in unexpected contexts, a good example of which comes from al-Ma'mūn's caliphate. This caliph's famous attempt to impose the doctrine of the created Qur'ān, the *miḥna*, was executed with the help of the *Barīd*, both in investigating the provincial judges in order to verify that they upheld this doctrine, and in sending out orders regarding the *miḥna* to his regional agents. In one instance, the caliph wrote to Isḥāq ibn Ibrāhīm in al-Raqqa, ordering him that judges interrogate people regarding the createdness of the Qur'ān, and that Isḥāq should 'find out people's affairs and write back to the caliph'.[183] That the caliph should correspond with distant officials on matters of policy was not extraordinary: when, for instance, al-Ma'mūn designated 'Alī al-Riḍā as his heir, letters to this effect were sent out to the outlying provinces,[184] just as previous caliphs had sent letters to all corners of their realms to secure the *bay'a* from distant subjects.[185] But in another account of al-Ma'mūn's implementation of the *miḥna*, the caliph declared that he is sending orders concerning the *miḥna* via 'an express mail-bag' (*kharīṭa bundāriyya*), rather than waiting to send these letters via the [slower] 'regular mail-bag' (*kutub kharā'iṭiyya*). The caliph then demanded that letters with reports on the state of the *miḥna* in the various regions of the caliphate be sent to him via the same 'express mail-bag, sent separately from the rest of the mail-bags'.[186] The implication is that there were two levels at which the *Barīd* could function, and in the *miḥna*'s case the faster of the two was to be employed. These are the earliest references to the term *bundār*,[187] and it is likely that both the term and the postal technique to which it corresponds were imported by al-Ma'mūn from Khurasan, where he had served as governor from 809 to 813. Similarly, in effecting the *miḥna*, al-Ma'mūn repeatedly ordered that suspected dissenters be spied upon,[188] and in one passage there is reference to a special *ṣāḥib al-khabar* by the name of Sulaymān ibn Ya'qūb charged with reporting on Bishr ibn al-Walīd's beliefs.[189] What the relationship between the *miḥna* and the *Barīd* demonstrates is that the *Barīd* was a caliphal tool to be used by rulers in whatever capacities deemed worthy of the hassle and

[183] Ṭabarī, *Ta'rīkh*, III, p. 1116.

[184] Ibid., III, p. 1012. The letters also stipulated that the troops replace their black uniforms (traditionally associated with the Abbasids) with green ones.

[185] E.g., Jahshiyārī, *Wuzarā'*, p. 34, where 'Abd al-Malik 'wrote to the countries' to receive the *bay'a* for his sons; Ṭabarī, *Ta'rīkh*, II, p. 1752, where, upon his accession to the caliphal throne, 'al-Walīd [II] appointed agents, and letters offering him the oath of allegiance reached him from far-flung areas'; and ibid., II, pp. 1755–6, where al-Walīd II had letters circulated widely proclaiming that the *bay'a* to his two sons had been taken.

[186] Ṭabarī, *Ta'rīkh*, III, p. 1137. [187] On this term, see above, p. 64.

[188] Ṭabarī, *Ta'rīkh*, III, pp. 1121, 1125, and 1130–1. [189] Ibid., III, p. 1132.

expense. It is for this reason that poets and peaches could be sent via the *Barīd* in addition to the expected prisoners and post-bags.

Conclusions: the origins and early development of the *Barīd*

Having surveyed the official methods of communication employed in ancient Iran, Byzantium, pre-Umayyad Arabia, and the early caliphal period, we are in a position to identify the pivotal stages of development through which the *Barīd* passed during this period and to assess the relative contributions of pre-Islamic postal systems to the early *Barīd*.

From pre-Umayyad Arabia to the Sufyanid period

At least a century before the establishment of Umayyad rule in Damascus, Arabians became familiar with the postal systems of their Byzantine and Sasanid neighbours. The imperial presence in Arabia meant that a number of postal terms enriched the Arabic language in the pre-Umayyad period, and during their campaigns of expansion the early Muslim forces made use of a simple network of mounted couriers that was inspired by the methods of communication that had been used in Arabia for centuries, as well as the imperial postal systems with which Arabians were familiar. Upon settling in conquered territories outside the Arabian Peninsula, the Muslims adapted the local postal infrastructures to their needs. Documents from the seventh century indicate that in Egypt and Syria the local postal arrangements were remarkably similar to the *Cursus Publicus*, while later literary sources suggest that in the eastern provinces of the caliphate Sasanid traditions persisted. But there is also evidence that methods of communication that were used in pre-Umayyad Arabia were incorporated into the *Barīd* during this period, some of which (e.g. the *risāla mughalghala*) were dropped in subsequent decades, while others (e.g. the practice of sending two couriers with a single message) endured for centuries thereafter.[190]

The Marwanid period

During this period, a calculated programme of Arabisation and expansion of the caliphal administration was carried out, one ramification of which was the attention paid to the road network that linked the caliph's provinces. Difficult passes were levelled, milestones (bearing little resemblance to Roman ones) were placed along the routes, and regional postal chiefs – *aṣḥāb al-barīd* – were

[190] On the fact that in the Middle Abbasid period 'at each station two mules [were] saddled and stationed on the road', see Silverstein, 'New Source', 131–2. As late as the reign of the Indian Sultan Shīr Shāh (r. 1472–1545), two horses and two riders are said to have been posted at each postal relay (in Sabahuddin, 'Postal System', 275). See also n. 4 above for further examples.

appointed to write reports to the central authorities and administer the facilities of the *Barīd*, although control of the system remained in the hands of provincial governors. An anecdote preserved in a relatively late source shows the *Barīd* during Hishām's reign to be following an unshakable routine: in an attempt to trick Hishām, the Khazar *khāqān* blackmailed a Mesopotamian Arab into travelling to the caliph in the guise of al-Jarrāḥ ibn ʿAbdallāh's messenger in order to deliver a falsely positive report to the caliph on the situation in the East and to receive information from the caliph on conditions in Syria. The *khāqān* managed to transport the mock-envoy on mounts of the caliphal *Barīd*, but Hishām sussed out the ruse from the fact that the envoy did not bear a written letter from al-Jarrāḥ and from the lack of any confirmation of the envoy's mission from postal chiefs along the road.[191] If nothing else, this anecdote indicates the high level of administrative uniformity that is said to have characterised the *Barīd* by this point.

Hishām's reign represents a turning-point in the *Barīd*'s development for two reasons. First, although the available evidence suggests that in the early eighth century postal stations continued to be funded by the local population, Hishām is the first caliph who is said to have invested a considerable amount (four million dirhams) of the Treasury's funds towards the *Barīd*'s facilities. This is a significant departure from the funding model set by the Byzantines and Sasanids, who relied on requisitions, corvées, and special taxes to maintain their postal systems. As such, the early Marwanid *Barīd* can be said to have been a Late Antique institution from which the post-Hishām *Barīd* distinguished itself.

Second, it is from Hishām's reign that 'eastern' bureaucratic practices were incorporated into the administration of regions that had not been part of the Sasanid Empire. Hishām's interest in Iranian traditions of statecraft has been argued in general terms by scholars,[192] and the case of the *Barīd* lends considerable support for the argument. Hishām is said to have taken an unprecedented measure of interest in the affairs of his provincial officials,[193] for which the caliph had 'eyes and ears of the highest [moral] standing' planted everywhere.[194] Hishām is also the first caliph on record as having used physically modified mounts (in this case, *ḍāmira* mounts) for the purpose of speedy communication, and it is from his reign onwards that proto-viziers such as the *kuttāb* Sālim ibn ʿAbd al-Raḥmān, ʿAbd al-Ḥamīd, and Ibn al-Muqaffaʿ achieved prominence at the court. Interestingly, the letters (*rasāʾil*) attributed to ʿAbd al-Ḥamīd and Ibn al-Muqaffaʿ repeatedly stress

[191] Ibn Manẓūr, *Mukhtaṣar taʾrīkh dimashq li ibn ʿasākir*, Damascus, 1985, vol. IX, p. 340.

[192] H. A. R. Gibb, *Studies on the Civilisation of Islam*, London, 1962, p. 63.

[193] Cf. Ṭabarī, *Taʾrīkh*, II, p. 1733, where it is said that 'Nobody amongst the Marwanids was more avaricious in dealing with his associates and *dīwān*s than Hishām, nor did any of the Marwanids investigate the activities of his officials with such extreme thoroughness as did Hishām.'

[194] '*ʿuyūn wa jawāsīs min khiyār al-nās*', in pseudo-Ibn Qutayba, *Imāma wa siyāsa*, vol. II, p. 206.

the importance of planting spies and agents throughout the caliphal realms.[195] Crucially, it is from the last decade of Umayyad rule that the Iranian term *furāniq* surfaces in administrative documents from Egypt, demonstrating that even before the Abbasids moved to Iraq, Sasanid postal terminology was introduced uniformly throughout the caliphate.

Linguistic evidence, however, can only attest to theoretical rather than actual continuity. That Iranian terminology persisted into the Islamic period may indicate that in a bureaucrat's mind an institution that is referred to by a Middle Persian term is the equivalent of the pre-Islamic one that went by the same name. But we cannot be certain that the caliphal version of this institution took the same shape as its Iranian namesake. Thus, the existence of a *furāniq* in Umayyad Egypt indicates that administrators there associated this functionary with Iranian practices, and yet it is impossible to determine whether or not the Egyptian *furāniq*s performed the same functions and in the same ways as Sasanid *parwānag*s did in the pre-Islamic East. And although Hishām was served by '*uyūn wa jawāsīs*', we cannot be certain that their activities resembled those of the 'eyes and ears' of Sasanid or Achaemenid times.

Another example – one that is, moreover, related to road networks – illustrates the problem. In late Medieval Iran, a functionary called the *rāhdār* ('owner of the roads') served to ensure that routes were patrolled, well-organised, and free from highway robbers.[196] The term *rāhdār* was also used in pre-Islamic Iran, where it referred to brigands and highway robbers who 'owned' the roads in their own way.[197] As such, the terms are concurrently homonyms and antonyms. Linguistic continuity can therefore yield only tentative conclusions that, in the best of cases, attest to the deliberate association of one institution with another but not to the existence of identical institutions. Be that as it may, even 'theoretical' continuity of this sort confirms that towards the end of the Umayyad period, uniform postal terminology – if not the practices to which it refers – was disseminated throughout the Near East, and Hishām's openness to Iranian ideas may be directly implicated in this regard.

The collapse of the Umayyad *Barīd*

The closing years of the Umayyad period were characterised by unrestrained factionalism amongst the ruling elite and surreptitious planning on the part of the regime's enemies. Although the Abbasids' ousting of the Umayyads has

[195] 'Abd al-Ḥamīd, *Rasā'il al-bulaghā'*, p. 192; Ibn al-Muqaffa', *Risāla fī al-ṣaḥāba*, (ed./trans. Ch. Pellat), Paris, 1976, p. 37, §29.

[196] See W. Floor and J. Emerson, 'Rahdars and their Tolls in Safavid and Afsharid Iran', *JESHO* 30 (1987), 318–27; and Chardin, *Journey to Persia*, pp. 39 and 95.

[197] MacKenzie, *Pahlavi Dictionary*, p. 70. It is a little-known fact that in Babylonian Aramaic from the Sasanid period (as reflected in the Talmud), the term for 'brigands' or 'robbers' was *gyys'*, a cognate of Arabic *jaysh* (in Jastrow, *Sefer millīm*, pp. 237ff.), suggesting perhaps that the early activities of the Muslim *juyūsh* were considered to be little more than the ravagings of unruly brigands.

been treated extensively by modern scholars in a number of sophisticated studies,[198] to Muslim authors writing not long after the events, what happened was really quite simple: the Umayyads neglected their postal and intelligence apparatus, and the Abbasids exploited this situation by overthrowing the Umayyad dynasty. The author of the *Siyāsat al-Mulūk* concludes his chapter on the *Barīd* with the following statement: 'It used to be said: "No kingdom has ever lost its power except with the cessation of [the flow of] intelligence." It has reached me that the Umayyads lost power with the cessation of intelligence.'[199] The same verdict, which is attributed to 'some veterans of the Umayyad period', is quoted by Masʿūdī. In this passage 'the concealment of intelligence from [the Umayyads]' was the leading cause of their demise.[200] Similar accounts are preserved by Ṭabarī and Jāḥiẓ, the latter of whom elaborates on this issue in his treatment of the *Barīd*.[201]

The problem with this account of the collapse of the Umayyad state is that papyri from Egypt that straddle the late Umayyad and early Abbasid periods indicate that not only was the *Barīd* functioning at the very end of the Umayyad period, but there appears to have been no change to administrative practices with the advent of the Abbasids.[202] Literary sources also make reference to the late Umayyad *Barīd*, but it is telling that they almost always depict an institution that is functioning imperfectly: rebels are repeatedly seen to disrupt the *Barīd* routes and stations, messengers are kidnapped, and in some episodes conspirators against the caliph are seen to use the *Barīd* for their own purposes.[203] Furthermore, even when the *Barīd* managed to transmit intelligence reports successfully, the caliph al-Walīd II is said to have dismissed their validity on more than one occasion.[204] What the final years of the Umayyad reign exemplify is a distinction between the existence of the *Barīd* (on some level) and the successful transmission and analysis of intelligence reports.

The early Abbasid *Barīd*

Under the early Abbasids, the *Barīd* was used for the purposes of internal surveillance to an unprecedented extent. Al-Manṣūr, in particular, made

[198] E.g. M. Sharon, *Black Banners from the East*, Jerusalem, 1983; M. Shaban, *The Abbasid Revolution*, Cambridge, 1970; H. Kennedy, *The Early Abbasid Caliphate*, Cambridge, 1981; Lassner, *Abbasid Rule*; S. S. Agha, *The Revolution which Toppled the Umayyads*, Leiden, 2003; and others.

[199] Silverstein, 'New Source', 131–4. [200] Masʿūdī, *Murūj*, vol. IV, p. 65, §2266.

[201] Jāḥiẓ, *Bighāl*, p. 55 (§78); Ṭabarī, *Taʾrīkh*, III, p. 414 (quoted above, p. 67). Although this assessment of the Umayyads' demise would appear to be simplistic, if not naïve, it is important to note that these authors agree that the Umayyad *Barīd* was in fact neglected.

[202] This point is argued in Raghib, 'Poste d'Ašmūn', 6. On the general issue of administrative continuity from late Umayyad to early Abbasid times, see: A. Elad, 'Aspects of the Transition from the Umayyad to the Abbasid Caliphate', *JSAI* 19 (1995), 89–132; and I. Bligh-Abramski, 'Evolution versus Revolution: Umayyad Elements in the 'Abbasid Regime 133/750–320/932', *Der Islam* 65 (1988), 226–43.

[203] E.g. Ṭabarī, *Taʾrīkh*, II, pp. 1851 and 1854. [204] Ibid., II, pp. 1795 and 1803.

what was deemed by some to be excessive use of the *Barīd* in spying on his subjects,[205] and ʿUmarī's statement that 'no saddle was strapped and no mount was bridled for the *Barīd*' until al-Mahdī's reign is manifestly untenable. In fact, it is from this period that some of the most interesting episodes in which the *Barīd* played an important role date. The *Barīd* during the early Abbasid period was characterised by a certain degree of malleability for two related reasons. First, the autocratic nature of caliphal rule meant that individual caliphs were able to tamper with and shape the *Barīd*'s infrastructure in a way that came to be impossible with the emergence of a robust and largely independent bureaucracy in the late ninth century. Second, the fact that most early Abbasid caliphs came to power either after having served as provincial governors or after staging a successful coup meant that the caliphs often brought their 'gubernatorial baggage' with them, a fact that has implications for the development of the central bureaucracy. As one scholar put it, 'The highly personal ties that bound each caliph to the army and governmental bureaucracy could not always be transferred to his successor with the same intensity.'[206] Accordingly, the central administration was significantly affected by the arrival of a new caliph and his personal entourage in the capital.

This lack of administrative continuity explains why the *Barīd*s of Hārūn al-Rashīd, al-Maʾmūn, and al-Muʿtaṣim were so distinctive. Hārūn's reliance on the Barmakids led to the temporary co-ordination of the *Barīd*'s activities throughout the caliphate under Yaḥyā ibn Jaʿfar. The sharp decline of the *Barīd* in the aftermath of the Barmakids' fall from grace indicates how pivotal they were to its operations. The *Barīd* played a prominent role in the civil war between al-Amīn and al-Maʾmūn, and the fact that the latter retained control over the postal system in Khurasan (as stipulated in Hārūn's document of succession)[207] enraged al-Amīn, who resolved to send his own postal agent to the region.[208] When al-Amīn attempted to secure the *bayʿa* to his son Mūsā, al-Maʾmūn shrewdly cut off the *Barīd* between Khurasan and the capital,[209] depriving his brother of news from this indispensable region and openly signalling his disobedience. Upon becoming caliph, al-Maʾmūn took an active interest in the *Barīd*'s affairs, using the system extensively to enforce the *miḥna* and introducing what appears to be the Iranian concept of *kharāʾiṭ bundāriyya*. Aspects of Iranian influence on the *Barīd* are also in evidence for al-Muʿtaṣim's caliphate, where other specimens of pre-Islamic terminology and methods of communication make a sudden appearance. Terms such as *dayādiba* (sing. *dīdabān*) and *kūhbān*, and postal techniques such as the use of runners, physically modified mounts (either dock-tailed or *muḍammara*), and

[205] Cf. ʿAsqalānī, *Rafʿ al-iṣr min quḍā miṣr*, Cairo, 1988, p. 255, where numerous references to al-Manṣūr's obsession with *Barīd* reports are provided.
[206] Lassner, *Abbasid Rule*, p. 245. [207] Ṭabarī, *Taʾrīkh*, III, p. 655. [208] Ibid., III, p. 780.
[209] Ibid., III, pp. 777 and 796.

relays of messengers (rather than relays of mounts for the same messenger) all demonstrate the continuation of pre-Islamic Iranian contributions to the *Barīd* even two centuries after the fall of the Sasanids. The malleability of the imperial routes and the use of horses in al-Muʿtaṣim's *Barīd* – perhaps due to the equestrian traditions of the *mamlūks* – also attest to the fluidity of the system throughout this period.

With the reign of al-Wāthiq, and the composition of Ibn Khurradādhbih's *Kitāb al-masālik wa al-mamālik*, the *Barīd* and its infrastructure achieved a measure of permanence. And it is shortly after al-Wāthiq's reign that the activities and administration of the *Barīd* were co-ordinated and placed under the direction of a special *dīwān*, which allowed the system to operate smoothly even in the absence of an autocratic caliph's input. It is to the *Dīwān al-Barīd* that we now turn.

CHAPTER 3

Dīwān al-Barīd: the Middle Abbasid period

Introduction

It would appear that al-Mutawakkil (r. 847–61) created the *Dīwān al-Barīd*, as he is the first caliph for whose reign both a *Dīwān al-Barīd* and a *Ṣāḥib Dīwān al-Barīd* are repeatedly mentioned in the Arabic sources.[1] There is no direct evidence for the motivations behind the creation of such a *dīwān* in this period: the fact that al-Mutawakkil's concern for public security and justice was fabled amongst later writers,[2] as was his willingness to expend large sums on the needs of the administration,[3] are interesting but fall short of explaining why previous caliphs with similar reputations did not have a *dīwān* for the postal system. Be this as it may, it is probable that al-Mutawakkil himself was behind this initiative. Our sources describe him as a caliph who took an interest in the practical details of his realms. The same cannot be said for his predecessor, al-Wāthiq, who was sufficiently curious about the fantastical peoples of Gog and Magog and the legendary Seven Sleepers to send official delegations to locate the former and describe the latter,[4] but was otherwise willing to perpetuate the policies and functionaries he inherited from al-Muʿtaṣim, and to defer to the wishes of such figures as the former *mamlūk* Ītākh and the *qāḍī* Aḥmad ibn Abī Duʾād. Al-Mutawakkil, on the other hand, dismissed both of these overbearing functionaries and wrote letters to the provinces instructing local officials to purge the administration of Christians and Jews, reflecting an active interest in the bureaucratic machinery of the empire.[5]

[1] Yaʿqūbī (*Kitāb al-buldān*, Leiden, 1861, p. 43) and Ibn al-Faqīh (*Buldān*, p. 267) mention a *Dīwān al-Barīd* for al-Mutawakkil's reign, while Masʿūdī (*Murūj*, vol. V, pp. 141–2, §3259) refers to Maymūn ibn Ibrāhīm as al-Mutawakkil's *Ṣāḥib Dīwān al-Barīd*. Other references, which will be examined below, make it clear that a *Dīwān al-Barīd* existed in subsequent caliphs' reigns.

[2] Masʿūdī, *Murūj*, vol. V, p. 6, §2874, and vol. V, p. 39, §2960.

[3] Contrast al-Muʿtaḍid's well-known stinginess (ibid., vol. V, pp. 137–8, §3243).

[4] These episodes, which represent a caliphal equivalent of the modern 'space programme', are described in Ibn Khurradādhbih, *Masālik*, pp. 162–70 (Gog and Magog), and pp. 106–7 (Seven Sleepers).

[5] Ṭabarī, *Taʾrīkh*, III, p. 1390.

Why was the *Barīd* centralised during this period? It has been suggested that the spread of paper in Islamic lands from the late eighth century 'contributed to the growth of the Abbasid . . . postal system',[6] presumably because paper was cheaper than papyrus, parchment, and other writing materials, and the volume of written letters would have increased for this reason. However, while the introduction of paper made writing and literacy more accessible to those for whom the cost of papyrus and parchment texts would have been prohibitive, this does not apply to the central bureaucracy. The papyri from the first two centuries of Islamic rule in Egypt show that caliphs and their administrators had plentiful writing materials and could afford to make multiple copies of official documents. If a ruler in the pre-paper age felt the need to send an urgent message to a provincial governor, it is unlikely that he would have hesitated on account of the cost of writing materials. But the spread of paper did have a tangible effect on the consumption of books amongst the general population, resulting in a remarkable surge of writing on subjects that would have been deemed non-essential to previous generations of scholars and rulers. For our purposes, the result of this phenomenon is that there are a number of detailed sources that discuss the *Barīd* during the ninth and tenth centuries, written by jurists, historians, poets, and travellers, in addition to the strictly administrative (and religious) literature that probably would have been written regardless of the costs involved. Whereas Ibn Khurradādhbih composed a geographical treatise on imperial routes for a caliph, drawing on the caliph's resources – both monetary and archival – al-Muqaddasī wrote a geography book for himself, for jurists, or for no one in particular.[7]

Many sources from this period provide us with details of the *Barīd*'s functions that were not available to us for previous periods. Furthermore, as some authors discuss the *Barīd* directly it is not necessary to draw a tentative and piecemeal picture of the institution on the basis of passing references in chronicles to the *Barīd* in action. And even those passing references in the same chronicles take on an added significance, for in many cases the author is a (near-) contemporary of the events described and less susceptible to anachronistic or teleological interpolations. From these sources a fairly clear picture of the routes and stations, administration, and functionaries of the *Dīwān al-Barīd* emerges.

[6] P. Lunde and C. Stone, *Masudi: The Meadows of Gold – the Abbasids*, London and New York, 1989, p. 14; and cf. J. Bloom, *Paper before Print*, New Haven, 2001, p. 48f.

[7] In quoting Ibn Khurradādhbih's account of the rampart built by Alexander the Great, Muqaddasī explains that the former has superior information on this issue since 'he was the *wazīr* of the caliph and had the resources of the caliph's library available to him' (*Aḥsan al-taqāsīm*, p. 362).

Routes and stations[8]

There are three facts about the imperial road network of the Abbasid caliphate that underpin any discussion of the *Barīd* and its routes. The first fact is that no matter how wealthy or powerful he might be, a pre-modern ruler was at nature's mercy. Topography and geography were not impressed by sceptres or signet rings, and it was up to a ruler to adjust his activities to the local terrain. Mountains, deserts, and rivers were the most obvious and daunting obstacles to travellers, and although measures could be taken to build bridges, level roads, or dig wells, man-made solutions were often fragile and imperfect.

The second fact is that this fragility of the postal infrastructure was easily exposed by those who were intent on restricting a ruler's reach. As in the Umayyad period, rebels would often sabotage the postal network in order to prevent news of their actions from reaching the authorities. During the Zanj revolt, for instance, the caliph al-Muʿtamid's (r. 870–92) brother al-Muwaffaq is repeatedly described as having to repair the roads and highways in order to mount an effective defence against the rebels.[9] References to bedouin 'cutting roads' – especially pilgrimage routes – are ubiquitous in the sources, even for periods of relative peace and internal stability. In some instances it seems that the bedouin are regularly poised to attack travellers, only requiring the slightest provocation to encourage them to unleash havoc on the routes.[10]

Of course, it is considerably easier to disrupt a road network than it is to maintain one: when ʿAlī ibn Muḥammad, the leader of the Zanj rebels and a skilled disrupter of caliphal networks, wanted to gather intelligence and communicate with his deputies, he was forced to settle for unsophisticated and amateurish techniques of espionage and correspondence. In one instance, he is said to have entrusted a batch of letters to a peasant and had him swear that he would deliver the correspondence to his supporters. In another episode, ʿAlī sent a scout (*ṭalīʿa*) to gather intelligence and – in order not to arouse suspicion – he selected an elderly man for the task. The man never returned.[11] These bumbling arrangements demonstrate the importance of an efficient system of communication but also show that rebels who were not

[8] The imperial routes described in Arabic geographical works from the ninth to twelfth centuries have been analysed and mapped by Sprenger (*Post- und Reiserouten*), G. Le Strange (*The Lands of the Eastern Caliphate*, Cambridge, 1905), N. Saʿdawi (*Niẓām al-barīd*, pp. 110–15), and G. Cornu, (*Atlas du monde arabo-islamique à l'époque classique: IXe–Xe siècles: répertoire des toponymes des cartes*, Leiden, 1983–5).

[9] Ṭabarī, *Taʾrīkh*, III, pp. 1973, 1976, 1986, 2021–2, etc. Conversely, depriving the rebels of their channels of communication and supply was a tactic used with great success by the caliph's supporters (ibid., III, pp. 2001 and 2017–18).

[10] For the reign of al-Muhtadī (r. 869–70), Masʿūdī (*Murūj*, vol. V, p. 94, §3118) tells us that when the revolt of the Kharijite Musāwir grew serious 'the lines of communication were cut and the Bedouin appeared'.

[11] Ṭabarī, *Taʾrīkh*, III, pp. 1762 (on a peasant serving as a courier), and 1769 (on an aged man as a scout).

possessed of such a system themselves were nevertheless able to cause considerable disruption to the caliphal *Barīd*.[12]

The third fact about the caliphal road network is that it also benefited travellers who were not entitled to use the postal system itself. The construction and maintenance of roads, caravanserais, and security along the routes were some of the responsibilities expected of just rulers in the Near East from ancient times through to the Islamic period.[13] For obvious reasons, rulers could derive prestige and legitimacy from publicly improving pilgrimage facilities on the roads to Mecca, but it was also deemed important to attend to the other routes of the empire, thereby allowing merchants, ṣūfīs, scholars, and others to travel freely. It is no coincidence that the height of the *Barīd*'s organisation in the ninth century coincided with a flourishing period of international trade and travel in the Islamic world. The traffic of merchants became regular and heavy enough to sustain a private, 'commercial' postal system in these regions, a point to which we shall return below. Other travellers, chief among whom were pilgrims and scholars, benefited from the infrastructure of the road network but also from the detailed descriptions of itineraries compiled originally for the benefit of the *Barīd*'s couriers. Ibn Khurradādhbih's geographical work – despite having been dismissed by Masʿūdī as being 'of no use . . . other than for couriers and bearers of mail-bags and letters'[14] – was used extensively by later travellers and geographers who often confess to having brought a copy of the work on their travels. The science of geographical writing in Arabic is thus indebted to the postal itineraries collected in the *Dīwān al-Barīd*, although later writers who were not functionaries in the administration would subsequently take the genre in other directions.[15] It is particularly telling that Qudāma ibn Jaʿfar's detailed description of the imperial routes of the caliphate is provided in his treatment of the *Dīwān al-Barīd* rather than in his geographical treatise.[16]

The *Barīd* routes, as described by the Arabic geographers, were measured in miles (*mīl*, pl. *amyāl*), parasangs (*farsakh*, pl. *farāsikh*, usually explained as equalling 3 *amyāl*), stages (*marḥala*, pl. *marāḥil*) or *barīd*s (pl. *burud*), this latter measure being the distance between two postal stations (*sikka*, pl. *sikak*). There is rarely any consistency in an author's use of these terms. Although *mīl* is a Latin word and *farsakh* an Iranian one, it is not the case that the former measurement is used for western regions and the latter for

[12] It is possible that these anecdotes are simply meant to poke fun at the Zanj leader, rather than depict accurately his methods of communication.
[13] Cf. P. Crone, *Medieval Islamic Political Thought*, Edinburgh, 2004, pp. 305–6.
[14] Masʿūdī, *Murūj*, vol. I, p. 241, §503. [15] Cf. S. Maqbul-Ahmad, *EI2*, s.v. 'Djughrāfiya'.
[16] P. L. Heck, *The Construction of Knowledge in Islamic Civilization: Qudāma ibn Jaʿfar and his Kitāb al-kharāj wa ṣināʿat al-kitāba*, Leiden, 2002, pp. 121–2.

eastern ones.[17] Often, in fact, both terms will be used indiscriminately in connection with different legs of a single itinerary. Furthermore, although a *marḥala* is meant to denote the distance covered by a caravan in one day, this is clearly not a precise measurement: caravans could cover widely varying distances based on the climate (bad weather hampered progress and speed) and season (longer days in summertime allowed travellers to cover more ground than in winter). On the *Ḥajj* route from Iraq, the *marāḥil* were calculated as equalling 4 *farsakh*s, or 24 kilometres, this being the *barīd* distance in the region,[18] though in most other cases the *marḥala* represented a distance of 35 kilometres or so.[19] The *barīd* distance itself was determined by the intervals at which stations were found.

As a general rule, stations were separated by 2 parasangs in Syria and Khurasan, and by 4 parasangs in the desert (*al-bādiya*) and in Iraq.[20] It is likely that these were only theoretical guidelines and that, as is often the case, topographical realities dictated the precise location of the stations. We know, for instance, that the routes of the Mamluk *Barīd* – for which we have both detailed, contemporary descriptions and archaeological evidence – were provided with stations at irregular intervals due to the existence (or lack) of water, amongst other considerations.[21] Not all caliphal roads were provided with postal stations, however.[22] This is apparent in the works of both Qudāma and Ibn Khurradādhbih. The former concludes his description of the imperial highways by saying: 'As we have mentioned the routes to the East, to the West, to the South, and to the North, it is fitting to mention the *sikak* where men have been stationed for the conveyance of mail-bags (*kharā'iṭ*), and which have come to symbolise the *Barīd*.'[23] Interestingly, the *sikak* mentioned are seen to cover only a small proportion of the routes that the author had previously described. Similarly, throughout his work Ibn Khurradādhbih frequently appends a list of the *sikak* of a particular region to

[17] *Contra* A. Mez, *The Renaissance of Islam*, (trans. S. Khuda-Bukhsh and D. S. Margoliouth), New York, 1975, p. 496. Although Mez seems surprised that the Roman *mille [passus]* was used 'even in places where the Romans never ruled', it is clear that Jews in Sasanid Iraq were familiar with the term, in addition to the expected 'parasang', rendered *parse'a* in Hebrew (for the term *mīl*, pl. *mīlīn*, in Rabbinic literature cf. Jastrow, *Sefer millīm*, p. 733b, s.v. 'mīl').

[18] Pseudo-Ibn Qutayba, *Imāma wa siyāsa*, vol. II, p. 308.

[19] Cf. *EI2*, s.v. 'Marḥala', vol. VI, pp. 639–40.

[20] Muqaddasī, *Aḥsan al-taqāsīm*, p. 66, and repeated by Yāqūt (in Jwaideh, *Introductory Chapter*, p. 53). As there are also deserts in both Syria and Khurasan, modern scholars have preferred to distinguish between 'eastern' lands (2-parasang intervals) and 'western' lands (4-parasang intervals), this being a distinction that tallies well with the information provided in Arabic geographical treatises.

[21] 'Umarī, *Ta'rīf*, pp. 184–5.

[22] This point has gone unnoticed by Sprenger (*Post- und Reiserouten*) and Darādkeh ('*al-Barīd wa ṭuruq al-muwāṣalāt fī bilād al-shām fī al-'aṣr al-'abbāsī*', in M. A. al-Bakhit, *Bilād al-Shām during the Abbasid Period, Proceedings of the Fifth International Conference – Arabic Section*, Amman, 1991, pp. 191–207), who assume that the roads detailed by the Arabic geographers are all postal routes.

[23] Qudāma, *Kharāj*, p. 124.

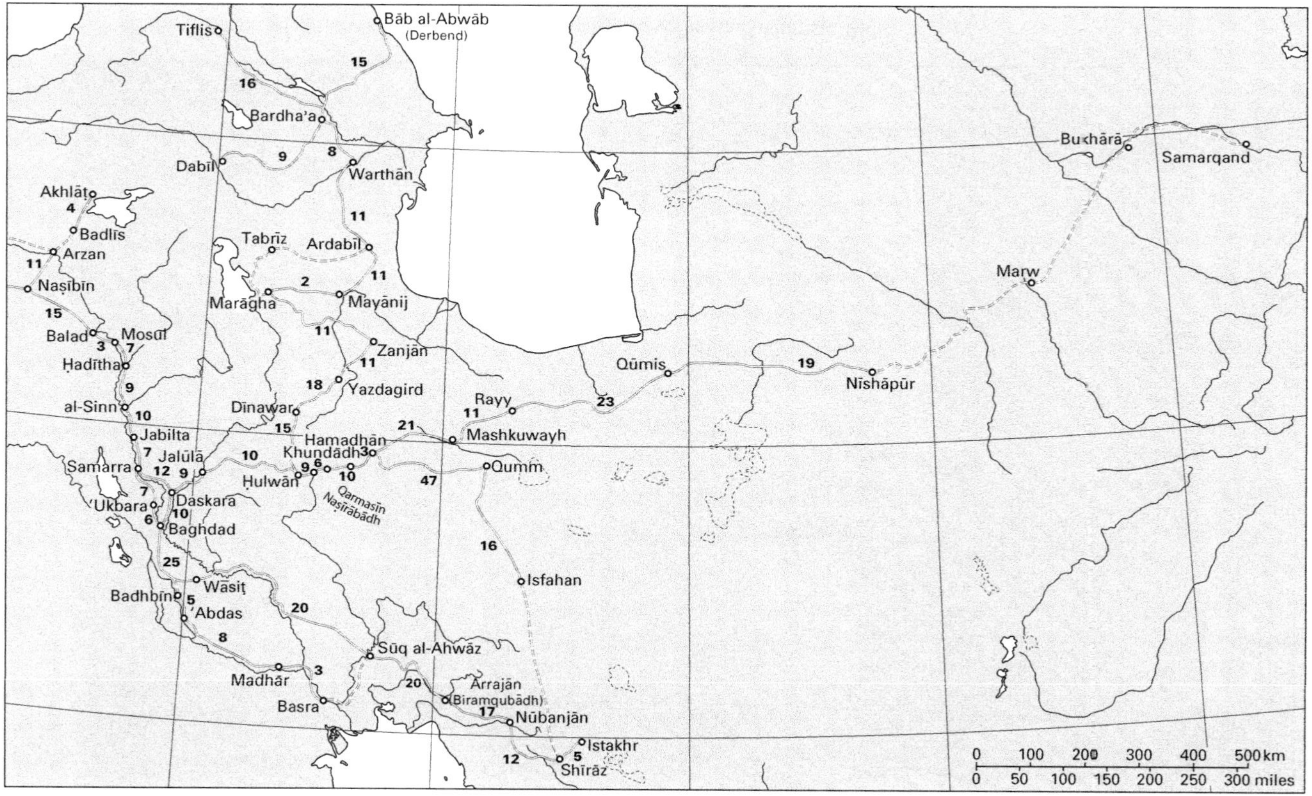

Map 2a. Routes of the Abbasid *Barīd*: the East

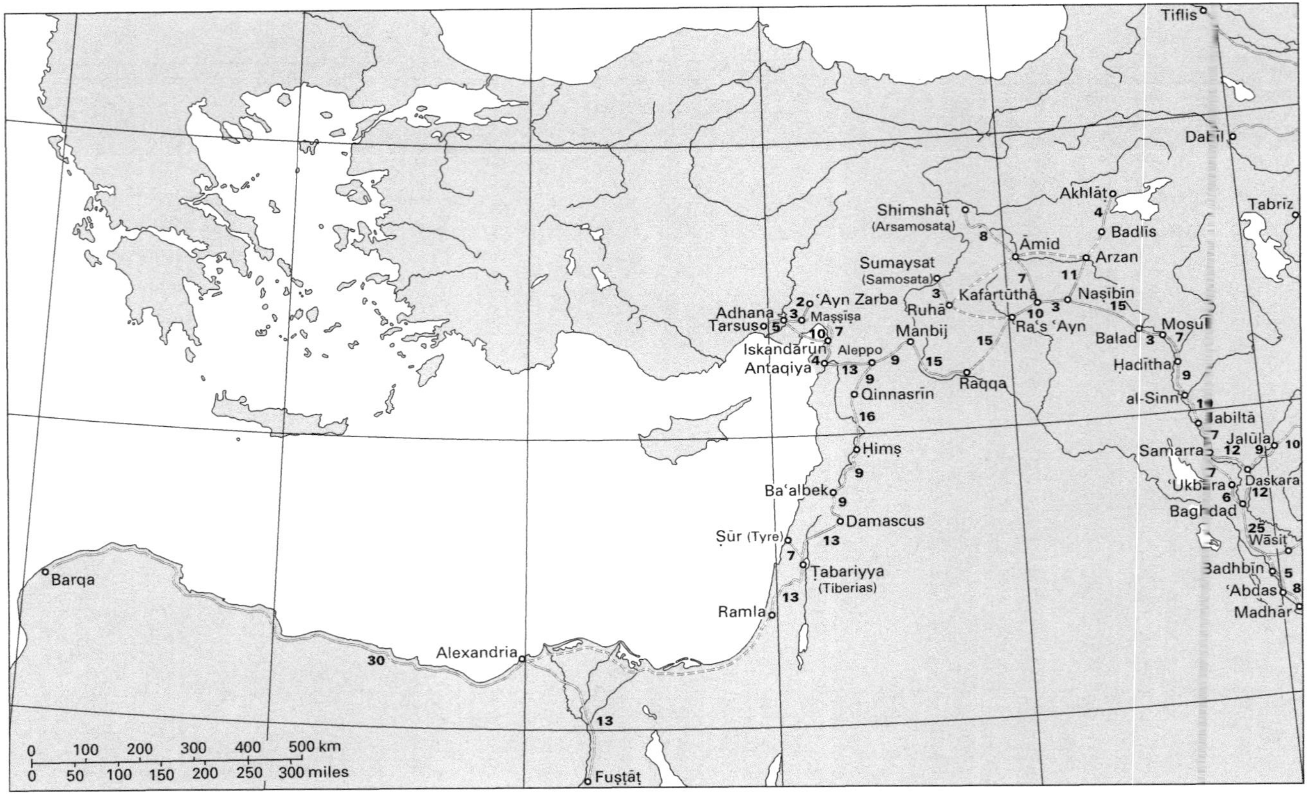

Map 2b. Routes of the Abbasid *Barīd*: the West

his more detailed and general treatment of the routes and distances between local towns.[24] Sometimes, of course, the ordinary and postal routes entirely overlap, in which case the author mentions that this is so.[25]

The postal stations appear to have been relatively simple constructions, which may explain why no clearly identifiable example of an Abbasid *sikka* has survived.[26] In describing the responsibilities of provincial postal chiefs (*aṣḥāb al-barīd*) the author of the mid tenth-century work *Siyāsat al-Mulūk*[27] mentions that they

> must ensure that every postal station is provided with the required number of mounts ... [and] that at each station two mules are saddled and stationed on the road, so that when the courier-guide (*furāniq*) calls out to him, the mount will be mounted and bridled – if it is eating and had not already been bridled, since this is more merciful to the mule[28] – and will meet him on the road so that [the courier] can take the mail-bag from him [and proceed to the next station]. The estimated distance that a mail-bag borne by a courier-guide can cover [in a day] is 60 parasangs, as this is the most the postal mounts can ride [in a day] ... The mules must not be stationed farther apart than 2 parasangs or nearer together than 2 parasangs, and the same applies to the station-masters.[29]

From this account we may conclude that, at least in the eastern provinces of the caliphate (ruled by the Buyid *amīr*s for whom the author composed this work), relays of mounted couriers could pass through up to 30 *sikak* a day, covering a distance of some 360 kilometres. It is worth mentioning that although the postal itineraries provided in Arabic geographical works are almost always confined to the lands of Islam, the postal systems of neighbouring states were, on occasion, also available to Muslims travelling in official capacities. Tamīm ibn Baḥr's journey through Central Asia *ca.* 821

[24] Hence, Ibn Khurradādhbih, *Masālik*, p. 41, where, having described the various routes of the East (*al-mashriq*), the author enumerates the *sikak* of the region, implying that not all routes are equipped with postal provisions.

[25] E.g. ibid., p. 98: 'The route from Ḥimṣ to Damascus via Ba'albek, which is the *Barīd* route. From Ḥimṣ to Jusiyya [is a distance of] four stations, then to Ba'albek [a distance of] six stations, then to Damascus [a distance of] nine stations.'

[26] See R. Hillenbrand, *Islamic Architecture: Form, Function, and Meaning*, Edinburgh, 1994, p. 334, for the fact that pre-Mongol postal stations in the Near East are 'irretrievably lost' to modern scholarship.

[27] On this source, see J. Sadan and A. Silverstein, 'Ornate Manuals or Practical Adab? Some Reflections on a Unique Work by an Anonymous Author of the 10th Century CE', *al-Qanṭara* 25ii (2004), 339–54. An edition and annotated translation of the sections of this manuscript that concern the *Barīd* may be found in Silverstein, 'New Source'. Although the source was composed in the early Buyid period, the author is summarising late ninth- and early tenth-century Abbasid practices for the Buyid *amīr*s, rather than describing the Buyid administration.

[28] Cf. Balādhurī, *Futūḥ*, p. 201, where a place is named 'Dhāt al-Lujūm', since the mules and horses there had been grazing without their bridles when the Muslims were attacked and could not be bridled in time.

[29] Silverstein, 'New Source', 131/132.

to the Khāqān of the Toghuzghuz was achieved by riding the Turkic '*Barīd*'. According to Ibn al-Faqīh's version of the travel-account,

> [Tamīm] journeyed ... via the *Barīd* on which the Khāqān sent him ... he was travelling through three stations (*sikak*) in a day and a night, travelling as hard and as fast as he could. He journeyed twenty days in steppes (*barārī*) where there were springs and grass but no villages or towns. Only the station-masters (*aṣḥāb al-sikak*) living in tents (*khiyām*).[30]

The *sikak* of the Turkic '*Barīd*' can hardly have been spaced at 2-parasang intervals if Tamīm was only able to cover three stations in a day and a night 'travelling as hard and as fast as he could'. If using the Turkic '*Barīd*' reduced a fifteen-day journey to three days, it is likely that these *sikak* were not relay-stations in the sense of Byzantine *mutationes* but rather caravanserais comparable with the Byzantine *mansiones*, which provided lodgings and provisions for travellers at the end of a day's journey. Indeed, as we have seen, Herodotus describes the number of Achaemenid postal stations on a route as being equal to the number of days in a rider's journey. Hence, Tamīm may be claiming to have been riding three times as fast as the 'ordinary' postal couriers would. This short passage also indicates that the stations on this route were 'tents'[31] and that Muslims had direct experience of foreign postal systems.

It is not only in Central Asia that Muslims during this period were exposed to the workings of extra-caliphal *Barīd*s: accounts of varying degrees of credibility refer to Muslim travellers and prisoners being transported in China and Byzantium via the local postal systems. For China we have Sulaymān the merchant's account, as preserved in *Silsilat al-Tawārīkh*.[32] As Sulaymān's travelogue is full of *mirabilia* it does not inspire confidence, though the fuller and more trustworthy sources from the Mongol period suggest that it would not have been exceptional for foreign delegates to use the Chinese *Yi*.[33] Evidence for Muslims being transported through Byzantine lands via the *Cursus Publicus* is more reliable. In 878, 'Abdallāh ibn Rashīd, the governor of the *thughūr* regions, was captured by the Byzantines and

[30] The account is provided with extensive commentary in V. Minorsky, 'Tamīm ibn Baḥr's Journey to the Uyghurs', *BSOAS* 12ii (1948), 275–305 at 278–9 (Arabic)/283 (trans.). Although he does not mention Tamīm by name, Ibn Khurradādhbih (*Masālik*, pp. 28–9) bases his description of the route through Central Asia to China on this account, including the fact that from K.bāl to Upper Nushajān (corrected by Minorsky as Barskhān), which is on the doorstep of China, it takes fifteen days by caravan (*li al-qawāfil*) but only three days using the Turkic '*Barīd*'.

[31] Compare *Psalms* 27: 5: 'For in the day of evil He shall hide me in His shelter (*sukkoh*), in the convent of his tent (*ohalo*) he shall hide me', demonstrating direct parallelism between *s.k.k.* and 'tent'.

[32] E. Renaudot, *Ancient Accounts of India and China*, Delhi, 1995 (reprint from London, 1733), pp. 77–8.

[33] See below, pp. 149–51.

taken to the Emperor (*al-ṭāghiya*) by post,[34] and Hārūn ibn Yaḥyā is also said to have had direct experience of the *Cursus Publicus* as a prisoner of the Byzantines in the second half of the ninth century.[35] Finally, from a number of accounts it is clear that the caliphal *Barīd* was routinely used in prisoner exchanges with the Byzantines,[36] although there may be a number of reasons for this: Muslims returning from Byzantine lands would probably have been interrogated by the authorities regarding the situation in *dār al-ḥarb*; and Muslims recently released from captivity would not have had any other way of returning home.

Administration

The network of routes and stations that connected the provinces of the caliphate with the capital represented the skeleton of the *Barīd*, while the couriers, guides, station-masters, and mounts of the postal system gave flesh to this skeleton and combined to provide rulers with a complex system of communication. In some ways, one would expect the *Barīd* to have been part of the military establishment. After all, the Umayyad *Barīd* was often used in military contexts, and, as we shall see, the Mongol and Mamluk postal systems were essentially military institutions. Moreover, during the early Abbasid period, influential Turkish military commanders would occasionally control the system,[37] and maintenance of the imperial routes undoubtedly served the interests of the military. In his discussion of the *Dīwān al-Barīd*, Qudāma explains that the *ṣāḥib* of this bureau must have detailed knowledge of the various routes and stations of the caliphate so that, should the need arise, the caliph could efficiently despatch troops to a battlefield.[38] Despite all this, the *Barīd* during this period was unmistakably a civilian bureau in its conception and execution: the uses to which the *Barīd* was put are overwhelmingly administrative in nature, and the day-to-day functioning of the system was entrusted to 'men of the pen'.

The situation of the *Barīd* within its wider bureaucratic context is known to us owing to the exceptionally detailed description of the Middle Abbasid bureaucracy provided by the tenth-century *Siyāsat al-Mulūk*. The anonymous author of this work most probably served in the *dīwān al-Kharāj*, but

[34] Ṭabarī, *Ta'rīkh*, III, p. 1917. As seen in the previous chapter (p. 57), even within caliphal lands prisoners were often transported to the authorities via the *Barīd*.

[35] Ibn al-Faqīh, *Buldān*, pp. 119–30, at p. 119. And cf. A. Vasiliev, 'Harun ibn Yahya and his Description of Constantinople', *Seminarium Kondakaovinium* 5 (1932), 149–63.

[36] E.g., Ṭabarī, *Ta'rīkh*, III, pp. 1352–3, where al-Wāthiq despatches Aḥmad ibn Sa'īd, the recently appointed governor of the *thughūr* and *'awāṣim* regions, to carry out a prisoner exchange with the Byzantines using seventeen postal couriers.

[37] Such Turks as Ītākh (under al-Mutawakkil) and Mūsā ibn Bughā (under al-Mu'tazz) are known to have served as *Ṣāḥib Dīwān al-Barīd*, amongst others (cf. D. Sourdel, *Le Vizirat Abbaside de 749 à 936*, Paris, 1959, pp. 273, 295–6, 734, and 736).

[38] Qudāma, *Kharāj*, pp. 77–8.

appears to be very well-informed regarding the entire administrative structure of the caliphate on a practical and detailed level.[39] In addition to his description of the workings of the *Barīd*, the author explains that the King, the *Wazīr*, the *Ṣāḥib Dīwān al-Kharāj*, the *Ṣāḥib al-Ma'ūna* and the *Ṣāḥib al Shurṭa* are all required to maintain independent information networks, served by trustworthy agents who would report to them regularly. The King is instructed to 'plant spies (*'uyūn*) overtly and covertly, amongst the general population and the elite, so that [news of] whatever happens publicly will reach him, and that [news of] whatever happens privately will not be hidden from him'.[40] The *Wazīr* is given similar advice, albeit in greater detail. He is told to 'intimidate his close associates and trustworthy agents by planting spies to watch over them, in both their private affairs and their public ones, so that they will be intensely cautious [in their behaviour] and so that their administrative decisions will be disinterested', for which purpose a special *ṣāḥib khabar* must be appointed. Furthermore, the roads must be safeguarded through the establishment of watch-posts (*arṣād*), and those working in this capacity must also be subjected to surveillance.[41] The impression one gets is that of spies infiltrating every nook and cranny of the realm with, rather absurdly, more spies charged with reporting on the spies themselves. In this vein, Tanūkhī preserves an account from the court of al-Mu'taḍid, where the caliph and his *wazīr* al-Qāsim ibn 'Ubaydallāh engage in a subtle espionage-tussle against one another. The caliph's informants report that the *wazīr* was neglecting his work in favour of wine and slave-girls, and the caliph rebuked him. Rattled by the realisation that the caliph is spying on him, al-Qāsim despatched his own spies to uncover the source of the caliph's information, illustrating a web of intrigue and espionage reminiscent of the one described in the *Siyāsat al-Mulūk*.[42]

Interesting though all this may be, the operations of intelligence agents within the capital are not, strictly speaking, dependent upon the infrastructure of the *Barīd*. More relevant is the information pertaining to the *Ṣāḥib Dīwān al-Kharāj* and the *Ṣāḥib al-Ma'ūna* provided in the *Siyāsat al-Mulūk*. The bureau of taxation had branches dispersed throughout the provinces of the caliphate. Thus, provincial centres had their own, local chiefs of taxation answerable to the central taxation authorities in the capital, and communication between the branches of the bureau and the capital had to be maintained. In this regard, we are told that

> The *Ṣāḥib Dīwān al-Kharāj* must order his deputy to examine the incoming and outgoing letters – and to endorse the latter with his signature – for there is information of relevance to him in these. [Doing so] will lessen the burden on [the *Ṣāḥib Dīwān al-Kharāj*] in that he will only have to read that which is absolutely necessary . . . As for

[39] On this source, see above, n. 27. [40] Silverstein, 'New Source', 125. [41] Ibid., 125–6.

[42] The episode is translated in B. Lewis, *Islam: From the Prophet Muhammad to the Capture of Constantinople*, Oxford, 1987, vol. I, pp. 34–9.

the outgoing letters, he [the deputy] must be present when they are sealed, and when the incoming letters are opened.[43]

Furthermore, the provincial tax officials are required to send reports of their affairs and of the affairs of the regions within their jurisdiction, including information on the state of local cultivation, changes in climate, prices, imported and exported luxury goods, and anything else related to the province's finances. Interestingly, the local postal chiefs (*aṣḥāb al-burud*) are then required to compose independent reports on the local prices, changes in climate, and the safety of the region from dangers, so as to provide an alternative source of information to that of the local tax officials.[44] This indicates that the bureaus of the *Barīd* and the *Kharāj* would overlap to a certain extent, and serve as mutual checks on the reliability of reports from the provinces. As if this was not enough, elsewhere in the text the *Wazīr* is implored to 'match the *Ṣāḥib al-Barīd* in [obtaining] information about the state of the *kharāj* and its causes'.[45]

Responsibility for the provincial postal infrastructure was in the hands of the local *aṣḥāb al-burud*, of course, but since the costs of supplying the postal stations were covered by the caliphal authorities, balancing the *Barīd*'s accounts in each province often fell to the local *'āmil al-kharāj*. As the author of the *Siyāsat al-Mulūk* was an experienced accountant, his information on the funding of the system is particularly detailed and authoritative. He writes:

[The *'āmil al-kharāj*] must draw up three accounts for the financial aspects of the *Barīd*: for that which is spent on the mules of the *Barīd* – for their needs and their treatment – and for the maintenance of the postal stations, and [for the expenses incurred] in exchanging that which has become weak and for the amount of their prices, and for selling off those that have become worthless and for the amount of their prices, and the cost of equipment needed, and the appointment and funding of the courier-guides. He must undertake this promptly and maintain this [system]. He must consult with the [local] *ṣāḥib al-barīd* if the responsibilities were entrusted to him, or at least consult him regarding that which is entrusted to him. And he must closely monitor the progress (in these affairs) in order to know the truth about these things, and write a report about the situation, keeping one draft with him with which he can work, and sending two copies to the *dīwān*s at the court.[46]

While this arrangement applied to most caliphal regions, on the northern frontiers of the Islamic world responsibility for the upkeep of the *Barīd* network was delegated to the *Ṣāḥib al-Ma'ūna*. This high-ranking military official must 'supervise the *thughūr* [frontier regions] near his jurisdiction and must undertake guarding the borders. He must write to the sultan with news of [this region] at all times and he must take care of the mounts of the *Barīd* and that which is done with them. [For] if the situation happened to deteriorate, the resulting corruption would revisit him.'[47]

[43] Silverstein, 'New Source', 127–8. [44] Ibid., 127. [45] Ibid., 128. [46] Ibid., 129. [47] Ibid.

The picture that emerges from this unique source indicates the impressive extent to which – at least in theory – the central authorities were to be kept updated regarding developments in the distant provinces of their rule. Both the *dīwān al-Kharāj* and its functionaries and the *Ṣāḥib al-Maʿūna* would despatch regular reports on the state of financial and military affairs in their respective regions, with the latter providing the financial and material resources that would maintain the postal infrastructure in the *thughūr*, and the former overseeing the funding of the *Barīd* in other provinces. But although other functionaries partook in the administration of the *Barīd* network throughout the caliphate, the figures central to the maintenance of the postal system were the *Ṣāḥib Dīwān al-Barīd* in the capital and his provincial agents, the *aṣḥāb al-barīd* (or *al-burud*). Information concerning the operations of these officials is relatively full, and the detailed treatment of this subject provided by the author of the *Siyāsat al-Mulūk* is complemented by numerous references to the postal chiefs during this period that are scattered in the literary sources.

Functionaries

Both Qudāma and the *Siyāsat al-Mulūk* deal with the *dīwān al-Barīd* and those functionaries that served in it, but whereas Qudāma's information focuses on the central administration of the *dīwān* in Baghdad, the author of the *Siyāsat al-Mulūk* restricts his coverage of the *dīwān* to some general observations on the composition of *Barīd* reports and chooses to elaborate, instead, on the provincial administrators of the system. The eleventh chapter of Qudāma's encyclopaedia is entitled 'On the bureau (*dīwān*) of the *Barīd*, and the stations (*sikak*), and routes (*ṭuruq*) to the eastern and western regions'. As mentioned, it is in this chapter that he provides detailed itineraries of the imperial routes of the caliphate, rather than in his chapter on geography, where such information might otherwise have been expected. Qudāma prefaces his description of the routes with a short explanation of the *Barīd*'s responsibilities.[48] He writes:

> Abū al-Faraj [Qudāma] said: The *Barīd* requires its own *dīwān*, and the letters despatched from all the regions are to be directed to [the *dīwān*'s] *ṣāḥib*, so that he [can] then despatch each item from among them to its proper destination. He is charged with presenting the letters of the postal and intelligence chiefs (*aṣḥāb al-barīd wa al-akhbār*) in all provinces to the caliph, or with the task of summarising them [for the caliph]. It is his [duty] to supervise the affairs of the courier-guides (*furāniqiyyīn*), the endorsers [of the mail-bags] (*muwaqqiʿīn*), and the station-masters (*murattabīn*) in the stations, and to [ensure] the payment of their salaries, and to appoint mail-bag carriers (*aṣḥāb al-kharāʾiṭ*) in all cities.

[48] On this passage, see Heck, *Construction of Knowledge*, pp. 87–8.

Qudāma then goes on to explain that the attributes demanded of the *Ṣāḥib Dīwān al-Barīd* are those of loyalty and dependability, as well as a thorough knowledge of the routes and stations of the realms, as mentioned.[49]

This passage brings two points to our attention. First, in opening this passage with the remark that the *Barīd* 'requires its own *dīwān*' (a statement that he does not make with reference to other bureaus), the author may be implying that this point is not a given. Although contemporary sources indicate that a *Dīwan al-Barīd* with its own *ṣāḥib* was in existence already from al-Mutawakkil's reign, that is to say, over half a century before Qudāma was writing, it is possible that in some periods a special bureau for the *Barīd* was deemed unnecessary. Under al-Mustaʿīn (r. 866–9), for example, we are told that Sīmā al-Shārābānī (or 'al-Sharābī') was put in charge of '*barīd al-āfāq*',[50] a phrase that echoes the label applied to Yaḥyā ibn Jaʿfar the Barmakid (under Hārūn) in pre-*dīwān* times.[51]

Second, the responsibilities of the *Ṣāḥib Dīwān al-Barīd* are described in clear terms. He is expected to gather incoming reports from the provinces and present their content (in full or in summary) to the caliph. He is also ultimately responsible for the employment of the various officials serving in the *Barīd*, from station-masters, to courier-guides, to the couriers themselves. The precise function of the 'endorsers of the mail-bags' would probably escape us, were it not for the survival of a station's log-book from Ptolemaic Egypt, in which the traffic of passing couriers was recorded,[52] and from a reference to the practice of endorsing mail-bags in the *Siyāsat al-Mulūk*, where it is the local postal chief (rather than a separate *muwaqqiʿ*) who must 'endorse every pouch (*jirāb*) and mail-bag (*kharīṭa*) that comes his way, with the time at which it reached him and the time at which it was sent off'.[53]

In his discussion of the *Barīd*, the author of the *Siyāsat al-Mulūk* provides us with further details concerning the functions and responsibilities of local postal chiefs. He writes:

> The [local] chiefs of the *Barīd* (*aṣḥāb al-burud*) must obtain information both covertly and overtly. They must be truthful in this and act quickly regarding the gradation in the urgency of reports. [They must] supervise the postal stations, the courier-guides, the express couriers (*banādira*), the fodder for the postal mounts and their equipment, and they must examine [the mounts'] appearance so as to know the fit from the weak, including the scribes, thereby perpetuating the efficiency of the system and its

[49] Qudāma, *Kharāj*, pp. 77–8.

[50] Ṭabarī, *Ta'rīkh*, III, p. 1550. Later (ibid., III, p. 1552), al-Mustaʿīn addresses letters that are intended for the provinces to Sīmā al-Shārābī, who is requested to despatch them. Thus, he is clearly filling the role of a *Ṣāḥib Dīwān al-Barīd*, despite the absence of this title.

[51] Jahshiyārī, *Wuzarā'*, p. 204.

[52] In N. N. Austin, *The Hellenistic World from Alexander to the Roman Conquest: A Selection of Ancient Sources in Translation*, Cambridge, 1981, document §247.

[53] Silverstein, 'New Source', 131/133.

> integrity. They must appoint trustworthy agents to carry out its affairs and to ensure that those in charge of expenditure spend the [necessary] funds on the system. They must ensure that every postal station is provided with the required number of mounts and that no mount should be loaded, besides its rider, with more than forty *riṭls*, using the Baghdadi measurement[54] ... The bags with accounting documents and other things that can bear a slight delay must be sent out twice per week; other (more urgent) things are to be sent as quickly as they need to be ... The [local] chief of the *Barīd* must guard himself from untruthfulness for he is the 'eye' of the sultan [regarding] his officials and his subjects ...[55]

As with Qudāma's account, it is stressed that the postal officials must be trustworthy, and they must ensure that all associated officials are paid. The *Siyāsat al-Mulūk* adds details about the maximum weight to be carried by postal mounts, and the fact that ordinary letters are to be sent out twice a week, whereas urgent correspondence was to be expedited immediately. It is noteworthy that in both accounts it is taken for granted that the stations, mounts, couriers, guides, and officials were all to be funded by the authorities. There is no hint of the corvées or requisitioning of mounts and labour associated with the Byzantine, Sasanid, early Islamic, and Mongol periods.[56] Although it is always wise to consider that these descriptions reflect an ideal situation rather than a more realistic, imperfect system, the attention to detail in this as in other chapters of the *Siyāsat al-Mulūk* suggests that the author was intimately familiar with all aspects of the bureaucratic machine, and most probably availed of administrative archives and notebooks. Furthermore, we know that as early as the reign of Hishām, steps were taken to ensure that the *Barīd* was – at least in part – funded by the Treasury. Hilāl al-Ṣābi' even details the salaries paid to various employees of the *Barīd* during al-Mu'taḍid's reign, including, for instance, the fact that the grooms who look after the postal mounts earned 150 dinars a month or five dinars a day.[57]

Passing references to the activities of postal chiefs in literary sources from this period illustrate the variety of purposes for which this expensive system was put to use. The period between al-Mutawakkil's accession and the arrival of the Buyids in Baghdad covers roughly a century. If, as the *Siyāsat al-Mulūk* suggests, letters from the provinces would be sent twice a week, it follows that tens of thousands of reports will have been sent to the *Dīwān al-Barīd*. Although this figure seems excessive, Jahshiyārī's reference to the 'four thousand' unopened mail-bags discovered in the aftermath of Hārūn's death indicates that the volume of correspondence during a caliph's reign

[54] For the *riṭl* or '*raṭl*', see W. Hinz, *Islamische Masse und Gewichte: umgerechnet ins metrische System*, Leiden, 1970, pp. 27–33 at p. 31, where a Baghdadi *riṭl* is estimated at 406.25 grams and is much lighter than other local measurements of the *riṭl*.

[55] Silverstein, 'New Source', 131/132–3.

[56] On the administration of the Mongol postal system, see chapter 4 below.

[57] Hilāl al-Ṣābi', *Kitāb al-wuzarā'*, Beirut, 1904, p. 18.

could be very substantial. Indeed, we hear of provincial postal chiefs acting in response to and reporting on important as well as trivial matters, suggesting that correspondence flowed freely.

Important roles played by postal chiefs include informing the central authorities of unscrupulous officials,[58] uprisings in the provinces,[59] the deaths of important individuals,[60] the arrival of rebels in a city,[61] the activities of a rebel leader,[62] the spread of detrimental rumours in Baghdad,[63] and exceptional weather conditions in the regions,[64] amongst other issues.[65] We also see them function as official witnesses in politically sensitive circumstances. The death of Ītākh, for instance, was officially 'witnessed' by the local *ṣāḥib al-barīd*,[66] while the former caliph al-Mustaʿīn (having been deposed by al-Muʿtazz) was guarded by the trustworthy postal chief.[67] Similarly, when al-Mutawakkil sent a craftsman to repair damage in Mecca caused by severe weather conditions, the local *ṣāḥib al-barīd* was amongst those who accompanied the craftsman into the Kaʿba.[68] In the *Siyāsat al-Mulūk*, the local *ṣāḥib al-barīd* is occasionally called upon to serve as an arbiter in cases where conflicting claims are brought before the authorities: in the event that tax-payers dispute the amount owed, it is the postal chief who must examine their claims, together with other upstanding members of the community (*ṣulaḥāʾ al-balad*). Other

[58] Ṣābiʾ, *Wuzarāʾ*, p. 82, where the *ṣāḥib al-barīd* in Mosul writes to Ibn al-Furāt regarding the embezzlement of monies by Abū Aḥmad al-Ḥasan.

[59] Ibn al-Athīr, *al-Kāmil fī al-taʾrīkh*, Beirut, 1965, vol. VII, pp. 126–7, on the revolt of a Ṭālibid rebel in Kufa; and vol. VII, p. 77, (cf. Ṭabarī, *Taʾrīkh*, III, p. 1429), where the *ṣāḥib al-barīd* in Egypt writes to al-Mutawakkil regarding the campaigns of the Būja people of Upper Egypt against the Muslims.

[60] Ṭabarī, *Taʾrīkh*, III, pp. 1406–7, where the *ṣāḥib al-barīd* in Medina writes to al-Mutawakkil regarding the death of Muḥammad ibn Isḥāq ibn Ibrāhīm. And ibid., III, p. 1465, where the *Barīd* brings news of the deaths of al-Mutawakkil and al-Fatḥ ibn Khāqān. In Ṣābiʾ, *Wuzarāʾ*, p. 102, Sulaymān ibn Ḥasan falls from grace and is imprisoned; subsequently the *ṣāḥib al-barīd* in Baghdad informs Ibn al-Furāt that Sulaymān's mother has died without being able to see her son on her deathbed.

[61] Ṭabarī, *Taʾrīkh*, III, p. 1517, where the local *ṣāḥib al-barīd* writes to al-Mustaʿīn that Yaḥyā the Ṭālibid rebel has arrived in Fallūja with his supporters. And ibid., III, p. 2203, where the *ṣāḥib al-barīd* in al-Ahwāz reports that Ṣaffārid forces have marched towards the region, followed by another letter concerning the appointment of Ismāʿīl ibn Aḥmad as governor of Sijistan.

[62] Ibid., III, p. 1852, where the *ṣāḥib al-barīd* in Basra reports that the leader of the Zanj has performed a prayer session in front of nine supporters, without the knowledge of the other local authorities. In a similar incident, the *ṣāḥib al-barīd* of Hamadhan writes to al-Muhtadī informing him that Mūsā ibn Bughā had departed from the town (ibid., III, p. 1740).

[63] Ṣābiʾ, *Wuzarāʾ*, p. 83, where al-Nushajānī reports on these rumours to al-Muʿtaḍid.

[64] Azraqī, *Akhbār makka*, (ed. R. S. Malḥas), Madrid, n.d., pp. 299–302, where the *ṣāḥib al-barīd* in Mecca writes to al-Mutawakkil concerning the extreme weather conditions that have damaged the Kaʿba. The caliph sends a craftsman to repair the damage and provides him with letters for the provincial governors on the road, ordering them to extend courtesies to the bearer. In another instance (Ṭabarī, *Taʾrīkh*, III, pp. 2183–4), the *ṣāḥib al-barīd* in Kufa writes to the capital about a mysterious yellow wind gusting through the town.

[65] E.g., when ʿĪsā ibn Jaʿfar blasphemes, it is reported by the *ṣāḥib al-barīd* in Baghdad (Ṭabarī, *Taʾrīkh*, III, p. 1424).

[66] Ibid., III, p. 1386. [67] Ibid., III, p. 1670. [68] Azraqī, *Akhbār makka*, pp. 301–2.

reports of injustices that reach the provincial *dīwān* must be confirmed in the presence of both the *ṣāḥib al-maẓālim* and the *ṣāḥib al-barīd*. Following this, a report must be sent to the postal chiefs 'with a letter on the true state of affairs, explaining the situation, and these must send trustworthy agents to investigate [the matter]'. Finally, we are told that the financial records produced by the *Kharāj* accountants are to be confirmed independently by the *ṣāḥib al-barīd* and the *qāḍī*.[69]

Postal chiefs could also deal with matters that are of little obvious relevance to the security of the caliphal realms. In one instance, upon hearing of a particularly impressive Indian sword, al-Mutawakkil had his *Ṣāḥib Dīwān al-Barīd* write to his deputy in Basra with instructions to acquire the sword in question. The local *ʿāmil* managed to track it down in Yemen, whence it was transported to the caliph.[70] In another episode, the *ṣāḥib al-barīd* in Dīnawar composed a report – the full text of which is preserved by ʿArīb al-Qurṭubī – concerning the alleged fact that a mule gave birth to a colt (*filwa*) in Qarmīsīn.[71] There are also contexts in which the *Barīd* was used that do not conform to the usual practices of pre-modern postal systems, but which, nonetheless, are easier to explain as serving the interests of the caliphate than the foregoing accounts are. An example of this is the little-known practice of sending mail-bags (*kharāʾiṭ*, sing. *kharīṭa*) between the capital and the pilgrimage in Mecca. In ordinary circumstances, the *kharīṭa* would contain reports on the security and successful organisation of the festivities (*salāmat al-mawsim*).[72] In one case, however, al-Mutawakkil despatched a special yellow *kharīṭa* with details of the time when the new moon of the month of Dhū al-Ḥijja was sighted,[73] in order to settle the confusion in Mecca concerning the date of the Day of Sacrifice (*yawm al-naḥr*).[74] This is reminiscent of the rabbinic Jewish practice of lighting beacons or sending messengers from Jerusalem to the Diaspora (particularly Babylonia) announcing the sighting of the new moon.[75] In order to ensure that the festivals were observed on the correct dates, the mail-bag, thus, had to arrive in the capital without

69 Silverstein, 'New Source', 128. 70 Masʿūdī, *Murūj*, vol. V, p. 36, §2952.

71 ʿArīb, *Ṣilat taʾrīkh al-ṭabarī*, Leiden, 1897, p. 39. ʿArīb also informs us that the *ṣāḥib al-barīd* in Egypt wrote to the central authorities to extol the virtues of al-Qāsim ibn Sīmā al-Farghānī in fighting against the Shiʿites (ibid., p. 68). The letter was sent with '*kutub ahl miṣr wa ṣāḥib al-barīd*', a point to which we shall return below. According to al-Iṣbahānī (*Ḥilyat al-awliyāʾ wa ṭabaqat al-aṣfiyāʾ*, Cairo, 1932–8, vol. V, p. 101), as early as the reign of al-Manṣūr, a local *ṣāḥib al-barīd* is said to have reported a miraculous occurrence to the authorities (drawn to my attention by Christopher Melchert).

72 E.g., Ṭabarī, *Taʾrīkh*, III, p. 1640.

73 This coloured *kharīṭa* is deemed special on account of the fact that ordinary *kharāʾiṭ* used for official correspondence were 'of black silk, and the head of the *kharīṭa* is pulled by another tassel in a sealed [bag] woven of palm-leaves' (Ṣābiʾ, *Rusūm*, p. 127).

74 Ṭabarī, *Taʾrīkh*, III, p. 1470.

75 The two cases are not, however, exactly comparable. In the Islamic period the pilgrimage mail-bag was sent via official couriers, whereas the Jews of the Mishnaic and Talmudic periods transmitted the message through privately organised methods (cf. *Rosh ha-Shana*, 22b–23b).

delay, and both Hilāl al-Ṣābi' and the *Siyāsat al-Mulūk* record impressive speeds achieved by the *kharīṭat al-mawsim*.[76] As was the case with the Samaritans who endeavoured to sabotage the rabbinic signalling system, sectarians would occasionally disrupt the course of this special mail-bag: in 882, for instance, an Alid rebel was imprisoned for intercepting and seizing the *kharīṭat al-mawsim*.[77]

Given the repeated stress on the need for trustworthiness in Qudāma's and the *Siyāsat al-Mulūk*'s descriptions of the *ṣāḥib al-barīd*, this was presumably the basis on which he was chosen. In some instances we may deduce additional attributes of particular postal chiefs. Some were known for their scholarship: in addition to Ibn Khurradādhbih, who was famously *ṣāḥib al-barīd* in the province of al-Jibāl, the scholar Ya'qūbī,[78] the poet Abū Tammām,[79] and the Ghaznavid historian al-'Utbī[80] had all served as postal chiefs at one point in their career,[81] while a postal chief in Nīshāpūr is said to have had the largest collection of books in Khurasan.[82] Others were appointed for less virtuous reasons: al-Mu'taḍid's *wazīr* al-Qāsim ibn 'Ubaydallāh offered the poet Ibn Bassām the post of *ṣāḥib al-barīd* in Qinnasrīn and the Syrian *'awāṣim* in order to blunt his tongue,[83] while another poet was awarded the same position in Khurasan as a reward for his eloquence.[84]

It is likely that most administrative centres had a resident *ṣāḥib al-barīd*. The references above attest to postal chiefs in Mosul, Mecca, Medina, Kufa, Basra, Egypt, Fallūja, al-Ahwāz, Dīnawar, Khurasan, Qinnasrīn, the frontier regions, and Baghdad (when the capital was at Samarra). It is reasonable to assume that other towns and cities had a postal chief,[85] although it would seem that occasionally the postal jurisdiction of more than one region would be combined under the same chief: Ya'qūb ibn Ibrāhīm al-Bādghīsī, for instance, served as *ṣāḥib al-barīd* in Egypt, though his job description is said to have included responsibility over the system in Fusṭāṭ, Alexandria, Barqa,

76 Ṣābi', *Rusūm*, p. 17; and Silverstein, 'New Source', 131/133. In both sources the mail-bag took four days between Mecca and Iraq.

77 Ṭabarī, *Ta'rīkh*, III, p. 2025.

78 In A. Miquel, *La Géographie humaine du monde musulman*, Paris, 1973, vol. I, p. 102.

79 In H. Ritter, *EI2* s.v. 'Abū Tammām'. He was *ṣāḥib al-barīd* in Mosul under al-Mu'taṣim.

80 In C.E. Bosworth, *EI2* s.v. "Utbī'. He served as *ṣāḥib al-barīd* in Nīshāpūr under the Samanids, and in Ganj Rustaq under the Ghaznavids.

81 It is worth noting that Wang Yangming (1472–1529 CE), the most famous Chinese philosopher and the founder of Neo-Confucianism, served as the Lungchang postmaster in Kwichow province during the Ming Dynasty, indicating that intellectuals served as postal chiefs elsewhere in the pre-modern world.

82 Ibn Ḥawqal, *Masālik*, p. 320. 83 Mas'ūdī, *Murūj*, vol. V, p. 202, §3420.

84 Tha'ālibī, *Yatīmat al-dahr*, Cairo, 1934, vol. IV, p. 62.

85 Iṣfahānī (*Maqātil al-ṭālibiyyīn*, Najaf, 1964, p. 412), for instance, refers to the *ṣāḥib barīd iṣfahān*; Buḥturī (*dīwān*, pp. 1225–6, 1544–5 in Ullmann, *Geschichte*, p. 34 nos. 91–2) mentions Nahshal the *ṣāḥib al-barīd* in Raqqa; and Miskawayh (*Eclipse*, vol. I, p. 25/vol. IV, p. 28) mentions Khāqānī as being in charge of the affairs of the *Barīd* in Masabādhān under al-Mu'taḍid.

and the Maghreb.[86] Similarly, although in one instance we hear of a postal chief particular to the region of Diyār Muḍar,[87] in another case we are told that al-Mu'tamid's *mawlā* Fātik was responsible for the *Barīd* in Mosul, Diyār Rabī'a, Diyār Muḍar, and the *thughūr* of Syria (*al-shām*) and Mesopotamia (*al-jazīra*).[88] Perhaps less surprising is the fact that *Barīd* affairs in Mecca and Medina could also be combined under a single *ṣāḥib*.[89]

Regardless of their status, attributes, or activities, local *aṣḥāb al-barīd* were directly answerable to the *Ṣāḥib Dīwān al-Barīd*, the Postmaster-General of the caliphate. Although high-ranking Turks would occasionally hold this position, it was more often the case that the head of this *dīwān* was a favoured civilian. Under al-Mutawakkil, Maymūn ibn Ibrāhīm was the Postmaster-General, and it would appear that he was not a popular figure. Mas'ūdī relates a poignant anecdote in which a blind poet describes Maymūn as 'A robbing hand, a flatulent anus. He is like a Jew who has been robbed of half his fortune.'[90] The poet may have been hinting at the fact that one postmaster was well-known for public flatulence: Wahb ibn Sulaymān ibn Wahb is reported to have passed wind in the middle of 'Ubaydallāh ibn Yaḥyā ibn Khāqān's *majlis* (assembly). News of this spread to such an extent that the saying 'More [in]famous than Wahb's fart' (*ashhar min ḍarṭat wahb*) entered common parlance.[91] Postmasters were often associated with homosexual practices, too, although this may simply be a formulaic accusation.[92] A hint of *Schadenfreude* may be detected in these references to public flatulence and homosexuality. It is not just that postmasters were unpopular and, hence, a common target for ridicule; but it may also be the case that ordinary people resented the prying eyes of the *Barīd* officials and saw a sort of poetic justice in the spread of intimate details of a postmaster's life.

The tenure of a *Ṣāḥib Dīwān al-Barīd* varied greatly. Under al-Mu'tazz no fewer than three people served in this position, these being Sīmā al-Sharābī, Aḥmad ibn Isrā'īl, and Mūsā ibn Bughā the elder.[93] By contrast, Abū Marwān 'Abd al-Malik ibn Muḥammad ibn 'Abd al-Malik al-Zayyāt held the position of '*Ṣāḥib Dīwān al-Kharā'iṭ*, which is called *Dīwān al-Barīd*' for thirty years, serving in this capacity under both al-Mu'taḍid and al-Muqtadir.[94] He was succeeded in this position by Shafī' al-Lu'lu'ī, a eunuch

[86] Ṭabarī, *Ta'rīkh*, III, p. 1429. [87] Ya'qūbī, *Ta'rīkh*, Leiden, 1883, vol. II, p. 612.
[88] Ṭabarī, *Ta'rīkh*, III, p. 2184. In 906, this same Fātik despatched a mail-bag from Egypt to Baghdad with news of campaigns there, suggesting that his jurisdiction extended even to that region.
[89] Ibid., III, p. 2274. [90] Mas'ūdī, *Murūj*, vol. V, pp. 141–2, §3259.
[91] Tha'ālibī, *Thimār al-qulūb fī al-muḍāf wa al-mansūb*, (ed. M.A.F. Ibrahim), Cairo, 1985, pp. 206–7, and Ullmann, *Geschichte*, p. 20 (no. 24), and pp. 35–6 (no. 102). For another account of famous flatulence in this period, see 'The Historic Fart' in *Tales from the Thousand and One Nights*, (trans. N.J. Dawood), London, 1973, pp. 163–4.
[92] Cf. Ullmann, *Geschichte*, p. 66, where various references of this nature are collected.
[93] Ṭabarī, *Ta'rīkh*, III, pp. 1640 and 1660; and Sourdel, *Vizirat*, pp. 735–6.
[94] Ṣābi', *Wuzarā'*, p. 159.

who spent ten years in charge of 'the *Dīwān al-Barīd* in Baghdad, and supervision (*ishrāf*) of the *wazīr*, the army, the bureaux-chiefs (*aṣḥāb al-dawāwīn*), the judges, and the police chiefs (*aṣḥāb al-shuraṭ*)',[95] only to be succeeded upon his death by Shafīʿ al-Muqtadarī, another eunuch.[96]

The significance of the *dīwān*

The postal system that served the caliphs from the mid ninth century was dissimilar to previous and contemporary postal systems in two important ways. The first is the co-ordination of the *Barīd*'s activities in a special *dīwān*; the second is the financial administration of the *Barīd* during this period. Importantly, both of these characteristics would have a perceptible impact on later postal systems in the pre-modern Islamic world.

The Abbasids' postal bureau does not appear to have been inherited from Late Antiquity or inspired by neighbouring empires. Although in the late eighth century the Byzantines revamped their administrative structure and assigned a considerable amount of influence to the Logothete of the Drome who controlled the *Cursus Publicus*, he controlled much besides it and cannot realistically be seen to have influenced the creation of a *Dīwān al-Barīd*.[97] And although there was a Ministry of Posts in medieval China, its founding is most probably later than the creation of a *Dīwān al-Barīd* and, in any event, China is too geographically removed from the Near East to have been of any real influence. Thus, while geography, topography, and pre-Islamic institutions continued to inspire and shape the caliphal postal system, the *Barīd* developed into an institution that was nonetheless unique.

The way in which this *dīwān* was funded is also atypical of comparable institutions of the pre-modern Near East. Although, as it will be seen, medieval Muslim rulers (including the Mamluk sultans, the post-Ghāzān Mongols, and the Ottomans) also drew on the Treasury in funding their postal systems, this was an exceptional measure by most standards,[98] and it was viewed by later writers in the Muslim world as being a caliphal legacy. In praising the Ottoman vizier Luṭfī Pāshā's reform of the Ottoman *Ūlāq* postal system, Quṭb al-Dīn al-Nahrawālī sheds light on late medieval perceptions of the Abbasid *Barīd*. In his words:

> Amongst the positive aspects of [Luṭfī Pāshā's] vizierate was that he cancelled the [practice of] *ūlāq*,[99] for it had got out of hand in those days and caused widespread

[95] Miskawayh, *Eclipse*, vol. I, p. 24 (Arabic)/vol. IV, p. 27 (trans.). [96] Sourdel, *Vizirat*, p. 661.

[97] On the Logothete of the Drome, see Miller, 'Logothete of the Drome'. Ibn Khurradādhbih (*Masālik*, p. 112) refers to the 'Logothete' alongside the Byzantine 'postal chief', suggesting that – at least according to his sources – this functionary was not tantamount to the *Ṣāḥib Dīwān al-Barīd*.

[98] See above, p. 104.

[99] In this instance, '*ūlāq*' refers not to the postal system itself, but to the practice of arbitrarily requisitioning mounts from passers-by for couriers on official missions.

damage to travellers. The routes were full of [*Ūlāq* couriers] and a courier would accost a traveller, hurl him off his mount and ride it until it would break down, at which point he would discard it and take another rider's mount . . . and when Luṭfī Pāshā became vizier he reduced their numbers [lit. 'cancelled their abundance'] and specified that couriers should be despatched only for the most important affairs of the Sultanate . . . and people celebrated him [Luṭfī Pāshā] for discontinuing this injustice [of requisitions for the postal system]. The caliphs had established their own mounts in every town and village under their rule, called *khayl al-barīd*, and when an important matter arose they despatched whosoever they wanted on the postal mounts, and he would ride them until he reached another village, where he found other postal mounts, which he would ride having left the first [mounts] behind, and so forth until he reached Baghdad; and he would return from [Baghdad] with the relevant command. [The caliphs] had servants appointed for this, and mounts with fodder and other provisions arranged, may Allāh have mercy on [the caliphs] and on him who put an end to the injustice of the *Ūlāq*, and lifted it entirely from the Muslims, and appointed for these purposes postal mounts (*khayl al-barīd*), just as the caliphs – may Allāh have mercy on them – had done before him.[100]

Although Nahrawālī does not distinguish between 'caliphs' in praising their *Barīd*, he can hardly have been referring to the system in the first two centuries of Islam; his sources for the funding of the 'caliphal' *Barīd* are our sources, and they date, without exception, to the ninth and tenth centuries at the earliest. But, to their credit, the ninth- and tenth-century sources can speak of the *Barīd* in the ninth and tenth centuries with considerable authority, and the postal system that they describe is complex, effective, and impressive by any standard.

The efficiency of the route-system and the ambitious caliphal programme of funding the *Barīd*, however, can be said to have contributed to the political decline of the Abbasid caliphs. The existence of a well-defined, maintained, and provisioned system of routes facilitated the flow of couriers, other envoys, and military personnel and their mounts. But the opening of routes from the capital to the battlefield also meant that routes were open from the battlefield to the capital, and Baghdad was easily targeted by conquerors,[101] the most successful of whom were the Buyids and Seljuks. The expenses associated with a system of routes, stations, couriers, mounts, station-masters, and other provisions could only be met by a robust Treasury, the likes of which did not always exist in post-Mutawakkil Iraq. The expanding bureaucracy and the increasingly factionalised Turkish military were a financial liability, while internal challenges such as the Zanj rebellion in the most fertile regions of Iraq contributed to the problems. Although the late ninth and early tenth centuries were characterised by an impressive flow of international

[100] Quṭb al-Dīn al-Nahrawālī, *Kitāb al-iʿlām bi-aʿlām bayt allāh al-ḥaram*, Leipzig, 1857, pp. 299–300 (drawn to my attention by Khaled el-Rouayheb).

[101] For an application of this idea to the spread of languages in the Near East, see N. Ostler, *Empires of the Word: A Language History of the World*, London, 2005, p. 35.

trade and commercial traffic in the Near East, a spendthrift court, greedy commanders, and a costly bureaucracy coincided with a gradual decrease in tax revenues from the provinces. On occasion, *wazīr*s could lean on the *jahābidha* or wealthy merchants for quick access to cash with which to pay a twitchy army, but the central authorities could not sustain a costly *Barīd* dependably.

Other than having the distinction of being an unprecedented institution in Near Eastern history, the *Dīwān al-Barīd* did serve an important purpose: al-Mutawakkil gave something that had essentially been a tool of communications technology its own bureau, with all that it entailed: a physical existence in the capital, a high-ranking functionary to manage its affairs, a network of employees in the exclusive service of the bureau, and a budget with which to support the system. When the political cohesiveness of the caliphate gave way to a fragmented pastiche of independent dynasties, these dynasties modelled their own bureaucracies on the Abbasid *dīwān*s. Accordingly, at a time when the Abbasid caliphs were losing the ability to maintain a *Barīd* in any meaningful way, the independent rulers who emerged in the former caliphal lands tended to include in their administrative structures a *Dīwān al-Barīd*. Before discussing the postal organisation of the successor states, it is worth examining the fate of the *Barīd* in the Abbasid heartland in light of the decline of the central authorities.

The tenth to twelfth centuries: continuities and discontinuities

The financial troubles that plagued the caliphate in the late ninth century were accompanied by – and in no small measure related to – the emergence of obstinate rebels and rebellions such as the Zanj and the Qarāmiṭa. Both movements caused significant disruption to the imperial routes of the caliphate, particularly in Iraq (the Zanj), and Arabia and the Maghreb (the Qarāmiṭa). As a result, it would seem, the *Barīd* had to be adjusted. The resulting adjustments may be treated under the rubrics of: mounts, pigeons, and intelligence chiefs. It will also be shown that merchant postal networks emerged in the late tenth century and came to complement – or in some cases replace – the official systems of communication that were in decline.

Mounts

The sources discussed above make regular reference to the use of mules (*bighāl*) in the Abbasid *Barīd*. Although more general terms such as *khayl* and *dawābb* may suggest that horses were also used, and although in Arabia and North Africa it may be assumed that camels were the mount of choice, mules recur in descriptions of the *Barīd* in action more regularly than any other type of mount. Ḥamza al-Iṣfahānī explains that mules were suitable for these purposes as they combined the sure-footedness of donkeys with the speed of horses.[102] Whether or not this is factually true, it was enough to dictate *Barīd*-practices that people at the time believed it to be so.[103]

From the last years of the ninth century onwards, however, mules begin to feature less frequently than before in descriptions of the *Barīd*, and instead swift she-camels called *jammāzāt* are seen to replace all other types of riding animal in postal contexts. In 892–3, for instance, Rāfiʿ ibn Harthama fled to Khwarazm with a guide (*dalīl*) on *jammāzāt*;[104] during the reign of al-Muktafī (r. 902–8) official correspondence was sent with *jammāzāt*;[105] in 918–19 Ibn al-Furāt wrote to ʿAlī ibn Aḥmad in Syria ordering him to arrest Ḥusayn ibn Aḥmad and his nephew in Egypt and to send them to Baghdad on *jammāzāt* – for this purpose a eunuch (*khādim*) from the caliph's inner circle (*thiqāt*) was sent on *jammāzāt* on the overland route (*ṭarīq al-bariyya*) to Damascus.[106] Most importantly, perhaps, al-Muqtadir's *wazīr*, ʿAlī ibn ʿĪsā, is said to have established a network of *jammāzāt* between Egypt and Baghdad in 915–16 in order to ensure the transmission of daily reports on the campaigns against ʿUbaydallāh.[107] The use of *jammāzāt* for the purpose of swift communication continued under the Buyids and the Samanids.[108]

Sending letters, transporting people to the capital, and transmitting intelligence reports from the provinces are unmistakably *Barīd* contexts, and the sudden widespread use of *jammāzāt* in these contexts must be beyond coincidence. The sources do not explain why she-camels suddenly emerge as the most popular mount for speedy communications, although it is possible that financial considerations and disruptions to the imperial routes were behind this change. A major distinction between camels and other mounts is that the former can travel for longer distances on less food and water. Camels would therefore require fewer relays, and the relays themselves could possess scantier provisions. Support for this hypothesis comes from the *Siyāsat al-Mulūk*, which makes reference to the use of both mules and *jammāzāt* by courier-guides, although when the *Barīd* stations are described only mules are mentioned.[109] Thus, when mules were used in the *Barīd* they were regularly

102 Iṣfahānī, *Taʾrīkh*, p. 25. And see A.C. Leighton, 'The Mule as a Cultural Invention', *Technology and Culture* 8i (1967), 45–52.
103 Jāḥiẓ (*Bighāl*, pp. 55–72) is particularly adamant about the fact that the mule is the most suitable mount for couriers and dedicates a chapter of his work to the use of mules in the *Barīd*.
104 Ibn al-Athīr, *Kāmil*, vol. VII, p. 459.
105 Ṭabarī, *Taʾrīkh*, III, p. 2211 (correspondence between Fārs and Baghdad).
106 ʿArīb, *Ṣilat taʾrīkh al-ṭabarī*, p. 65. Later (ibid., p. 74), Ḥusayn ibn Aḥmad is again summoned to the caliph and transported on *jammāzāt*.
107 Ibid., p. 53.
108 Buyids: Ibn al-Athīr, *Kāmil*, vol. VIII, p. 653; and cf. Mez, *Renaissance*, p. 502, where in 975 the Buyid *wazīr* is said to have travelled hurriedly on *jammāzāt* from Baghdad to Shiraz. Samanids: L. Treadwell, 'Ibn Ẓāfir al-Azdī's Account of the Murder of Aḥmad ibn Ismāʿīl al-Sāmānī and the Succession of his Son Naṣr', in C. Hillenbrand (ed.), *Studies in Honour of C. E. Bosworth*, vol. II, Leiden 2000, pp. 397–419, at p. 400 (Arabic)/p. 409 (trans.), where *jammāzāt* are despatched to accompany the coffin of Aḥmad ibn Ismāʿīl on the road to Bukhara.
109 Silverstein, 'New Source', 131/132–3.

changed at the stations (to ensure the freshness of the mounts), whereas *jammāzāt* would not have had to be provided as regularly, on account of their superior endurance.[110] In other words, substituting camels for mules may have been a money-saving measure that would have allowed the *Barīd* to function even when – on account of marauding Qarāmiṭa, for example – the network of relay-stations was in disarray. Another possible explanation for the decrease in mules and horses is that the equestrian *mamlūk*s may have had an (indeterminable) impact on the availability of horses during this period. Horses tend to be expensive, and *mamlūks* in the late ninth/early tenth centuries tended to be protective of their resources, and a proportionate dearth in horses and mules could have been the result. Both explanations are mere conjecture, however.

Pigeons

The use of pigeon-couriers to transmit messages speedily across vast distances is far better understood. Ragheb's thorough study of the topic obviates the need to treat this subject here in any detail,[111] but it is worth demonstrating how homing pigeons solved some of the problems that affected the *Barīd* during this period.

On account of their unique ability to sense their way home even from hundreds of kilometres away, pigeons could be relied upon to return to a pigeon tower in their hometown bearing small notes attached to their legs. Although elaborate pigeon networks were often developed to enhance the efficiency of the system, on a basic level, using pigeon-couriers entailed little more than providing local pigeons to the person with whom communication was desired. This is considerably less complex and expensive than establishing relays of mounts and station-masters over thousands of kilometres of roads. Additionally, pigeons were considerably speedier than mounted couriers:[112] according to one source, during the reign of Hārūn al-Rashīd the pigeon-couriers that transmitted messages between Baghdad and Mecca could cover 30 *marāḥil* a day, whereas swift camels (*najā'ib*) could only cover 8 *marāḥil* in the same time-span. As the *marḥala* in this instance was estimated at 24 kilometres, it is clear that impressive speeds were achieved using this method.[113]

But for the central authorities during this period, the fact that pigeons were not reliant on the increasingly fragile overland routes was perhaps the most

110 As early as Hishām's reign, a man is reported to have covered the enormous distance of 80 parasangs in 24 hours by riding *jammāzāt* (see above, p. 66).
111 Y. Ragheb, *Les Messagers volants en terres d'Islam*, Paris, 2002. A shorter treatment of this subject may be found in Mez, *Renaissance*, pp. 503–4.
112 For a discussion of the relative speeds attainable by pigeons and mounted couriers respectively, see Ragheb, *Messagers*, pp. 181–6.
113 Pseudo-Ibn Qutayba, *Imāma wa siyāsa*, vol. II, p. 309.

important consideration. Pigeons could deliver an important message at a relatively low cost, irrespective of the state of the routes and stations. In fact, not only could the Qarāmiṭa do little to sabotage the traffic of pigeon-couriers, they are also known to have used homing pigeons themselves.[114] The comparative simplicity of the system made it affordable and accessible to rebels and private citizens alike,[115] and frequent use of homing pigeons is in evidence from the late ninth century onwards.[116] There can be little doubt that the sudden increase in the official use of pigeon-couriers was directly related to the decline in safety along the routes during this period, and to the fact that employing homing pigeons was cheaper than maintaining a network of mounted couriers.

Intelligence chiefs (*aṣḥāb al-akhbār*)

The relationship between the *Barīd* as an overland system of communication and the gathering of political intelligence is clear: as local postal chiefs were charged with transmitting news from afar, they naturally became involved in the collection of the news that was to be transmitted. However, when the traditional *Barīd* system was deteriorating in the early tenth century, and when pigeons (and, as we shall see, merchant networks) came to replace the *Barīd* as a communications system, it was no longer practical to restrict intelligence-gathering duties to the local *ṣāḥib al-barīd.* Although there is no defining moment at which the *Barīd* relinquished its intelligence responsibilities to 'intelligence chiefs' (*aṣḥāb* – sing. *ṣāḥib* – *al-akhbār*) or 'supervisors' (sing. *mushrif*) there is evidence that these functionaries were introduced already in the mid ninth century. We know, for instance, that in addition to a *Ṣāḥib Dīwān al-Barīd* called Maymūn ibn Ibrāhīm, al-Mutawakkil had an intelligence chief (*mutawallī al-akhbār*) by the name of Ibrāhīm ibn ʿAṭāʾ in Samarra who reported the death of al-Ḥasan ibn Sahl to the caliph.[117] Similarly, during the reign of al-Mustaʿīn, al-Muʿtazz (who was, at this point, siding with the Turks against the caliph) had both a *ṣāḥib al-khabar* and a chief of military intelligence (*ṣāḥib khabar al-ʿaskar*) in his service.[118] Al-Muʿtaḍid is said to have had *aṣḥāb al-akhbār* in all provinces, and Hilāl al-Ṣābiʾ has preserved an example of a short intelligence report despatched by one such intelligence chief.[119]

[114] Mez, *Renaissance*, pp. 503–4.
[115] On homing pigeons in the service of private individuals, see Ragheb, *Messagers*, pp. 169–74.
[116] For a concise chronological overview of the Abbasid pigeon network, see Ragheb, *Messagers*, pp. 4–7.
[117] Ṭabarī, *Taʾrīkh*, III, p. 1406. In the same source we are told that al-Fatḥ ibn Khāqān was put in charge of – amongst other things – the *akhbār* of the elite and the commoners in Samarra and in the Hārūnī Palace. It would appear that al-Fatḥ was Ibrāhīm's co-ordinator, on account of the former's rank.
[118] Ibid., III, pp. 1556–7. [119] Ṣābiʾ, *Rusūm*, p. 72.

The use of intelligence chiefs was widespread (and undoubtedly more significant) when the ruling authorities did not possess a *Barīd*. As we shall see below, neither the Seljuks nor the Fatimids availed themselves of a formal *Barīd* system, but both had intelligence chiefs: the Fatimid caliph al-Ḥākim, for instance, had a *ṣāḥib al-khabar* called ʿUqayl,[120] while the Geniza documents from over a century later show intelligence agents functioning in Fatimid Cairo.[121] In the late eleventh century, none other than the poet al-Ḥarīrī, the author of the *Maqāmāt*, was *ṣāḥib al-khabar* in Baṣra, a position that his descendants held well into the twelfth century,[122] indicating that as with the *ṣāḥib al-barīd* the intelligence chief could be a well-respected poet or litterateur. The Uqaylid *amīr* Sharaf al-Dawla (d. 1084–5), who, at the height of his power, ruled over lands from Aleppo to Mosul to Baghdad, is said to have had a *ṣāḥib khabar* in every town and village of his realms to ensure justice.[123] And the Abbasid caliph al-Nāṣir (r. 1180–1225), ruling long after the *Barīd* had disappeared from the central Islamic lands, is said to have had such a developed network of *aṣḥāb al-akhbār* in Iraq and in all other provinces that men were wary of what they told their wives out of fear that the caliph would find out what was said.[124] Just as Qudāma and the *Siyāsat al-Mulūk* described the qualities and responsibilities of the *Barīd* chiefs, in the mid tenth century other writers began to treat the *ṣāḥib al-khabar* in works dealing with the caliphal bureaucracy. In his chapter on intelligence chiefs, the *kātib* Ibn Wahb (writing after 946 CE) describes this functionary in terms distinctly reminiscent of the *Siyāsat al-Mulūk*'s description of the postal chiefs.[125]

Despite the fact that *ishrāf* ('supervision') is likely to have been practised by the late ninth century in central Islamic lands,[126] *mushrif*s operated predominantly in eastern provinces, under the Seljuks[127] and the Ghaznavids.[128] Their role varied according to the region and period, but in general terms the *mushrif* was similar to the old *ṣāḥib al-barīd*, in that both were officials sent to the provinces to observe and report on local administration to the central authorities. On account of the similarities between the two positions,

120 Maqrīzī, *Mawāʿiẓ*, vol. IV, p. 183.

121 In M. Gil and E. Fleischer, *Yehuda Ha-Levi and his Circle: 55 Geniza Documents*, Jerusalem, 2001, document 50, p. 471 ll. 15, 18 (Arabic) and p. 473 (Hebrew). Gil/Fleischer's translation of *ṣāḥib khabar* as '*mishṭara ḥashaʾīth*' ('secret police') is imprecise: from the context, and from what we know of the *aṣḥāb al-akhbār* in general, the functionary was not undercover.

122 Cf. D. S. Margoliouth [Ch. Pellat], *EI2* s.v. 'al-Ḥarīrī'.

123 Ibn al-Athīr, *Kāmil*, vol. X, p. 140.

124 Maqrīzī, *Kitāb al-sulūk li maʿrifat duwal al-mulūk*, Cairo, 1939–73, vol. I, p. 217.

125 Ibn Wahb, *al-Burhān fī wujūh al-bayān*, (eds. A. Maṭlūb and Kh. al-Ḥadīthī), Baghdad, 1967, pp. 417–19.

126 E.g. Miskawayh, *Eclipse*, vol. I, p. 24 (Arabic)/vol. IV, p. 27 (trans.), where, during the reign of al-Muqtadir, Shafīʿ al-Luʾluʾī was in charge of *ishrāf* over the *wazīr* and other functionaries in the capital, in addition to heading the *Dīwān al-Barīd*.

127 A. K. S. Lambton, *Continuity and Change in Medieval Persia: Aspects of Administrative, Economic and Social History, 11th–14th centuries*, London, 1988, pp. 36–7.

128 Bosworth, *The Ghaznavids*, Edinburgh, 1963, pp. 93–6.

al-Māwardī felt the need to distinguish clearly between the roles of the *mushrif* and the *ṣāḥib al-barīd* – either because the distinctions were not at first clear to him, or in order to prevent confusion in any future sultanate that might use his work as a blueprint for proper governance.[129] Māwardī draws three distinctions between the responsibilities of the two functionaries. In his words,

> The duties of the *mushrif* are different from those of the *ṣāḥib al-barīd* in three ways. First, an official (*'āmil*) has no right to have sole responsibility for his work to the exclusion of the *mushrif*, although he may exclude the *ṣāḥib al-barīd*. Second, the *mushrif* may exclude an official from the activity in which he proved corrupt, but the *ṣāḥib al-barīd* is not empowered to do so. Third, the *mushrif* does not have to report correct or incorrect actions of an official that are reported to him, while the *ṣāḥib al-barīd* has to, because the *mushrif*'s information constitutes a call for punishment, but the *ṣāḥib al-barīd*'s [information constitutes] mere reporting.[130]

What Māwardī's distinctions boil down to is the fact that the *mushrif* is a supervisor who oversees the operations of other local administrators and intervenes in bureaucratic affairs. His job is to ensure that things run efficiently and to correct them when they do not. The *ṣāḥib al-barīd* is a mere reporter who has no stake in the efficiency of the local administration; his job is simply to let the ruler know what is going on in the bureaus. This distinction would have been obvious had it not been for the fact that, as seen in the *Siyāsat al-Mulūk*, the local *aṣḥāb al-barīd* often did much more than simply despatch reports to the caliph.

By the mid tenth century, however, the local *aṣḥāb al-barīd* were not doing very much, certainly not for the ineffectual Abbasid caliphs. The employment of novel methods of swift communication – specifically *jammāzāt* and pigeons – and the emergence of *aṣḥāb al-akhbār* and *mushrifs* must have made imperial communications more practicable in light of the political developments and disturbances that characterised this period. But while these changes were significant, they did not alter the fact that news and official correspondence were arranged by the authorities who were the sole benefactors of the postal systems. The appearance of private communications networks that were controlled by powerful merchant groups represents a sharp break in the official hold on the flow of news and correspondence in the early medieval Islamic world, and in the tenth to twelfth centuries merchant networks came to complement (and, in one instance, even replace) official postal systems in much of the Near East.

Merchant networks

Due to the itinerant nature of their activities, international merchants have always played a role in the transmission of news. Ancient Near Eastern

[129] If, as H. A. R. Gibb ('Al-Mawardi's Theory of the Caliphate', *Islamic Culture* 11 (1937), 291–302) argues, this is the intention of Māwardī's work. And see Crone, *Political Thought*, pp. 222–3.

[130] Māwardī, *Ordinances*, pp. 230–1 (translation modified).

sources such as the Sumerian *Epic of Enmerkar and the Lord of Aratta* (*ca.* 1800 BCE) and the Eblaite Tablets (third millennium BCE) refer to merchants (lit. 'purse-carriers') operating as emissaries, messengers, or spies.[131] Similarly, in the Biblical story of Joseph, the latter suspects his brothers – who claim to be grain-merchants – of espionage, reflecting the widespread association of merchants with gathering and disseminating information.[132] In the Near East on the eve of Islam, Procopius refers to spies in the guise of merchants operating in both Byzantine and Sasanid lands.[133] And in the Umayyad period, 'Abd al-Malik is said to have received news of a provincial rebellion from merchants, while news of Yazīd's irresponsible behaviour was brought to 'Umar II's attention by traders from Khurasan.[134]

There are two distinct ways in which merchants and messages interacted. On the one hand, those travelling to distant lands could put their itinerary to use in delivering private letters and returning to their homelands with incidental news and reports from afar.[135] Such reports informed both geographers and government officials – these two being categories that had considerable vocational overlap in Antiquity. This function of merchants may be referred to as 'occasional' postal activity.[136] On the other hand, in periods and regions that could support extensive trading networks, merchants could establish 'commercial' postal systems through which news of relevance to their trading activities would be circulated amongst partners and colleagues. This type of merchant activity may be termed 'organised' postal activity. Both the occasional and the organised roles played by merchants became increasingly important in the Near East from the ninth century onwards.

With regard to the 'occasional' activity of merchants, Yāqūt relates a (possibly fictitious) account of a Byzantine envoy's visit to the caliph al-Manṣūr. Having toured al-Manṣūr's new capital, the envoy registered his positive verdict on the city's architecture, but warned the caliph that the city's markets might contain enemy spies, since 'Spies enter [Baghdad] under the pretext of trade, traders being the *barīd*s from the outlying regions; they gather intelligence, come to know what they wish, and return [to their lands of origin] with none being the wiser.'[137] The reference to traders being the

131 W. Hallo, *Origins: The Ancient Near Eastern Background of Some Modern Western Institutions*, Leiden 1996, pp. 75–6. See also: G. H. Oller, 'Messengers and Ambassadors'; and A. D. Crown, 'Tidings and Instructions: How News Travelled in the Ancient Near East', *JESHO* 17 (1974), 244–71.

132 *Genesis* chapter 42, *passim*. 133 Procopius, *Anecdota*, XXX: 12.

134 'Abd al-Malik: Ṭabarī, *Ta'rīkh*, II, p. 916; 'Umar II: ibid., II, p. 1313.

135 E.g. *A Mirror for Princes: The Qābūs Nāma by Kay Qā'ūs ibn Iskandar*, (trans. R. Levy), London, 1951, p. 160, where Kay Qā'ūs ibn Iskandar, the late eleventh-century ruler of Gurgān, advises merchants to deliver letters or report news from foreign lands (but only if the letters and reports contain good news).

136 In the late ninth century, for instance, al-Mu'taḍid's fear of ghosts became known in the capital amongst both commoners and the elite, and was spread to other parts 'by the caravans (*al-rukbān*)' (Mas'ūdī, *Murūj*, vol. V, pp. 161–2, §3319).

137 Yāqūt, *Mu'jam al-buldān*, (ed. F. Wustenfeld), Leipzig, 1869, vol. IV, p. 254.

*barīd*s from outlying regions is phrased in the Arabic text '*al-tujjār burud al-āfāq*'. This saying is also found in the *Siyāsat al-Mulūk*, where the author distinguishes between foreign envoys visiting the lands of Islam and merchants arriving from distant lands. Of the former he has the following to say: 'The *wazīr* must closely watch the envoys arriving from outlying regions, for they are the greatest spies. He must prevent them and their followers from mingling with the king's associates and from frequenting the markets for any reason.'[138] Concerning the merchants, however, the author succinctly states: 'The *wazīr* must treat merchants kindly, for they are the *barīd*s from the outlying regions.'[139] In the view of the Byzantine envoy, foreign traders were the ones to act as spies. But to the author of the *Siyāsat al-Mulūk* it was just the likes of the Byzantine envoy upon whom the suspicion of espionage should fall.[140]

The 'organised' postal activities carried out by merchants are more relevant to us, as it was the commercial postal networks that came to interact with and even replace official postal systems. The pivotal Arabic phrase in this context is *kutub al-tujjār*, 'letters of the merchants', and this phrase occurs in a number of fascinating episodes preserved in literary sources. In one of the earliest such episodes, the *Kitāb al-aghānī* relates the circumstances of Ṭāhir's rebellion against al-Ma'mūn while the latter was governor of Khurasan:

> Shortly after Ṭāhir arrived in Khurasan, he omitted [the compulsory] reference to the caliph's name from the Friday pulpit. ʿAwn ibn Mujāshiʿ ibn Masʿada, the local postal chief (*ṣāḥib al-barīd*), said to him: 'Have you not mentioned the caliph in the prayers?', and Ṭāhir replied: 'It was just a lapse; do not report it.' The same happened the next week and [Ṭāhir] said to ʿAwn: 'Do not report it.' On the third week ʿAwn said: 'The letters of the merchants are uninterrupted between [here and] Baghdad and should this information reach the caliph from sources other than us it will surely result in my fall from grace.' Ṭāhir replied: 'So write whatever you want to.'[141]

What this exchange between Ṭāhir and the postal chief says is that if the *Barīd* and its agents do not write letters with the news, then it is only a matter of time before merchants will. It is important to point out that the content of these letters (specifically, the omission of the caliph's name from the *khuṭba*) would hardly have been the stuff of private or even mercantile correspondence.

Two other episodes, both from the early tenth century, indicate that *kutub al-tujjār* were arriving in Baghdad from northern and western regions,

[138] Niẓām al-Mulk (*Siyāsat Nāma*, Tehran 1985, p. 128; trans. H. Darke, *The Book of Government*, London 1978, p. 95) states that 'when kings send ambassadors to one another their purpose is not merely the message or the letter which they communicate openly, but secretly they have a hundred other points and objects in view'.

[139] Both references may be found in Silverstein, 'New Source', 126.

[140] For some general remarks on the use of merchants as spies, see P. Crone, *Pre-Industrial Societies*, Oxford, 2003, p. 70, where further examples are provided.

[141] *Kitāb al-aghānī*, vol. XV, p. 237. Another version of this episode appears in Ṭabarī (*Taʾrīkh*, III, p. 1064), where the local postal chief is called Kulthūm ibn Thābit.

bearing news of political, rather than strictly commercial, interest. In the first account, we are told that in the year 901,

Letters of the merchants reached Baghdad from Raqqa stating that the Byzantines had arrived in many vessels. Some Byzantines had also come on horseback to the region of Kaysūm. They had driven off more than fifteen thousand Muslims, men, women and children. They had left with them, including some protected non-Muslims whom they had seized.[142]

Here, what may be described as military intelligence is obtained from the 'letters of the merchants'. In the second account, Ṭabarī informs us that,

On the fifteenth of Jumāda I, 290 AH (903 CE), letters of the merchants dated the twenty-second of Rabīʿ II arrived at Baghdad from Damascus with the information that the Qarmaṭī nicknamed al-Shaykh had routed Tughj more than once and killed all but a few of his men ... A number of Baghdādī merchants gathered the very same day to go to the *qāḍī* Yūsuf ibn Yaʿqūb. They had him read their letters and asked him to go to the *wazīr* and inform him about the inhabitants of Damascus. He promised them that he would do that.[143]

This account clarifies the procedure through which the contents of these letters would reach the authorities. It also informs us that it took three weeks for merchants' letters to reach Baghdad from Damascus. By *Barīd* standards, covering this 750-kilometre stretch in three weeks is unimpressive.[144] Nonetheless, the authorities still deemed the news to be current. As with the previous two episodes, the letters here contain information of political interest, and they are deemed *kutub al-tujjār* not because they represent correspondence between merchants but because they are transmitted by them.

It could be argued, of course, that these letters are in fact the correspondence of merchants who treated political affairs in their missives since the political conditions in a particular region could have a direct effect on the local markets. This is borne out in one episode where the 'letters of the merchants' dealt with issues that were primarily of interest to the traders themselves. Ibn al-Jawzī reports that in 1065,

Letters of the merchants arrived from a distance reporting that twenty-six vessels were captured from the coastline en route to Oman. All of the ships sank ... and 18,000 people perished, and all the merchandise was lost, including 10,000 drums of camphor.[145]

142 Ṭabarī, *Taʾrīkh*, III, p. 2205. 143 Ibid., III, p. 2222.

144 According to Ibn Khurradādhbih (*Masālik*, pp. 116–18), the route from Iraq (Samarra) to Damascus traverses 145 *sikak*, this being roughly 1,740 kilometres (assuming that stations were 2 parasangs or 12 kilometres apart), although the actual distance overland is closer to 1,200 kilometres. Bearing these figures in mind, the speed achieved by 'letters of the merchants' is a more respectable 60–80 kilometres a day.

145 Ibn al-Jawzī, *al-Muntaẓam fī taʾrīkh al-mulūk wa al-umam*, (ed. N. Zarzūr), Beirut, 1992, vol. XVI, p. 95.

From these letters merchants could infer that the Persian Gulf was unsafe and the price of camphor was set to skyrocket.[146] A particularly compelling anecdote of this nature is related by Tanūkhī, who describes the fortunes of a depressed merchant from tenth-century Baghdad in some detail. The merchant decided to shun his mercantile interests and retreat to a garden. On his way there, however, he chanced upon a *fayj* bearing 'letters of the merchants', travelling from Raqqa to Baghdad. The depressed trader eventually succeeded in peeking at the letters, which disclosed to him many details of other merchants with whom he had dealings. The letters advised his rivals to hang onto their stockpiles of olive oil, as its market value had risen sharply. The protagonist of the story then went about securing as much olive oil as he could, and he eventually made a profit of 10,000 dinars from his investment.[147]

The eastern Islamic world of the eleventh to twelfth centuries may not benefit from a Geniza-type archive, but literary sources suggest that merchants functioned in similar contexts in Iran and Central Asia. In the *Kutadgu Bilig*, for example, it is clear that in the late eleventh century the relationship between merchants and the dissemination of news was appreciated by inhabitants of the Islamic East. In his discussion of international merchants, Yūsuf Khāṣṣ Ḥājib tells his son:

> Treat them kindly and you may be sure that your good name will travel far. For these are they who spread one's name abroad, be it good or bad . . . If you would spread your name abroad, be sure to treat travellers hospitably. If you desire good repute, then give merchants good recompense. If you want a good name, my son, continually favour the traveller and the merchant caravan. Deal with merchants in this way and you will enjoy contentment and good repute.[148]

This passage captures the basic association of long-distance travellers – who usually engaged in trade – with the spread of news and information. It does not, however, hint at any formal organisation of letter-carrying traders.

[146] In a similar vein, a Geniza document from 1050 CE refers to a courier (*fayj*) travelling from Mahdiyya to Alexandria bearing letters that detail the arrival and contents of six ships in the port (in M. Gil, *Be-malkhūth yishmaʿel be-tekūfath ha-ge'onīm*, Tel-Aviv, 1997, vol. III, p. 306 (no. 385)). Other such cases are ubiquitous in the Geniza documents.

[147] Tanūkhī, *Nishwār al-muḥāḍara wa akhbār al-mudhākara*, Beirut, 1972, vol. II, pp. 79–82.

[148] Yūsuf Khāṣṣ Ḥājib, *The Wisdom of Royal Glory (Kutadgu Bilig): A Turko-Islamic Mirror for Princes*, (trans. R. Dankoff), Chicago, 1983, ll. 4429ff. Interestingly, in ll. 3811–20 the author outlines the Central Asian Steppe attitude to foreign envoys and messengers, and stresses that messengers and envoys are inviolable, as the Khwārazm-Shāh's governor of Utrār would find out in 1218 (see below, p. 141). And cf. M. Hinds and H. Sakkout, 'A Letter from the Governor of Egypt concerning Egyptian–Nubian Relations', in M. Hinds (eds. J. Bacharach, L. Conrad, and P. Crone), *Studies in Early Islamic History*, Princeton, 1996, pp. 160–87, at 183 ll. 21–3, where in 758 the Abbasid governor of Egypt complains to the Nubian authorities that messengers and merchants from Egypt had been detained, and states that nobody – even heathens – detains wayfarers.

The relationship between merchants and messages in the eastern Islamic world is illuminated in another late eleventh-century source: Maḥmūd Kashghārī, who wrote his dictionary of Turkic dialects in 1076–7, explains the term *Yukurka'n* (*yügürgān*), as meaning 'a courier, *barīd*, who goes out in advance of the merchants of Ṣīn toward the lands of Islam and brings news of them and their communications'.[149] Although the relationship between the *Barīd* – in this case, the term '*barīd*' itself – and mercantile communications systems in Central Asia is highlighted in this source, there is no evidence to suggest that the activities of merchants' letter-carriers in these parts of the Islamic world were regulated or centrally co-ordinated. Taken together, the evidence suggests that, in these regions, merchants played an occasional rather than an organised role in the transmission of news and correspondence. It is only in the Fatimid period (969–1171) that a 'commercial mail-system' was created, and the efficiency of this system had a perceptible effect on the Fatimids' '*Barīd*'.

The Fatimid '*Barīd*'

The early, pre-Cairo Fatimids directed a complex and clandestine missionary movement that must have benefited from a centrally organised system of communication, although – as is often the case with covert political movements – our information on the co-ordination of the *dā'īs* ('propagandists') is limited.[150] What we do know is that by the reign of the Mahdī (r. 909–34) the rudimentary administration of the Fatimid polity in North Africa was modelled – at least in its broad outlines – on the Abbasid administration.[151] Ibn al-Qadīm, for instance, served as the Mahdī's *ṣāḥib dīwān al-kharāj* and was also in charge of his *Barīd*.[152] Additionally, we are told that during the pilgrimage season the Mahdī had spies in Mecca who sent news of his enemies' movements to him, through *dā'īs* and a *Barīd* system,[153] and the Mahdī 's successor, al-Qā'im (r. 934–46), is said to have had the *kātib* al-Baghdādī serve as his *Barīd* chief.[154] The eunuch Jawdhar, who served as a trusty administrator under the Mahdī, al-Qā'im, al-Manṣūr (r. 946–53), and al-Mu'izz (r. 953–75), endowed the early Fatimid court with a significant measure of bureaucratic

[149] *Dīwān lughāt al-turk*, (ed./trans. R. Dankoff), *Compendium of the Turkic Dialects*, Cambridge Mass., 1984, vol. II, pp. 176–7.

[150] Similar constraints hamper our assessment of the early Abbasid state that emerged from the secretive operations of *du'ā*, although we have seen that shortly after going public the Abbasids had control of the *Barīd* system.

[151] Hence, the Fatimid state-secretary al-Muhallabī (d. 990 CE) wrote a *Kitāb al-masālik wa al-mamālik*, reflecting the influence of Abbasid geographers (in S. Munajjid, '*Qiṭ'a min kitāb mafqūd al-masālik wa al-mamālik li al-muhallabī*', *Majallat ma'had al-makhṭūṭāt al-'arabiyya* 4 (1958), 43–72).

[152] H. Halm, *The Empire of the Mahdī*, Leiden, 1996, p. 151.

[153] Ibid., p. 247.

[154] Ibid., p. 278.

continuity.[155] He controlled the Treasury, the *ṭirāz* (manufacture of ceremonial textiles), and, under al-Muʿizz, administered the outgoing and incoming correspondence of the caliph, having also been al-Qāʾim's *safīr* – a predominantly Shiʿite term for an intermediary between the *imām* and the uninitiated public.[156]

However, it was with the expansion of the Fatimids' realms eastwards and westwards that their system of communication took on its own identity. In 958, during his campaigns to the far west of North Africa, the celebrated Fatimid general Jawhar al-Rūmī is said to have sent a fish in a bottle to al-Muʿizz via 'the *Barīd*', as a sign that he had reached the Atlantic Ocean.[157] This, together with his impressive conquest of Egypt in 969, suggests that Jawhar's campaigns throughout North Africa were most probably realised with the help of an efficient, overland system of communication. Once they were established in Egypt, however, the Fatimid state appears to have favoured the pigeon-post and merchant networks over the more traditional *Barīd* system. The Fatimids' preference for pigeons is reflected in a well-known story, according to which the Fatimid caliph al-ʿAzīz (r. 975–96) said to his famous *wazīr* Yaʿqūb ibn Killis,

> 'I have never seen Baʿalbak cherries and I would like to see them'... The *wazīr* wrote a message and despatched it by one of the pigeons to Damascus. He ordered them in Damascus to attach to each wing of the Egyptian pigeon berries of Baʿalbak cherries. The pigeon arrived with this message and they immediately attached the berries to the wings of the bird as he had instructed them and they released it in the direction of Egypt. The *wazīr*, upon its arrival, went up to the caliph with the cherries on the same day that he ordered them. This astonished him greatly.[158]

This anecdote mirrors the earlier story in which al-Maʾmūn, while campaigning in Byzantine lands, had myrobalan fruit brought to him from Kabul via the *Barīd*.[159] Although the speeds achieved by al-ʿAzīz's pigeon-post are more realistic than those claimed for al-Maʾmūn's *Barīd*, both stories served the purpose of propagating the mythical efficiency of the ruler's communications system amongst the general population who, it was hoped, would be intimidated by the thought of an omniscient caliph. According to ʿUmarī, the Fatimids' employment of the pigeon-post 'was so excessive that they set

[155] For Jawdhar's career, see M. K. Ḥusayn and M. A. F. Shaʿīra, *Sīrat al-ustādh jawdhar*, Cairo, 1954.

[156] The institution of the *safīr* is probably based on the Assyrian *sepīru*, an imperial scribe who acted as an intermediary between Babylonian kings and foreign rulers with whom they had dealings, by translating official correspondence. Etymological explanations that link the Shiʿite *safīr* with the Arabic root *s.f.r.* ('to travel') appear to be incorrect. On the *sepīru*, see: J. Lewy, 'The Problems Inherent in Section 70 of the Bisutun Inscription', *Hebrew Union College Annual* 25 (1954), 169–208 at 188ff.; and H. J. Polotsky, 'Aramäisch *prš* und das "Huzvaresch"', *Le Muséon* 45 (1932), 273–83.

[157] Nuwayrī, *Nihāyat al-arab fī funūn al-adab*, Cairo, 1992, vol. XXVIII, p. 120. See also M. de Goeje, 'Paltiel-Djauhar', *ZDMG* 52 (1898), 75–80 at 76.

[158] On this episode, see Ragheb, *Messagers*, p. 170.

[159] See above, p. 82.

aside a *dīwān* for it',[160] a judgement that is all the more notable when considering that he was writing during the Mamluk period, when an official pigeon-post network was used regularly and efficiently.

The Fatimids' reliance on courier-pigeons does not in itself mean that they did without a *Dīwān al-Barīd*. There is, in fact, evidence that both al-Ḥākim (r. 996–1021) and al-Ẓāhir (r. 1021–36) had officials responsible for *Barīd* affairs: the former is said to have had a man 'in charge of the *Barīd* and the composition of documents (*inshā'*)',[161] while under the latter Ibn Khālid al-Ghurābīlī is described as being in charge of *Dīwān al-Barīd* in the year 1024.[162] Similarly, a modern study of Fatimid administration observes that '[The Fatimid *Dīwān al-Barīd*] was of great importance to the caliph, for it took care of correspondence reaching its point of destination', followed by the confusing detail that 'This bureau used carrier-pigeons.'[163] The problem is that those sources that detail the bureaus of the Fatimid state make no reference to a *Dīwān al-Barīd* in their thorough lists,[164] and al-Maqrīzī even speaks of a certain *Dīwān al-Tartīb*, which was instituted by the Fatimids and placed under an official whose duties in other periods of Islamic history would be covered by the *Ṣāḥib* [*Dīwān*] *al-Barīd*.[165] Furthermore, when the Mamluk Sultan Baybars I (r. 1260–77) decided to create an overland courier service in his lands, he is said to have modelled his *Barīd* on either Abbasid or Mongol precedents, rather than on any Fatimid institution that would have seemed a more natural source of inspiration.[166] It is possible, then, that the few references to a Fatimid *Barīd* in the post-Cairo era pertain to pigeon networks and other methods of despatching official correspondence, chief among which was the commercial postal system established by merchants.[167]

Goitein has described the merchant postal networks that operated in Fatimid lands in detail,[168] and his findings may be summarised as follows. At very reasonable rates, merchants would deliver letters to and from

[160] 'Umarī, *Ta'rīf*, p. 196.

[161] Maqrīzī, *Itti'āẓ al-ḥunafā' bi-akhbār al-a'imma al-fāṭimiyyīn al-khulafā'*, Cairo, 1973, vol. II, p. 6.

[162] Ibid., vol. II, p. 141.

[163] L. S. al-Imad, 'The Fāṭimid Vizierate 969–1172', unpublished PhD thesis, New York University, 1985, pp. 18–19.

[164] For a summary and analysis of the Fatimid administration, see *EI2* s.v. 'Dīwān' ii (2): the Fāṭimid period'.

[165] Maqrīzī, *Itti'āẓ*, vol. III, pp. 194–5.

[166] See below, p. 169. Communications in Medieval Europe, however, appear to have been influenced by the situation in Fatimid lands, which explains why in Europe postal networks were established by merchants and not by governments.

[167] On the basis of papyri from ninth-century Egypt, it would appear that merchants referred to the private networks of communication by the term '*Barīd*'. On this point, see: G. Levi della Vida, *Arabic Papyri in the University Museum in Philadelphia (Pennsylvania)*, Rome, 1981, doc. 74; and A. Dietrich, *Arabische Papyri*, p. 64 l. 13 (drawn to my attention by Petra Sijpesteijn).

[168] The following is based on S. D. Goitein, 'The Commercial Mail Service in Medieval Islam', *JAOS* 84 (1964), 118–23, and *A Mediterranean Society Volume I*, pp. 281–95.

scholars, other merchants, pilgrims, and their families. The documentary evidence shows that although mail on the route from Egypt westwards was subject to delays, irregularities, and a large measure of chance, letters sent from Egypt to the eastern provinces of the Fatimid state were transmitted by a regular, weekly system that proved to be efficient and safe. Senders would even receive confirmation of the safe receipt of their letters at the other end of the route. The term for ordinary couriers was *fuyūj* (sing. *fayj*) in Arabic, or *raṣṣīm* (sing. *raṣ*) in Hebrew. Although in a list of Jewish taxpayers from Fusṭāṭ the term *rasūl* appears as the name of an occupation, it is evident from other sources that most couriers were Muslims.[169] On the eastern routes of this merchant network, delivery times were moderately impressive, if irregular. However, for a higher price one could choose to send letters with a special courier, referred to as a *rasūl* in Arabic or a *shalīʾaḥ* in Hebrew. This commercial service was well organised, and certain families even arranged professional postal agencies, such as those of 'Muḥammad ibn Ṭāhir' or the 'House of ʿAbd'. In these agencies, incoming letters were sorted and sent on to another agency or to the addressee.

The Fatimid rulers benefited from the existence of these merchant networks both directly and indirectly. Directly, they may have utilised the merchants who were the *burud al-āfāq* when they needed to send or receive official correspondence. Indirectly, the constant and regular flow of information as reported in the *kutub al-tujjār* may have obviated the need for an entirely independent overland system of communication. There are Geniza documents that strongly suggest that the lines distinguishing private communication from imperial systems were hazy, in two ways. First, there is evidence that private individuals made use of the official pigeon-courier service.[170] Second, two recently published documents from the mid eleventh century suggest that local rulers may have made use of the commercial *fuyūj* and *rusul*. In the first document, an Alexandrian Jew wrote the following message to his correspondent in Fusṭāṭ:

> I already sent you a letter with the *fayj*. But afterwards, I wrote you another one prior to the fixed time [of the messenger's departure] but the *fayj* did not set out. He remained in my presence while I wrote this letter; I gave it to him when he was [finally] about to depart but the *amīr* – may God grant him success – delayed him.[171]

In the second document, the writer states that the *fuyūj* have collected the letters and are all set to leave, but they will not depart until the sultan's ship arrives. Presumably, the sultan insisted that commercial messengers wait for

[169] E.g., W. Diem, *Arabische Geschäftsbriefe des 10. bis 14. Jahrhunderts: aus der Österreichischen Nationalbibliothek in Wien*, Wiesbaden, 1995, pp. 7–9, no. 1, line 3, where a contemporary refers to one "Abdallāh al-Fayj', suggesting that he was a professional courier. Moreover, many of the couriers mentioned in Geniza documents had identifiably Muslim names.

[170] In Ragheb, *Messagers*, pp. 169–74.

[171] Gil and Fleischer, *Be-malkhūth yishmaʿel*, vol. III, p. 484 (no. 447).

him before setting off in order to make use of their services.[172] Co-operation between merchant networks and the ruling authorities would not have been out of the ordinary in tenth-century Egypt: in 917, for instance, letters of the *ṣāḥib al-barīd* in Egypt extolling the achievements of al-Qāsim ibn Sīmā al-Farghānī in his campaigns against the Shiʿites were sent to Baghdad together with 'the letters of the people of Egypt' (*kutub ahl miṣr*).[173]

The Fatimids thus benefited from the existence of private, merchant networks to an extent that was both unprecedented and unmatched by contemporary dynasties in the Islamic world. For although Tanūkhī, Yūsuf Khāṣṣ Ḥājib, and Maḥmūd Kashgharī indicate that merchants played a role in the transmission of news and correspondence in the eastern Islamic world, the political context of this activity did not encourage (or necessitate) the creation of highly regulated private postal networks in these regions, as will now be shown.

The eastern provinces: the Samanid and Ghaznavid *Barīd*s

In the eastern Islamic world from the tenth century until the Mongol invasions, overland postal systems modelled (at least initially) on the Abbasid *Barīd* were in operation. Passing reference has already been made to the use of *jammāzāt* in Buyid and Samanid lands, and to the existence of *mushrif*s and *aṣḥāb al-barīd* in the Samanid and Ghaznavid realms. But the communications arrangements in these successor states deserve more focused attention here, both because they preserved the *Dīwān al-Barīd* at a time when the Abbasids were struggling to maintain their own postal system, and because in these states the *Barīd* underwent changes that add depth and texture to our understanding of communications technology in the pre-modern Islamic world.

Although they emerged as provincial rulers of the Islamic world at roughly the same time, the Samanids differed from the Fatimids in two significant ways. First, the Samanids were genuinely loyal to the Abbasid caliphs of Baghdad who conferred upon them governorships of Transoxania, Khurasan, and – for a short while during the reign of Naṣr II (914–43) – Rayy, whereas the Fatimids could never reconcile their Ismaʿīlī mission with the illegitimate rule of the Abbasids. Thus, despite striking similarities between the messianism of the early Abbasid and the early Fatimid movements, the Fatimids unequivocally rejected any association with the Abbasid regime, while the Samanids were the successors of the caliphs – taking subordinate titles such as *amīr* and minting Samanid–Abbasid coins that openly displayed their allegiance to the Abbasids. Second, although the Samanids were loyal to the Abbasids while the Fatimids

172 Ibid., vol. III, p. 848 (no. 558). It is possible that rulers insisted that private couriers set out only after their return in order to read all outgoing letters (cf. Herodotus, *Histories*, VII: 239). There is, however, no evidence that this was the case in Fatimid Egypt, especially as some of the letters unearthed make derogatory references to public officials.

173 ʿArīb, *Ṣilat taʾrīkh al-ṭabarī*, p. 68.

were not, it was a more realistic proposition for the Abbasids to attempt to rule Egypt and its environs than it was to exert any measure of real influence on the affairs of Khurasan and Transoxania. Thus, for all that the Samanids officially deferred to the Abbasids, they were economically, politically, and militarily unfettered by their association with the caliphs. And yet the Abbasid court, despite its increasingly apparent feebleness, held an enormous amount of prestige within the courts of the successor states, and it is not surprising that the Samanids modelled their *Barīd* on the caliphal one.

The Samanids' first taste of power came as governors in Transoxania, subordinated to the Ṭāhirids who ruled the East on behalf of the caliphs from *ca.* 820. When they achieved autonomy as Abbasid governors in Transoxania (874) and Khurasan (875), the Samanids were therefore heirs to both the Ṭāhirid and the Abbasid systems of government. In 821, Ṭāhir ibn al-Ḥusayn composed for his son an epistle on governance, one item of which concerns the duty to establish an intelligence system in the province to which he had been appointed by the caliph. In Ṭāhir's words,

> In every district of your governorship you should appoint a trusted observer (*amīn*) who will keep you informed of the activities of your local officials and will write to you regularly about their policies and doings, in such a way that you will be, as it were, an eyewitness of every official's activities within his sphere of responsibility.[174]

There is no explicit reference here to the *Barīd*, although in his commentary on the text Bosworth rightly appends to the term '*amīn*' the remark 'Here obviously the equivalent of the *Ṣāḥib al-Barīd*, postmaster and intelligence officer, of the Abbasid caliphate and of the later *mushrif al-mamlaka* of eastern Iranian states.'[175] By 900, when Ismāʿīl I (r. 892–907) defeated ʿAmr ibn Layth al-Ṣaffār, Samanid rule in eastern Iran was achieving a measure of stability; with the reign of Naṣr II (r. 914–43) the administrative bureaus of the Samanid state reached a level of complexity that could support an independent *Barīd* system, and Narshakhī's list of the Samanid *dīwāns* makes it clear that it was an Abbasid rather than a Ṭāhirid precedent that was being followed.[176] Moreover, Khwārazmī's treatment of the terms employed in the Samanid administration reflects the unique evolution of Abbasid postal terminology in Persian-speaking lands.[177] Although it is undoubtedly true that Khwārazmī was drawing on sources that depict the

[174] C. E. Bosworth, 'An Early Arabic Mirror for Princes: Ṭāhir Dhū al-Yamīnayn's Epistle to his Son ʿAbdallāh (206/821)', *Journal of Near Eastern Studies* 29 (1970), 25–41, at 38.

[175] C. E. Bosworth, *The History of al-Ṭabarī vol. XXXII: The Reunification of the Abbasid Caliphate*, New York 1987, p. 123 n. 374; and cf. Bosworth, 'Mirror for Princes', 28–9 for a similar observation.

[176] In his enumeration of the ten bureau-chiefs in Bukhara, Muḥammad Narshakhī specifically includes the *Barīd* (in R. Frye, *The History of Bukhara*, Cambridge Mass., 1954, p. 26).

[177] C. E. Bosworth, 'Abū ʿAbdallāh al-Khwārazmī on the Technical Terms of the Secretary's Art', *JESHO* 12 (1969), 113–64 at 141ff. ('The Expressions used in the Department of the Postal Service (*Dīwān al-Barīd*)').

Abbasid, not the Samanid, administration,[178] the existence in this work of Persian words such as *askudār* (meaning here a register of the courier-traffic between stations) suggests that the author was influenced by local practices and terminology. And the fact that the *Dīwān al-Barīd* merits its own sub-chapter in this work is indicative of the high standing that this Abbasid institution enjoyed in the Samanid bureaucracy.

The Samanids also emulated the Abbasids' patronage of scholars through whom their rule was legitimised and extolled. The Samanids' answer to Ṭabarī was Balʿamī, and – with particular relevance to the route system – their answer to Ibn Khurradādhbih was Jayhānī, who could not but call his own work *Kitāb al-Masālik wa al-Mamālik*. Both Balʿamī and Jayhānī served as *wazīr*s under Naṣr II, and this period represents a high-point in Samanid fortunes. Writers such as Muqaddasī and Ibn Ḥawqal, whose wide-ranging travels afforded them a comparative perspective on the various regions of the Islamic world in the tenth century, were unrestrained in their praise of conditions under the Samanids. Muqaddasī quotes a popular saying that captures the Samanids' reputation for centralised administration: 'Were a tree to revolt against the Samanids, it would wither.'[179] In describing the customs (*rusūm*) particular to the Samanid dynasty, he mentions the curious fact that 'on occasion they communicated on important matters through messengers'.[180] Of course, Muqaddasī cannot be implying that other rulers do not employ messengers. What his statement indicates is the high degree of centralisation that characterised the Samanid state: when important matters present themselves, consultation between the various authorities – distant though they may be – is to be undertaken through couriers.

Unfortunately, Jayhānī's geographical treatise does not survive except in extensive quotations by other Muslim geographers,[181] and it is impossible to reconstruct the postal routes and stations of the Samanid realms. Ibn Ḥawqal, however, mentions a number of details pertaining to the employment and funding of *Barīd* administrators in the Samanid state. In every district (*nāḥiya*) of Sīstān, we are told, there was a local *ṣāḥib khabar wa-barīd*,[182] and from other references we know that this arrangement pertained to other regions too.[183] In fact, on the basis of what would appear to be

[178] In the words of Bosworth (ibid., 116): 'Khwārazmī's material here should accordingly be regarded as pertaining to practice in the central lands of the Caliphate.'

[179] Muqaddasī, *Aḥsan al-taqāsīm*, p. 338. Muqaddasī supports this with the observation that when a powerful ruler such as ʿAḍud al-Dawla challenged the Samanids, he was defeated.

[180] *wa-rubbamā shāfahū al-rusul ʿind al-muhimmāt* (ibid., p. 339).

[181] Cf. J.-C. Ducène, 'al-Ğayhani: Fragments (Extraits du Kitāb al-Masālik wa al-Mamālik d'al-Bakrī)', *Der Islam* 75 (1998), 259–82.

[182] Ibn Ḥawqal, *Kitāb ṣūrat al-arḍ*, Leiden, 1939, vol. II, p. 424. Interestingly, in the same line Ibn Ḥawqal refers to the *bundār* as an official involved in tax-collection, in contrast to the *banādira* (sing. *bundār*) who expedited urgent mail-bags in the Abbasid period.

[183] Ibid., vol. II, p. 430, where all the districts of Khurasan have '*aṣḥāb al-burud wa al-banādira … ṣāḥib barīd wa bundār … wa aṣḥāb akhbār wa burud*'.

chancery documents, Ibn Ḥawqal tabulates the stipends (*ʿishrīnāt*) of the postal chiefs of every region of the Samanid state.[184] The data he provides suggests that the local *aṣḥāb al-barīd* earned decent salaries, although their precise wages appear to have varied by region.[185] Some districts may have had both a *ṣāḥib al-khabar* and a *ṣāḥib al-barīd*: an intelligence chief was based in Marw in 914,[186] but we also know that at the end of the Samanid period al-Faḍl ibn Aḥmad al-Isfarā'inī was *ṣāḥib al-barīd* in Marw before becoming a Ghaznavid *wazīr*.[187]

As with the Abbasids in the second half of the ninth century, towards the end of their reign the Samanids were weakened by both financial problems and the machinations of Turkish commanders whose ostensible role was to preserve Samanid power but whose actual activities caused irreversible instabilities. Already Aḥmad II had been murdered by a *ghulām* in the early tenth century, and by the last decades of the century Nūḥ II (r. 976–97) was forced to draw on the military assistance of Sebüktigin, the founder of the Ghaznavid dynasty, in attempting to overcome the unruly Turks. But despite the influence of slave-soldiers on the Samanid court and on the Ghaznavid state that would succeed it, and despite the fact that under the slave-soldier dynasty of the Mamluks the *Barīd* was part of the military, the Samanid *Barīd* was a civilian institution. The civilian character of the Samanid *Barīd*, coupled with the overwhelmingly Abbasid terminology employed in the system, bears witness to the fact that the Samanid and Ghaznavid postal systems were modelled on the Abbasid *Barīd*.

Although Maḥmūd (r. 998–1030) and Masʿūd (r. 1030–40) are the sultans most commonly associated with Ghaznavid power, it was Maḥmūd's father Sebüktigin who laid the foundations of Ghaznavid rule and who is said to have composed a testament of advice to his son in which the importance of maintaining a postal and intelligence system is stressed.[188] In this testament Sebüktigin tells his son that,

> It is most important that you keep yourself well-informed about the condition of the army, their pay and daily allowances. Their condition should be as well-known to you as the recitation of '*qul huwa allāh*' every day … You should always keep spies (*jāsūsān*) to bring you news of foreign kingdoms and armies, and distant cities. In your own kingdom and cities, you should keep honest postal chiefs (*ṣāḥib-i barīdān-i amīn*) so that they may keep you acquainted with the condition of the people, and of

184 Ibid., vol. II, p. 470.

185 The *ṣāḥib al-barīd* in smaller regions such as Arbinjān, Khujanda, Zamm, Bādhghīs, Ṭūs, Ṭāliqān, Kish, Bust, Tirmidh, and others, received only 300 dirhams; by contrast the postal chief in Nīshāpūr received as much as 3,000 dirhams (ibid.).

186 Treadwell, 'Murder of Aḥmad ibn Ismāʿīl', 398/404.

187 Cf. M. Nazim, *EI2* s.v. 'al-Faḍl ibn Aḥmad al-Isfarā'inī'. Another Samanid postal chief who became an influential figure in Ghaznavid times was the historian Abū Naṣr al-ʿUtbī, who had been *ṣāḥib al-barīd* in Ganj Rustāq under the Samanids, as we have seen.

188 If, indeed, the *Pand-Nāma* was genuinely penned by Sebüktigin, it is likely that the son in question was Ismāʿīl rather than Maḥmūd.

the justice and righteousness of your *ʿāmil*s.[189] Every night before you have said your night prayer, you should have obtained detailed information about your country, so that your affairs should prosper.[190]

There is nothing surprising about the contents of this passage, and the advice offered is so general and so typical of the genre as to be uninformative about the particularities of Ghaznavid practices (or the Samanid practices of which the writer had experience).[191] That said, the terminology used is instructive, in that it is the *ṣāḥib al-barīd* who is charged specifically with internal surveillance (external surveillance being the responsibility of the *jāsūs*), and who is required to be 'honest', *amīn* – this being the term for the 'trusted observers' already encountered in Ṭāhir's *waṣiyya* to his son ʿAbdallāh.

Evidence for the Ghaznavid *Barīd* is relatively detailed, and modern studies of the period often include full descriptions of it.[192] Two officials play a central role in Ghaznavid communications, both of whom have been encountered above. On the one hand, the *ṣāḥib al-barīd* (rendered in the Persian sources as *ṣāḥib(-i) barīd*) continued to serve in capacities bequeathed to the Ghaznavid administration from the Abbasid and Samanid states. Under the Ghaznavids, the status of the postmaster in the capital probably exceeded that under either the Abbasids or Samanids, as evidenced by the fact that frequently the head *ṣāḥib barīd* would be promoted to the role of *wazīr*.[193] The provincial postal chiefs would compose and despatch reports to the central chancellery (*Dīwān-i Risālat*), reports that could be written in code (*muʿammā*) or transported in intricate hiding places (hollowed-out staffs, shoes, saddle cloths, and the like) for safety, since although roads were provided with watchmen (*ṭalāʾiʿ*), there was always the worry that the messages would fall into the wrong hands. On the other hand, the Ghaznavids made extensive use of the *mushrif*s[194] who continued to function as inspectors of the court officials and other members of the ruling elite. Although the precise functions of the *mushrif* appear to have evolved during this period, his basic responsibility was still to ensure that government functionaries carried out their duties loyally and efficiently.

189 In the early Islamic period, by contrast, local *ʿāmil*s controlled the *Barīd* in their region.

190 In M. Nazim, 'The Pand-Nāmah of Sebuktigīn', *JRAS* (1933), 605–28, at 616/625 and 620/627 (translation modified).

191 On this point, see Crone, *Political Thought*, p. 157.

192 M. Nazim, *The Life and Times of Sulṭān Maḥmūd of Ghazna*, Cambridge, 1931, pp. 144–6; and Bosworth, *Ghaznavids*, pp. 93–7. The following description of Ghaznavid communications is based on Bosworth, unless stated otherwise.

193 And, as with the *aṣḥāb al-barīd* in previous Islamic states, local postal chiefs were often poets and scholars (in Bosworth, *Ghaznavids*, p. 95, and 279 n. 105). Conversely, there is no evidence of Abbasid postal chiefs rising to such positions, although the fortunes of the Barīdī family in the tenth century indicate that a postal chief's descendants could achieve roles of such prominence. Muqaddasī's suggestion that Ibn Khurradādhbih was a *wazīr* (*Aḥsan al-taqāsīm*, p. 362) appears to be incorrect.

194 The full title of the *mushrif* is given in contemporary sources as *mushrif dar umūr-i mamlakat*, that is: 'supervisor of the kingdom's affairs' (Bosworth, *Ghaznavids*, p. 94).

While both the postal chiefs and the supervisors were associated with internal surveillance on a number of levels, we also hear of intelligence chiefs (*ṣāḥib khabarān*) and reporters (*munhiyān*) gathering news and intelligence in Ghaznavid lands. Niẓām al-Mulk is best remembered as a Seljuk *wazīr*, but his *Siyāsat Nāma* was written largely on the basis of experience gained as a Ghaznavid functionary,[195] and his chapter on 'Intelligence agents (*ṣāḥib khabarān*) and reporters (*munhiyān*) and [their importance in] administering the affairs of the country'[196] is therefore pivotal in this context. In a well-known passage, Niẓām al-Mulk states:

It is the king's duty to enquire into the condition of his peasantry and army, both far and near, and to know everything that goes on. If he does not do this he is at fault and people will charge him with negligence, laziness and tyranny . . . Inevitably, therefore, he must have a postmaster (*ṣāḥib barīd*) . . . But this is a delicate business involving some unpleasantness; it must be entrusted to the hands and tongues and pens of men who are completely above suspicion and without self-interest, for the wealth of the country depends on them. They must be directly responsible to the king and not to anyone else; and they must receive their monthly salaries regularly from the treasury so that they may do their work without any worries, and nobody but the king should know what they report. In this way the king will know of every event that takes place and will be able to give his orders as appropriate . . . Thus the employment of intelligence agents (*ṣāḥib khabar*) and reporters (*munhī*) contributes to the justice, vigilance, and prudence of the king, and to the prosperity of the country.[197]

This advice was dispensed to the Seljuk sultan and, as we shall see, it was rejected. But in this context Niẓām al-Mulk's framework of surveillance is undoubtedly a Ghaznavid one, and in another passage he explains how news that is gathered in the provinces is to be relayed to the central authorities:

Couriers (*paykān*) must be posted along the principal highways, and they must be paid monthly salaries and allowances. When this is done, everything that happens throughout the 24 hours within a radius of 50 parasangs will come [to their knowledge]. In accordance with established custom they must have sergeants (*naqībān*) to see that they do not fail in their duties.[198]

Here too, the author is describing a system with which he was familiar from Ghaznavid lands, and a number of conclusions may be drawn from these two passages. First, the postal and intelligence system was to be funded by the Ghaznavid Treasury, mirroring Abbasid practice. Second, although the term *paykān* (sing. *payk*)[199] ordinarily signifies runners rather than mounted couriers, the distance of 300 kilometres a day could only be a realistic goal for

[195] On this source cf. M. Simidchieva, '*Siyāsat Nāme* Revisited: The Question of Authenticity', in *Proceedings of the Second European Conference of Iranian Studies* (ed. B. Fragner et al.), Rome, 1995, pp. 657–74.
[196] Niẓām al-Mulk, *Siyāsat Nāma*, pp. 85–95/pp. 63–71.
[197] Ibid., pp. 85–6/pp. 63–4. [198] Ibid., p. 117/p. 87. [199] On this term, see above p. 20.

messengers riding swift mounts.[200] Third, maintaining an efficient postal and intelligence system is directly associated in the author's mind with the ruler's reputation for justice (rather than with preserving the ruler's authority and power).[201]

The Ghaznavid systems of *Barīd* and *Ishrāf* appear to have been sophisticated and well-maintained. There is little direct information on the state of the routes or the postal stations in Ghaznavid lands, and although sultans such as Maḥmūd and Masʿud are often praised for the attention they paid to the road system, such praise is formulaic in the Iranian world and tells us little about the actual state of the roads. In fact, in a passage describing the conditions in Seljuk lands, Niẓām al-Mulk suggests that the official routes were not always maintained satisfactorily. He writes:

> When the Exalted Stirrup (*rikāb-i ʿālī*) proceeds on a journey, there may not be fodder and provisions ready at every stage (*marḥala*) where he halts, and so the rations for the day will have to be procured at great trouble and inconvenience, or even seized from the peasants by shares. This is bad procedure. On all the roads by which the king is going to pass, at every village which is a stopping place, if it and its environs are held in fief, supplies should be requisitioned; but in places where there is no village and no caravanserai (*ribāṭ*), [before requisitioning supplies] they must wait at the nearest village in the district while the harvest is being gathered; then if the provisions are required, they will be used . . . In this way the peasants will suffer no distress, there will be no breakdown in the supply of fodder, and the king will not fail in the important task which he has undertaken.[202]

The reference to the ruler as being 'The Exalted Stirrup' suggests that the author had the Seljuk road system in mind rather than that of the Ghaznavids, about whose road system he has only good things to say.[203] The Seljuks are known to have neglected all aspects of communication and intelligence-gathering, a fact that is all the more baffling considering that they had both the Ghaznavid model of their contemporaries and the Buyid model of their predecessors on which to build. It is to the Buyid successes and the Seljuk failures that we now turn.

The central provinces: communications under the Buyids and Seljuks

The Buyids

In his summary of the historical development of the *Barīd*, ʿUmarī concludes his statements on the Abbasid *Barīd* by saying: 'When the Buyids took

200 As we have seen for the Achaemenid period, 'runners on horses' was an acceptable phrase for mounted couriers.
201 Conversely, Kay Kāʾūs' rationale for maintaining an internal surveillance mechanism is that only through knowledge of internal affairs can one keep abreast of one's enemy's affairs (*Qābūs Nāma*, p. 234).
202 Niẓām al-Mulk, *Siyāsat Nāma*, p. 133/pp. 98–9 (translation modified).
203 E.g., ibid., pp. 87ff./pp. 64ff.

control of the caliphate, they discontinued (*qaṭaʿū*) the *Barīd* in order to deprive the caliph of intelligence about them and their movements, at the time when they were heading towards Baghdad . . .'.[204] We have seen that much of what ʿUmarī has to say about the pre-Mamluk *Barīd* is inaccurate, and this statement may be no different. It is difficult to imagine that Daylamite conquerors hailing from a relatively harsh region of the Islamic world would have been so mindful of the pivotal role that the caliphal *Barīd* could play in the early Buyid campaigns against Iraq. What is more probable is that – as with the Zanj and Qarmaṭī movements before it – the Buyid advance had a disastrous effect on the caliph's ability to communicate and to maintain a road system. Thus, in his account of the Buyids' rise to power, Masʿūdī admits that his knowledge of events in Iraq is limited due to the 'distances, cut roads, and the cessation of news' while he was in Egypt and Syria.[205] The arrival of the Buyids probably disrupted the flow of news to and from Iraq unintentionally rather than as a planned tactic aimed at keeping the caliph in the dark. Whatever the case may be, when ʿImād, Rukn, and Muʿizz al-Dawla established their authority in Iraq and much of Iran, they came to appreciate the value of efficient communications and set up a courier service that was derivative of Abbasid precedent and yet unique in many ways.

Despite ruling a large, land-based region in the caliphal heartland, the Buyids did not create a centrally controlled empire. The familial division of the realm into three provinces centred on Rayy, Baghdad, and Shiraz meant that decisions could be taken at a regional level, as each provincial capital was administered independently of the others.[206] In the first half of the Buyid period, rulers such as Muʿizz al-Dawla (r. Baghdad, 945–67) and ʿAḍud al-Dawla (r. Fārs, 949–78, Baghdad, 978–83) ruled efficiently, ensuring stability and a large degree of co-ordination amongst the respective provincial rulers. The splintered nature of Buyid rule allowed each province to benefit from the attention of a local but influential ruler, yet the (relative) lack of internal rivalries meant that the three regions co-operated with each other and remained tightly knit. In the second half of the period, however, the provincial nature of Buyid rule proved to be a weakness, as it encouraged regional rulers with interests (and pressures) of their own to pursue independent policies. It is during the first, co-ordinated period of Buyid rule that the *Barīd* functioned efficiently.

We have seen that the Buyids made use of *jammāzāt* and pigeon-couriers during their reign. It is not surprising that methods of communication that

[204] ʿUmarī, *Taʿrīf*, p. 186.

[205] *buʿd al-dār wa fasād al-subul wa inqiṭāʿ al-akhbār* (Masʿūdī, *Murūj*, vol. V, p. 258, §3670).

[206] On this subject, cf. J. Donohue, *The Buwayhid Dynasty in Iraq 334H/945 to 403H/1012*, Leiden, 2003; M. Kabir, *The Buwayhid Dynasty of Baghdad*, Calcutta, 1964; H. Busse, *Chalif und Grosskönig: Die Buyiden im Iraq (945–1055)*, Beirut, 1969; and H. Munaymana, *Taʾrīkh al-dawla al-buwayhiyya: al-siyāsī wa al-iqtiṣādī wa al-ijtimāʿī wa al-thaqāfī: muqāṭaʿat fāris*, Beirut, 1987.

became popular in the Islamic world during the tenth century would have been adopted by the Buyids too. But in addition to these methods the Buyids are said to have introduced a novel solution to the problem of swift communication. Numerous authors credit Muʿizz al-Dawla with the creation of a network of runners (*suʿā*) in Buyid lands. According to Qalqashandī,

> The first ruler to use runners (*suʿā*) was Muʿizz al-Dawla ibn Buwayh, the first of the Daylamite rulers, after the year 330 A.H. (941/2 C.E.). The reason for this was that he was based in Baghdad while his brother Rukn al-Dawla ibn Buwayh was in Isfahan, far away from him, and Muʿizz al-Dawla wanted to inform his brother Rukn al-Dawla quickly of the up-to-date news (*mutajaddidāt al-akhbār*). For this reason, he introduced runners. In his day, two runners emerged, one called Faḍl, the other Marʿūsh. One was the runner of the Sunnis, the other of the Shiʿites, each having a fan-base supporting him. [Either] one of them could cover some 40-odd parasangs in a single day.[207]

It is worth considering the speed that these runners are alleged to have achieved. Covering 216 kilometres – assuming Ibn Taghribirdī's more conservative estimate of 36 parasangs – in 10 to 12 hours would require a runner to maintain a speed close to 20 kilometres an hour. This pace is not, in itself, unreasonable. Leading marathon runners, who cover a distance in excess of 40 kilometres, complete the distance in just over 2 hours, thereby averaging the same 20 kilometres an hour. But modern marathon runners who achieve such speeds tend to collapse upon reaching the finish-line, and it is difficult to believe that either Faḍl or Marʿūsh could maintain the pace over a twelve-hour period.[208] The *Siyāsat al-Mulūk*, it should be remembered, mentions 60 parasangs as the farthest a mail-bag can travel – using relays of mounted messengers – in one day, while Niẓām al-Mulk speaks of news arriving on a daily basis from within a radius of 50 parasangs. What these exaggerated speeds tell us, of course, is that Muʿizz al-Dawla's couriers were believed to be extremely fast and, as with other postal fables encountered above, it was in a ruler's interest that the general public should believe that official couriers could cover extraordinary distances at superhuman speeds.[209]

The reasons behind the introduction of runners are unclear. It may be that – as with *jammāzāt* and pigeons – using runners was a cheap option that did away with the need to maintain relays of horses (and grooms, fodder, etc.) along the routes. It is also possible that in preferring unmounted couriers over

[207] Qalqashandī, *Ṣubḥ*, vol. I, pp. 126–7. It is important to stress that unlike the *fuyūj* mentioned for the Ghaznavid period, the term *suʿā* did not refer to 'runners on horses', as Qalqashandī discusses Muʿizz al-Dawla's couriers in his treatment of the Mamluk '*quṣṣād*' (sing. *qāṣid*) who carry letters when the *Barīd* routes hampered and were unsuitable for mounted couriers. Ibn Taghribirdī (*Nujūm*, vol. III, p. 285) has a similar account, but says that the runners could cover only 36 parasangs a day. In his discussion of the year 480 AH (1087/8 CE), Ibn al-Athīr mentions that two couriers attained fame at this time, provoking comparisons with Faḍl and Marʿūsh (*Kāmil*, vol. X, p. 162).

[208] According to legend, the runner who, in 490 BCE, brought news of the Greeks' victory over the Persians from Marathon to Athens dropped dead upon completing the 25-mile run.

[209] Cf. Busse, *Chalif*, p. 311.

mounted ones, the Daylamite rulers were reflecting their own traditions of infantry- rather than cavalry-based movement.[210] Muʿizz al-Dawla's introduction of runners notwithstanding, the Buyids otherwise perpetuated the bureaucratic framework of the Abbasid caliphs. The *Siyāsat al-Mulūk*, for instance, was written in the early years of the Buyid period and suggests that the only difference between working under the old regime and the new one is that now copies of official documents had to be submitted to a Shiʿite supervisor.[211] We hear specifically of a *Dīwān al-Khabar wa al-Barīd* under Sharaf al-Dawla (r. 961–89),[212] and for his father ʿAḍud al-Dawla's reign we have a detailed description of the ruler's postal routine. According to Miskawayh,

As the day advanced, [ʿAḍud al-Dawla] would ask about the arrival of the [postal] rounds (*al-nuwab al-mutaraddida bi al-kutub*), for which there was a fixed time of day which they were expected to observe. If they were late, there was a terrible disturbance, and inquiries were instituted into the cause of the delay. If it was something obviously excusable, the excuse was accepted; if it was due to a preventable cause, the cause was removed; if the postal officials (*nuwabiyyīn*) were to blame, they were punished. One of the carriers (*ṭurād*) narrated how once a station-master (*murattab*) was told by his wife that some rice had just been cooked and he might as well stay and eat it before proceeding. He waited just the time it took him to eat and the [postal] round was delayed that amount of time. More than 3,000 lashes were in consequence inflicted on the carriers and station-masters between Shiraz and Baghdad.[213]

The author adds that post from Shiraz to Baghdad took only seven days,[214] and that 'fruit and flowers came perfectly fresh from the districts of Fars and Khuzistan', bringing to mind other accounts of the *Barīd* transporting perishables, as discussed above. We are also told that it was a common custom for officials to send money home using the postal service and that, in one case, when the money did not reach its destination, ʿAḍud al-Dawla ordered a strict inquiry into the matter; the guilty postman (*kharāʾiṭī*) was discovered and his hand amputated. Miskawayh then describes the routine by which the ruler received and replied to official letters as follows:

When the post arrived, the seals were broken and the bags (*kharāʾiṭ*) were opened, and the letters taken out in the prince's presence. He would select such as were addressed to his throne, and despatch the rest to the *Dīwān al-Barīd*, whence they would be distributed to their addresses. He would then read the letters one by one, and toss them to Abū al-Qāsim ʿAbd al-ʿAzīz. When he had finished their perusal, Abū al-Qāsim would read them to him afresh, and receive instructions about the reply to

210 The mountainous terrain of Daylam was not conducive to cavalry-based armies.
211 In Sadan and Silverstein, 'Ornate Manuals', 342.
212 Ṣābiʾ, *Rusūm*, pp. 73–4, where the *ṣāḥib* of this *dīwān* is named as al-Ḥasan ibn Muḥammad ibn Naṣr. On the Buyid *dīwāns* of *Barīd* and *Khabar* in general, see Busse, *Chalif*, pp. 310–12.
213 Miskawayh, *Eclipse*, vol. III, pp. 40ff./vol. VI, pp. 36ff. (translation modified). Cf. Sabahuddin, 'Postal System', 279, where Mughal couriers who were late in delivering mailbags were punished harshly.
214 According to Hilāl al-Ṣābiʾ (*Rusūm*, p. 18), it took eight days.

be inserted under each section; such as the prince thought fit would then be communicated to Muṭahhar ibn ʿAbdallāh (or his substitute) ... Abū al-Qāsim would now arrive, squat according to custom in his presence, and lay before him the replies written by himself or the *kuttāb* to the letters which had arrived. The prince would occasionally suggest additions or omissions; the letters would then be corrected accordingly, be sealed, and placed in their portfolio (*askudār*), and then conveyed to the *Dīwān al-Barīd*, whence they would be despatched at the right time.[215]

From this detailed account a number of points emerge. First, both Abbasid and 'Iranian' terminology is used in the context of the Buyid *Barīd*. The system and its headquarters are still the *Dīwān al-Barīd* and the mail-bags are *kharāʾiṭ*, relayed between stations under the administration of the familiar *murattab*s, but the Persian term *askudār* also occurs. The couriers themselves are referred to either as *ṭurād* or by the term *kharāʾiṭī*, neither of which occurred regularly in earlier periods, and the absence of Muʿizz al-Dawla's celebrated *suʿā* is conspicuous.[216] Second, the *Barīd* under ʿAḍud al-Dawla followed a stringently enforced timetable: the ruler would receive official correspondence at a specific time every day; even the slightest delay would be punished harshly; and inefficiencies would not be tolerated at any level. Third, if it took seven or eight days for the *Barīd* to travel between Shiraz and Baghdad – at a distance, according to Qudāma,[217] of 91 *sikak*, or just under 1,100 kilometres – the speeds attained by ʿAḍud al-Dawla's strictly disciplined couriers did not exceed 130–60 kilometres a day.

Clearly, things improved greatly from when the Buyids are alleged to have 'cut off' the *Barīd* until the reign of ʿAḍud al-Dawla. As with the Abbasids before them, the Samanids to their east, and the Fatimids to their west, in al-Iṣṭakhrī the Buyids had their own author of a *Masālik wa Mamālik* work,[218] and Iṣṭakhrī's use of *kishwar*s in lieu of *iqlīm*s in delineating the regions of the world must have satisfied the neo-Sasanid fetish of his Buyid patrons. That said, the high level of centralisation under ʿAḍud al-Dawla was not maintained after his death. Muqaddasī's statement that 'there was not a thing that crawled that was not registered in one of [ʿAḍud al-Dawla's] books'[219] resonates with those who are familiar with the ruler's *Barīd*, but also implies that he was rather exceptional amongst Buyid rulers in this regard. As Niẓām

215 Miskawayh, *Eclipse*, vol. III, p. 41/vol. VI, pp. 37–8.
216 It is difficult to establish conclusively the evolution of *Barīd*-terminology during this period. The term *askudār*, for instance, may either have been borrowed from the Samanids or simply a Persian word common to all eastern states at the time. The regional variation in postal terminology will be discussed below.
217 Qudāma, *Kharāj*, pp. 125–9. The distance is measured on the assumption that *sikak* in this eastern region were calculated at 2 parasangs, or 12 kilometres a *sikka*. As the crow flies, it is *ca.* 900 kilometres from Shiraz to Baghdad.
218 As Iṣṭakhrī was a native of Kharkh (Charax), his *Kitāb al-masālik wa al-mamālik*, Leiden, 1870, is another instalment in the Characene contribution to Iranian geography, following Isidore of Charax's *Parthian Stations* by some nine centuries.
219 Muqaddasī, *Aḥsan al-taqāsīm*, p. 338.

al-Mulk put it: 'None of the Daylamite kings was more vigilant, clever and farsighted than 'Aḍud al-Dawla; he was a great builder and had lofty aspirations and strong authority.'[220]

The Seljuks

The decline of Buyid power following 'Aḍud al-Dawla's death and the ensuing (and related) lack of centralisation in Buyid realms cannot be held to account for the Seljuks' lack of a *Barīd.* Rather, it would appear that this resulted from an active decision taken by early Seljuk rulers, as Niẓām al-Mulk remarked: 'From ancient times onwards kings have preserved this system [of intelligence agents], except for the house of Seljuk who have shown no interest in the matter.'[221] In his account of the emergence of the Ismā'īlīs and the terror they spread, Bundārī attributes the movement's success to a lack of political surveillance in Seljuk lands and says,

> [The Ismā'īlīs] managed to conceal their affairs since there were no *aṣḥāb akhbār* in the [Seljuk] state. It was customary in the days of the Daylamites and among previous rulers that they would not leave an inch of their country without a *ṣāḥib khabar wa barīd*, and thus they were never unaware of news from remote regions or nearby ones, or of the affairs of obedient and disobedient subjects alike. But then Alp Arslān took charge of the Seljuk state and consulted Niẓām al-Mulk in the matter. [Alp] said to him: 'We do not need a *ṣāḥib khabar* because in every region we have friends and enemies. If the *ṣāḥib khabar* [in a particular region] was motivated by selfish interests he would report our friends as being enemies and our enemies as being friends.' For this reason, the sultan abandoned the custom [of maintaining intelligence agents] on account of this whimsical idea that occurred to him.[222]

Niẓām al-Mulk relates a similar anecdote but says that it was Abū al-Faḍl Sigzī who consulted with Alp Arslān on this issue, rather than himself. In Niẓām al-Mulk's version of the account, the corrupting 'selfish interests' mentioned by Bundārī are plainly described as bribes. If, as Alp Arslān protested, one's intelligence agents are untrustworthy, then the system is pointless. And if the postal systems that were ultimately based on the Abbasid *Barīd* were to be funded and supplied by the central authorities, then this pointless system would be a very expensive one, although Alp Arslān stops short of making this point.[223] Nonetheless, Niẓām al-Mulk concluded

[220] Niẓām al-Mulk, *Siyāsat Nāma*, pp. 101ff./pp. 75ff., where the author follows this statement with a story about 'Aḍud al-Dawla's espionage system.

[221] Ibid., p. 95/p. 71.

[222] Bundārī, *Tārīkh dawlat āl saljūq*, (ed. M. Th. Houtsma), *Histoire des Seldjoucides de l'Iraq par al-Bondari d'après Imâd ad-dîn al-Kâtib al-Isfahânî: texte arabe*, Leiden, 1886, vol. II, pp. 66–7.

[223] It is also possible that the Seljuks' lack of a *Barīd* was entirely the result of their uncouth background: according to Niẓāmī, (*Chahār maqāla*, trans. E. G. Browne, *The Four Discourses*, London, 1921, p. 26), 'Being nomads, ignorant of the conduct of affairs and the high achievements of kings, most of these royal customs became obsolete in [the Seljuks']

that it is better to have intelligence agents, 'because having *aṣḥāb barīd* is one of the rules of state-craft; and when they can be relied upon sufficiently to perform the function we have described, there is no anxiety'.[224] It is possible that it was the Seljuk tribal commanders who rejected the idea of a *Barīd*, not because they feared that the system would be ineffective but because they feared that an effective postal system would compromise their independence.[225] Either way, the important point is that the Seljuks chose not to create and maintain such a system, and it is hardly surprising that they were initially unaware of the Crusaders' arrival in the Near East on the eve of the eleventh century and ill-informed of subsequent developments in Syria.[226]

Thus, by the late eleventh century, in central lands of the Islamic world the *Barīd* was abandoned by the Seljuks,[227] in western lands it was replaced under the Fatimids by pigeon and merchant networks, and in eastern lands under the later Ghaznavids the system was in decline. Nonetheless, the Abbasid *Barīd* continued to exert its influence in the medieval Near East. Not only, as we shall see, did the early Mamluk *Barīd* owe a significant debt to its Abbasid namesake, but from the late tenth century onwards the *Barīd* came to serve in an altogether unexpected context.

The philosophers' *Barīd*

The decline of the *Barīd* as an official system of communication coincided with the use of *Barīd*-related metaphors in the works of leading Muslim philosophers. This is not to say that the two processes were causally related, and it is most unlikely that the philosophers were attempting to immortalise this institution by using its terminology in their works. Rather, the adoption of *Barīd*-terminology in such contexts demonstrates that philosophers and other scholars considered this terminology to be familiar and intelligible throughout the Islamic world, owing to the fact that provincial dynasties perpetuated the Abbasid *Barīd* long after the Abbasids had all but abandoned the institution.

The use of 'roads' as a metaphor in religious contexts was widespread in Near and Far Eastern cultures for centuries. Release from the state of suffering, according to the Buddha, was 'an ancient path, an ancient road, trodden

time, and many essentials of dominion fell into disuse. One of these was the *Dīwān al-Barīd*, from which one can judge of the remainder.' That the equally uncouth Buyids managed to maintain a postal system disproves Niẓāmī's theory.

224 Niẓām al-Mulk, *Siyāsat Nāma*, p. 95/p. 71. 'Umarī, (*Ta'rīf*, pp. 186–7) also holds that the Seljuks abandoned the *Barīd* and only used irregular messengers as and when needed.

225 This is M. Hodgson's view (in *The Venture of Islam. Volume II: The Expansion of Islam in the Middle Periods*, Chicago, 1974, p. 45).

226 On which, see C. Hillenbrand, *The Crusades: Islamic Perspectives*, Edinburgh, 1998, pp. 31–48, esp. pp. 38–40.

227 On the (expected) lack of archaeological evidence for Seljuk postal stations, see Hillenbrand, *Islamic Architecture*, pp. 370–1.

by Buddhas of a bygone age',[228] while the term *ṣirāṭ al-mustaqīm* appears in the Qur'ān 45 times and *sabīl* appears no fewer than 176 times. Accordingly, in Islamic political theory, life was considered to be a caravan-journey through a perilous desert; one's salvation would be achieved through the guidance of an *imām*,[229] and for this reason *imāms* were regularly compared to milestones on the road.[230] Moreover, the fact that God communicates with mankind via messengers, *rusul*, suggests that postal terminology could easily lend itself to metaphors of an Islamic nature.

It was also a commonplace of ancient cultures to speak of divine surveillance in ways that could invite comparisons between the all-knowing postmaster and an omniscient God. In the Bible we are told that angels (from the Greek *angelos*, 'messenger')[231] 'were sent out by the Lord to roam the earth. And ... they reported to the angel of the Lord ... [saying] "we have roamed the earth and have found all the earth dwelling in tranquillity".'[232] Similarly, the Indian gods Varuna and Mitra are said to have had their spies wander the earth and survey the affairs of man.[233] Thus, the *Barīd* and its associated terminology could fit neatly into a metaphorical framework of either divine guidance or divine surveillance.

However, when the *Barīd* surfaces in the works of Muslim philosophers, it is used to express the writer's analysis of sensory perception. The earliest Muslim writer to draw the comparison is Fārābī (d. 950), who writes:

> Sensory perception has both main and subordinate [elements]. The subordinate ones are those famous five senses, consisting of the eyes, the ears, and others. Each of these perceives a particular sensation. As for the main [element], this is where all the information that the five senses have perceived is gathered together. It is as though these five senses are the warners [of the main element] ... and the main [element] is like the king in whose presence the news (*akhbār*) from the provinces is gathered from amongst the reports of his intelligence chiefs (*aṣḥāb akhbārihi*).[234]

The metaphor is taken up by the Ikhwān al-Ṣafā', writing in late tenth-century Basra. In their view,

> All that which is perceived by the senses gathers together around the 'compositive imagination' (*al-mutakhayyila*) just as the letters of the intelligence chiefs [gather] around the *ṣāḥib al-kharīṭa*, who despatches all of these letters to the king.

[228] *Samyutta-Nikaya part two*, London, 1888, p. 106. To Confucius (551–479 BCE) is attributed the statement that 'News of deeds travels faster than the mail.'
[229] In the Qur'ān, Allāh Himself is referred to as a guide (*dalīl*) five times.
[230] Crone, *Political Thought*, pp. 21–2. Similarly, in the modern world, people often refer to the 'milestones' that are reached during one's lifetime.
[231] See above, p. 19.
[232] *Zachariah* 1: 10–11. The New Testament (*1 Peter* 3: 12) states, 'For the eyes of the Lord are on the righteous and His ears are attentive to their prayer.'
[233] *Atharvaveda*, 4.6.14.
[234] Fārābī, *Āthār ahl al-madīna al-fāḍila*, Cairo, 1323 AH, p. 49.

Thereafter, the king reads them, understands their significance, and hands them over to his treasurer (*khāzin*) for safekeeping until they are needed once again.[235]

In a subsequent discussion the authors elaborate on the contribution of each respective sense and state that the sense of sight (*al-quwwa al-bāṣira*) brings the intelligence it gathers 'to the composite imagination (*al-quwwa al-mutakhayyila*), which resides in the front of the brain, and plays the same role for the soul as that played by a watchman (*dīdabān*) and a postmaster (*ṣāḥib al-barīd*) who bring news to the king from one of his provinces'.[236]

This *Barīd* metaphor gathers both momentum and tantalising details in the versions of Ibn Sīnā (d. 1030) and Ghazālī (d. 1111). According to the former,

The five senses are like scattered spies, while the faculty of representation (*al-mutaṣawwira*) is like the prince's postmaster (*ṣāḥib al-barīd*) to whom the spies ultimately return. The compositive imagination (*al-mutakhayyila*) is like the courier (*fayj*) who runs between the *wazīr* and the postmaster, while the estimative faculty (*al-wahm*) is like the *wazīr* and the memory is like a repository of secrets.[237]

The arrangement depicted here has spies delivering information to the postmaster who then sends couriers with the reports to the *wazīr*. The latter analyses the information and deposits it with the treasurer (whose presence is implied by the reference to 'the memory'). Ghazālī's adaptation of the metaphor is similar to Ibn Sīnā's, though for him the 'retentive imagination' (*al-khayāliyya*) is equivalent to the postmaster, while the senses are not spies but 'intelligence chiefs' (*aṣḥāb akhbār*).[238] Owing, no doubt, to the prestige and influence of these authors, this metaphorical framework was repeated and reworked by subsequent Muslim philosophers.[239]

Although Fārābī is the first Muslim writer to employ the analogy, he did not create it, and the origins of this metaphorical framework – known as the 'theory of the inner senses' – is Greek.[240] The postmaster is generally compared in these passages to the human imagination, and as 'al-Fārābī owes his concept of imagination to Aristotle',[241] we should not be surprised to find that Aristotle makes the analogy repeatedly in his *Parva Naturalia*.[242] But this kind of analogy has roots in the Near East that are older than Aristotle: the Memphite Theology (mid third-millennium BCE Egypt) states that 'sight of

[235] Ikhwān al-Ṣafā', *Rasā'il*, vol. II, p. 347. [236] Ibid., vol. III, p. 15.

[237] Ibn Sīnā, *Aḥwāl al-nafs*, Cairo, 1952, p. 160.

[238] Ghazālī, *Iḥyā' ulūm al-dīn*, Cairo, 1348 AH, vol. III, pp. 5, 8; and *Kīmiyā' al-sa'āda*, Cairo, 1343 AH, p. 10, where the *ṣāḥib al-barīd* is inexplicably replaced by a *ṣāḥib al-kharīṭa*.

[239] E.g., al-Rāghib al-Iṣfahānī, *Tafṣīl al-nash'atayn wa taḥṣīl al-sa'ādatayn*, Beirut, 1988, pp. 92–3.

[240] On the 'inner senses', see: E. R. Harvey, *The Inward Wits*, London, 1975. Harvey (ibid., p. 6) quotes the author of the Hippocratic treatise on epilepsy as saying 'to consciousness the brain is the messenger'.

[241] S. Kemal, *The Poetics of al-Fārābī and Avicenna*, Leiden, 1991, p. 89.

[242] Ed. I. Bekker, Berlin, 1831, 437a, 2 and 6; and 461b, 3 (drawn to my attention by Fritz Zimmermann).

the eyes, hearing of the ears, [and] breathing of the nose – they report to the heart. It makes come forth every understanding. As to the tongue, it says what is in the heart.'[243] That senses 'report' to the heart or mind just as spies or messengers report to a postmaster is an obvious comparison to draw and brings to mind the use of the phrase 'eyes and ears' to denote spies in ancient Iran. But even the more developed metaphor of senses/spies in the service of the mind/king was widespread: the Kalachuris of Karnataka (twelfth-century CE India) employed intelligence agents (*karṇams*) that were dubbed 'the five senses of the supreme government'.[244]

What is important here is not the provenance of Fārābī's postal metaphor but its eventual popularity: by the time some of these authors were writing, the *Barīd* was a shadow of its former self in the central lands of the Islamic world. But the use of the *Barīd* in philosophical contexts hardly compensates for the demise of the institution as an efficient system of imperial communication. By the time the Mongols and Mamluks came to establish their own postal systems in the Near East, the *Barīd* was probably more familiar to philosophers than it was to administrators and bureaucrats.

[243] In Ostler, *Empires of the Word*, pp. 113–14. The Qur'ān itself (90: 8–10) states: 'Did We not assign to him two eyes and a tongue and two lips, and guide him on the two highways (*al-najdayni*)?' Although [some of] the senses are related here to 'highways', an unbridged gap between the two remains, and these verses probably played no role in the development of the metaphor.

[244] In A. S. Altekar, *State and Government in Ancient India*, Delhi, 1958, p. 191.

PART III

Conquest and centralisation – the Mongols

CHAPTER 4

The Mongol *Yām* and its legacy

Introduction

Bearing in mind the roles that merchants played in the transmission of news in Near Eastern history, we should not be surprised that the Khwārazm-shāh's governor of Utrār suspected a delegation from Chinggis Khān of espionage, and putting enemy spies to death would have shocked few in the pre-modern world. Unfortunately for the Khwārazm-shāh 'it was the custom of the Tartars never to make peace with those who have killed their envoys until they have wrought vengeance upon them', as one medieval observer put it.[1] In the interest (or with the pretext) of revenge for the massacre of the Mongol merchants and envoys, Chinggis Khān and his successors embarked on a devastating campaign of conquest through Central Asia. Amongst the numerous consequences of these conquests and of the establishment of a Mongol polity in their wake, the one relevant to this study is the creation of a postal system that both provided communications during the conquests and facilitated imperial administration in their aftermath.

The Mongol postal system, usually referred to as the *Yām*,[2] is generally agreed to have been adopted from the Chinese *Yi* (or *Li*) system of communication, which was introduced to Chinggis through the Uighur and Khitan advisors who had a formative influence on the development of Mongol bureaucratic practices and institutions.[3] Prominent examples of such functionaries include T'a-T'a-Tung'a, Chinggis' Uighur secretary, and Chinkai,

[1] John Pian Carpini, *The Journey of Friar John of Pian de Carpine to the Court of Kuyuk Khan, 1245–1247*, (trans. W. W. Rockhill), London, 1900, p. 30. The inviolability of envoys in Mongol society and the episode at Utrār are described in *The Secret History of the Mongols*, (trans. U. Onon), London, 2001, §254, (pp. 241–5).

[2] The term *yām* is explained as an 'early loanword in Mongolian, probably direct from Chinese *cham*' in G. Clauson, *Etymological Dictionary of Pre-13th Century Turkish*, Oxford, 1972, p. 933 s.v. YM. We shall return to the question of this term's etymology below. See also G. Doerfer, *Türkische und mongolische Elemente im Neupersischen*, Wiesbaden, 1963–75, no. 1812.

[3] Gazagnadou, *La Poste*, pp. 45–7; D. Morgan, *The Mongols*, Oxford 1986, p. 107; and others.

the Nestorian Kereit advisor to Chinggis, Ögödei, and Güyüg, who established the Mongols' chancery. The conquest of Khitan territories was another important step in this process, and Khitan administrators are credited with establishing many of the Mongols' administrative tools.[4] Thus, the basic idea that non-Mongols contributed significantly to the development of Mongol bureaucratic institutions is beyond debate. Quantifying the relative measure of influence that each group or nation had in this regard is trickier, and the issue is still debated by scholars.[5] But the Uighurs and Khitans were undoubtedly influential, and these groups transmitted Chinese practices to the Mongols indirectly.

There are, however, three reasons why associating the Mongol *Yām* with the Chinese *Yi* may be misleading and even unhelpful. First, it has been argued that regardless of the Mongols' dependence on their conquered populations for most administrative needs, the basic idea that one can send a message with a mounted courier would have been obvious to Mongol leaders during the earliest stages of their conquests.[6] And although a Khitan administrator is famously recorded as having said to Ögödei, 'The Empire was created on horseback, but it will not be governed on horseback',[7] this statement did not hold true for the *Yām*. By this logic, the Mongols would not have had to rely on conquered peoples in establishing a basic system of communication. Second, those features that are common to the *Yām* and the *Yi* and that have been adduced to show direct Chinese influence on the postal system are not as persuasive as they may seem. The word *yām* itself and the use of a tablet of authority by couriers (Persian *pā'iza*, from Chinese *p'ai-tse*, Mongolian *gerege*) are generally assumed to clinch the argument for Chinese origins. However, the term *yām* is attested in an eighth-century Judeo-Persian document from Central Asia, with the meaning of 'postal courier'. This indicates that the word entered Inner Asian vocabulary centuries before the Mongols are said to have adopted

4 For in-depth and influential discussions of the Uighur/Khitan influence on Mongol administration, see: P. Buell, 'Sino-Khitan Administration in Mongol Bukhara', *JAH* 13 (1979), 121–51; I. de Rachewiltz, 'Personnel and Personalities in North China in the Early Mongol Period', *JESHO* 9 (1966), 88–144; and 'Sino-Mongol Culture Contacts in the 13th Century', unpublished PhD thesis, Australian National University, 1960.

5 Cf. D. O. Morgan, 'Who Ran the Mongol Empire?', *JRAS* (1982), 124–36, who argues that Uighurs, Khitans, Persians, and Chinese each deserve some of the credit. In a subsequent article, which deals with the Īl-khānid period, Morgan adjusts his previous conclusions to make room for Mongol influence (D. O. Morgan, 'Mongol or Persian: The Government of Īl-khānid Iran', *HMEIS* 3 (1996), 62–76).

6 As argued by D. O. Morgan, 'Reflections on Mongol Communications in the Ilkhanate', in *Studies in Honour of C. E. Bosworth*, vol. II (ed. C. Hillenbrand), Leiden, 2000, pp. 375–85 at p. 384.

7 The administrator was Ch'u Ts'ai, who served both Chinggis and Ögödei (in. J. J. Saunders, 'The Nomad as Empire-Builder: A Comparison of the Arab and Mongol Conquests' in his *Muslims and Mongols*, (ed. G. Rice), Christchurch, NZ, 1977, pp. 36–66, at p. 48). That the Mongol postal system *was* an institution that could 'be governed on horseback' is a point to which we shall return below.

the Chinese *Yi* and the term *yām*,[8] a fact that appears to have escaped scholars of the *Yām*.[9] Similarly, the term for postal mounts used in the *Yām* is *ūlāgh*, which is a Central Asian rather than a Chinese word.[10] Furthermore, although the *pā'iza* of the Mongols is strikingly similar in its form, usage, and name to the Chinese *p'ai-tse*, such tablets of authority had been in use in these regions for centuries: Apollonius of Tyana, writing in the first century CE, tells us that on his travels from Ecbatana to India 'The guiding camel bore a golden tablet on the forehead, as a sign for all they met with, that the traveller was one of the king's friends and travelled with royal authorization.'[11] Third, the assumption that the *Yi* was simply lifted by the Mongols in creating their *Yām* does not appreciate the unique topographical conditions that characterised China on the one hand and Central Asia, the Near East, and Southern Russia on the other. The importance of rivers in China and the virtual absence of them along the Eurasian steppe route and in most of Iran, to name but one example,[12] meant that even the conscious adoption of a Chinese system of communications by the Mongols would have resulted in a *Yām* that diverged in many respects from the *Yi*. This point not only concerns the origins of the *Yām* but also pertains to the postal systems employed contemporaneously by various branches of the Mongol Empire; Olbricht's oft-quoted study on the Mongol postal system in China may tell us a lot about the *Yām* in China, but much less about the *Yām* elsewhere.[13] Indeed, scholars have noticed

[8] The document is published in B. Utas, 'The Judeo-Persian Fragment from Dandān Uiliq', *Orientala Suecana* 17 (1968), 123–36 at 128 (Persian text)/130 (translation). The text reads: '[*niga*]*r kū jāmak-ī man pa chē rasad* . . .'; the term *jāmak* was translated by Utas as 'little bowl', but a revised translation by V. B. Moreen, in conjunction with Utas, has amended the word to mean 'postman, post-horse' in light of the previous line that refers to twenty letters (*nāma*) sent by the writer (in V. B. Moreen, *In Queen Esther's Garden*, New Haven, 2000, pp. 22ff.), a possibility that Utas had considered in the notes to his original translation (Utas, 'Judeo-Persian Fragment', 131–2 n. 3).

[9] It should be noted that Utas's publication of this document was not available to P. Pelliot ('Sur yam ou jam, "relais postale" ', *T'oung Pao* 27 (1930), 192–5). Clausen (*Etymological Dictionary*, p. 933) and Gazagnadou (*La Poste*, p. 45 and p. 135 n. 16) also appear to be unaware of the contents of this document.

[10] For the etymology of *ūlāgh*, see W. Kotwicz, 'Contributions aux études altaïques A: les termes concernant le service des relais postaux', *Rocznik Orientalistyczny* 16 (1950); and G. Doerfer, *Türkische und mongolische Elemente im Neupersischen*, no. 617. This is in stark contrast to the prevalence of foreign (mainly Persian) terms in the early *Barīd*.

[11] In Herzfeld, *Zoroaster*, p. 230.

[12] Another example is the complete lack of wheeled vehicles in the Near East during this period, despite the use of such vehicles in China (cf. Bulliet, *Camel and the Wheel*; and J. Masson-Smith Jr., 'Mongol Nomadism and Middle Eastern Geography', in R. Amitai-Preiss and D. O. Morgan, *The Mongol Empire and its Legacy*, Leiden, 1999, pp. 39–56 at p. 45).

[13] P. Olbricht, *Das Postwesen in China unter der Mongolenherrschaft im 13. und 14. Jahrhundert*, Wiesbaden, 1954. Even within China, the topographical conditions were considerably varied, and methods of transport and communication differed from one region to another. As an ancient Chinese proverb has it: 'South boat, North horse.'

that Olbricht's description of the Chinese *Yām* portrays a system that is far better organised and less susceptible to maladministration than that of the Īl-khānids.[14]

Despite these objections, it is very likely that at least initially the Mongols used the *Yi* as the model for their *Yām*. The argument that riding a horse while bearing a message is an idea that would have come naturally and independently to the Mongols is unsatisfactory on two grounds. First, the *Yām* was a sophisticated postal system that comprised way-stations, written documents allowing the bearer to claim fresh mounts, lodgings, and food, and so forth. This level of bureaucratisation was atypical of traditional (pre-Chinggis) Mongol society. Second, although riding horses was an essential part of the Mongols' cultural baggage, being posted at permanent stations and manning those stations go against the grain of Central Asian nomadic life – especially along roads that did not overlap with the pastoral routes.[15] Thus, the perceptible influence of Uighur and Khitan officials in most other aspects of the early Mongol state would suggest that these Sinified officials were also instrumental in establishing the *Yām*,[16] even if we are to dismiss the term *yām* and the use of postal tablets as evidence for this argument.

Creation of the *Yām*

Wherever the idea of creating a postal system originated, there is little doubt that in some regions it was already in use during Chinggis' lifetime. In many ways, Chinggis' career and legacy mirror those of Muḥammad. Both are said to have been illiterate members of nomadic societies who managed to unite the fragmented tribes of their homeland and create a polity in regions that were unaccustomed to such structures. Both also created a supra-tribal identity and brought an original code of law to their respective nations; and both enjoyed military successes that would embolden and inspire their successors long after their deaths. It is also noteworthy that in both cases, upon

[14] Morgan, 'Reflections', 379–80. Morgan suggests that the difference may be due to the nature of Chinese and Persian sources; as the latter were concerned with the Īl-khāns' reforms, it is natural that they focused on those aspects of the *Yām* that were in need of reform and in doing so give the impression that the Īl-khānid *Yām* was constantly in disarray.

[15] As argued in J. Masson-Smith Jr., 'Mongol and Nomadic Taxation', *HJAS* 30 (1970), 46–85 at 70–1.

[16] Moreover, the Khitans had recent experience in gathering and transmitting intelligence in military contexts, experience that would have been acquired in regions that shared topographical features with the central lands of the Mongol Empire. For Khitan espionage on the eve of the Mongol conquests, see M. Biran, 'Like a Mighty Wall: The Armies of the Qara Khitai', *JSAI* 25 (2001), 44–91 at 70; and her *The Empire of the Qara Khitai in Eurasian History*, Cambridge, 2005, part 2. Chinggis' own arrangements for gathering intelligence are described in *Secret History*, §141–2 (pp. 115–16).

that leader's death, the energies of the newly created armies were redirected, in the first case by ʿUmar I, in the second by Ögödei, against the sedentary societies who were unfortunate enough to be neighbours of the nascent conquest-states.[17] The major difference between the two cases is that the Arab conquerors had a lasting impression on the civilisations they conquered, eventually imposing their language and religion on others, whereas the Mongols tended to be absorbed into the civilisations they conquered.[18] They never quite left their *ordus* ('camps'), but nor did their subject populations ever adopt the Mongolian language or embrace Shamanism. The obvious consequence of this is that the caliphate lasted for over five centuries, while the Mongols never managed to rule for more than a century anywhere outside of Mongolia itself.

For the purposes of this study, what is interesting is how these conquests were actually effected, given the huge expanses of land involved. It has been argued above that during the Arab conquests the idea of the *Barīd*, which had been known to the inhabitants of Arabia owing to the imperial (Byzantine and Sasanid) penetration of this region, was adopted from the neighbouring states and adapted to the Arabs' needs. As is often the case with early Islamic history, the evidence is debatable: documents and inscriptions make it clear that the term *barīd* had entered the Arabs' lexicon at a very early stage, but details of the implementation of this idea can only be sketched with broad strokes. The Mongol conquests, by contrast, afford us a unique glimpse into the consolidation and extension of a nomadic conquest movement and may serve as an historical paradigm that illuminates the situation in the Near East of the seventh century. Most of the sources for the *Yām* during the conquests are near contemporary – one, the travels of the Buddhist priest Ch'ang Ch'un, was written in the 1220s – and even those that are not are based on traceable sources that date from this period.

According to these sources, Chinggis availed himself of *īlchīs*, or 'envoys', whose traffic along the routes is ubiquitous in accounts from the period.[19] In his descriptions of Chinggis' *yāsās*, Juwaynī explains that when the Mongol territories increased,

[17] A useful but somewhat dated comparison between the Arab and Mongol conquests may be found in Saunders, 'The Nomad'. Saunders saw a religious dimension to the Mongol conquests (ibid., pp. 41–2) and even compares the Prophetic *ḥadīths* with the sayings or *bilik* of Chinggis. A. Khazanov's more recent essay ('Muhammad and Jenghiz Khan Compared: The Religious Factor in World Empire Building', *Comparative Studies in Society and History* 35iii (1993), 461–79) focuses on religious aspects of the two conquest movements to the exclusion of military and administrative issues, and appears to be indebted to P. Crone, *Slaves on Horses*, Cambridge, 1980, pp. 18–26.

[18] Compare Horace's statement that 'Greece, once captured, captured its wild conqueror, and instilled arts into boorish Rome ...' (*Epistles Book II*, 1.156, quoted in Ostler, *Empires of the Word*, p. 250).

[19] Cf. Gazagnadou, *La Poste*, pp. 45ff.

> [I]t became essential to ascertain the activities of their enemies, and it was also necessary to transport goods from the West to the East and from the Far East to the West. Therefore, throughout the length and breadth of the land, they established *yams*, and made arrangements for the upkeep and expenses of each *yam*, assigning thereto a fixed number of men and beasts as well as food, drink, and other necessities.[20]

Juwaynī's data may well be anachronistic, but the point he makes is important: the *Yām* was established in response to a practical need that arose in light of the Mongol conquests. That this happened during Chinggis' lifetime is beyond doubt – the formal agreement to erect postal lines within the various conquered regions is said to have taken place at a Mongol assembly (*quriltay*) in 1218,[21] and the travel account of Ch'ang Ch'un, who made his way from China by land to eastern Iran between 1220 and 1224, confirms that a postal system was in place. Ch'ang Ch'un himself used the system, witnessed postal couriers on his travels, and followed delineated postal routes throughout his journey to Samarqand, Balkh, and Northern India.[22] Chinggis even sent him a special *pā'iza*,[23] on which was written, 'This man is empowered to act with the same freedom as I myself should exercise, had I come in person.'[24]

The *Secret History of the Mongols*, a near-contemporary source which, unlike most sources for Mongol history, is not tainted by the embittered perspective of a conquered population, concludes with three sections on the establishment of the *Yām* in light of the early Mongol conquests.[25] A superficial reading of these passages suggests that it was Ögödei who ordered and carried out the establishment of a regular system of communication. However, a nuanced reading of the text alludes to the realities of communication before Ögödei's innovations and sheds light on both Chinggis' own arrangements in this regard and on the precise nature of Ögödei's reforms.[26] The decision to establish the *Yām* is said to have been taken in 1229, although it appears to have been implemented no earlier than 1234, and in some regions perhaps even later.[27] The text of these reforms reads as follows:

[20] Juwaynī in J. A. Boyle (trans.), *The History of the World Conqueror*, Manchester, 1958, vol. I, p. 33.

[21] Gazagnadou, *La Poste*, p. 45.

[22] In A. Waley (trans.), *Ch'ang-Ch'un: The Travels of an Alchemist*, London, 1931. On Ch'ang Ch'un using postal horses: pp. 50, 119, 125, 133 and 158 n. 4; on postal couriers along the way: pp. 52, 54, 72, 75, 77, and 95; on specific postal routes: pp. 66 and 121.

[23] On the *pā'iza*, see S. S. Blair, 'A Mongol Envoy', in B. O'Kane (ed.), *The Iconography of Islamic Art: Studies in Honour of Robert Hillenbrand*, Edinburgh, 2005, pp. 45–60, esp. 50–4; and A. Qūchānī, '*Pā'iza*', *Mīrāth-i Farhangī* 17 (1997), 42–5.

[24] In Ch'ang Ch'un, *Travels*, p. 48. Later, Chinggis orders that Ch'ang Ch'un be allowed to 'travel in comfort, by easy stages' (ibid., pp. 60–1).

[25] *Secret History*, §279–81 (pp. 274–8).

[26] This was first argued by Morgan, 'Reflections', pp. 377–9.

[27] For the dates 1229 and 1234, see Olbricht, *Postwesen*, pp. 40–1. For evidence that some of these measures were only introduced *ca.* 1237, see de Rachewiltz, 'Sino-Mongol Culture Contacts', 428–32, n. 271.

[At present,] our messengers gallop across people's [settlements] and [thus not only] delay [our] official business [but] cause suffering to the people [of] the nation. We shall now settle [this matter] once and for all by providing post-station keepers and post-horse keepers from among the various thousands in every quarter and establishing post-stations at various places. Does it not make sense for our messengers to gallop along [the lines of] post-stations rather than across the people's [settlements], except in urgent cases? When Chanai and Bolqadar, who understand [these things], made [these suggestions] to Us, I thought that they were right and said: 'Let elder brother [Chaghadai] decide whether the suggestions deserve to be implemented and whether he approves them'... elder brother [Chaghadai] replied: 'You ask my opinion on these matters. I approve all [of the suggestions]. Act in accordance with them.' Elder brother [Chaghadai] sent a further [message] saying: 'I will have post-stations [established] here that join [yours] to mine. I will send a messenger to Batu and get him to [establish] post-stations that join [his to mine].' He sent [the following message]: 'Of all the matters [that have been discussed], establishing post-stations is the most suitable proposal.'[28]

The implication of this crucial text is that messengers (*īlchīs*) travelled between the Mongol leaders even before routes and stations were established – the irony of sending official messengers to discuss the creation of a messenger system being immediately obvious. The pre-*Yām* messengers do not appear to have followed established postal routes or to have benefited from the existence of postal stations. This cannot have been the case everywhere, as Ch'ang Ch'un's travels indicate, but whatever rudimentary arrangements had existed lacked systematisation, which caused delays for the couriers and was a nuisance to anyone unlucky enough to be in their way.[29] That Chaghadai and Batu were consulted in the matter and complied with the suggestion suggests that the *Yām* was an 'international' institution, uniformly diffused throughout the Mongol territories.[30]

Whether Ögödei created the *Yām* or merely reformed an existing system is debatable, but either way his order was heeded. The *Secret History* tells us that 'He got them to measure the locations of the various stages [along the route] and to establish the post-stations. He put Arajan and Toquchar in charge, and provided [exactly] twenty post-horse keepers at each of the stages [where there were] post-stations and roughly twenty post-horse keepers at each of the [other] stages.'[31] Ögödei was immensely proud of his achievement in this regard and considered it to be the second most important deed of his

[28] *Secret History*, §279 (pp. 274–5).
[29] Even Ch'ang Ch'un was described by Sun Hsi in 1228 as 'setting out to cover thousands of miles of most difficult country, through regions never mapped, across deserts unwatered by rain or dew' (in Ch'ang Ch'un, *Travels*, p. 44), attesting to the fact that the availability of a postal infrastructure was irregular.
[30] Already in Chinggis' lifetime, we hear of Ögödei (Ch'ang Ch'un, *Travels*, p. 76) and Chaghadai (ibid., pp. 85 and 95–6) constructing roads and bridges during military campaigns.
[31] *Secret History*, §280 (p. 276).

reign as *Qā'ān*.[32] Interestingly, his fourth most important deed was to post scouts amongst the people of all cities, to establish civic order.[33]

The reports of Juwaynī and the *Secret History* are confirmed by Rashīd al-Dīn, according to whom Ögödei established the *Yām*, since 'there was [much] coming and going of envoys both from the princes [to the court of *Qā'ān*] and from the court to the prince upon important and necessary business'.[34] Rashīd al-Dīn, perhaps drawing on older Mongolian works such as the *Altan Debter*, then enumerates the names of the various officials appointed to help establish the *Yām*. The consensus about the *terminus post quem* of the *Yām* establishes that within a single generation of the early Mongol conquests a complex postal network served the nomadic conquerors in the basic capacities of transmitting goods, people, and information across vast expanses of land. It is likely that the Arab conquests were no different in this regard, as argued in our treatment of the early *Barīd*. As with the *Barīd*, the initial creation of the *Yām* was followed by a series of improvements, innovations, and reforms under subsequent leaders.

The *Yām* until Möngke

Routes and stations

Although the highest echelons of society were greatly affected by the Mongol invasions, everyone else in the Near East and Central Asia was more or less untouched, until the second half of the thirteenth century. While many factors contributed to this, perhaps the most important one is climatic: the Mongols, as nomads of the Eurasian steppe, felt at home on the road. Seasonal migrations from north-east to north-west had been part of the natural rhythm of nomadic life in Eurasia since time immemorial, and millennia of experience contributed to cultural and civilisational methods of dealing with the natural (and often harsh) conditions that prevailed in this horizontal slice of the world. However, vertical migration and conquests are less appealing to the Eurasian steppe nomads, the seasonal migrations between winter quarters (*qishlāq*) and summer quarters (*yailāq*) notwithstanding. It is not just that Mongol migration routes are determined by grazing pastures (though this is certainly a central consideration), they are also determined by the weather. Ancient Greeks and, later, Muslims divided the world into climatic zones (Greek *klima*, Arabic *iqlīm*) because they recognised the impact that one's proximity to or distance from the equator had on life in a world that had not mastered the elements. Hence, when Chinggis and Ögödei made headway into Persia, it was the north that was

[32] Ibid., p. 277. The most important deed was conquering the 'Jaqut' people of Northern China.
[33] Ibid.
[34] Rashīd al-Dīn, in J. A. Boyle (trans.), *The Successors of Genghis Khan*, New York and London, 1971, vol. III, pp. 55–6 (translation modified).

affected, while southern Persia would have to wait for Hülegü to experience directly the effects of Mongol rule. The reality was that neither central China nor the Near East was really in the Mongols' climatic comfort zone, and for this reason these regions were initially spared.

One important ramification of this horizontal expansion is that, within a few decades of Mongol rule, a politically unified route from eastern Europe to East Asia was open to travellers, and the famous *pax mongolica* ('Mongol peace') allowed merchants, pilgrims, messengers, and envoys to make the entire journey from West to East and back.[35] Although Roman envoys (or Western traders claiming such official status) are said to have reached China in 166 CE, as a general rule the Silk Road trade was made up of a chain of intermediaries who transported goods across their own lands, only to transfer them to neighbouring merchants who did the same.[36] The *pax mongolica* had two effects on relations between East and West during this period. First, it allowed European political envoys to make the entire journey to the Far East, in what was fast becoming a routine (though arduous) journey, rather than a miraculous one. Consequently, knowledge of the East was generally purged of the *mirabilia* that had characterised attitudes towards China and India in ancient times. Second, it meant that a wide array of trade goods was considerably cheaper at both ends of the route owing to the lack of intermediaries demanding progressive mark-ups. For the purposes of this study, the *pax mongolica* was important for two further reasons. First, the improbably long overland route opened to travellers was provided with postal stations and horses and, this being so, represents perhaps the longest postal route in pre-modern history. Second, the European travellers who used this route often wrote detailed accounts of their journeys, providing us with eye-witness testimony of the workings of the *Yām* in various regions and periods.

Three accounts of the route from Europe to Asia during this period are worth our attention here. The first is that of John Pian Carpini, who travelled to the court of Güyüg from 1245 to 1247; the second is that of C. de Bridia, a mysterious figure who was on the road *ca.* 1247; and the third is that of William of Rubruck, who made his famous journey eastwards from 1253 to 1255.[37] In many ways, Carpini's account is the most interesting of the three. All de Bridia has to say in this context is that,

[35] It has long been recognised that a decisive majority of travellers along this route were Westerners journeying eastwards, and not vice versa.

[36] An enormous amount of scholarship is dedicated to Silk-Road studies. A good summary may be found in T. Allsen, *Culture and Conquest in Mongol Eurasia*, Cambridge, 2001, chapter 2.

[37] Carpini: John Pian Carpini, *Journey*; C. de Bridia, *The Vinland Map and the Tartar Relation* (R. A. Skelton, T. E. Marston, and G. D. Painter), New Haven and London, 1965, section 3: 'The Tartar Relation' (ed./trans. G. D. Painter); William of Rubruck: *The Journey of William of Rubruck to the Eastern Parts of the World, 1253–55, as Narrated by Himself, with Two Accounts of the Earlier Journey of John of Pian de Carpine*, (trans. W. W. Rockhill), London, 1900.

Envoys sent by [the Mongol ruler] or to him are given their keep free of charge together with post-horses, but foreign envoys are given only meagre keep ... I therefore shudder to describe or enumerate the hardships undergone by our friars ... O, how often they rode more than 30 Bohemian miles [*ca.* 210 kilometres] in a single day on the Tartars' post-horses, tasting neither bread nor water but obtaining with difficulty at noon or in the night only a little thin broth of boiled millet! That they rode so far is not surprising, for as soon as their horses grew weary, even before they could begin to rest, the Tartars brought up fresh strong mounts.[38]

Although his tone is generally negative, it would appear that de Bridia had a grudging admiration for the efficiency of the *Yām*. William of Rubruck, by contrast, has nothing even remotely positive to say about his journey; an obese man, he found the journey particularly trying, and his constant whingeing about the conditions under which he travelled contributes little to our understanding of the *Yām* during this period.[39]

Carpini's account is relatively full and informative. On the first leg of his journey, through Germany and eastern Europe, the 'King of Bohemia' gave him official letters, escorts, and horses, as well as general funds to defray the costs of his travels.[40] Upon reaching Eurasian steppe terrain, however, he and his entourage were told that the horses they were riding would not be able to negotiate the snowy routes in the way that Mongol ('Tartary') horses could, and they acquired suitable mounts in their stead,[41] reminding us that even in the smallest of ways the local topography and climatic conditions dictated the details of travel. Mongols patrolling the routes interrogated Carpini as to the nature of his journey, and when it became clear that he was an official envoy, he was supplied with packhorses and a guide and set off to Batu's camp 'riding as fast as horses could go trotting, for we had fresh horses three or four times nearly every day, we rode from morning to night, and very often even at night ...'.[42] Having entered Mongol lands, he travelled for three weeks,

[R]iding hard ... along all this [part of the] route we travelled very fast, for our Tartars had been ordered to take us to the solemn court [of Güyüg] which had already been convened for several years for the election of an emperor, so that we might be present at it. So we had to rise at dawn and travel till night without a stop; often we arrived so late that we did not eat at night, but that which we should have eaten at night was given

[38] C. de Bridia, *Vinland Map*, pp. 95–6. Painter (ibid., pp. 95–6, n. 2) compares the alleged speed of de Bridia's postal journey with those of Carpini and William of Rubruck, and concludes that de Bridia must be exaggerating, as a 'Bohemian mile' was estimated at 7 kilometres, and neither of the other envoys achieved anything near the 200 kilometres a day claimed by de Bridia. It should be noted, however, that although the figure of 30 Bohemian miles is almost certainly an exaggeration, express couriers are known to have achieved much quicker speeds using the *Yām*, as we shall see below.

[39] The fact that he repeatedly misuses the term *iam* in referring to the station-masters of the postal system may reflect his imperfect grasp of the contemporary situation (William of Rubruck, *Journey*, pp. 101, and 160–1).

[40] Carpini, *Journey*, p. 2. [41] Ibid., p. 4. [42] Ibid., pp. 6, and 8.

us in the morning; and we went as fast as the horses could trot, for there was no lack of horses, having usually fresh horses during the day, those which we left being sent back ... and in this fashion we rode rapidly along without interruption.[43]

Carpini appears to be more understanding about the variable standards of treatment offered along the road by his Mongol hosts, accepting that the need to arrive at Güyüg's court as soon as possible entailed discomforts. These travel accounts demonstrate that the *pax mongolica* benefited from a postal infrastructure that, in turn, allowed the unified Mongol lands to enjoy the fruits of their considerable efforts in facilitating the journeys of envoys and foreign merchants.

But all this came at a cost and – as is often the case in the pre-modern world – it was the simple peasants living along the routes who were expected to meet that cost. Although the *Secret History* makes it clear that Ögödei's postal reforms were meant to alleviate the chaos created by the traffic of couriers, there is little doubt that these reforms were not entirely successful, if at all. Rashīd al-Dīn tells us that Möngke instituted reforms aimed at 'relieving the people and alleviating all manner of compulsory labour',[44] reforms that included limiting the use of the *Yām* throughout the empire. It is not just that the general population had to serve as station-masters and supply the stations with fodder and associated supplies, but Möngke's reforms of the *Yām* are specifically mentioned in the context of easing the burden of relinquishing horses to the envoys, merchants, and couriers who swept through their towns. Rashīd al-Dīn writes:

And since after the death of Güyüg Khān many of the *khātūns* and princes had issued *yarlīghs* and *pā'izas* without number to the people, had dispatched ambassadors to all parts of the empire, and had given protection to noble and base on the pretext of their being *ortaqs*, etc., [Möngke] issued a *yarlīgh* instructing each one of them to conduct an inquiry in his own territory and call in all the *yarlīghs* and *pā'izas* which the people had received from them and the other princes during the reigns of Chinggis-Khān, Ögödei Qā'ān, and Güyüg Khān ... As for the great *īlchīs*, they were not to have the use of more than fourteen post-horses: they should proceed from *yām* to *yām* and not seize the people's animals en route. In the reign of Qā'ān it had been the custom for merchants to come to Mongolia on post-horses. [Möngke] denounced this practice, saying: 'Merchants journey to and fro for the sake of gain. What is the point in their riding post-horses?' And he commanded them to travel on their own animals. [Möngke] likewise commanded ambassadors not to enter any town or village in which they had no business and not to take more than the amount of provisions allotted to them.[45]

[43] Ibid., p. 18. [44] In Rashīd, *Successors*, p. 218.
[45] Ibid., p. 219 (translation modified). Juwaynī (*World Conqueror*, pp. 598–9) has a near-identical passage, suggesting that he and Rashīd al-Dīn were drawing on a common source.

Administration

Möngke's postal reforms intended to solve three inter-related problems. The first problem was the proliferation of *pā'iza*s, particularly those authorised by previous rulers, which clearly increased the volume of official traffic along the routes.[46] This traffic disrupted and inconvenienced ordinary travellers, and ensuring that *pā'iza*s (and the *Yām* in general) were used only sparingly promised to improve the situation considerably. The second problem was the practice of requisitioning mounts from ordinary travellers in the name of official service. Ögödei's reform of the *Yām* was meant – at least in part – to rectify similar practices that were current during an earlier period, and it would appear that, although *īlchī*s do not seem to have been straying from the official roads into neighbouring villages as before, they still tended to interrupt their missions to seize horses, at a cost both to ordinary travellers and to the speed of the mission. The third problem was the use of the *Yām*'s facilities by merchants. This is related to the first problem in that it meant that more mounts and fodder had to be provided by the local population. We have already seen that merchants had a complex relationship with official systems of communication: on occasion they helped to provide a postal service in the absence of more reliable, official options; in other cases they made use of an official postal system themselves, usually by way of abuse of the system. In the pre-Möngke period, however, merchants appear to have legitimately enjoyed full use of the *Yām*. Möngke's objection to this situation may be over-simplistic: the roles that international merchants played in the dissemination of information about distant lands and in supplying the political elite with merchandise explain why the *Yām* was at their disposal.[47] Thus Möngke's measures not only lifted a considerable burden from the shoulders of the local population but must also have cut into the profits of merchants, who would now have to cover their own travel expenses.[48]

Möngke's reign as *Qā'ān* also had an effect on the *Yām* in less direct ways. It is well known that Möngke's succession in 1251 was not a smooth affair, as it represented a victory for Tolui's branch of the family at the expense of Ögödei's. Chaghadai's branch of the family was also displeased with the outcome, although the descendants of Jochi prospered as the 'Golden Horde' under Batu. In other words, the empire disintegrated into various 'nations' as a result of Möngke's succession. Some have even seen this period

[46] Juwaynī tells us that in the region of Khurasan during this period Körgüz 'established *yām*s in various places complete with horses and other necessities in order that the people might not be put to inconvenience by the *īlchī*s', suggesting that the problem was being addressed throughout Mongol lands (in Juwaynī, *World Conqueror*, p. 501).

[47] It is worth remembering that in Juwaynī's account of the establishment of the *Yām*, the system was created since it was 'necessary to transport goods from the West to the East and from the Far East to the West', amongst other reasons.

[48] As perceptively noted by T. Allsen (*Mongol Imperialism*, London, 1987, p. 160).

as 'the dissolution of the Mongol Empire',[49] and in many ways it was. The fragmentation of the empire had serious ramifications for the integrity of Mongol territories, and relations between the various 'nations' of the empire were often strained. Berke, who succeeded Batu as ruler of the Golden Horde, converted to Islam and clashed continuously with the early Īl-khāns, to whom we shall return. This rivalry lasted nearly a century and affected Mongol advances in the Near East, especially in light of Berke's alliance with the Mamluks. Stability on the roads was affected, and it is no coincidence that we have few accounts of foreign envoys making their way from Europe to the Far East during the ensuing decades.

But this dissolution of the empire meant that the various regional leaders could focus on their own, more manageable lands, and Möngke's brothers Qubilai and Hülegü were able to conquer China and Iran–Iraq respectively. Thus it is with Hülegü's career and the establishment of the Īl-khānid dynasty that the *Yām* became a Near Eastern institution, and within a few decades – with the careers of Aḥmad/Tegüder and, more importantly, Ghāzān – it became an 'Islamic' postal system.

The *Yām* under the Īl-khāns[50]

Although Qubilai's conquest of China and Hülegü's conquest of the Near East were set into motion by the same political and historical forces, their outcomes from the perspective of contemporary Chinese and Near Eastern populations could not have been more different. Qubilai's Sinophilia had no parallel in Hülegü's attitude to Iran, Iraq, and those small parts of Syria where he made progress. Both universal histories (often written under the patronage of Mongol rulers) and local accounts of Hülegü's campaigns in the Near East give the unambiguous impression that these campaigns were traumatic for a decisive majority of inhabitants in the regions affected. The best efforts of Mongol-friendly revisionism can do little more than put a positive spin on what was a bloody and destructive episode of Mongol history.[51] The almost inevitable deaths associated with military conquest, the economic devastation caused by upsetting the fragile *qanāt* system that supported Iranian agriculture, and the symbolism of sacking the Abbasid capital at Baghdad all contribute to the negative image of the Mongols in Near Eastern memory.

49 Cf. P. Jackson, 'The Dissolution of the Mongol Empire', *Central Asiatic Journal* 22 (1978), 186–244.

50 The only treatment of this subject is that of Morgan, 'Reflections', which, though very useful, is confessedly preliminary and limited in scope. Although, strictly speaking, the term Īl-khāns refers only to those Mongol rulers in Persia who assumed this title (ending with Ghāzān, who styled himself a 'Khān'), here 'Īl-khānate' will refer to the period of the Mongols in Iran, until 1335, in conformity with modern usage.

51 For recent statements of the revisionist case, see G. Lane, *Early Mongol Rule in Thirteenth-Century Iran*, London, 2003; and C. V. Findley, *The Turks in World History*, Oxford, 2004.

As may be expected, the Mongol penetration of the Near East was less than incisive; the establishment of capitals at Marāgha, Ujān, Tabrīz, and Sulṭāniyya confirms what we know about the Mongols' loyalty to their natural climatic zones, and these cities had the added distinction of serving both caravan traffic and the pasturage needs of the Mongol rulers.[52] Similarly, the armies of the Īl-khāns were concentrated in three regions: Anatolia, Azerbayjān, and greater Khurasan, regions that were convenient both for pasturage/climate reasons[53] and for their proximity to the Īl-khānate's borders with hostile neighbours. Furthermore, the early Īl-khāns appear to have maintained close ties with Mongols in China, the very title 'Īl-khān' indicating a certain measure of deference to the Yüan ruler. This ensured a steady flow of envoys between the two courts, requiring an efficient route system and resulting in exchanges of political and military intelligence that was vital to the Īl-khāns, who were surrounded by enemies and rivals.[54] But there were two aspects of the *Yām* during this period that were in urgent need of attention: the state of the routes and the funding and general administration of the system.

The official routes – both within the Īl-khānate and between it and the other Mongol regions – were not always well maintained or secure, and political instabilities made overland travel unsafe and caused delays. This explains why it took almost five years for Qubilai's envoys (from China) to reach Abaqa (in Iran) and deliver an official patent, a crown, and the customary robe of honour that were central to the process of investiture. Other envoys endured similar delays or opted to travel by sea.[55] As distinct from the sources for the *Cursus Publicus*, the caliphal *Barīd*, or the Mamluk *Barīd*, contemporary descriptions of the *Yām* do not provide detailed descriptions of the imperial overland routes used by couriers in the Īl-khānate.[56]

It can only be assumed that couriers adhered to the traditional roads of Iran and Iraq, and there is little doubt that the existence of the *Yām* in this region was affected by the state of the roads, rather than *vice versa*. Although there are dissenters,[57] most scholars would agree that roads during this period

[52] For a fascinating case-study of a Mongol ruler's travel considerations, see Melville, 'Itineraries', 55–70, esp. 60. The general lack of overlap between caravan routes and pasturage routes is analysed in J. Aubin, 'Réseau pastoral et réseau caravanier: Les grand-routes du Khurasan a l'époque Mongole', *Le Monde Iranien et l'Islam* 1 (1971), 105–30, esp. 107, where it is argued that the postal stations did not conform to the military routes followed by Mongol armies, as the latter with their attendant cavalry were dependent on pasturage.

[53] Masson-Smith Jr., 'Mongol Nomadism', 41.

[54] The fullest account of the co-operation and interaction between the Mongols in Iran and China during this period is Allsen, *Culture and Conquest*.

[55] Cf. Allsen, *Culture and Conquest*, p. 25 and n. 5; and ibid., p. 29.

[56] Allsen, however, believes that Rashīd al-Dīn composed detailed descriptions of the *Yām* routes (*Culture and Conquest*, pp. 103ff.). A graphic depiction of the Īl-khānid road system may be found in *Tübinger Atlas des Vorderen Orients*, Wiesbaden, 1977, map B VIII 15 'Irān: Das Reich der Īlḥāne 656–736 h/1258–1336 n. Chr.' (pp. 271–2).

[57] E.g. G. Lane, *Genghis Khan and Mongol Rule*, London, 2004, p. 66.

were generally unsafe, at least until the reign of Ghāzān, and probably thereafter too. As Lambton succinctly puts it, 'However much the postal system, the *yam*, may have facilitated the movement of merchants and goods in Central Asia and the Far East, inside Persia it failed to do so, except so far as the facilities of the post stations were used (or abused) by the ortaqs.'[58] The *ortaqs* were (predominantly Muslim) merchant associations or partnerships that arose in large part due to the lack of security on the roads, which compelled merchants to travel in large caravans for safety. The lack of security along the roads reflected poorly on the Īl-khāns in this regard, and it was to the restoration of security in particular and of the ruler's reputation for 'justice' in general that Ghāzān's reforms were intended.

Another aspect of the Īl-khānid *Yām* that required reform was the funding and administration of the system. The basic problem was that the *Yām* was costing the general population more time and money than was deemed reasonable by the populace. As a general rule, pre-modern populations were expected to shoulder the burden of supplying the imperial postal system with mounts, fodder, manpower, and other services, a burden that was normally accepted as incontestable. However, occasionally the population felt that their service was being exploited by employees of the system, and this was a grievance to which rulers felt the need to respond: in the Roman period, Diocletian and Constantine instituted well-documented reforms; during the Mongol period, it was Ögödei, Möngke, and – most importantly – Ghāzān who rose to the challenge. While Ögödei and Möngke are to be credited with fine-tuning the basic infrastructure of the *Yām* – the former in delineating and supplying the routes, the latter in restricting the system to official envoys and couriers – Ghāzān focused on finances.[59]

The precise details of the *Yām*'s finances during the pre-Ghāzān period are difficult to ascertain for two reasons. First, our main source for this issue is Rashīd al-Dīn, who was in the service of Ghāzān and had a habit of exaggerating the appalling state of affairs that his patron was coming to ameliorate. Moreover, according to Waṣṣāf (d. 1329), Rashīd al-Dīn was actually involved in reforming the *Yām*,[60] which, if true, would further undermine his credibility. Second, funding the *Yām* was integral to the Mongol system of taxation in Iran, a system that was so complex that the logic behind it has largely eluded both people living in the Īl-khānate and modern scholars. The confusion hinges on the fact that the Persian systems of taxation in place on the eve of the Mongol conquests were based on land surveys, whereas the Mongol taxes (introduced as early as the reign of Möngke, in some parts of the Near East) were based on population surveys. Since these two systems did

58 Lambton, *Continuity and Change*, p. 333.
59 Naturally, Ögödei's and Möngke's reforms also had financial ramifications, but the focus on extortionate taxation in the context of supplying the *Yām* is particularly stressed in Ghāzān's reforms.
60 Cf. Morgan, 'Reflections', 383.

not clash, both were applied in the Īl-khānate, meaning that taxpayers were doubly burdened.[61] The Mongols introduced three new types of taxation: *qūbchūr*, *qālān*, and *ṭamghā*. Although the precise meaning of each term changed based on the period and region, it is believed that *ṭamghā* referred to a tax on commercial goods payable by merchants, while the *qūbchūr* – whatever its exact meaning – was the category through which postal taxes were extracted.[62]

In the aftermath of Hülegü's campaigns, a witness to the events recorded a short description of the Mongol conquests, in which he describes the arrangement by which the *Yām* was funded in his native Armenia. He writes:

> [Hülegü] began to rebuild the devastated places and from each inhabited village he selected householders, one from the small and two from the large villages, and he called them *iam* and he sent them to all destroyed places to undertake rebuilding. They paid no taxes at all but gave only bread and broth for Tat'ar travellers.[63]

It would appear that this relatively benign method of funding *Yām* stations did not last long. As with other parts of the Mongol Empire, the administration of the regional systems of taxation was entrusted to a *darughachī*.[64] The *darughachī* was a regional governor of sorts, who represented the [Īl-]Khān and had executive responsibilities over the collection of taxes, official communication, and the military in his jurisdiction. These categories overlapped considerably: the taxes were collected for the funding of the needs of the military and communications, and moreover, the amount of taxation levied helped establish a census of the population that, by a confusing and circular logic, determined the amount of *qūbchūr* to be raised. Such a complex system was bound to lead to confusion, maladministration, and general discontent. This situation was further complicated by the flight of peasants from taxable lands, the disruption of agriculture in areas dependent on a well-maintained canal system, and the fact that in addition to the three newly introduced categories of taxation, Mongol officials passing through various regions would make unsystematic demands on locals to supply them with food and mounts.[65]

61 An influential attempt to make sense of this situation may be found in A. K. S. Lambton, 'Mongol Fiscal Administration in Persia', *Studia Islamica* 64 (1986), 77–99; continued in *Studia Islamica* 65 (1987), 97–123.

62 The *qālān* may have been a labour service associated with military operations (Lambton, 'Mongol Fiscal Administration', 93).

63 Gregory of Aknac: *History of the Nation of Archers*, tr. R. P. Blake and R. Frye, Cambridge, Mass., 1954, p. 345 (and cf. p. 389 n. 54 on the term *iam*). As we have seen, William of Rubruck also uses the term *iam* with reference to the station-masters of the *Yām*, suggesting either that there was a common misconception concerning the imported terminology or that the terms were fluid in their usage.

64 On the function of the *darughachī*, who was also referred to as a *bāsqāq* or a *shaḥna*, see Buell, 'Sino-Khitan Administration'; and Lambton, *Continuity and Change*, pp. 51 and 132–3.

65 Lambton, 'Mongol Fiscal Administration', 95.

The needs of the *Yām* were occasionally disruptive to the local population in ways that exceeded the 'inevitable' burden of supplying and serving in the postal stations. In some cases, entire tribes were uprooted and resettled in distant regions in order to draw on their particular expertise: the Bekrin tribe, who were natives of eastern Turkestan and expert mountaineers (*qīāchī*), were sent by Hülegü to serve as *īlchīs* in the mountainous regions of the realm, an indication of the Mongols' sensitivity to the topographical concerns that might have escaped a ruler from a sedentary background, and of the fact that service in the *Yām* could be a nuisance in a variety of ways. The evidence shows that the Bekrin were still active in Georgia for decades thereafter.[66]

As for the relationship between the *Yām* and the provincial administration, the situation can best be described as complex and even perplexing. Ibn al-Ṭiqṭaqā, writing in 1302, after having travelled extensively in Īl-khānid lands, makes reference to the Mongol '*Barīd*' of his day in his discussion of the caliphal postal system. He writes:

> 'Alā' al-Dīn 'Aṭā Malik [Juwaynī] wrote in [his work] 'Jihān Kushāy' ('The World Conqueror') that, among other things, the purpose of establishing the *Barīd* (read: *Yām*) everywhere was to preserve wealth and [ensure] the speedy transmission of news and ever-changing affairs. But I do not see in the *Barīd* any purpose other than the speedy transmission of news. As for the preservation of wealth, what connection does it have with that?[67]

It is telling that a highly educated native of the Īl-khānate with a keen interest in administrative history could not make sense of the precise role of the *Yām* or of the relationship between the *Yām* and the provincial finances.[68] Clearly, many things were wrong with the Īl-khānid postal system, and it is to the problems of the *Yām* in particular and to the maladministration of the Īl-khānid realms in general that Ghāzān applied himself.

Ghāzān's reforms

Rashīd al-Dīn's description of the pre-Ghāzān *Yām* – despite the well-known caveats concerning this source – depicts a chaotic postal system that threatened to destabilise the countryside, and it is likely that the deterioration of the *Yām* was so severe that it was simply in Ghāzān's interests to act.[69] According

[66] Allsen, *Mongol Imperialism*, p. 211.

[67] Ibn al-Ṭiqṭaqā, *Fakhrī*, p. 148. On Ibn al-Ṭiqṭaqā's use of Juwaynī, see J. Boyle, 'Ibn al-Ṭiqṭaqā and the Ta'rīkh Jahān Gushāy of Juvaynī', *BSOAS* 14 (1952), 175–7.

[68] It is possible that Ibn al-Ṭiqṭaqā was merely disputing the efficacy of the *Yām* in 'preserving wealth', rather than expressing bafflement about the *Yām*'s theoretical role in this regard. The interaction between international merchants and the *Yām* appears to have escaped him.

[69] On abuses of the *Yām* during the pre-Ghāzān period, see also D. O. Morgan, 'Cassiodorus and Rashīd al-Dīn on Barbarian Rule in Italy and Persia', reprinted in G. Hawting (ed.), *Muslims, Mongols, and Crusaders*, London and New York, 2005, pp. 151–69 at 160–1.

to Rashīd al-Dīn, the number of *īlchīs* circulating in Īl-khānid lands was so great that 'even if five thousand mounts had been stationed at each *yām*, they would not have been enough for them'.[70] The *īlchīs* therefore requisitioned mounts from all travellers – including other officials and merchants. The proliferation of *īlchīs* and their escalating need for mounts had been a problem in earlier periods of Mongol rule, as we have seen. But according to Rashīd al-Dīn, a novel problem emerged during the Īl-khānid period whereby highway robbers would impersonate *īlchīs* with the purpose of commandeering mounts, food, and supplies from ordinary passers-by,[71] on occasion even tying up the travellers who were targeted. As Rashīd al-Dīn adds in another context, 'How many thousands of *ra'iyyat* had their heads, arms and legs broken by the messengers!'[72] Furthermore, we are told that even legitimate *īlchīs* would exploit their privileges and take more provisions than needed in order to profit from selling the surplus. For this reason, honest *īlchīs* also came to be loathed and would suffer delays or only be offered malnourished mounts on their missions. Even if the details of this situation have been exaggerated by Rashīd al-Dīn, the general point is clear: the *Yām* was not in need of reform because it was not being used, but rather because it was being over-used and abused.

Ghāzān's reforms concerned several aspects of the administration, only one of which was the *Yām*. That said, many of these other issues were tangentially related to the postal system. The rationalisation of the taxation system and the distribution of *iqṭā*'s alleviated the burden of supporting the *Yām* as land-holding soldiers came to supply mounts ('two or three well-nourished horses') for use in military communications.[73] The fact that peasants' mounts were placed under the protection of the crown was also a significant improvement, while the favours that Ghāzān bestowed on the *qāḍīs* included exemption from postal taxes and associated services.[74] Of most relevance are those stipulations that deal directly with the *Yām*, which concern three categories: routes and stations; administration of the system; and the use of runners.[75]

[70] Rashīd al-Dīn discusses the pre-Ghāzān *Yām* in *Jāmi' al-tawārīkh*, (ed. A. A. Alizade), Baku, 1957, vol. III, pp. 480–3; this source is analysed in Morgan, 'Reflections', 381f.

[71] Compare the activities of rebels during the late Umayyad and early Abbasid period, who often impersonated *Barīd* couriers or officials entitled to *Barīd* mounts (see above, pp. 65, 70, 80).

[72] Rashīd al-Dīn, *Jāmi' al-tawārīkh*, vol. III, p. 556.

[73] Lambton, *Continuity and Change*, p. 126.

[74] Ibid., p. 91, esp. n. 73. This mirrors the Chinese 'Edict of Mangala' of 1276, which prohibited messengers from taking horses and provisions from clergymen. In N. Poppe (trans. J. R. Krueger), *The Mongolian Monuments in HP'AGS-PA Script*, Wiesbaden, 1957, pp. 46–7.

[75] Ghāzān's reform of the *Yām* is described in Rashīd al-Dīn, *Jāmi' al-tawārīkh* vol. III, pp. 483–5, and in Waṣṣāf, *Tajziyat al-amṣār wa tajziyat al-a'ṣār*, in J. Hammer-Purgstall, *Geschichte Wassafs*, Vienna, 1856, p. 387. The reforms are analysed in Morgan, 'Reflections', 382f.

Routes and stations

Stations were to be established at regular intervals and supplied with fifteen well-nourished mounts. Rashīd al-Dīn mentions that the stations were to be 3 parasangs apart, while Waṣṣāf specifies 4 parasangs. In all likelihood, the distance between stations was determined by the same factors that shaped other postal infrastructures – the proximity of villages, the topography, and the availability of water.[76] The important point is that the stations were situated at intervals far more frequent than one day's travel, making them specifically 'postal' stations rather than way-stations or caravanserais that could also be used by couriers. The stipulation that only (or at least) fifteen mounts be available at each station also limited the system to couriers, as military or merchant caravans would ordinarily require more than fifteen mounts. These, however, can hardly be said to have been unprecedented measures, as establishing postal stations and preventing *īlchī*s from making costly and inefficient detours through towns and villages had been attempted before.[77]

Administration

The administration of the system was tightened through the appointment of an official (*amīr*) who supervised the functioning of the *Yām*. Couriers would be required to provide suitable documentation, including a 'golden seal' (*altun ṭamghā*) at the stations, and their course along the routes was to be registered by officials who would be paid for their efforts, not pressed into service. Most importantly, the system would be financed by the Khān, and although the finances (which were undoubtedly still controlled by the regional *darughachī*) must have ultimately been derived from tax revenues, the population would no longer fear the irregularities of *īlchī*s and other official travellers. With the establishment of postal stations with officials and mounts at the ready, and with the bureaucratisation of the system in the Īl-khānid period, the *Yām* finally came to resemble a great imperial postal system in the Near Eastern tradition. Considering that Iran on the eve of the Mongol conquests did not have a functioning *Barīd*, we are left to wonder whence Ghāzān and Rashīd al-Dīn drew their inspiration for these reforms. It is possible that the Chinese *Yām*, which had been recently reformed by Qubilai, served as a model for Ghāzān.[78] The frequent exchanges between

[76] The lack of clear guidelines concerning the distance between stations suggests that route-books such as the one Rashīd al-Dīn is supposed to have composed (*pace* Allsen, *Culture and Conquest*, pp. 103ff.) did not in fact exist.

[77] Apparently, even Geikhatu – infamous for his disastrous attempt to introduce paper currency to Īl-khānid lands as a quick fix for the Treasury's problems – is said to have ordered a reform of the *Yām* (Ḥamdallāh Mustawfī Qazwīnī, *Tārīkh-i guzīda*, Tehran, 1958–61, p. 608).

[78] In 1281, the Chinese postal system was reformed (Allsen, *Culture and Conquest*, p. 105). The Chinese *Yām* during this period is discussed in Olbricht, *Postwesen*, and Gazagnadou, *La Poste*, pp. 47–52.

the Īl-khānid and Yüan courts could have precipitated such cross-cultural influence,[79] and the introduction of runners (*paykān*)[80] to Ghāzān's *Yām* smacks of Chinese origins. However, the fact that the system was funded by the Treasury may indicate that the Mamluk *Barīd* served as a model.[81]

Runners

The runners that served in the Chinese *Yām* are known to us thanks to Marco Polo's hackneyed account of the system. According to him,

> Every three miles, between the stations, there is a village, of some forty houses, where live foot-runners who also carry messages for the Great Lord. I will tell you how. They wear a broad belt, hung all around with bells, that they may be heard from afar when they are on the road. They always go at full speed, and only run three miles. At the end of the three miles, there is another messenger standing ready, waiting for the one who is coming, having heard him a long way off. When this messenger arrives, the other takes from him whatever he is carrying, receives a slip of paper from the clerk, and sets off at a run; he then goes three miles, when the same thing happens as at the previous station. And I assure you that in this way, by means of these runners, the Great Lord has news in a day and a night from places at a distance of ten days' journey.[82]

The runners in Ghāzān's service could cover 30 (or 40, according to Waṣṣāf) parasangs a day, this being 180 (or 240) kilometres.[83] Two runners were to be posted at the stations and relay their message sequentially. Presumably, any speed benefits that mounted couriers had over runners were offset by the advantageous fact that runners did not require the postal mounts that seemed to be at the root of the *Yām*'s problems.

The extent to which Ghāzān's reforms were implemented is difficult to ascertain. We do know that, during his reign, overland travel to, from, and within the Īl-khānate was unsafe: when Ghāzān sent two envoys on an official mission to the Yüan court, they were forced to travel by sea to avoid disturbances along the land routes.[84] And it is only during the reign of Öljeitü that peace amongst the Mongol 'nations' was achieved, a fact that had a direct bearing on the fate of the *Yām*: in a letter to King Philip of France sent by Öljeitü in 1305, the latter proudly states that after forty-five years of

[79] Cf. Allsen, *Culture and Conquest*, pp. 59–80.

[80] The term *payk*, it should be remembered, was used in Ghaznavid Iran. In retaining the initial 'p' of Pahlavi *payg* ('courier'), it would appear that this term resisted the Arabisation that characterises the Arabic *fayj*. The term lived on in the Delhi Sultanate, where couriers were referred to as *pykes* (Sabahuddin, 'Postal System', 271).

[81] On which, see below, pp. 173–6.

[82] *The Travels of Marco-Polo*, (ed./trans. A. Ricci), London, 1950, pp. 154ff.

[83] As we have seen, under the Buyids, Faḍl and Mar'ūsh are supposed to have covered a similar distance each day. In the Buyid case, the alleged speeds were deemed unrealistic since, although runners can achieve 20 kilometres an hour, they cannot do so continuously over a 10-hour stretch. In this case, however, the existence of *relays* of runners meant that fresh couriers could achieve such speeds realistically.

[84] Allsen, *Culture and Conquest*, p. 34.

internal fighting the descendants of Chinggis Khān have settled their differences and restored their postal links (*jamud*) in order to connect their realms.[85] Furthermore, it is only during Öljeitü's reign that roads within Iran were measured and milestones erected along them for the benefit of travellers.[86] But there is evidence that already during Ghāzān's reign, improvements to the *Yām* were also being made in Temür Qā'ān's China, and it is tempting to view Ghāzān's reforms within this larger context.[87] To some extent at least, the *pax mongolica* was restored. The Franciscan Friar Odoric, travelling from Europe to the Far East between 1318 and 1321, recorded a very positive impression of a *Yām* which comprised both mounted couriers and runners.[88] A similar account is provided by John of Cori, the Archbishop of Sulṭāniyya, who travelled to China in 1330,[89] and Pegolotti's *Treatise on the Practice of Trade*, written *ca.* 1340, mentions that the entire route from Tana to Cathay is perfectly safe for travellers.[90] The very fact that these envoys could even make the journey from West to East is already an improvement on the earlier state of affairs.

From a Near Eastern perspective, the Mongol achievement in establishing the largest pre-modern postal system in history, which served and impressed travellers from many regions and periods, was not an unbridled success: Great Khāns such as Chinggis, Ögödei, and Möngke ruled an enormous empire, and their *Yām* is remarkable for it. But the *Yām* only became a Near Eastern institution when the empire became fragmented. Thus, for all that Rashīd al-Dīn praised Ghāzān's postal innovations, by Mongol standards it was merely a regional *Yām* that he was praising.

The legacy of the *Yām*

The *Yām* appears to have outlasted the Mongol rulers in southern Russia,[91] China, and the Near East. More importantly, perhaps, there is persuasive evidence to suggest that it had a formative influence on the postal systems

[85] In Morgan, 'Reflections', 384; and Allsen, *Culture and Conquest*, p. 36.
[86] Ḥamdallāh Mustawfī Qazwīnī, *Nuzhat al-qulūb*, (ed./trans. G. le Strange), London, 1915–19, vol. II, pp. 161–2. And see Melville, 'Itineraries', for the state of imperial routes during Öljeitü's reign.
[87] According to Rashīd al-Dīn (in Boyle, *Successors*, p. 326), four years into his reign, Temür had set up *yāms* linking the East with the West, and stationed couriers therein.
[88] Odoric: in *Cathay and the Way Thither: Being a Collection of Medieval Notices on China*, (ed./trans. H. Yule and H. Cordier), London, 1913, vol. II, pp. 232–4.
[89] John of Cori: in *Cathay and the Way Thither*, vol. II, pp. 240–1.
[90] Pegolotti: in *La pratica della mercatura*, (ed. A. Evans), Cambridge, Mass., 1936, chapter 2.
[91] For the survival of the *Yām* in Russia, see: Dvornik, *Origins*, pp. 306–16; and G. Alef, 'The Origins and Early Development of the Muscovite Postal Service', *Jahrbücher für Geschichte Osteuropas* 15 (1967), 1–15. On the more general issue of the Mongol impact on the early Russian state, see D. Ostrowski, 'The Mongol Origins of Muscovite Political Institutions', *Slavic Review* 49 (1990), 525–42.

established in the Delhi Sultanate, the Ottoman Empire, and in the Mamluk state.

The state of the *Yām* in the post-Mongol Near East is known to us through Ruy González de Clavijo's description of his journey to Tīmūr's court. Travelling with an official embassy between 1403 and 1406, Clavijo writes:

All along this route . . . Tīmūr causes horses to be kept stationed ready for use at post-stages, in one place there may be a hundred in another two hundred horses, and this is the case right up to Samarqand. These are kept for the service of the special messengers or envoys sent to distant places by Tīmūr, or for the use of such envoys as may be coming to him, and such as come and such as go may ride these horses day and night without halt. These government studs are stationed both in those desert or uninhabited regions along the route, and in places where there is a settled population. Further for this service there have been built caravanserais at diverse intervals, where there are stables for the horses with hostelries: the same being supplied with needful provender provisioned from the towns and villages adjacent. These government horses are cared for by men appointed to see to them, who are as we say postillions, being known here under the name of *yamchi*s. When any envoy sent by Tīmūr, or any messenger carrying despatches to him arrives at one of these post-houses forthwith they unsaddle the horses that have come in, and saddle fresh beasts of those they keep. Then forward with the envoy will ride a postillion or maybe two of those *yamchi*s, aforesaid, who are in charge of their horses, and these on arrival at the next post-house return thence with the beasts that they have brought thus far. After this fashion the messenger will pass along continuously.

Although Clavijo credits this system to Tīmūr himself, it would appear that a version of the Mongol *Yām* was available nearly two centuries after Chinggis or Ögödei established it. The use of the term *yāmchī* with reference to the station-masters implies that the system was influenced by the Mongol one, although it is possible that Tīmūr had to re-establish aspects of the system that may have fallen out of use following the demise of the Īl-khāns. The large number of horses at each station, and the fact that the stations did not always bypass inhabited regions (thus sparing the locals from the whims of the *īlchī*s), suggests that not very much had improved since pre-Ghāzān times.[92] Importantly, the mounts are said to have been provided by the government, as stipulated in Ghāzān's reforms. Even the chance requisitioning of private mounts was arranged in a way that did not disadvantage non-official travellers along the routes. As Clavijo tells us:

. . . should ever the horse that envoy is riding tire on the road, and by chance should he meet with any other horse whatever in these parts – for instance should he come on one riding a horseback for his pleasure or business – the messenger will take that horse, making the rider give it up, the *yamchi* in attendance being then held responsible for the animal thus taken on loan, in place of the government horse discarded. Indeed the

[92] As does the fact that supplies for the stations are provisioned 'from the towns and villages adjacent'.

universal custom is that any man riding his way, be he ever so great a lord, or any merchant or private citizen, should such anyone meet an ambassador going to Tīmūr, or some messenger riding with despatches from his Highness by post, forthwith, on demand, he must set foot to ground and give him up his horse, namely to him who thus comes from Tīmūr or to him who rides to his Highness. No one in this case can refuse, or it will cost him his head, such is the invariable order.[93]

The fact that the *yāmchī* was expected to reimburse locals for any mounts seized by the *īlchī*s would, if true, make Tīmūr's *Yām* a model of justice and efficiency,[94] and one cannot help but be both impressed with Tīmūr's organisation and suspicious of Clavijo's accuracy.[95] It is also noteworthy that Clavijo makes no mention of runners, although Ḥāfiẓ Abrū's account of an embassy from the Timurid Shāh Rukh to the Ming court suggests that only two decades later runners operated in Persia. In describing the Chinese postal system, the use of whose facilities the embassy enjoyed, Ḥāfiẓ Abrū states that grooms run in front of the postal wagons 'in such a manner that even the swift couriers (*paykān*) would hardly be able to do in our country'.[96] Elsewhere in this account, the Ming postal system is described in great detail, indicating that at least in China the *Yām* did in fact survive the change in dynasty.[97]

The influence of the *Yām* on other 'Islamic' postal systems is an important and often overlooked aspect of the Mongols' legacy.[98] For the Delhi Sultanate, we have the testimony of Ibn Baṭṭūṭa, whose description of the Indian postal system is remarkably similar in certain points of detail with Marco Polo's account of the *Yām*. According to Ibn Baṭṭūṭa,

The postal service in India is of two kinds. The horse-post, which they call *ūlāq*, consists of horses belonging to the sultan [with relays] every four miles. The service of couriers on foot has within the space of each mile three relays, which they call *dawā*, the *dawā* being a third of a mile, and a mile itself is called by them *kuruh*. The manner of its organization is as follows. At every third of a mile is an inhabited village, outside which there are three pavilions. In these sit men girded up ready to move off, each of whom has a rod two cubits long with copper bells at the top. When a courier leaves the town he takes the letter in the fingers of one hand and the rod with the bells in the other, and runs with all his might. The men in the pavilions, on hearing the sound of the bells, get ready to meet him and when he reaches them one of them takes the letter

93 Clavijo: *Embassy to Tamerlane 1403–1406*, (trans. G. le Strange), New York and London, 1928, pp. 177–80 (translation modified).

94 Whether or not the authorities kept their promise to reimburse ordinary travellers in this way is impossible to determine.

95 A similarly impressive account of Tīmūr's postal and intelligence system is described in the Ẓafarnāma attributed to Tīmūr's grandson (Sharafuddin Ali Yezdi, *The Political and Military Institutes of Tamerlane*, (trans. J. Davy), New Delhi, 1972, pp. 126–9). The authenticity of this source is beyond confirmation.

96 Ḥāfiẓ Abrū: *A Persian Embassy to China*, (ed./trans. K. M. Maitra), Lahore, 1934, p. 35.

97 Ibid., pp. 26–7, 34–6, and 42–3.

98 Occasionally, however, the case has been overstated – Gazagnadou's argument concerning the diffusion of postal technology from China to Medieval Europe is unconvincing on a number of accounts (cf. Silverstein, 'Abbasid *Barīd*').

in his hand and passes on, running with all his might and shaking his rod until he reaches the next *dawā*, and so they continue until the letter reaches its destination. This post is quicker than the mounted post, and they often use it to transport fruits from Khurasan which are regarded as great luxuries in India . . .[99]

Although the distance between the stations is not comparable to that of the *Yām*, the dual system of mounted couriers and runners, and the use of bells as an early-warning system for the station-masters echo Marco Polo's description of the *Yām*, as does the use of the system to bring fresh fruit to the ruler. That the postal mounts were called *ūlāq* strongly suggests that these similarities are not incidental.[100] The topography of (northern) India invites comparisons with China rather than Iran, but this does not challenge the general point that the Mongol *Yām* lived on, in some form or another, in the Delhi Sultanate.

The Ottoman postal system may also have been indebted, at least in its early stages, to the *Yām*. In general terms, the Ottoman rise to power resembles that of the Mongols, especially in the relationship between *ghāzī*-conquest and political centralisation that we have stressed with regard to the Arab and Mongol campaigns. Furthermore, it is clear that the Ottomans drew considerably upon Mongol influences in setting up their state.[101] With particular regard to the Ottoman postal system, Mongol fingerprints are discernable in the system's name, the *Ulāq*, and Luṭfī Pāshā actually describes the *Ulāq* as being a continuation of the 'Chinggisid' postal system in his historical discourse on the Ottoman institution.[102]

Most famously, perhaps, the *Yām* is said to have been the model for the Sultan Baybars I in his creation of the Mamluk *Barīd*. It is to this question of Mongol influence in particular, and to the Mamluk *Barīd* in general, that we now turn.

[99] Ibn Baṭṭūṭa, *The Travels of Ibn Battuta AD 1325–1354*, (trans. H. A. R. Gibb), London, 1956, vol. III, pp. 594ff.

[100] On the Delhi Sultanate's postal system, see Sabahuddin, 'Postal System'.

[101] Cf. R. P. Lindner, 'How Mongol were the Early Ottomans?', in R. Amitai-Preiss and D. O. Morgan (eds.), *The Mongol Empire and its Legacy*, Leiden, 1999.

[102] Luṭfī Pāshā, *Tewārīkh-i āl-i osmān*, p. 373. I would like to thank Murat Menguç for help with the Turkish text. For Luṭfī Pāshā's role in reforming the *Ulāq*, see above pp. 109–10. It should be noted, however, that Nahrawālī's description of the *Ulāq* compares it to the caliphal *Barīd* rather than to the *Yām*.

CHAPTER 5

The Mamluk *Barīd*

Introduction

The postulate that the Mamluk *Barīd* is indebted to the Mongol *Yām* was pointed out by Sauvaget,[1] and the hypothesis has been adopted and expanded by other scholars.[2] The basic argument is that the early Mamluks were repeatedly exposed to Mongol military and administrative culture and adopted some of their military techniques, one of which was the postal system. In support of the argument, Gazagnadou has highlighted similarities between the Mongol and Mamluk systems, such as the existence of *pā'iza*s in the Mamluk *Barīd*, where they are referred to as *alwāḥ al-barīd* ('*Barīd* tablets'). On the whole, the case is convincing, with three important caveats: first, there are significant aspects of the Mamluk *Barīd* that do not resemble the *Yām* and, moreover, are clearly distinct from Mongol practices. Second, in addition to their Mongol heritage, the Mamluks were heirs to a number of political and administrative traditions, some of which were at least as potent as the Mongol factor and most of which were of particular relevance to the administration of Egypt and Syria.[3] Third, although Mamluk writers who treat the *Barīd* were aware of the *Yām* and had no qualms about crediting the Byzantines and Sasanids with influencing the caliphal *Barīd*, they do not ascribe the creation of the *Barīd* under Baybars I (r. 1260–77) to Mongol influences.[4] The most important account of the Mamluk *Barīd*'s establishment is that of 'Umarī, according to whom,

[1] Sauvaget, *Poste aux chevaux*, p. 13.

[2] Most notable amongst whom is Gazagnadou, *La Poste*, pp. 73–80. The central argument of Gazagnadou's book hinges on the assumption that the origins of the Mamluk *Barīd* are in the *Yām*.

[3] On the continuity of pre-Mamluk institutions in the early Mamluk period, see R. S. Humphreys, 'The Emergence of the Mamluk Army', *Studia Islamica* 45 (1977), 67–99, continued in 46 (1977), 147–82.

[4] In fact, Qalqashandī (*Ṣubḥ*, vol. XIV, p. 400) states that the Mamluks' use of beacons to signal enemy manoeuvres was adopted from India, which suggests that Mamluk writers recognised the non-Muslim provenance of some of their bureaucratic institutions.

[When] kingship came to al-Ẓāhir Baybars – may God have mercy on him – and when he united Egypt, Syria, and Aleppo to the Euphrates, he endeavoured to establish [provincial] administration in Damascus, for which he appointed a representative (*nā'ib*), a *wazīr*, a *qāḍī*, and a chief secretary (*kātib li al-inshā'*). My uncle al-Ṣāḥib Sharaf al-Dīn Abū Muḥammad al-Wahhāb – may God have mercy on him – was appointed chief secretary, and when he appeared before [the sultan] to bid him farewell, [the sultan] made numerous suggestions to him, amongst the most important of which was that [my uncle] communicate to him intelligence and ever-changing news of the Mongols and Franks, saying 'If you can ensure that every night I go to sleep [having received] news and every morning I wake up to news, then do so!' [My uncle] then explained to him that which the *Barīd* had achieved in ancient and caliphal times and proposed [this system] to him; [the sultan] liked the idea and ordered [its establishment]. My uncle said: 'It was I who established this in his presence.' This was reported to me in great detail from my uncle by Jamāl al-Dīn 'Abdallāh al-Dawādārī al-Barīdī, known as Ibn al-Shadīd. And [the *Barīd*] is [functioning] in this manner even now.[5]

Thus, according to 'Umarī, whose family connections afforded him a unique glimpse into early Mamluk administration (even if we are not to take this vignette literally), the Mamluk *Barīd* was modelled on the caliphal one. The very fact that the Mamluks labelled their system '*al-Barīd*' confirms that they were mindful of caliphal precedent and distinguishes the Mamluk case from those of the Delhi and Ottoman Sultanates, where the local postal terminology was permeated by 'Mongol' words.

The problem with accepting this version of events is that, as we have seen, the caliphal *Barīd* had fallen out of use centuries before Baybars established his postal system. As Sauvaget noted, it is unlikely that the Mamluk system was created on the basis of scattered references to the Abbasid *Barīd* in literary sources,[6] and the existence of *Yām*-like features such as the *alwāḥ al-barīd* in the Mamluk system reduces the status of 'Umarī's version to that of propaganda. Understanding the motivation behind this propaganda and the actual conditions that dictated the creation of the Mamluk *Barīd* may tell us a great deal about the Mamluk Sultanate in general and its *Barīd* in particular.

The sources

Unlike the pre-Islamic, caliphal, and Mongol postal systems, for which disparate literary sources and documentary evidence have to be combed and combined to arrive at even a bare outline of the respective systems, the Mamluk *Barīd* benefits from exceptionally detailed descriptions by (near-) contemporary writers. 'Umarī's informative chapter on the *Barīd* covers the history of the system until the third reign of al-Nāṣir Muḥammad (r. 1310–41). Qalqashandī continues 'Umarī and annotates the latter's

[5] 'Umarī, *Ta'rīf*, p. 187. [6] Sauvaget, *Poste aux chevaux*, p. 13.

discussion with considerable elaboration, from the perspective of the 'men of the pen', while Anṣarī, his contemporary, offers a discussion of the system within a military context. Maqrīzī's information does not rely on 'Umarī and is of interest both for that reason and because he is a post-*Barīd* historian – that is to say, one writing only in hindsight after the system had collapsed.[7] Additionally, the enormous amount of contemporary material found in Mamluk historical chronicles shows the *Barīd* in action and generally confirms the data provided in the aforementioned sources.[8] Conversely, documentary sources for this period are relatively lacking, especially compared with the Geniza resources from the preceding period and the Ottoman archives from the subsequent one.[9] Only the Ḥaram documents stand out in this regard,[10] but this relative deficiency hardly limits our knowledge of the postal system, as the literary sources provide us with a clear and detailed picture of every aspect of the institution. Not surprisingly, the Mamluk *Barīd* is the only system of its kind to have benefited from extensive scholarly attention. Outstanding amongst studies is Sauvaget's classic exposition on the subject, which was preceded and followed by a number of other studies but never equalled.[11] On the basis of this generous corpus of material the creation and evolution of the Mamluk *Barīd* may be analysed.[12]

Creation of the Mamluk *Barīd*

Although he was not the first Mamluk sultan, Baybars is widely regarded as having been the founder of the sultanate, not least because it was under him that Syria was incorporated into the Mamluk realms. The circumstances

7 'Umarī, *Ta'rīf*, pp. 184–96; Qalqashandī, *Ṣubḥ*, vol. I, pp. 114–28 and vol. XIV, pp. 366–400; Anṣarī, *Tafrīj*, pp. 12–15; and Maqrīzī, *Khiṭaṭ*, vol. I, pp. 614–16.

8 A considerable amount of this material is analysed by Sauvaget, *Poste aux chevaux*. References to the *Barīd* in chronicles that were unavailable to Sauvaget will be discussed in what follows.

9 On documentary sources for the Mamluk period in general cf. D. P. Little, 'Documents as a Source for Mamluk History', *Mamluk Studies Review* 1 (1997), 1–13.

10 Discussed in D.S. Richards, 'The Mamluk Barīd: Some Evidence from the Haram Documents' in M.A. al-Bakhit (ed.), *Studies in the History and Archaeology of Jordan III*, Amman 1987, pp. 205–9.

11 Sauvaget's *Poste aux chevaux* was preceded by the pioneering work of E. Quatremère, *Histoire des Sultans Mamelouks*, Paris, 1837–44, vol. II (ii), pp. 87–92; and M. Gaudefroy-Demombynes, *La Syrie à l'époque des Mamelouks d'après les auteurs arabes*, Paris, 1923, pp. 239ff. Short summaries of Sauvaget's work are found in Dvornik, *Origins*, pp. 225–35; Gazagnadou, *La Poste*, pp. 63–72; and Sa'dawi, *Niẓām al-barīd*, pp. 123–33. A translation and short discussion of 'Umarī's chapter on the *Barīd* may be found in R. Hartmann, 'Zur Geschichte der Mamlukenpost', *Orientalische Literaturzeitung* 46 (1943), 266–70.

12 The aim of the present chapter is not to supersede Sauvaget's work, but rather to contextualise the Mamluk *Barīd* in relation to previous and contemporary postal systems, a subject in which Sauvaget was uninterested. In his words: 'As for the other postal systems in Islam ... we possess only skeletal documentation made up of the most laconic hints that have to be assembled by exacting sweat and toil from the immense historiographical production of the Arabs, Persians, and the Turks, and from which we can deduce only the mere fact of the *Barīd*'s existence' (*Poste aux chevaux*, pp. 1–2).

through which Syria – and even Egypt – were taken by the Mamluks were unmistakably military: just as Saladin had swept into (a reluctant) Syria with the expressed intention of waging *jihād* against infidel invaders, the early Mamluks justified their presence and control over Egypt and Syria by invoking the cause of *jihād* against the Crusaders and Mongols. The political unification of Egypt and Syria on the one hand, and the need for military intelligence in wars against refractory enemies on the other, made the establishment of an official system of communication attractive to Baybars. But establishing a *Barīd* was not the only option available to him, as both military intelligence and political correspondence could be transmitted reliably without resorting to a complex, fragile, and expensive postal system.[13] With regard to military intelligence, homing pigeons had been used for centuries in this region and were used by Nūr al-Dīn (*atabeg* of Syria, 1146–74) for just this purpose. In a well-known passage, Ibn al-Athīr explains the role of pigeons as follows:

> The reason for this is that [Nūr al-Dīn's] territories had become so extensive and his realm so great that it reached from the border of Nubia to the gate of Hamadan, with only the land of the Franks intervening. The Franks, may God curse them, sometimes attacked some of the border areas, but by the time news of this reached him and he was able to set out against them, they had already in part achieved their purpose. He therefore issued orders concerning this matter and sent them in writing to all his territories ... In this way the borders were protected, and when a band of Franks attacked one of them, news reached him on the same day ... May God have mercy on Nūr al-Dīn and be pleased with him. How great was his concern for his subjects and his realms![14]

Homing pigeons had been used in Egypt and Syria since the late ninth century and were still in use on the eve of the Mamluks' ascendancy: Joinville reports that when St Louis landed in Damietta in 1249 'for a moment the sky was darkened' with a cloud of carrier pigeons bringing news of this to the capital.[15] Unsurprisingly, Baybars and subsequent sultans would continue to use them for the speedy transmission of intelligence and other news, but only in conjunction with the *Barīd*.

Nor did the flow of political correspondence between Egypt and Syria necessitate a *Barīd*. The Tell al-Amarna documents from the fourteenth century BCE show that twenty-six centuries before the Mamluk period official letters between the Pharaoh and his vassals in Canaan and Syria were exchanged freely. The 350 or so letters (out of roughly 400 documents that survive in total) demonstrate that imperial messengers could link Egypt with Syria without relying on a *Barīd*.[16] More importantly, neither the

[13] The complexities and costs of the system will be discussed below.
[14] In Lewis, *Islam*, vol. I, pp. 223–4 (translation modified).
[15] In *EI2*, s.v. 'Ḥamām', vol. III, p. 108.
[16] For the Amarna documents see *The Amarna Letters*, (ed./trans. W. L. Moran), Baltimore, 1992.

Fatimids and Ayyubids, who exerted considerable influence on Mamluk administration, nor the Great Seljuks (and their Syrian appanages), who shaped the contours of the Mamluk military establishment, had availed themselves of a postal system. The basic fact is that the region of Egypt and Syria was manageable without depending on a *Barīd* in a way that the Mongol or caliphal lands were not. And for the purposes of transmitting urgent messages on military affairs pigeons were effective, proven, and available.

Despite this, there are two attributes of the *Barīd* as an overland system of communication that may account for its attraction to Baybars. The first is the 'mounted' nature of the *Barīd*, specifically as a horse-based system. The *Barīd* under Baybars was an unequivocally military institution; although, as we shall see, control over the *Barīd* was contested by both 'men of the sword' and 'men of the pen' (and generally despised by 'men of the turban'), the frequent references to the system as *al-barīd al-manṣūr* ('made victorious by God') leave little doubt as to the martial character of the system.[17] As such, its functionaries were royal *mamlūks* – particularly the *khāṣṣakiyya*, the most trustworthy of the sultan's *mamlūks*.[18] 'Mamluks' in the original sense of the word had been imported into the lands of Islam as military slaves since the ninth century, and in Egypt they had been used by the Tulunids, Ikhshidids, and Fatimids. The advantage of slave soldiers in general is their unconditional loyalty to their recruiters; the advantage of Turkish slave soldiers in particular is their cavalry skills. From the ninth century onwards Turkish *mamlūks* provided the essential manpower of cavalry-based armies that came to replace the traditional, infantry-based armies of the Islamic world. Therefore, in restricting *Barīd* affairs and missions to his trusty *mamlūks* Baybars was all but ensuring that the system would be a mounted one. This explains why, unlike the Mongols, who made increasingly frequent use of runners in their *Yām*, the Mamluks only employed runners (*quṣṣād* or *suʿā*) in their *Barīd* reluctantly, when the postal routes were hindered or rendered impractical.[19] In other words, a mounted postal system was an entirely natural institution for Mamluk sultans and their *mamlūks*.

17 As noted by Sauvaget, *Poste aux chevaux*, p. 27, and stressed in D. Ayalon, 'On One of the Works of Jean Sauvaget', *Israel Oriental Studies* 1 (1971), 298–302, at 300.

18 On the *khāṣṣakiyya*, see D. Ayalon, 'Studies on the Structure of the Mamluk Army', *BSOAS* 15 (1953), 203–28. It is worth mentioning that E. Whelan ('Representations of the Khāṣṣakīyah and the Origins of Mamluk Emblems', in P. Soucek (ed.), *Content and Context of Visual Arts in the Islamic World*, New York 1988, pp. 219–43, at pp. 230ff.) argues that the *khāṣṣakiyya* did not hold a central role in the *Barīd*, since their functions were limited to ceremonial contexts, and since being stationed along the routes would not befit their social standing. However, unlike in the postal systems in some other pre-modern states the Mamluk couriers would have made the entire journey on the *Barīd* from start to finish, changing mounts but not handing over to relay-couriers. Thus, serving as a *Barīd* courier in the Mamluk period is unlikely to have involved being stationed along the routes.

19 '*ind taʿadhdhur wuṣūl al-burud ilā nāḥiya min al-nawāḥī*', as Qalqashandī put it (*Ṣubḥ*, vol. I, p. 126).

The second attribute is the caliphal pedigree of the *Barīd*. That ʿUmarī (or his uncle) claims that the Mamluk system was fashioned after caliphal precedents and that this system was called *al-Barīd* may be explained in the context of Baybars' atavistic tendencies; the use in Mamluk ceremonies of black robes and turbans that typify the Abbasids, the guardianship over the *ḥaramayn al-sharīfayn*, the very public championing of the *jihād*, and – most of all – the installation of an Abbasid caliph in Cairo all served to legitimise the rule of self-conscious usurpers.[20] The early Mamluks did not have to worry about lacking royal lineage, as this was one of their strengths. But legitimacy in Islamic terms was clearly important to them, and reviving a distinctively Abbasid institution such as the *Barīd* can be interpreted in this light.[21]

Thus the Abbasid caliphs had *mamlūks* and the Mamluks had an Abbasid caliph, and both had a postal system they called *al-Barīd*. But these parallels aside, the Mamluk *Barīd* was different from its Abbasid namesake in a number of significant ways. It is not just that the Mamluk realm was more compact – and easier to control – than that of the Abbasids: a careful examination of the postal routes from Egypt to Syria in the itineraries of Ibn Khurradādhbih (for the Abbasids) and ʿUmarī (for the Mamluks) shows that even within the same regions the Abbasid and Mamluk networks differed.[22] Furthermore, there are three major features of the Mamluk *Barīd* that distinguished it from the caliphal system: the bureaucratic context of the *Barīd*, the funding of the network, and the use of associated methods of communication that co-existed and interacted with the Mamluk postal system.

Bureaucratic context

The Mamluk *Barīd* was distinguished from the caliphal system in that the former was part of the military. Although the caliphal *Barīd* probably originated during the Islamic conquests, just as the *Yām* was employed during the

[20] This sort of atavism has ancient roots in the region: in the sixth century BCE the neo-Babylonian king Nabonidus famously revived ancient practices and ceremonial to provide legitimacy for his usurpation of power and compensate for his lack of royal lineage (cf. P. A. Beaulieu, *The Reign of Nabonidus: King of Babylonia 556–539 B.C.*, New Haven, 1989).

[21] On Mamluk succession practices and ceremonial, see: P. M. Holt, 'Some Observations on the Abbasid Caliphate of Cairo', *BSOAS* 47 (1984), 501–7; and D. Ayalon, 'Studies in the Transfer of the Abbasid Caliphate from Baghdad to Cairo', *Arabica* 7 (1960), 41–59.

[22] Saʿdawi (*Niẓām al-barīd*, p. 126) argues that the Mamluk postal route from Egypt to Syria was the same route used since ancient times, even by the Israelites in their Exodus from Egypt to Canaan. Not only does one question the wisdom of establishing a postal route along a road that famously took forty years from Egypt to Palestine, but Maqrīzī himself (*Khiṭaṭ*, vol. I, p. 614) notes that the Mamluk *Barīd* route from Egypt to Syria followed a relatively recently established itinerary. ʿUmarī (*Taʿrīf*, p. 184) suggests that the caliphal *Barīd* followed a Byzantine or Sasanid model in establishing stations at rigidly calculated intervals, in contrast to the Mamluk *Barīd*, whose routes were influenced by topography. ʿUmarī is wrong to assume the caliphal *Barīd* to have been any different in this regard, but it is interesting that he distinguishes it from the Mamluk system in points of detail.

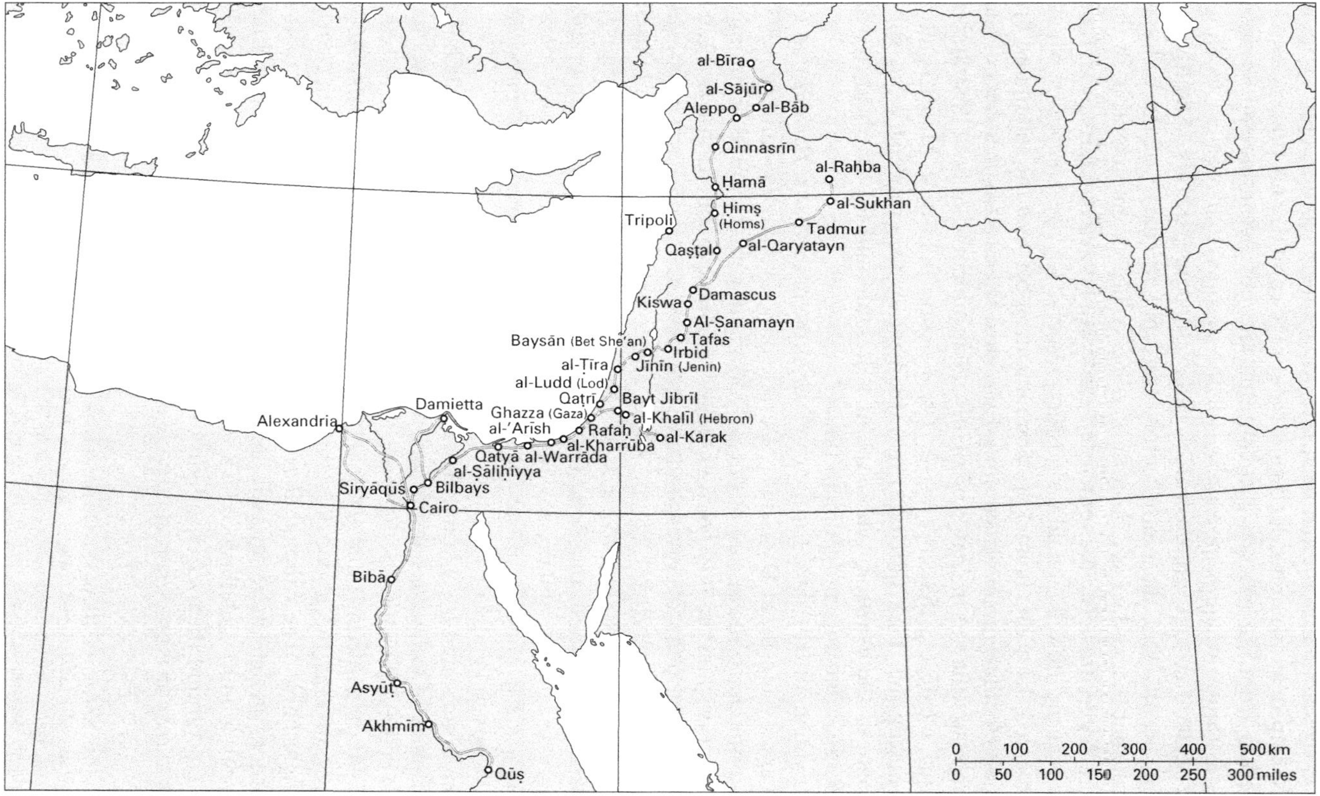

Map 3. Routes of the Mamluk *Barīd*

earliest years of Mongol expansion, it is clear that by the early Abbasid period the caliphal *Barīd* had been integrated into the bureaucratic regime of the empire and assigned its own *dīwān* in the capital. This practice was a reflection – but not necessarily a continuation – of Byzantine and Sasanid administration, where responsibility for the postal system was entrusted to state secretaries and administrators rather than to generals. Admittedly, leading *mamlūks* of the ninth century were put in charge of the caliphal system, but they did so as *aṣḥāb dīwān al-barīd*, not as 'commanders' of the system. By contrast, Baybars entrusted control of his *Barīd* to the *dawādār*, or 'bearer of the inkwell', a military position reserved for royal *mamlūks*, which represented the main channel of communication between the sultan and his officials. As the *dawādār* was amongst the most trustworthy members of the sultan's circle he was in charge of all official documents that bore the sultan's insignia, a category that covered the *Barīd*'s correspondence. Maqrīzī states that during the 'Turkish' (Baḥrī) era, the head of the chancellery was subordinate to the *dawādār*, 'whose status is [tantamount to] that held by the *ṣāḥib al-barīd* in ancient (caliphal) times'.[23]

A contemporary source for the *dawādār*'s role in the Baḥrī *Barīd* is that of Baybars al-Manṣūrī al-Dawādār.[24] Despite only rising to this rank *ca.* 1293, the author charts the history of the early Mamluk period from its beginnings and demonstrates the *Barīd* being used for military communication (*ca.* 1266 and 1300), for political correspondence (*ca.* 1268, 1280, and 1282), to convey the news of a death (*ca.* 1268 and 1283), and to transport the sultan himself between Egypt and Syria (*ca.* 1272).[25] In one instance, during the reign of al-Nāṣir Muḥammad, the *Barīd* between Egypt and Syria was temporarily disrupted, and the sultan was forced to send a courier via 'side-roads' (*mulaṭṭafāt*); as *dawādār*, it was the author's duty to choose a trusty *mamlūk* for the mission and despatch him.[26]

The *Barīd*'s military character is also reflected in Anṣarī's work, which is a description of techniques and tactics used in warfare.[27] Anṣarī discusses the *Barīd* in the first chapter of the work, the third section of which deals with the methods of 'gathering intelligence about the enemy' (*istiṭlāʿ akhbār al-ʿadūw*). In previous eras, the 'abode of Islam' and the 'abode of war' had been clearly distinguishable. The caliphal *Barīd* was concerned with the former to the exclusion of the latter; internal surveillance was its business rather than external military intelligence. The unique situation in which the early Mamluks found themselves in light of the Crusades and the Mongol incursions into Syria is one where the abode of war came to the abode of Islam, and

[23] Maqrīzī, *Khiṭaṭ*, vol. III, p. 733. On the *dawādār* cf. ibid., vol. III, pp. 720–1.
[24] Baybars al-Manṣūrī al-Dawādār, *Zubdat al-fikra fī taʾrīkh al-hijra*, (ed. D.S. Richards), Berlin, 1998. This source was unavailable to Sauvaget.
[25] Military communications: pp. 30, 207, and 323. Political correspondence: pp. 119, 181, and 229. News of a death: pp. 119 and 246. Sultan rides the *Barīd*: pp. 119 and 136.
[26] Ibid., p. 422. [27] Anṣarī, *Tafrīj*. This source was unavailable to Sauvaget.

internal surveillance *became* external, military intelligence. As ʿUmarī's passage quoted above shows, it was in response to military threats that the Mamluk *Barīd* was established. It is significant that although Anṣarī discusses the postal system at the beginning of his work, Qalqashandī, who is only concerned with chancellery practices and their historical development, relegates his detailed and important chapter on the *Barīd* to the very end of the last volume of his encyclopaedic treatise on administrative practices. The two authors were contemporaries coming at the same subject from opposed perspectives, and the result is unambiguous. The caliphs had their *Dīwān al-Barīd*; the Mamluk sultans had their *Barīd al-Manṣūr*.

Funding

The funding of the system is the second distinguishing trait of the Mamluk *Barīd*, not only *vis-à-vis* the Abbasid postal system but also in relation to most pre-modern ones. Although both the caliphal and Mongol postal systems would eventually be funded by the state, they were originally based on requisitions, corvées, and special tax arrangements. The Mamluk *Barīd*, by contrast, was conceived as a state-funded institution from the outset. Maqrīzī informs us that, in establishing the *Barīd*, Baybars 'expended an enormous sum of money (*anfaqa mālan ʿaẓīman*) until it was completed'.[28] Unlike the other antiquarian ideas that he adopted, the *Barīd* had both a practical function and tangible costs. Baybars established postal routes along which stations (*marākiz*) were available to couriers, where fresh horses (as opposed to the mules and camels of previous systems), water, and food for both couriers and mounts were provided. Stations were manned by station-masters who registered the couriers' traffic in log-books and by grooms (sing. *sā'is*) and drivers (sing. *sawwāq*), the latter being the Mamluks' equivalent of the caliphal *furāniq*. The routes went from Cairo to Qūṣ in Upper Egypt and to Alexandria (two routes), Damietta, and to 'Syria'. The couriers (sing. *barīdī*) were housed in the Citadel in Cairo and despatched on their missions by a 'commander of the couriers' (*muqaddim al-barīdiyya*). Couriers were furnished with a copper or silver 'postal tablet' (*lawḥ al-barīd*) through which was threaded a yellow silk scarf (*shurrāba*) that was tied around the courier's neck. The tablet – as with the Mongol *pā'iza* – indicated to station-masters that the bearer was a royal courier; the scarf served to warn all others of the courier's official identity.[29] In provincial centres a local *wālī al-barīd* was in charge of maintaining the system in his region, and both in the capital and in the provinces there were stables specifically designated for *Barīd* purposes

[28] Maqrīzī, *Khiṭaṭ*, vol. I, pp. 615–16.

[29] Interestingly, Qalqashandī (*Ṣubḥ*, vol. I, p. 114) explains that this scarf would serve as a distinguishing feature of couriers, using the phrase *ʿalāmatan lahu*, which echoes the words used with reference to the practice of tail-docking in the postal system of ancient Iran (see above, p. 8).

(*iṣṭabl khayl al-barīd*), administered by an *amīr ākhūr al-barīd*. In addition to all this, the pigeon post and beacon networks were also paid for by the sultan's Treasury.[30]

With dozens of costly stations to build and maintain, and scores of functionaries to pay, one would expect the *Barīd* either to drain the Treasury or to suffer from maladministration and corruption. If Maqrīzī is to be trusted on the issue, we can assume that the system functioned smoothly. He tells us that 'The Syrian routes were well-furnished; at each *Barīd* [station], provisions, fodder and anything else the traveller needed was to be found. Due to the excellent security [on the routes] a woman could travel alone from Cairo to Syria – riding or walking – carrying neither provisions nor water.'[31] It is not clear why this woman would have been entitled to benefit from the postal infrastructure,[32] but the general point is that the *Barīd* was administered competently.

The potentially exorbitant costs of this system were defrayed in two ways. First, at least with regard to the Baḥrī period, most of the functionaries involved in the system – both as administrators and as couriers – were royal *mamlūk*s (usually *khāṣṣakiyya*) who did not need to be reimbursed for their services. Second, on certain stages of the route – particularly on the road to Syria, between al-Saʿīdiyya and al-ʿArīsh – local Bedouin maintained the postal stations. ʿUmarī explains that Bilbays is 'the last of the stations (*marākiz*) for the sultan's horses; these are the horses that are purchased with the sultan's funds and for which grooms and fodder are provided [by the sultan]. Following [Bilbays] are the postal mounts assigned to Arabs who [are rewarded with] *iqṭā*ʿs.' The Bedouin would provide horses, fodder, and manpower for the stations, sharing the responsibilities amongst local tribes in monthly cycles, for which reason they were termed *khayl al-shahāra* ('the monthly horses').[33] Interestingly, ʿUmarī compares this arrangement with the stations of 'the sons of Hülegü' that are called '*khayl al-ūlāq wa-khayl al-yām*', which are 'not purchased with the ruler's funds and do not cost him a thing, rather they are the responsibility of the local population, just as the Bedouin stations [are arranged] in the Egyptian desert'.[34] ʿUmarī's statement is interesting for two reasons: first, it reflects a Mamluk administrator's (rather

[30] For a detailed analysis of the administration of the system, see Sauvaget, *Poste aux chevaux*, pp. 16–23 and 42–55. The most complete description in Mamluk sources is that of Qalqashandī, *Ṣubḥ*, vol. I, pp. 114–28, and vol. XIV, pp. 366–400.

[31] Maqrīzī, *Khiṭaṭ*, vol. I, p. 616. Admittedly, Maqrīzī's statement is followed by his description of the collapse of the system, and his tone may be one of uncritical nostalgia. Nonetheless, references to the *Barīd* in action in Mamluk chronicles indicate that the system functioned properly in the early period.

[32] Although there is evidence to suggest that women played an important role in the transmission of messages in the ancient Near East (cf. S. A. Meier, 'Women and Communication in the Ancient Near East', *JAOS* 111 (1991), 540–7), it is unlikely that women served as official couriers in the Mamluk period.

[33] ʿUmarī, *Taʿrīf*, pp. 189–90. [34] Ibid., p. 196.

superficial) understanding of the Mongol *Yām*. Second, it shows that in Mamluk eyes the *Barīd* and the *Yām* were equivalent but distinguishable institutions.

It is important to bear in mind that even disregarding the ways in which the financial burden caused by the *Barīd* was occasionally relieved, the very fact that in most regions the sultan funded and provided for the system demanded a considerable investment of the sultan's resources to maintain it. The cost of the system was justifiable in two ways. First, the *Barīd* was strictly limited to important regions and people. Maqrīzī's treatment of the *Barīd* is provided under the rubric of 'The route from the capital of Egypt to Syria';[35] and although ʿUmarī and Qalqashandī also describe the routes to Arabia, it is clear that these routes are not part of the *Barīd* network. The Arabian routes were of central importance to the thousands of annual pilgrims from Mamluk lands to Mecca, but this did not rationalise extending the costly *Barīd* network to those regions. Thus, compared with the great expanses of land covered by the *Yām* or the caliphal *Barīd*, the routes within Egypt and from Egypt to Syria represented a relatively light burden on the Treasury. Furthermore, use of the *Barīd* during the Baḥrī period was limited to travellers on official missions to an extent that eluded other pre-modern postal systems. Not only were postal warrants (and 'tablets') required of those using the service, but the routes did not conform to the regional trade and pilgrimage itineraries, and the relay-stations were intentionally constructed on a scale that would not benefit large caravans even in cases where corruption could allow non-official travellers to enjoy the postal facilities.[36]

Second, the costs of the *Barīd* were justifiable on account of the extensive use of the system in a variety of contexts. Although the Mamluk sources that focus on the *Barīd* describe the remit of the system in terms no more specific than the sultan's *muhimmāt* or 'important affairs',[37] the chronicles that describe the *Barīd* in action inform us of the many uses to which the system was put. Military intelligence and orders were transmitted, as was political and diplomatic correspondence, and envoys – to and from the sultanate – as well as other officials travelled using the postal network. Additionally, internal political disturbances were reported, and those whom the sultan wished to interrogate were transported to Cairo via the *Barīd*. The swords of important *amīrs* were returned to the capital by post, and the oath of allegiance (*bayʿa*) to the sultan was pledged by remote tribesmen in the presence of a *Barīd* courier.[38] Although ʿUmarī mentioned that Baybars demanded twice-daily reports on the situation in Syria, according to Maqrīzī 'news from the provinces would reach [Baybars] twice a week', as the *Barīd* journey from

35 Maqrīzī, *Khiṭaṭ*, vol. I, p. 614. Anṣarī (*Tafrīj*, p. 15) also makes it clear that the *Barīd* was limited to Egypt and Syria.
36 On this important point, see Sauvaget, *Poste aux chevaux*, pp. 28–9.
37 E.g., Qalqashandī, *Ṣubḥ*, vol. XIV, p. 370; and Maqrīzī, *Khiṭaṭ*, vol. I, p. 616.
38 Cf. Sauvaget, *Poste aux chevaux*, pp. 15–16 and nn. 55–8, and 62.

Cairo to Damascus took four days in each direction.[39] Compared with other archaic symbols adopted by Baybars, the *Barīd* proved to be particularly useful on a practical level, and amongst his many military innovations establishing a postal system was perhaps the most successful.[40]

Associated methods of communication

The third distinguishing feature of the Mamluk *Barīd* was its interaction with carrier pigeons and optical signals or 'beacons' (*manāwir*, sing. *manār*).[41] These systems were considered to be complementary to the *Barīd* and, generally speaking, served the same military purposes for which the *Barīd* was originally established, albeit with advantages and disadvantages particular to each system. In his chapter on 'Seeking intelligence about the enemy' Anṣarī describes the pigeon and beacon networks with characteristic clarity. He says, 'for the gathering and transmission of intelligence, when quick arrival of reports is sought, there are methods', and explains as follows:

> The quickest of these is the kindling of fires (*nīrān*) on the summits of mountains; for, if something happened in an extremity of the kingdom, such as the movement of the enemy and similar matters, and there were high mountains: then, if it happened at night, fire [signals] can be lighted on the summit of a high mountain; while by daylight smoke signals can be sent from the top of one mountain to the one which comes after it. This is repeated until [the information] reaches the place for which it is intended. In the beginning of the Mamluk rule, when war broke out between the rulers of the Egyptian lands and the Mongols, men were stationed on the summits of mountains, paid for this work by arrangements with the sultan, and [concentrated] along a line from the Euphrates to Gaza. If any movement of the Mongols was noticed, the fire would be kindled and they would make smoke [signals], and this [information] would be relayed from the Euphrates to Gaza in the shortest time. Thus it would be known generally that an incident had occurred. Then pigeons would be sent from Gaza to Egypt. News of this event would be known in one day. The achievement of peace between the Mongols and the rulers of the Egyptian lands obviated this [mode of communication] and its [various] components fell into desuetude.[42]

From Anṣarī's account four important points emerge. First, the system of beacons was deemed the quickest of all methods of communication, relaying news from northern Syria to Egypt in just one day. Second, as with the *Barīd*, this method was created in response to military needs and funded by the sultan's Treasury. Third, beacons worked in conjunction with homing

39 Maqrīzī, *Khiṭaṭ*, vol. I, p. 615.

40 Introducing fighting elephants was one of Baybars' less successful ideas (on which, see R. Amitai-Preiss, *Mongols and Mamluks*, Cambridge, 1995, pp. 71ff.).

41 The main sources for these systems are ʿUmarī, *Taʿrīf*, pp. 196–7 (pigeons), and pp. 199–201 (optical signals); Qalqashandī, *Ṣubḥ*, vol. I, pp. 118ff., and vol. XIV, pp. 389–94 (pigeons), and pp. 398–400 (optical signals); and Anṣarī, *Tafrīj*, pp. 13–14 (pigeons), and pp. 12–13 (optical signals). And see Sauvaget, *Poste aux chevaux*, pp. 36–41.

42 Anṣarī, *Tafrīj*, pp. 12–13/pp. 46–7 (translation modified).

pigeons that linked Gaza with Cairo. And fourth, the achievement of peace between the Mamluks and Mongols led to the discontinuation of this system. We shall return to these points below.

Immediately following his description of optical signals, Anṣarī turns to the pigeon network, saying:

Less speedy is the arrival of news by pigeon and that is [because] the pigeon travels from only one country to another. If in one of the countries which have pigeons an incident took place, notes (*baṭā'iq*) are written and attached to the wings of pigeons and despatched. The pigeons would seek the tower which is in their country, and arrive in the shortest time possible. But it is not possible by this method to obtain [complete] information; rather the necessity of the matter is merely hinted at, vital information alone being cited ... The pigeon towers in the kingdom of the Egyptian regions in those times (*fī al-zamān al-mutaqaddim*) extended from the Citadel in Cairo to Qūṣ, and to Aswān and to ʿAydhāb, and to Alexandria and Damietta and Suez on the Pilgrimage route; and likewise to Damascus and Aleppo and the rest of the administrative districts (*niyābāt*) ...[43]

According to this passage, the pigeon network does not only complement the system of beacons but also serves as an independent (albeit slower) method of communication. That Anṣarī describes this system as having operated 'in those times' suggests that it too had fallen out of use.

Anṣarī follows his discussion of beacons and pigeons with passages on the *Barīd*, which is 'less swift than the pigeons in the dispatching of news', on runners (*suʿā*) who are yet 'less speedy' and, finally, on spies (*ʿuyūn wa jawāsīs*, 'eyes and ears') who are the slowest of all.[44] Although in the hierarchy of speed the *Barīd* ranked below beacons and pigeons, the postal system offered rulers a distinct advantage when compared to the quicker methods. Regarding pigeons, Anṣarī noted that 'it is not possible by this method to obtain [complete] information; rather the necessity of the matter is merely hinted at', and he describes the *Barīd* as being the system 'which conveys lengthy written despatches (*kutub muṭawwala*) and detailed information (*akhbār mufaṣṣala*)'.[45] The very nature of optical signals meant that only a very general message could be communicated from one hilltop to another, while the fact that notes were to be attached to a pigeon's wing meant that messages had to be abbreviated, and therefore pigeons could not convey the detailed reports that human couriers could.

More importantly, perhaps, is the fact that both beacons and pigeons were susceptible to sabotage. Regarding the latter, the worry was that the pigeon would be felled by the enemy, thereby revealing sensitive information to the wrong people while also depriving the authorities of the message. Qalqashandī explains that this danger necessitated the despatch of two pigeons with the same message, to ensure that at least one of them would

[43] Ibid., pp. 13–14/ pp. 48–9 (translation modified). [44] Ibid., p. 15. [45] Ibid.

reach its destination (while the fact that the other did not would presumably alert authorities to the intelligence leak).[46] Beacons could be sabotaged by enemies who were able to mislead authorities by triggering false alarms. The danger was that armies would be mobilised and trade disrupted simply by lighting a fire on a hilltop.[47]

Both beacons and carrier pigeons were used in the Islamic Near East long before the Mamluk period. And although Sauvaget argues that the pigeon network became more regular and extensive under Baybars than it had ever been,[48] we know that the Fatimids' use of carrier pigeons was just as extensive and, to the extent that the Fatimids did not avail themselves of a *Barīd*, more important to their administration than pigeons would be under the Mamluks.[49] The Mamluk achievement was thus strategic and administrative rather than technological. The successful interplay between the three major methods of communication distinguished the Mamluk system of communication from previous systems in which certain elements of the Mamluk system may have been available but the harmonisation of the elements in the ruler's service was lacking.[50] It is not just that the various methods of communication were all in use under a single ruler, but the three systems combined to deliver a single piece of news as quickly and efficiently as possible: beacons would relay a message from Northern Syria to Gaza, whence carrier-pigeons or *Barīd* couriers would deliver the message to Cairo. Alternatively, the optical signal would be continued by carrier pigeons to Cairo while the *Barīd* made its way to the capital at a slower pace, bearing detailed information of which the small pigeon-notes could only provide a summary.[51]

[46] Qalqashandī, *Ṣubḥ*, vol. I, p. 119. The despatch of more than one pigeon in transmitting a single message brings to mind the use of two couriers in Arabia to ensure that at least one of them completed the journey successfully. Qalqashandī (ibid., p. 117) says that Ardashīr ibn Bābak recommended sending a message with multiple couriers (independently of each other) to deprive a single courier of the ability to distort the (oral?) message. Multiple couriers would thus serve to ensure the accurate transmission of the message.

[47] This danger was not merely hypothetical; as we have seen, the beacon network operated by Rabbinite Jews in the first centuries CE was intentionally disrupted by sectarians (see above, p. 26). In his discussion of Jewish festivals, Maqrīzī (*Khiṭaṭ* vol. IV, p. 943) actually recounts this episode of Jewish history, though he does not draw a parallel between it and Mamluk practices.

[48] Sauvaget, *Poste aux chevaux*, pp. 36–7; and Ragheb, *Messagers*, p. 29.

[49] Sauvaget (ibid., pp. 40–1) assumes that Baybars created the system of optical signals, whereas Gazagnadou (*La Poste*, pp. 79–80) argues that this system was borrowed from the Chinese via the Mongols. Interestingly, Qalqashandī (*Ṣubḥ*, vol. XIV, p. 400) states that the method was adopted from the Indians, who may, of course, have been perpetuating a Sino-Mongol practice of which Qalqashandī was unaware.

[50] For example, during the early Abbasid period the *Barīd* often operated in parallel with a commercial postal system, while the Abbasids' enemies would make efficient use of carrier pigeons. The Fatimids used both carrier pigeons and merchant networks but did not have a *Barīd*.

[51] The co-ordination of the three methods of communication is described in Qalqashandī, *Ṣubḥ*, vol. I, pp. 118 and 128; ʿUmarī, *Taʿrīf*, p. 201; and Anṣarī, *Tafrīj*, pp. 12–13.

The associated methods of communication provided news more speedily than a more basic postal system would allow. But whereas the *Barīd* and comparable systems served in a variety of capacities, optical signalling or a pigeon network could only transmit news (or, in the case of the Fatimid pigeon post, cherries). Moreover, as mentioned, the news transmitted via such methods was necessarily limited in scope; hence, these systems served as effective early-warning systems in military contexts but little else. Thus, when the Mamluks defeated the Crusaders in the late thirteenth century and achieved peace with the Mongols in the early fourteenth century, a prolonged period of peace that militated against maintaining these systems ensued, for the costs of maintaining the beacon and pigeon networks were shouldered by the Treasury (just as the *Barīd*'s costs were).[52] It is therefore not surprising that the *Barīd* outlasted both systems. And although, as a result of the peace treaty with the Mongols in 1323, the beacons were the first to go,[53] the carrier pigeons were not far behind, and by the time Qalqashandī was writing the pigeon service had been suspended.[54] Eventually, the *Barīd* would also decline and, as we shall see, it would predecease the Mamluk sultanate by decades.

Decline of the system

Despite the early successes of the *Barīd*, the three unique features of the Mamluk system were eventually eroded: the bureaucratic context – specifically the military nature of the system – changed; the funding of the system was deprived of its access to a strong and willing Treasury; and the associated networks of beacons and pigeons no longer combined with the *Barīd* to provide a three-pronged system of communication.

The de-militarisation of the *Barīd* was the result of a more general trend initiated by al-Nāṣir Muḥammad in his third reign (1310–41). The sultan had previously served as a mere figurehead, placed on the throne during power struggles amongst manipulative *mamlūk*s. However, by the time of his third reign, al-Nāṣir Muḥammad had gained the benefits of age, political experience, and – perhaps most importantly – a *mamlūk* household that supported him. In a bold move that was more likely than not to get him assassinated, al-Nāṣir Muḥammad appointed his royal *mamlūk*s to positions hitherto occupied by established veterans, and the cadastral survey (*al-rawk al-nāṣirī*) that he ordered led to a redistribution of land grants skewed in favour of his supporters. The fiscal reforms were not short-lived; Ibn Jīʿān's historical geography of Egypt, which was written in the late fifteenth century, was

52 On which, see: Qalqashandī, *Ṣubḥ*, vol. I, pp. 127–8; Anṣarī, *Tafrīj*, p. 12 (beacons); and Ragheb, *Messagers*, p. 42 (pigeons).

53 As stated explicitly by ʿUmarī (*Taʿrīf*, p. 201), and followed by Qalqashandī (*Ṣubḥ*, vol. I, p. 128), and Anṣarī (*Tafrīj*, p. 13).

54 Qalqashandī, *Ṣubḥ*, vol. XIV, p. 394.

based almost entirely on al-Nāṣir Muḥammad's *rawk*, showing how little had changed in over a century. Although one result of the reforms was that irregular taxes (*mukūs*, sing. *maks*) were abolished – undoubtedly a popular move amongst civilians – the financial reforms in general were considerably less well-received amongst the powerful *mamlūk* elites. Al-Nāṣir Muḥammad did manage to overcome his rivals, including the *amīr*s with whom most sultans had to contend on near-equal footing, and an unprecedented level of autocracy and a high degree of centralised power were achieved at the expense of the traditional, militarised elites.[55] Not only were civilians appointed to positions within the military, a shocking departure from Mamluk norms in itself, but the administrative apparatus was also reformed. The position of *wazīr* was abolished, and financial administration was delegated to the *nāẓir al-khāṣṣ*, the new chief financial officer who was almost always a Christian.

These reforms did not succeed in replacing the Mamluk military structure with a purely administrative one (nor did they intend to do so). The main result of the reforms was that the 'men of the pen' were allowed to compete with the 'men of the sword' in a governmental tug-of-war that may be compared with the situation in ninth-century Iraq, where slave-soldiers and state-secretaries competed for primacy and decisive influence. The 'men of the pen' were allowed to emerge in the fourteenth century because al-Nāṣir Muḥammad and his successors were less reliant on the military prowess of the *mamlūk*s, owing to the waning of the Crusader and Mongol threats. Although the last Īl-khān only died in 1335, a peace treaty had been concluded with the Mongols in 1323, roughly ten years after the last battle between the two sides and three decades after the Crusader threat had passed. We have already seen that an immediate consequence of these developments was the discontinuation of beacons as an early-warning system, but a long-term effect was the attempted bureaucratisation of the *Barīd* by chancellery officials. Maqrīzī relates that Awḥad al-Dīn, the chief of the *Dīwān al-Inshā*ʾ under Barqūq, managed to wrest control of the *Barīd* from the *dawādār* in an episode that typified the rivalry between the two branches of government.[56] The fluctuation in the *Barīd*'s administrative status is also a recurring theme in Qalqashandī's treatment of the system.[57]

[55] On these reforms and their long-term effects, see A. Levanoni, *A Turning Point in Mamluk History: The Third Reign of al-Nās Qalāwūn (1310–41)*, Leiden, 1995. Levanoni argues that the de-mamlukisation instigated by the sultan ultimately led to the collapse of the Mamluk system. For a response to this argument, see W. W. Clifford's review of Levanoni's book in *Mamluk Studies Review* 1 (1997), 179–82.

[56] Maqrīzī, *Khiṭaṭ*, vol. III, pp. 254–6. Only a few years earlier (assuming that his *Muqaddima* was completed between 1375 and 1379), Ibn Khaldūn wrote that the *Barīd* belonged to the 'men of the sword', along with the *Shurṭa*, the army, and administration of the *thughūr* (*Muqaddima*, vol. I, p. 14).

[57] Qalqashandī, *Ṣubḥ*, vol. I, pp. 114ff.

An illustration of the effects that de-militarisation had on the *Barīd* is al-Nāṣir Muḥammad's use of overland routes to transport ice (or 'snow', *thalj*) from Syria to Cairo to chill his drinks. The transportation of ice was not an innovation of this sultan: 'Umarī and Qalqashandī recognise that previous rulers in Islam (including Mamluk sultans) had imported ice for the same purpose, but al-Nāṣir Muḥammad was said to be the first sultan to use overland routes – including 'the official mules' (*al-bighāl al-sulṭāniyya*) and postal couriers (*barīdī*) and horses (*faras al-barīd*) – in addition to the old sea-based system.[58] Although in the mid eleventh century Nāṣir-i Khusraw specifically mentions the use of camels to transport ice to Cairo,[59] it is likely that al-Nāṣir Muḥammad was the first Mamluk sultan to do so. The use of the *Barīd*'s facilities for such frivolous matters indicates that the sultan found uses for the system following a sharp decrease in military reports that resulted from the prolonged periods of stability along the borders of the sultanate. As Baybars and Qalāwūn did before him, al-Nāṣir Muḥammad acquired a large household of royal *mamlūk*s who could administer and serve in the *Barīd*. But he was succeeded by a series of twelve, generally ineffectual, descendants who were considerably less powerful and autocratic. Only al-Nāṣir Ḥasan (r. 1347–51, 1354–61), who intensified the trend of the de-militarisation of society, wielded a meaningful measure of authority, and his own *mamlūk*s killed him for it. The weakness of al-Nāṣir Muḥammad's successors created a climate of internal instability that hampered the operations of bureaucratic institutions. Worse yet was the series of financial and social disasters that would further destabilise Mamluk society and severely disrupt the unique conditions of the *Barīd*'s funding that the early sultans enjoyed.

The funding of the system in the early period relied on three conditions: First, the *Barīd* would justify its costs by providing regular military intelligence, and by serving in a variety of other capacities. Second, the costs of the system would be kept to a minimum by ensuring that the *Barīd* would be used only for important affairs (*muhimmāt*), and the fact that the routes and stations did not comply with the needs of merchants and caravans was of central importance in this regard. Third, the cost of supporting postal employees would be lessened by using trusty royal *mamlūk*s who did not require special salaries for their service. All three of these conditions went unsatisfied in the aftermath of al-Nāṣir Muḥammad's death. The lack of external enemies reduced the traffic of couriers bearing military intelligence considerably, as discussed. Furthermore, in the second half of the fourteenth century the *Barīd* was being used 'to transport a handsome *mamlūk* or to summon a singer with a beautiful voice [to the capital]', as Subkī complained.[60] Moreover, the routes were gradually restructured to favour

[58] 'Umarī, *Ta'rīf*, pp. 197–9; and Qalqashandī, *Ṣubḥ*, vol. XIV, pp. 395–7.
[59] *Naser-i Khusraw's Book of Travels*, (trans. W. M. Thackston Jr.), Costa Mesa, 2001, p. 57.
[60] Subkī, *Mu'īd*, p. 46.

caravan traffic, and the postal stations themselves were constructed with the needs of merchants in mind, as Sauvaget has shown.[61] Admittedly, these infrastructural reforms were meant to pad the sultan's coffers through tax revenue extracted from traders, but the significant point is that the *Barīd*'s facilities were deprived of their exclusivity, and the traffic of passing merchants would certainly have opened the floodgates of institutional corruption. Finally, drawing on one's royal *mamlūk*s to serve in the *Barīd* was becoming more difficult. Using one's own *mamlūk*s for *Barīd* missions was only practicable insofar as the *mamlūk*s were entirely trustworthy; according to Levanoni, *amīr*s and sultans could no longer count on the loyalty of their *mamlūk*s as a result of al-Nāṣir Muḥammad's reforms.[62] The fact that Qalqashandī includes in his description of the *Barīd* a section on the qualities required from a trustworthy *barīdī* – a section that is tellingly replete with stories of unscrupulous couriers – suggests that a sultan could no longer simply dispatch his *khāṣṣakiyya* on missions as earlier sultans had done.[63]

Even had these three conditions been upheld, the financial crises of the mid fourteenth century and thereafter would arguably have prohibited the sultans from supporting the system financially. Two interrelated developments had a devastating impact on the Mamluk economy from the mid fourteenth century and thereafter: the arrival of epidemics in lands of the sultanate and the decline of Egypt's role in international trade. Bubonic plague arrived in Egypt in 1347–8 and was followed by a succession of epidemics – of both bubonic and pneumatic plague – many of which were severe. Some twenty-five recurrences of plague in Syria and twice that amount in Egypt, between 1348 and 1517, had irreversible effects on the Mamluk economy in two ways: first, the mortality rate amongst the *mamlūk*s was particularly high, and maintaining a large *mamlūk* household became increasingly expensive. Accordingly, the number of royal *mamlūk*s dropped from *ca.* 12,000 under al-Nāṣir Muḥammad to *ca.* 6,000 in the Burjī period.[64] Second, the flight of peasants from arable lands had deep financial implications for Egypt's agricultural sector.

The decline in trade during this period is also of importance. The Mamluks had relied on international trade to maintain a steady flow of weapons, luxury items, and, most importantly, military slaves. As *mamlūk*s were imported from foreign lands to the north of the sultanate, fragile diplomacy was conducted to ensure the free traffic of merchants between and within these

[61] Sauvaget, *Poste aux chevaux*, pp. 54–5. For the fact that couriers began to use buildings external to the *Barīd*'s infrastructure, see Hillenbrand, *Islamic Architecture*, p. 202, where a *madrasa* is shown to have been used for these purposes (drawn to my attention by Robert Irwin).

[62] Levanoni, *Turning Point*, pp. 86 and 115.

[63] Qalqashandī, *Ṣubḥ*, vol. I, pp. 116–18. The increase in the number of *khāṣṣakiyya* during this period also served to devalue their prestige as members of the sultan's inner circle.

[64] On the effects of the 'Black Death' in Egypt and the difficulties that Mamluk society faced in dealing with epidemics, see S. Borsch, *The Black Death in Egypt and England*, Austin, 2005.

regions.[65] On occasion, political rivals such as the Īl-khāns and Ottomans would attempt to restrict the flow of *mamlūk*s with the aim of depriving the sultans of their power-base. Additionally, Italian merchants attempted to forge trade alliances with the Īl-khāns to undermine Mamluk trade interests in the Mediterranean. Most of these schemes amounted to nothing, as peace with the Mongols averted Īl-khānid interferences and promoted co-operation along the trade routes. More significant was the threat of the Mamluks' rivals in the Mediterranean. Genoese, Venetian, and Cypriot merchants all had designs on the region's commerce, and the Mamluk sultans became increasingly dependent on the revenues extracted from foreign traders to an extent that dismayed even Mamluk observers.[66] These economic crises, coupled with decades of political instability following al-Nāṣir Muḥammad's death, created an atmosphere in which the facilities of the *Barīd* were repeatedly abused: Subkī decries not only the frivolous purposes for which the system was used by sultans but also the maltreatment of postal mounts and the spreading of false reports by couriers.[67] Naturally, being a 'man of the turban' Subkī was more concerned with the tenets of religion than the practical demands of politics – his work is a sort of moral guide for functionaries in the administration – but his portrayal of the *Barīd* during this period depicts a system in decline and disarray.

A rare glimpse into the finances of a provincial *Barīd* station during this period is provided by the Ḥaram documents of Jerusalem. Although, as Richards has pointed out, Jerusalem is not mentioned as being a staging-point on the postal itineraries described by ʿUmarī and Qalqashandī, it is clear from these documents that the *Barīd* infrastructure was in place there in the last decade of the fourteenth century.[68] The relevant documents concern the uses to which escheated inheritances were put, including supplying the personnel and facilities of the local *Barīd*. The postal stable (*iṣṭabl al-barīd*) is mentioned as though it were a permanent topographical feature, and funds are set aside for the courier's travel expenses (*tasfīr*, comparable to the *jawāʾiz al-barīd* of caliphal times), for the courier's 'driver' (*sawwāq*) and mount, to hire runners (*suʿā*) on official business, and to pay for expenses associated with the pigeon network, amongst other costs. The postal tablets (*alwāḥ*) that would hang on a yellow silk scarf as a distinguishing emblem for couriers appear to have been discontinued: one document refers to the silk scarves used in the *Barīd* without reference to the tablets,[69] and Qalqashandī admits that in his time the tablets were no longer used in conjunction with the

[65] Cf. P. M. Holt, *Early Mamluk Diplomacy*, Leiden, 1995.

[66] On Maqrīzī's criticisms of the economic policies of Burjī sultans, see O. R. Constable, *Housing the Stranger in the Mediterranean World*, Cambridge, 2003, p. 236.

[67] Subkī, *Muʿīd*, pp. 46–8. It should be noted that kindness to animals is stressed throughout the work, not only with reference to the *Barīd*.

[68] Richards, 'Mamluk Barīd', *passim*.

[69] On this document (Ḥaram no. 556), see ibid., 206 n. 10.

scarves.[70] The finances of the station are not controlled by a *Barīd* administrator (the expected *wālī al-barīd* does not appear), perhaps indicating the reduced scale on which the system was functioning in this region. Not only is the *Barīd* funded through escheated inheritances, but we also hear of the arrest of one Muḥammad al-Khallā'ī, who was charged with misuse of the *Barīd* horses. The picture that emerges from these documents is that of a postal system in decline. Within a decade, the rate of decline accelerated under external pressures.

Tīmūr's invasion of Syria in 1400–1 is frequently cited as the moment of the *Barīd*'s demise. According to Maqrīzī,

> When Tīmūrlank took Damascus and besieged its people and razed it in the year 803 [A.H.], the *Barīd* stations were destroyed and the local population concerned itself with the trials that had befallen them and with the internal strife, to the detriment of the *Barīd*. The Syrian route thus became shamefully disorganised, a situation that persists until the present time, this being the year 818 [A.H.].[71]

Qalqashandī also offers us a frank picture of the *Barīd*'s operation in the early fifteenth century. After recounting 'Umarī's short history of postal systems in Islam, Qalqashandī adds morosely:

> The *Barīd* remained firmly established in the lands of Egypt and Syria until Tīmūrlank, ruler of Transoxania, swept through the Syrian regions and conquered Damascus, destroying and razing it in the year 804 [AH]. This caused the wings of the *Barīd* to be clipped and [the system] to be discontinued in the rest of the northern provinces. This poison then spread to Egypt, where [the *Barīd*] was impaired and neglected, and all traces of the *Barīd* were obliterated from Egypt and Syria. What happened then is that when an official mission presented itself within Egypt or Syria, the *barīdī* would ride one of his own horses, travelling slowly at the rate of an ordinary traveller on his way somewhere, then [the *barīdī*] would return in the same manner, thereby achieving slowness on both legs of his journey.[72]

Unlike the Mongol and Crusader threats, Tīmūr's invasion did not trigger a chain of beacons; the combined system of couriers, pigeons, and beacons that provided military intelligence in the Baḥrī period was no longer available – pigeons and couriers were still operating on some level, as the Ḥaram documents show, but clearly the system was not what it used to be. By this point, for nearly a century the only political threat that had confronted a Mamluk sultan was the ambition of other *mamlūks* to usurp the throne. As a result of this, the decadence that the slave-soldier system was engineered to prevent had gradually managed to set in, a trend that may have started as early as the third reign of al-Nāṣir Muḥammad. In some ways, the Burjī Sultans' adherence to the traditional Mamluk model of succession hindered their ability to

[70] Qalqashandī, *Ṣubḥ*, vol. I, pp. 115–16. According to him, *Barīd* tablets were employed only if a *barīdī* was travelling to a remote province where outdated practices were still current.
[71] Maqrīzī, *Khiṭaṭ*, vol. I, p. 616. [72] Qalqashandī, *Ṣubḥ*, vol. XIV, p. 370.

maintain a sophisticated *Barīd*. The regular substitution of the military elite with a fresh batch of *mamlūks* meant that bureaucratic institutions required a robust and well-defined infrastructure to which the newly arrived functionaries and commanders could swiftly adapt. The general instabilities of the fourteenth and fifteenth centuries deprived the sultanate of the solid foundation on which such infrastructures could be built and maintained.[73] Thus, although Mamluk writers generally accuse Tīmūr's invasion of having delivered the fatal blow to the *Barīd*, considering the chaotic state of Mamluk administration, finances, and institutions in the early Burjī period, Tīmūr's *Barīd*-icide seems more like euthanasia than murder.

The foregoing analysis of the Mamluk *Barīd* indicates that the prevalent view of this institution as a mere heir to the Mongol *Yām* is unsatisfactory. While it is undeniable that some aspects of the Mamluk *Barīd* unmistakably resemble the *Yām* and appear to be based on Mongol practices, some attributes of the Mongol system seem to have been inspired by Mamluk precedent. And yet, although the skeleton of the Mamluk *Barīd* was caliphal, as part of a conscious programme of atavism, in many ways it was fleshed out through interaction with the Mongols, both on the battlefield and, perhaps, in the lands of the Golden Horde, whence most of the early Mamluks were imported at a young age. It is very likely that the *Yām* was an institution with which Baḥrī *mamlūks* had direct experience. But the Mongols' influence runs deeper than mere points of detail: the need for an effective system of communication was encouraged by the Mongol threat, and the military character of the *Barīd* clearly attests to the context in which it was established. It is not surprising, then, that when the Mongol threat passed, the Mamluks' military tools – of which the postal system was one – lost their edge. As such, it is more fitting to view the Mamluk *Barīd* as an indirect product of the Mongol empire, rather than as the direct heir to one of its institutions. Moreover, the distinguishing features of the Mamluk postal system described above demonstrate that although it benefited from caliphal and Mongol models, the Mamluk *Barīd* was essentially an unprecedented institution.

[73] The Mamluk chronicles still, on occasion, mention the *Barīd* in action during the late Mamluk period. For specific examples, see: Gazagnadou, *La Poste*, p. 71 n. 28; and W. Popper, *Egypt and Syria under the Circassian Sultans: 1384–1468: Systematic Notes to Ibn Taghrībirdī's Chronicle of Egypt*, California, 1955–7, vol. I, pp. 45–54 and 81–110, for a general picture of the imperial routes during this period. Despite this, the practical decline of the system in the aftermath of Tīmūr's invasion is described in unequivocal terms by contemporary authors.

Conclusions

In the Sumerian *Epic of Enmerkar and the Lord of Arrata* (*ca.* 1800 BCE), a royal envoy's ineptitude is said to have had significant consequences: 'The messenger's mouth was heavy, he could not repeat the message. [Thus] the Lord of Kulab patted some clay, he put the words on it as on a tablet. Before that time, words put on clay had never existed' (ll. 500–14). According to this legend, one of the greatest inventions of all – writing – resulted from the actions of a Near Eastern courier. It would be an overstatement to suggest that couriers played roles of comparable importance in the pre-modern Islamic world, but the foregoing chapters have shown that their activities have been of enough significance to justify the creation and maintenance of complex postal systems throughout pre-modern Islamic history. A thorough analysis of these systems teaches us much about communications technology in the Near East in general and about Islamic state-building in particular.

I) The relationship between pre-modern postal systems and the exercise of political power was complex, for two reasons. First, the existence of well-maintained routes from the capital to the borders of the state also meant that a clear path from enemy territories to the capital was open to invaders, and it is no coincidence that some of the greatest conquest movements in history were accomplished along the Near East's venerable arteries of communication. Second, the very visible trappings of a postal network unquestionably bolstered a ruler's reputation for justice while also serving as a reminder to the population that the ruler was watching his subjects closely. But this aspect of postal systems made them particularly attractive targets for rebels and other enemies of the state, for whom such systems both symbolised and helped implement the ruler's authority.

More often than not, however, postal systems contributed to the creation and maintenance of geographically vast states in the pre-modern Islamic world. The nature of this contribution is twofold. On the one hand, postal systems played a passive role of propaganda and intimidation. The wide dissemination of 'postal myths' in pre-modern Near Eastern history bears witness to the fact that ordinary people attributed extraordinary abilities to such systems, which thereby served as a deterrent to would-be troublemakers.

That postal mounts are believed to have had carved hooves, removed spleens, docked tails, or *muḍammar* physiques explained in the popular mind how postal systems managed to transport perishables to a ruler from thousands of kilometres away. And it is hardly surprising that, due to his preoccupation with *Barīd* reports, al-Manṣūr was believed to have a magic mirror that showed him an updated picture of the world's affairs.[1] On the other hand, postal systems played an active and actual role in ferreting out insurgents, transmitting military intelligence, and conveying anything – dignitaries, poets, prisoners, correspondence, ice, and exotica – from one end of an empire to another. The numerous references to such postal activity analysed above attest to the large variety of contexts in which postal systems played an essential role and hint at the many other episodes that did not make it into our primary sources or documents.[2]

Perhaps the best indication of the significance of postal systems to the regions and periods treated here is the effect that *not* having a *Barīd* is believed to have had on Islamic history. According to such weighty authorities as Jāḥiẓ, Masʿūdī, Ṭabarī, and the *Siyāsat al-Mulūk*, the Umayyad dynasty was overthrown not because of *mawālī* discontent, the spread of Shiʿism, or any other ideological challenge to its legitimacy, but rather because the late Umayyads neglected the gathering of the political intelligence (*akhbār*) that these authors associated with the *Barīd.*[3] For ʿUmarī, the Buyids succeeded in capturing Baghdad by 'cutting off' the *Barīd* and depriving the caliphs of information about their movements, just as al-Maʾmūn overcame al-Amīn by depriving him of *Barīd* reports from Khurasan. Bundārī attributes the rise of Ismaʿīlī terrorism to the Seljuks' lack of a *Barīd*, and Alp Arslān's obstinate refusal to make use of such a system may account for the Seljuks' initial ignorance of the Crusaders' movements and operations. We can only speculate as to whether or not the existence of a well-oiled *Barīd* in the Near East of the 1250s would have thwarted the Mongols' offensive or, failing that, shaped the *Yām* in subsequent decades.

II) The postal systems surveyed here also contribute to our understanding of the various dynasties and states whose institutions have been analysed above. Despite the implied insistence to the contrary throughout this book, pre-modern postal systems were conceptually simple institutions: in order to deliver something quickly, a series of fresh messengers or mounts would sequentially relay the object over large distances. And yet this simple formula

[1] Crone, *Pre-Industrial Societies*, p. 41. Compare the fact that the Indian Sultan Sikandar Lodi's (r. 1489–1517) knowledge of provincial affairs was so extensive that his postal agents were believed to have been genii (in Sabahuddin, 'Postal System', 275).

[2] On the pivotal relationship between information-gathering and the exercise of imperial power in early modern India, see: C. A. Bayly, *Empire and Information: Intelligence Gathering and Social Communication in India 1780–1870*, Cambridge, 1997, pp. 10–55.

[3] It should be stressed that both the *Siyāsat al-Mulūk* and Jāḥiẓ make the connection between the fall of the Umayyads and the lack of political intelligence in their chapters on the *Barīd.*

was expressed and elaborated upon in manifestly different ways throughout Islamic history. The idiosyncratic ways in which different states chose to interpret the basic postal formula offer us rare insights into the political traditions of particular dynasties and rulers. That the infantry-based Buyids introduced runners and that the equestrian Mamluks introduced a horse-based *Barīd* to lands that had not seen runners or mounted postal systems for centuries are two examples that illustrate the point. Similarly, it is clear that dynasties loyal to the Abbasids chose to model their bureaucracies on the caliphal *dīwāns*, and both the Samanids and the Buyids had a *Dīwān al-Barīd*. Conversely, counter-caliphs such as the Fatimids consciously distinguished themselves from the Abbasids and – despite having truly 'international' aspirations – did not make use of a *Barīd* system.

The particular form that a postal system would take in any given region or period of Islamic history was also shaped by topography and technology. Topography and the natural conditions of the Near East's varied terrain almost always influenced the contours of a region's postal system. As the word implies, 'elements' were truly basic to ancient decision-making processes,[4] especially when large distances and harsh conditions were involved. The use of camels as postal mounts in Arabia or North Africa was not the result of a strategic decision taken by an administrator or ruler; rather, it was a reflection of the physical realities that characterised these regions and of the time-tested ways that were developed in response to these realities.[5] The introduction and availability of new technologies of communication also conditioned postal systems noticeably. Just as alphabets did away with cumbersome and elitist cuneiform tablets, and paper did away with papyrus and parchment, the widespread domestication of the camel did away with wheeled vehicles and paved roads in the Near East. The impact of the stirrup is still debated,[6] but the general point remains that new technologies of communication were introduced to the Near East in the centuries immediately preceding and following Islam's rise. To the extent that pigeon-couriers were speedier, cheaper, and easier to organise than mounted networks were, they too represented a technological advance that influenced the function and

4 'Elements' were quite literally the 'A-B-C' of pre-modern life. The Phoenician alphabet (on which the Greek and Latin alphabets are based) comprised twenty-two letters that were divided into the alphabet's first and second halves. The second half began with the letters L-M-N, just as the first half began with A-B-C. The 'eLeMeNts' were thus as basic as 'A-B-C' to ancient civilisations (cf. A. Dillmann, *Grammatik der äthiopischen Sprache*, Leipzig, 1899, p. 17 n. 4).

5 Conversely, the use of (she-)camels in the central Islamic lands was probably a conscious measure taken by rulers at a time when routes and stations could not be secured.

6 L. White Jr. (*Medieval Technology and Social Change*, New York, 1966) has forcefully argued for a direct causal link between the introduction of the stirrup to Western Europe and the development of feudalism in France. Although his conclusions have been heavily criticised by reviewers (e.g. B. S. Bacharach, 'Charles Martel, Mounted Shock Combat, the Stirrup and Feudalism', *Studies in Medieval and Renaissance History* 7 (1970), 49–75), it is undeniable that the stirrup transformed equestrianism in the early Middle Ages, and as a mounted relay-system the *Barīd* is likely to have been affected.

organisation of postal systems; in some cases (the Fatimids) they obviated postal systems, in other cases (the Mamluks) they complemented them.

III) Having analysed the various postal systems employed in pre-modern Islamic history, we may return to the question posed at the beginning of this book: in what way (if any) were Islamic postal systems 'Islamic'? There are two answers to this question, one of which is more satisfactory than the other. The less satisfactory answer is that the distinguishing feature of the postal systems discussed in this book is that they did not make use of wheeled vehicles. While it is factually true, this answer is unsatisfactory, since the domestication of the camel at the expense of the wheel is a process that began before the rise of Islam. Although the impact of this development was felt most strongly in the Islamic Near East, it cannot be argued that 'Islam' had much to do with it.[7] Accordingly, Near Eastern postal systems would probably have been wheel-less during this period had seventh-century Arabians stayed put.

The more satisfactory answer is that 'Islamic' postal systems were distinguished from others by their relatively benign funding arrangements. Requisitions and corvées were the 'death and taxes' of the pre-Islamic Near East, and the fact that from the Middle Abbasid period we hear nothing of such practices in the context of the *Barīd* is truly remarkable. Although the Mongol *Yām* was financially burdensome to local populations, it is a strange coincidence that Ghāzān Khān, the Mongol ruler famous for shifting the financial burdens incurred by the *Yām* from the population to the Treasury, was also famous for converting to Islam.[8] An unexpected implication follows from this analysis: the fact that the early caliphal *Barīd* was based on the same requisitions and irregular taxes that characterised the Byzantine and Sasanid postal systems suggests that, at least in this respect, the early *Barīd* resembled a Late Antique institution more than it did an Islamic one.

IV) Another feature of the early *Barīd* that emerges from this study is that the institution was adopted by the Muslims *before* the Umayyad period. Taking the Mongol conquests as a case-study, it has been shown that nomads conducting campaigns of expansion from regions steeped in long traditions of travel and riding can organise rudimentary postal systems even before a suitable administrative framework into which such systems can be integrated has been created. Arabic sources that describe the Muslim conquests make repeated reference to the operations of 'the *Barīd*', but the historiographical problems associated with these sources mean that such accounts have hitherto been rejected by cautious scholars.[9] The impact that the Barbarian

[7] Bulliet, *Camel and the Wheel*, p. 226.

[8] On Ghāzān's conversion, see C. Melville, 'Padishah-i Islam: The Conversion of Ghazan to Islam', *Pembroke Papers* 1 (1990), 159–77. The case of 'Umar II lends support to this hypothesis, as he is the only Umayyad caliph who is believed to have exonerated the populace from paying 'fees for couriers', just as he is the only Umayyad caliph whose 'Islamic' credentials were not questioned by later authors.

[9] See above, p. 49 n. 246.

invasions had on the Roman road system established a conquest paradigm according to which marauding conquerors are expected to disrupt rather than promote organised systems of communication. But the Mongol conquests – about which we are relatively well informed – demonstrate that the conquest of the Near East can take a different form, and the fact that pre-Umayyad Arabians were well acquainted with the Byzantine and Sasanid postal systems explains why it is the Mongol rather than the Barbarian model that applies to the Muslim conquests.

Without exception, rulers in the pre-modern Islamic world benefited from postal systems that were unparalleled in contemporary Europe. But where our story ends another begins, and in it European powers had the upper hand with regard to communications technology. Although Europeans who visited the Near East during the Middle Ages returned home with enthusiastic reports on the postal systems from whose services they benefited, by the nineteenth century the tables had turned. Muḥammad al-Saffār, a Moroccan who visited France in 1845–6, has the following to say about conditions of travel in France:

> Nor are the animals exhausted, for the horses and drivers are changed every hour. On the road are stables that they call in their language the *poste*, where many horses are kept. When a traveller arrives here, he leaves his horses and takes fresh ones, along with a [new] driver. They go for an hour or so to another post-house, where horses and driver are changed once again, so that the horses are always rested and may continue at the same fast pace. On our trip from Marseilles to Paris, more than eight hundred horses were changed. We were in three coaches, each one drawn by ten horses: three, three, and four . . . Whoever follows this road, travelling day and night, will arrive in Paris from Marseilles in about three days. Letters and correspondence going from one city to the other take three days or less, even though the distance between them for a person travelling on horse-back is close to a month.[10]

From al-Saffār's tone, a reader might deduce that comparable institutions had never existed in the Islamic world. As the preceding chapters show, this clearly was not the case. But by the nineteenth century, inhabitants of the Near East were taking postal lessons from the West: it was the Europeans who introduced the telegraph to the Muslim world,[11] and it was based on modern European postal systems that inhabitants of the modern Near East created their own postal organisations. In the contemporary Arab world, postal systems are still called '*al-Barīd*', a word that is surely one of the most historically loaded terms in the modern Arabic language.

[10] Muḥammad al-Saffār, *Disorienting Encounters: Travels of a Moroccan Scholar in France in 1845–6*, (ed./trans. S. G. Miller), Berkeley, 1992, pp. 94–5.

[11] Bektas, 'Sultan's Messenger', *passim*.

Appendix: distances and speeds of the *Barīd*

Those using the *Barīd* (or the *Yām*) could achieve very impressive speeds. In some cases, the postal speeds recorded in our sources appear to have been exaggerated: neither Faḍl nor Marʾūsh could really have covered over 200 kilometres a day on foot, and al-Maʾmūn could not have instantly received myrobalan fruits from Kabul while campaigning in Byzantine lands. That said, there is usually little reason to dismiss accounts that mention notable rates of travel, especially when various independent sources confirm that a particular speed was achievable. What should be remembered is that, by definition, historians chose to make note only of those speeds that were deemed to be noteworthy, and we cannot draw conclusions about the speeds routinely achieved by a postal system on the basis of such exceptional accounts. Hence, references to the 80 or 85 parasangs that *jammāzāt* traversed in a 24-hour period during Hishām's reign indicate that it may not have been impossible for mounted couriers to cover some 500 kilometres in a day and a night,[1] but also that we should not expect this to have been a commonplace occurrence.

What speeds can we realistically expect the *Barīd* and the *Yām* to have achieved on a regular basis? The *Siyāsat al-Mulūk* mentions that a mail-bag can travel no more than 60 parasangs (360 kilometres) in a day, while Niẓām al-Mulk states that a network of couriers (*paykān*) can relay news from 50 parasangs (300 kilometres) away within 24 hours. Herodotus also speaks of 300 kilometres as the maximum distance that express couriers using the postal system can cover in a day, and we know that although the *Cursus Publicus* only averaged about 75 kilometres on a daily basis, Procopius suggests that couriers could at times reduce a 10-day journey to a single day – thereby covering some 300 kilometres. Marco Polo also estimates that Mongol couriers were ten times as fast as ordinary travellers, and in Muḥammad al-Saffār's evaluation the French *poste* reduced a thirty-day

[1] Racehorses, for instance, are known to achieve well in excess of 30 kilometres an hour. A relay network of speedy horses could therefore cover more than 600 kilometres over a 24-hour period. Racing-camels and even mules are known to be only slightly slower than swift horses.

journey to three days (representing the same 10:1 ratio).[2] Runners in the Buyid and Mongol periods are said to have operated at a daily rate of approximately 200 kilometres (30 to 40 parasangs), although these speeds can only have been achieved when relays of runners were used, as a single man cannot physically maintain a rate of 20 kilometres an hour over more than 2 or 3 hours.

In most instances, postal systems were considerably less efficient than these speeds suggest, either because travel conditions were sub-optimal or because the circumstances did not justify the enormous effort required to clock a speed of 300 kilometres a day. Moreover, when dignitaries used the services of the postal system, they were not expected to travel as capably as professional riders could. And yet, using the postal system was still significantly quicker than travelling by ordinary means: scholars have shown that Öljetü averaged only 40 kilometres a day on his travels, whereas al-Mahdī used the *Barīd* to reach Baghdad from Jurjān, a 2,000-kilometre distance, in 13 days (achieving a daily speed of *ca.* 150 kilometres).[3] De Bridia mentions that envoys riding the *Yām* covered some 200 kilometres every day, a speed that modern scholars have dismissed as exaggerated. It may well be that envoys using the *Yām* could not cover this distance on a daily basis, but there is no doubt that couriers could.

The following table provides a summary of the recorded speeds at which the *Barīd* accomplished selected itineraries, coupled with data on the postal stations and distances provided by Ibn Khurradādhbih (IK) and Qudāma ibn Jaʿfar (Qud.) that allow us to calculate the average speeds achievable on these routes.

[2] That the communications network established by al-Afshīn during his campaigns against Bābak managed to convey news from a month away in less than four days represents a similar rate of speed.

[3] According to H. Kennedy (*The Courts of the Caliphs: The Rise and Fall of Islam's Greatest Dynasty*, London, 2004, p. 85), the 150 kilometres a day that the eunuch Rajā covered in transmitting news of Hārūn's death by riding the *Barīd* between Ṭūs and Baghdad was a rate that was 'not bettered before the coming of motor transport in the twentieth century'. This estimate of the *Barīd*'s maximum speed appears to be unnecessarily conservative.

Table: Distances and speeds of the *Barīd*

Route	Distance (overland)	Postal Stations	Recorded Speed	Period	Distance covered in a day
Damascus to Samarra	*ca.* 1,200/*ca.* 1,740 km[4]	145	6 days[5]	Abbasid (al-Muʿtaṣim)	200–300 km
Damascus to Baghdad	*ca.* 1,200/*ca.* 1,740 km	n/a[6]	3 weeks[7]	Merchant letters	60–80 km
Damascus to Medina	*ca.* 1,500 km	n/a[8]	12 days[9]	Umayyad (Yazīd I)	125 km
Samarra to Baghdad	*ca.* 180 km	15	1 hr 20 mins[10]	Abbasid	n/a
Baghdad to Shiraz	*ca.* 1,100 km	94(IK)/91(Qud.)	7–8 days[11]	Buyid	140–160 km
Baghdad to Mecca (*kharīṭat al-mawsim*)	*ca.* 1,650 km	n/a[12]	4 days[13]	Abbasid	410 km
Cairo to Damascus	*ca.* 730 km[14]		2–4 days[15]	Mamluk	180–360 km
Rayy to Marw	*ca.* 1,270 km	n/a[16]	3 days[17]	Abbasid (al-Maʾmūn)	420 km
Jurjān to Baghdad	*ca.* 2,000 km	n/a[18]	13 days[19]	Abbasid (al-Hādī)	150 km

4 See above, p. 66.
5 Ṣābiʾ, *Rusūm*, p. 19. In the Umayyad period, it took seven days from Damascus to 'Iraq' (Ṭabarī, *Taʾrīkh*, II, p. 1309).
6 This itinerary is recorded for the *kutub al-tujjār*, who did not make use of official postal facilities.
7 Ṭabarī, *Taʾrīkh*, III, p. 2222.
8 As the *masālik wa mamālik* literature that would ordinarily provide the number of *Barīd* stations was composed after the Umayyad period, the stations on this route are not mentioned.
9 Ṭabarī, *Taʾrīkh*, II, p. 406. The *Barīd* is not mentioned in this instance, though its use is assumed.
10 *Siyāsat al-Mulūk*, in Silverstein, 'New Source', 131/133. Ibn Khurradādhbih (*Masālik*, p. 59) specifies that it is 15 *sikak* from Samarra to Baghdad. Even if the stations were only 2 parasangs apart, this would still mean that covering this 180-kilometre distance in 1 hour and 20 minutes would entail riding at a rate of 135 kilometres an hour, an impossible speed.
11 Miskawayh, *Eclipse*, vol. III, p. 40; and Ṣābiʾ, *Rusūm*, p. 18.
12 The pilgrimage route was not a 'postal route', though pseudo-Ibn Qutayba mentions that *najāʾib* could cover eight *marāḥil* of 24 kilometres each a day during Hārūn's reign.
13 See above, p. 107.
14 This is Ibn Khurradādhbih's figure ('365 *mīl*'), as given by Maqrīzī (*Khiṭaṭ*, vol. I, p. 615). Popper (*Egypt and Syria*, vol. I, pp. 45–54, at pp. 48–9) estimates the distance as 475 [modern] 'miles', that is to say 760 kilometres.
15 Maqrīzī (*Khiṭaṭ*, vol. I, p. 615) states that the journey took four days by *Barīd*, though according to Popper (*Egypt and Syria*, vol. I, p. 45) 'it is recorded that once only four days were required for the combined journey there and back'.
16 The stations of 'the East' in Ibn Khurradādhbih (*Masālik*, pp. 41–2) reach no farther than Nīshāpūr.
17 Jahshiyārī, *Wuzarāʾ*, p. 294.
18 Neither Ibn Khurradādhbih nor Qudāma makes reference to this route.
19 See above, p. 66.

Bibliography

Abbott, N., *The Ḳurrah Papyri*, Chicago, 1938
ʿAbd al-Ḥamīd ibn Yaḥyā, *Rasāʾil al-bulaghāʾ*, ed. M. Kurd Ali, Cairo, 1946
ʿAbd al-Laṭīf, M. A., *Mudun wa qurā miṣr fī nuṣūṣ baʿḍ al-bardiyyāt al-ʿarabiyya fī al-ʿaṣr al-umawī*, unpublished MA thesis, University of Helwan, 2001
ʿAdiyy ibn Zayd, *Dīwān*, Baghdad, 1965
al-Afghānī, S., *Aswāq al-ʿarab fī al-jāhiliyya wa al-islām*, Damascus, 1960
Agha, S. S., *The Revolution which Toppled the Umayyads*, Leiden, 2003
Ahlwardt, W., *The Divans of the Ancient Arabic Poets Ennabiga, ʿAntara, Tharafa, Zuhair, ʿAlqama, Imruulqais*, London, 1870
Alef, G., 'The Origins and Early Development of the Muscovite Postal Service', *Jahrbücher für Geschichte Osteuropas* 15 (1967), 1–15
al-ʿAlī, S. A., '*Muwazzafū bilād al-shām fī al-ʿaṣr al-umawī*', *al-Abḥāth* 19 (1966), 44–79
Allsen, T., *Mongol Imperialism*, London, 1987
Culture and Conquest in Mongol Eurasia, Cambridge, 2001
ʿAlqama al-Faḥl, *Fuḥūl al-ʿarab fī ʿilm al-adab: sharḥ dīwān ʿalqama*, Algiers, 1925
Altekar, A. S., *State and Government in Ancient India*, Delhi, 1958
Amarna Letters, (ed./trans. W. L. Moran), Baltimore, 1992
Amitai-Preiss, R., *Mongols and Mamluks*, Cambridge, 1995
Anṣarī, ʿUmar ibn Ibrāhīm, *Tafrīj al-kurūb fī tadbīr al-ḥurūb*, ed./trans. G. T. Scanlon as *A Muslim Manual of War*, Cairo, 1961
ʿArīb, ibn Saʿd al-Qurṭubī, *Ṣilat taʾrīkh al-ṭabarī*, Leiden, 1897
Aristotle, *Parva Naturalia*, ed. I. Bekker, Berlin, 1831
Ashtor, E., *The Levant Trade in the Later Middle Ages*, Princeton, 1983
ʿAskarī, Abū Hilāl, *Dīwān al-maʿānī*, Cairo, 1933–4
Kitāb al-awāʾil, Beirut, 1997
ʿAsqalānī, *Rafʿ al-iṣr min quḍā miṣr*, Cairo, 1988
Aubin, J., 'Réseau pastoral et réseau caravanier: les grand-routes du Khurasan a l'époque Mongole', *Le Monde Iranien et l'Islam* 1 (1971), 105–30
Audollent, N., 'Les Veredarii: émissaires impériaux sous le Bas Empire', *Mélanges d'Archéologie et d'Histoire* 9 (1889), 249–78
Austin, N. J. E., and B. Rankov, *Exploratio: Military and Political Intelligence in the Roman World*, New York and London, 1995
Austin, N. N., *The Hellenistic World from Alexander to the Roman Conquest: A Selection of Ancient Sources in Translation*, Cambridge, 1981

Ayalon, D., 'Studies on the Structure of the Mamluk Army', *BSOAS* 15 (1953), 203–28

'Studies in the Transfer of the Abbasid Caliphate from Baghdad to Cairo', *Arabica* 7 (1960), 41–59

'On One of the Works of Jean Sauvaget', *Israel Oriental Studies* 1 (1971), 298–302

Eunuchs, Caliphs, and Sultans: A Study in Power Relationships, Jerusalem, 1999

Azraqī, Abū al-Walīd Muḥammad, *Akhbār makka*, ed. R. S. Malḥas, Madrid, n.d.

Bacharach, B. S., 'Charles Martel, Mounted Shock Combat, the Stirrup and Feudalism', *Studies in Medieval and Renaissance History* 7 (1970), 49–75

Bagnall, R. S., *Egypt in Late Antiquity*, Princeton, 1993

Balādhurī, Aḥmad ibn Yaḥyā, *Futūḥ al-buldān*, Leiden, 1866; trans. P. Hitti and F. Murgotten, *The Origins of the Islamic State*, New York, 1916

Kitāb jumal min ansāb al-ashrāf, ed. S. Zakkār, Beirut, 1996

Ansāb al-ashrāf, vol. III: ed. A. A. Duri, Wiesbaden, 1978; vol. IVa: ed. M. Schloessinger, Jerusalem, 1971; vol. IVb: ed. M. Schloessinger, Jerusalem, 1938; vol. V: ed. S. D. Goitein, Jerusalem, 1936; vol. VIb: ed. Kh. Athamina, Jerusalem, 1993

Baybars al-Manṣūrī al-Dawādār, *Zubdat al-fikra fī ta'rīkh al-hijra*, ed. D. S. Richards, Berlin, 1998

Bayhaqī, Ibrāhīm ibn Muḥammad, *Kitāb al-maḥāsin wa al-masāwī*, Cairo, 1906; and ed. M. A. F. Ibrāhīm, Cairo, 1991 (reprint from 1961)

Bayly, C. A., *Empire and Information: Intelligence Gathering and Social Communication in India 1780–1870*, Cambridge, 1997

Beaulieu, P. A., *The Reign of Nabonidus: King of Babylonia 556–539 BC*, New Haven, 1989

Becker, C. H., 'Arabische Papyri des Afroditofundes', *Zeitschrift für Assyriologie und verwandte Gebiete* 20 (1906), 68–104

Beitzel, B. J., 'The Old Assyrian Caravan Road According to Geographical Notices Contained in the Royal Archives of Mari', in G. D. Young (ed.), *Mari at 50*, Indiana, 1990, pp. 35–57

'Roads and Highways (pre-Roman)' in *ABD* vol. V pp. 776–82

Bektas, Y., 'The Sultan's Messenger: Cultural Constructions of Ottoman Telegraphy', *Technology and Culture* 41 (2000), 669–96

Bell, H. I., *Greek Documents in the British Library IV*, London, 1910

Ben-Shemesh, A., *Taxation in Islam III*, London, 1969

Biddle, D. W., 'The Development of the Bureaucracy of the Islamic Empire during the Late Umayyad and Early Abbasid Period', unpublished PhD dissertation, University of Texas at Austin, 1970

Biran, M., 'Like a Mighty Wall: The Armies of the Qara Khitai', *JSAI* 25 (2001), 44–91

The Empire of the Qara Khitai in Eurasian History, Cambridge, 2005

Blair, S. S. 'A Mongol Envoy', in B. O'Kane (ed.), *The Iconography of Islamic Art: Studies in Honour of Robert Hillenbrand*, Edinburgh, 2005, pp. 45–60

Bligh-Abramski, I., 'Evolution versus Revolution: Umayyad Elements in the ʿAbbasid Regime 133/750–320/932', *Der Islam* 65 (1988), 226–43

Bloom, J., *Paper before Print*, New Haven, 2001

Borsch, S., *The Black Death in Egypt and England*, Austin, 2005

Bosworth, C. E., *The Ghaznavids*, Edinburgh, 1963

'Abū 'Abdallāh al-Khwārazmī on the Technical Terms of the Secretary's Art', *JESHO* 12 (1969), 113–64

'An Early Arabic Mirror for Princes: Ṭāhir Dhū al-Yamīnayn's Epistle to his Son 'Abdallāh (206/821)', *Journal of Near Eastern Studies* 29 (1970), 25–41

The History of al-Ṭabarī vol. XXXII: The Reunification of the Abbasid Caliphate, New York, 1987

The History of al-Ṭabarī vol. XXXIII: Storm and Stress along the Northern Frontiers of the Abbasid Caliphate, New York, 1991

Bowerstock, G., P. Brown, and O. Grabar (eds.), *Late Antiquity: A Guide to the Post-Classical World*, Cambridge Mass., 1999

Boyle, J., 'Ibn al-Ṭiqṭaqā and the Ta'rīkh Jahān Gushāy of Juvaynī', *BSOAS* 14 (1952), 175–7

Bravmann, M., 'The State Archives in the Early Islamic Era', *Arabica* 15 (1969), 87–9

Briant, P., *From Cyrus to Alexander: A History of the Persian Empire*, trans. P. T. Daniels, Indiana, 2002

Bridia, C. de, in R. A. Skelton, T. E. Marston, and G. D. Painter, *The Vinland Map and the Tartar Relation*, New Haven and London, 1965, section 3: 'The Tartar Relation' (ed./trans. G. D. Painter)

Brocklemann, C., *Lexicon Syriacum*, Halle, 1928

Brown, F., S. R. Driver, and C. A. Briggs, *A Hebrew and English Lexicon of the Old Testament*, Oxford, 1962

Bryce, T., *Letters of the Great Kings of the Ancient Near East*, London, 2003

Buell, P., 'Sino-Khitan Administration in Mongol Bukhara', *JAH* 13 (1979), 121–51

Bulliet, R., *The Camel and the Wheel*, Cambridge Mass., 1975

Bundārī, al-Fatḥ ibn 'Alī, *Tārīkh dawlat āl saljūq*, ed. M. Th. Houtsma, *Histoire des Seldjoucides de l'Iraq par al-Bondari d'après Imâd ad-dîn al-Kâtib al-Isfahânî: texte arabe*, Leiden, 1886

Burhān, Muḥammad Ḥusayn ibn Khalaf, *Burhān-i qāṭi'*, ed. M. Mu'īn, Teheran, 1951–63

Busse, H., *Chalif und Grosskönig: Die Buyiden im Iraq (945–1055)*, Beirut, 1969

Cameron, G., *The Persepolis Treasury Tablets*, Chicago, 1948

Carpini, John Pian, *The Journey of Friar John of Pian de Carpine to the Court of Kuyuk Khan, 1245–1247*, trans. W. W. Rockhill, London, 1900

Casson, L., *Travel in the Ancient World*, New York, 1994

Ch'ang Ch'un: trans. A. Waley, *Ch'ang-Ch'un: The Travels of an Alchemist*, London, 1931

Chardin, J., *A Journey to Persia: Jean Chardin's Portrait of a Seventeenth-Century Empire*, trans. R. W. Ferrier, London, 1996

Christensen, A., *L'Empire des Sassanides*, Copenhagen, 1907

L'Iran sous les Sassanides, Copenhagen, 1944

Chronicon Paschale 284–628 AD, (trans. M. Whitby and M. Whitby), Liverpool, 1989

Clauson, G., *Etymological Dictionary of Pre-13th Century Turkish*, Oxford, 1972

Clavijo, Ruy Gonzales de, *Embassy to Tamerlane 1403–1406*, trans. G. le Strange, New York and London, 1928

Codex Iustinianus: in P. Krueger, *Corpus Iuris Civilis II*, Berlin, 1954

Codex Theodosianus, (ed. Th. Mommsen and P. M. Meyer), Berlin, 1905

Constable, O. R., *Housing the Stranger in the Mediterranean World*, Cambridge, 2003

Cooper, R. S., 'Ibn Mammati's Rules for the Ministries: Translation with Commentary of the *Qawānīn al-Dawāwīn*', unpublished PhD dissertation, Berkeley, 1973

Cornu, G., *Atlas du monde arabo-islamique à l'époque classique: IXe–Xe siècles: répertoire des toponymes des cartes*, Leiden, 1983–5
Corpus Inscriptionum Semiticarum, Paris, 1881–1930
Coxon, R., 'Ashpenaz' in *ABD*, vol. I pp. 490–1
Crone, P., *Slaves on Horses*, Cambridge, 1980
Pre-Industrial Societies, Oxford, 2003
Medieval Islamic Political Thought, Edinburgh, 2004
Crown, A. D., 'Tidings and Instructions: How News Travelled in the Ancient Near East', *JESHO* 17 (1974), 244–71
Darādkeh, Ṣ, '*al-Barīd wa ṭuruq al-muwāṣalāt fī bilād al-shām fī al-ʿaṣr al-ʿabbāsī*', in M. A. al-Bakhit, *Bilād al-Shām during the Abbasid Period, Proceedings of the Fifth International Conference – Arabic Section*, Amman, 1991, pp. 191–207
Dawood, N. J., trans., *Tales from the Thousand and One Nights*, London, 1973
Diem, W., *Arabische Geschäftsbriefe des 10. bis 14. Jahrhunderts: aus der Österreichischen Nationalbibliothek in Wien*, Wiesbaden, 1995
Dietrich, A., *Arabische Papyri aus der Hamburger Staats- und Universitäts-Bibliothek*, Leipzig, 1937
Arabische Briefe aus der Papyrus-Sammlung der Hamburger Staats- und Universitäts-Bibliothek, Hamburg, 1955
Dillmann, A., *Grammatik der äthiopischen Sprache*, Leipzig, 1899
Dīnawarī, Aḥmad ibn Dāwūd, *al-Akhbār al-ṭiwāl*, Leiden, 1888–1912
Dio Cassius, *Roman History*, trans. E. Cary, Cambridge Mass., 1914–27
Dion, P. E., 'Aramaic words for "Letter"', *Semeia* 22 (1981), 77–88
Diodorus of Sicily, (trans. R. M. Geer), Cambridge Mass., 1984
Doerfer, G., *Türkische und mongolische Elemente in Neupersischen*, Wiesbaden, 1963–75
Donner, F., 'The Formation of the Islamic State', *JAOS* 86 (1986), 283–96
Donohue, J., *The Buwayhid Dynasty in Iraq 334H/945 to 403H/1012*, Leiden, 2003
Driver, G. R., *Aramaic Documents of the Fifth Century BC*, Oxford, 1957
Drower, E. S., and R. Macuch, *A Mandaic Dictionary*, Oxford, 1963
Ducène, J.-C., 'al-Ǧayhani: Fragments (Extraits du Kitāb al-Masālik wa al-Mamālik d'al-Bakrī)', *Der Islam* 75 (1998), 259–82
Dvornik, F., *The Origins of Intelligence Services*, New Jersey, 1974
Eilers, W., 'Iranisches Lehngut im arabischen Lexikon', *Indo-Iranian Journal* 5 (1962), 203–32
Elad, A., 'Aspects of the Transition from the Umayyad to the Abbasid Caliphate', *JSAI* 19 (1995), 89–132
'The Southern Golan in the Early Muslim Period: The Significance of Two Newly Discovered Milestones of ʿAbd al-Malik', *Der Islam* 76 (1999), 33–88
Eliot, C. W. J., 'New Evidence for the Speed of the Roman Imperial Post', *Phoenix* 9ii (1955), 76–80
Fārābī, Abū Naṣr Muḥammad, *Āthār ahl al-madīna al-fāḍila*, Cairo, 1323 AH
Findley, C. V., *The Turks in World History*, Oxford, 2004
Fletcher, J., 'The Mongols: Ecological and Social Perspectives', *HJAS* 46i (1986), 11–50
Floor, W., 'The *Chapar-Khāna* System in Qajar Iran', *Iran* 39 (2001), 257–92
Floor, W., and J. Emerson, 'Rahdars and their Tolls in Safavid and Afsharid Iran', *JESHO* 30 (1987), 318–27

Forbes, R. J., *Studies in Ancient Technology II*, Leiden, 1955
Foss, C., 'The Persians in the Roman Near East (602–630 AD)', *JRAS* 13ii (2003), 149–70
'The *Sellarioi* and Other Officers of Persian Egypt', *Zeitschrift für Papyrologie und Epigraphik* 138 (2002), 169–72
Friedman, S., *Talmūd arūkh: Babā meṣīʿā VI*, Jerusalem, 1990, pp. 153–69
Fries, C., 'Babylonische Feuerpost', *Klio* 3 (1903), 169–70
'Zur babylonischen Feuerpost', *Klio* 4 (1904), 117–21
Frye, R., *The History of Bukhara*, Cambridge Mass., 1954
The Heritage of Persia, London, 1962
The History of Ancient Iran, Munich, 1984
Gardīzī, ʿAbd al-Ḥayy ibn Ẓaḥḥāq, *Zayn al-akhbār*, Teheran, 1969
Gazagnadou, D., *La Poste à relais: la diffusion d'une technique de pouvoir à travers l'Eurasie – Chine – Islam – Europe*, Paris, 1994
'Note sur le mot *Barīd* (*al-barīd*)', *Luqmān* 15i (1999), 35–42
Geiger, B., 'Zum Postwesen der Perser', *Wiener Zeitschrift für die Kunde des Morgenlandes* 29 (1915), 309–14
Ghazzālī, *Iḥyāʾ ulūm al-dīn*, Cairo, 1348 AH
Kīmiyāʾ al-saʿāda, Cairo, 1343 AH
Gibb, H. A. R., 'Al-Mawardi's Theory of the Caliphate', *Islamic Culture* 11 (1937), 291–302
Studies on the Civilisation of Islam, London, 1962
Gil, M., and E. Fleischer, *Be-malkhūth yishmaʿel be-tekūfath ha-geʾonīm*, Tel-Aviv, 1997
Yehuda Ha-Levi and his Circle: 55 Geniza Documents, Jerusalem, 2001
Gillet, A., *Envoys and Political Communication in the Late Antique West, 411–533*, Cambridge, 2003
Goeje, M. J. de, 'Paltiel-Djauhar', *ZDMG* 52 (1898), 75–80
Goitein, S. D., 'The Commercial Mail Service in Medieval Islam', *JAOS* 84 (1964), 118–23
A Mediterranean Society. Volume I: Economic Foundations, Berkeley, 1967; and *Volume II: The Community*, Berkeley, 1971
Goldsmid, Sir F. J., *Eastern Persia: An Acccount of the Journeys for the Persian Boundary Commission 1870–71–72*, London, 1876
Gregory of Aknac: *History of the Nation of Archers*, trans. R. P. Blake and R. Frye, Harvard University Press, 1954
Grenet, F., and E. de la Vaissière, 'The Last Days of Panjikent', *Silk Road Art and Archaeology* 8 (2002), 155–96
Grohmann, A., *Papyri in the Egyptian Library*, Cairo, 1934–8
Arabische Paläographie, Vienna, 1967–71
Groom, N., *Frankincense and Myrrh*, London, 1981
Grossfeld, B., *The First Targum to Esther: According to MS Paris Hebrew 110 of the Bibliothèque Nationale*, New York, 1983
Guillaume, A. *The Life of Muhammad*, Karachi, 1955
Ḥāfiẓ Abrū: *A Persian Embassy to China*, ed./trans. K. M. Maitra, Lahore, 1934
Hallo, W., *Origins: The Ancient Near Eastern Background of Some Modern Western Institutions*, Leiden, 1996
Hallock, R., *The Persepolis Fortification Tablets*, Chicago, 1969

Halm, H., *The Empire of the Mahdī*, Leiden, 1996
Hartmann, R., 'Zur Geschichte der Mamlukenpost', *Orientalische Literaturzeitung* 46 (1943), 266–70
Harvey, E. R., *The Inward Wits*, London, 1975
Heck, P. L., *The Construction of Knowledge in Islamic Civilization: Qudāma ibn Jaʿfar and his Kitāb al-kharāj wa ṣināʿat al-kitāba*, Leiden, 2002
Hendy, M. F., *Studies in the Byzantine Monetary Economy c. 300–1450*, Cambridge, 1985
Herodotus, *Histories*, trans. A. D. Godley, Cambridge Mass., 1963–9
Herzfeld, E., *Zoroaster and his World*, Princeton, 1947
Heyd, U., *Ottoman Documents on Palestine, 1552–1615*, Oxford, 1960
Heywood, C., 'The Ottoman *Menzilḥāne* and *Ulaḳ* System in Rumelī in the Eighteenth Century', in O. Okyar and H. Inalcik (eds.), *Türkiye-nin Sosyal ve Ekonomik Tarihi (1071–1920)*, Ankara, 1980, pp. 179–86
'The Via Egnatia in the Ottoman Period: The *Menzilḥānes* of the *Ṣol Ḳol* in the Late 17th/Early 18th Century', in E. Zachariadou, *The Via Egnatia under Ottoman Rule*, Crete, 1996, pp. 129–44
'Two Firmans of Muṣṭafā II on the Reorganisation of the Ottoman Courier System (1108/1696)', *Acta Orientalia Academiae Scientiarum Hungaricae* 54iv (2001), 485–95
Hill, D. R., 'The Role of the Camel and the Horse in the Early Arab Conquests', in V. J. Parry, and M. E. Yapp (eds.), *War, Technology, and Society in the Middle East*, London, 1975
Hillenbrand, C., *The Crusades: Islamic Perspectives*, Edinburgh, 1998
Hillenbrand, R., *Islamic Architecture: Form, Function, and Meaning*, Edinburgh, 1994
Hinds, M., and H. Sakkout, 'A Letter from the Governor of Egypt Concerning Egyptian-Nubian Relations', in M. Hinds (eds. J. Bacharach, L. Conrad, and P. Crone), *Studies in Early Islamic History*, Princeton, 1996, pp. 160–87
Hinz, W., *Islamische Masse und Gewichte: umgerechnet ins metrische System*, Leiden, 1970
Hirsch, S. W., *The Friendship of the Barbarians: Xenophon and the Persian Empire*, London, 1985
Hodgson, M., *The Venture of Islam. Volume II: The Expansion of Islam in the Middle Periods*, Chicago, 1974
Holmberg, E. J., *Zur Geschichte des Cursus Publicus*, Uppsala, 1933
Holt, P. M., 'Some Observations on the Abbasid Caliphate of Cairo', *BSOAS* 47 (1984), 501–7
Early Mamluk Diplomacy, Leiden, 1995
Hoyland, R., *Arabia and the Arabs from the Bronze Age to the Coming of Islam*, New York, 2001
Hudsailian Poems: The Hudsailian Poems Contained in the Manuscript of Leyden: Edited in Arabic and Translated with Annotations by John Godfrey Lewis Kosegarten, London, 1854
Humphreys, R. S., 'The Emergence of the Mamluk Army', *Studia Islamica* 45 (1977), 67–99; and 46 (1977), 147–82
Ḥusayn, M. K., and M. A. F. Shaʿīra, *Sīrat al-ustādh jawdhar*, Cairo, 1954
Ḥusrī, *Zahr al-ādāb wa thimār al-albāb*, Cairo, 1969–70

Ibn ʿAbd al-Ḥakam, Muhammad, *Sīrat ʿumar ibn ʿabd al-ʿaziz*, ed. A. Ubayd, Damascus, 1964
Ibn al-Athīr, ʿAlī ibn Muḥammad, *al-Kāmil fī al-taʾrīkh*, Beirut, 1965–7
Ibn Baṭṭūṭa: *The Travels of Ibn Battuta AD 1325–1354*, trans. H. A. R. Gibb, London, 1956
Ibn al-Faqīh al-Hamadhānī, Aḥmad, *Kitāb al-buldān*, Leiden, 1888
Ibn Ḥawqal, Abū al-Qāsim Muḥammad, *Kitāb al-masālik wa al-mamālik*, Leiden, 1873
Kitāb ṣūrat al-arḍ, Leiden, 1939
Ibn al-Jawzī, ʿAbd al-Raḥmān ibn ʿAlī, *al-Muntaẓam fī taʾrīkh al-mulūk wa al-umam*, ed. N. Zarzūr, Beirut, 1992
Ibn Khurradādhbih, Abū al-Qāsim, *Kitāb al-masālik wa al-mamālik*, ed. M. J. de Goeje, Leiden, 1889
Ibn Mājah, Muḥammad ibn Yazīd, *Sunan*, Cairo, 1952
Ibn Manẓūr, Muḥammad ibn Mukarram, *Lisān al-ʿarab*, Cairo, 1883–91
Ibn Miskawayh, *The Eclipse of the Abbasid Caliphate: Original Chronicles of the Fourth Islamic Century*, ed./trans. H. F. Amedroz and D. S. Margoliouth, Oxford, 1920–1
Mukhtaṣar taʾrīkh dimashq li ibn ʿasākir, Damascus, 1985
Ibn al-Muqaffaʿ, *Risāla fī al-ṣaḥāba*, ed./trans. Ch. Pellat, Paris, 1976
Ibn al-Nadīm, *al-Fihrist*, trans. B. Dodge, *The Fihrist of al-Nadīm*, New York, 1970
Ibn Qutayba, ʿAbdallāh ibn Muslim, *Taʾwīl mukhtalaf al-ḥadīth*, Cairo, 1326 AH
(pseudo-)Ibn Qutayba, *Kitāb al-imāma wa al-siyāsa*, Cairo, 1904
Ibn Rusta, Aḥmad ibn ʿUmar, *Kitāb al-aʿlāq al-nafīsa*, Leiden, 1891
Ibn Sīnā, *Aḥwāl al-nafs*, Cairo, 1952
Ibn Taghribirdī, Yūsuf, *al-Nujūm al-ẓāhira*, Cairo, 1929–38
Ibn al-Ṭiqṭaqā, Muḥammad ibn ʿAlī, *al-Fakhrī fī al-ādāb al-sulṭāniyya wa al-duwal al-islāmiyya*, Paris, 1895
Ibn Wahb, Abū al-Ḥusayn, *al-Burhān fī wujūh al-bayān*, eds. A. Maṭlūb and Kh. al-Ḥadīthī, Baghdad, 1967
Ikhwān al-Ṣafāʾ, *Rasāʾil*, Cairo, 1928
al-Imad, L. S., 'The Fāṭimid Vizierate 969–1172', unpublished PhD thesis, New York University, 1985
Isaac, B., 'Trade Routes to Arabia and the Roman Presence in the Desert', in T. Fahd (ed.), *L'Arabie préislamique et son environment historique et culturel*, Leiden, 1989, pp. 241–56
The Limits of Empire, Oxford, 1992
Iṣbahānī, Abū Nuʿaym, *Ḥilyat al-awliyāʾ wa ṭabaqat al-aṣfiyāʾ*, Cairo, 1932–8
Iṣfahānī, Abū al-Faraj, *Kitāb al-aghānī*, Cairo, 1927
Maqātil al-ṭālibiyyīn, Najaf, 1964
Iṣfahānī, Ḥamza, *Taʾrīkh sinī mulūk al-arḍ wa al-anbiyāʾ*, Berlin, 1921–2
Iṣfahānī, al-Rāghib, *Tafṣīl al-nashʾatayn wa taḥṣīl al-saʿādatayn*, Beirut, 1988
Iṣṭakhrī, Ibrāhīm ibn Muḥammad, *Kitāb al-masālik wa al-mamālik*, Leiden, 1870
Ivanov, A. A., 'Seal of the Eighth Century Secret Service', in *Sphragistica and History of Culture: Volume of Articles Dedicated to the Jubilee of V. S. Shandrovskaya*, St Petersburg, 2004, pp. 142–6
Jackson, P., 'The Dissolution of the Mongol Empire', *Central Asiatic Journal* 22 (1978), 186–244

Jāḥiẓ, ʿAmr ibn Baḥr, *Kitāb al-ḥayawān*, Cairo, 1940
Kitāb al-bayān wa al-tabyīn, Cairo, 1947
Kitāb al-qawl fī al-bighāl, Cairo, 1955
Jahshiyārī, Muḥammad ibn ʿAbdūs, *Kitāb al-wuzarāʾ wa al-kuttāb*, Cairo, 1938
Nuṣūṣ ḍāʾiʿa min kitāb al-wuzarāʾ wa al-kuttāb, ed. M. Awwad, Beirut, 1965
Jarīrī, al-Muʿafā ibn Zakariyya, *al-Jalīs al-ṣāliḥ al-kāfī*, Beirut, 1987
Jastrow, M., *Sefer millīm: Dictionary of the Targumim, Talmud Babli, Yerushalmi, and Midrashic Literature*, New York, 1992
John of Cori, *Cathay and the Way Thither: Being a Collection of Medieval Notices on China*, vol. III, ed./trans. H. Yule, and H. Cordier, London, 1916
John Lydus, *On the Magistrates*, ed./trans. T. F. Carney, in *Bureaucracy in Traditional Society: Roman-Byzantine Bureaucracies Viewed from Within*, vol. II, Kansas, 1971
Jones, A. H. M., *The Later Roman Empire 284–602*, Oxford, 1964
Juwaynī, ʿAtāʾ Malik, *Tārīkh-i jahān gushā*, ed. M. M. Qazwīnī, 3 volumes, Leiden and London, 1912, 1916, and 1937; trans. J. A. Boyle, *The History of the World Conqueror*, 2 volumes, Manchester, 1958
Jwaideh, W., *The Introductory Chapter to Yāqūt's Muʿjam al-Buldān*, Leiden, 1959
Kabir, M., *The Buwayhid Dynasty of Baghdad*, Calcutta, 1964
Kaegi, W., *Byzantium and the Early Islamic Conquests*, Cambridge, 1992
Kāfaḥ, Y., *Ḥamesh megīlloth*, Jerusalem, 1962
Kalīla wa Dimna, Tunis, 1997
Kashghārī, Maḥmūd, *Dīwān lughāt al-turk*, ed./trans. R. Dankoff, *Compendium of the Turkic Dialects*, Cambridge Mass., 1984
Kelly, C., *Ruling the Later Roman Empire*, Cambridge, Mass., 2004
Kemal, S., *The Poetics of al-Fārābī and Avicenna*, Leiden, 1991
Kennedy, H., *The Early Abbasid Caliphate*, Cambridge, 1981
The Courts of the Caliphs: The Rise and Fall of Islam's Greatest Dynasty, London, 2004
Khan, G., *Arabic Documents from Early Islamic Khurasan*, London, 2006
Khazanov, A., 'Muhammad and Jenghiz Khan Compared: The Religious Factor in World Empire Building', *Comparative Studies in Society and History* 35iii (1993), 461–79
Kindī, Muḥammad ibn Yūsuf, *Wulā miṣr*, Beirut, 1959
Kinnier Wilson, J., *The Nimrud Wine Lists*, London, 1972
Kitāb al-tāj fī akhlāq al-mulūk, trans. Ch. Pellat, *Le Livre de la couronne*, Paris, 1954
Klein, E., *A Comprehensive Etymological Dictionary of the Hebrew Language for Readers of English*, Jerusalem, 1987
Kogan, L., 'Addenda et Corrigenda to the Hamito-Semitic Etymological Dictionary by V. Orel and O. Stolbova', *JSS* 47 (2002), 183–202
Kolb, A., *Transport und Nachrichtentransfer im römischen Reich*, Berlin, 2000
Kotwicz, W., 'Contributions aux études altaïques A: les termes concernant le service des relais postaux', *Rocznik Orientalistyczny* 16 (1950)
Krachkovsky, I., *Izbranniye Sočineniya (= Selected Works)*, Moscow, 1955
Kraemer, C. J., *Excavations at Nessana III: Administrative Documents*, Princeton, 1950
Kramer, N., 'Das Itinerar Stathmoi Parthikoi des Isidor von Charax: Beschreibung eines Handelsweges?', *Klio* 85 (2003), 120–30

Kurz, O., 'Cultural Relations between Parthia and Rome', *The Cambridge History of Iran III*, Cambridge, 1983

Lambton, A. K. S., 'Mongol Fiscal Administration in Persia', *Studia Islamica* 64 (1986) 77–99; and 65 (1987), 97–123

Continuity and Change in Medieval Persia: Aspects of Administrative, Economic and Social History, 11th–14th Centuries, London, 1988

Lane, E. W., *Arabic-English Lexicon*, London and Edinburgh, 1863

Lane, G., *Early Mongol Rule in Thirteenth-Century Iran*, London, 2003

Genghis Khan and Mongol Rule, London, 2004

Lassner, J., *The Shaping of Abbasid Rule*, Princeton, 1980

Le Strange, G., *The Lands of the Eastern Caliphate*, Cambridge, 1905

Lee, A. H., *Information and Frontiers: Roman Foreign Relations in Late Antiquity*, Cambridge, 1993

Leighton, A. C., 'The Mule as a Cultural Invention', *Technology and Culture* 8i (1967), 45–52

'Secret Communication amongst the Greeks and Romans', *Technology and Culture* 10ii (1969), 139–54

Transport and Communication in Medieval Europe AD 500–1100, Newton Abbot, 1972

Levanoni, A., *A Turning Point in Mamluk History: The Third Reign of al-Nāṣir Muḥammad ibn Qalāwūn (1310–41)*, Leiden, 1995

Levi della Vida, G., *Arabic Papyri in the University Museum in Philadelphia (Pennsylvania)*, Rome, 1981

Lewis, B., *Islam: From the Prophet Muhammad to the Capture of Constantinople*, Oxford, 1987

Lewy, J., 'The Problems Inherent in Section 70 of the Bisutun Inscription', *Hebrew Union College Annual* 25 (1954), 169–208

Lindenberger, J. M., *The Aramaic Proverbs of Aḥīqar*, Baltimore and London, 1983

Lindner, R. P., 'How Mongol were the Early Ottomans?', in R. Amitai-Preiss and D. O. Morgan (eds.), *The Mongol Empire and its Legacy*, Leiden, 1999

Lunde, P., and C. Stone, *Masudi: The Meadows of Gold – the Abbasids*, London and New York, 1989

Luṭfī Pāshā, *Tewārīkh-i āl-i osmān*, Istanbul, 1341 AH

Das Asafname des Luṭfī Pāschā, ed./trans. R. Tschudi, Berlin, 1910

MacKenzie, D., *A Concise Pahlavi Dictionary*, Oxford, 1990

Maqrīzī, Tāqī al-Dīn Aḥmad, *Kitāb al-sulūk li maʿrifat duwal al-mulūk*, Cairo, 1939–73

Ittiʿāẓ al-ḥunafāʾ bi-akhbār al-aʾimma al-fāṭimiyyīn al-khulafāʾ, Cairo, 1973

Kitāb al-mawāʿiẓ wa al-iʿtbār fī dhikr al-khiṭaṭ wa al-āthār, ed. A. F. Sayyid, London, 2002–4

Marco Polo, *The Travels of Marco Polo*, ed./trans. A. Ricci, London, 1950

Margoliouth, D. S., *Catalogue of Arabic Papyri in the John Rylands Library*, Manchester, 1933

Masʿūdī, ʿAlī ibn al-Ḥusayn, *Murūj al-dhahab wa maʿādin al-jawhar*, Beirut, 1965

Masson-Smith Jr., J., 'Mongol and Nomadic Taxation', *HJAS* 30 (1970), 46–85

'Mongol Nomadism and Middle Eastern Geography' in R. Amitai-Preiss and D.O. Morgan (eds.), *The Mongol Empire and its Legacy*, Leiden, 1999, pp. 39–56

Māwardī, ʿAlī ibn Muḥammad, *al-Aḥkām al-sulṭāniyya*, trans. W.H. Wahba, *al-Mawardi: The Ordinances of Government*, Beirut and London, 1996

Meier, S., *The Messenger in the Ancient Semitic World*, Cambridge Mass., 1988
'Women and Communication in the Ancient Near East', *JAOS* 111 (1991), 540–7
Melville, C. P., 'The Itineraries of Sultan Öljeitü, 1304–16', *Iran* 28 (1990), 55–70
'Padishah-i Islam: The Conversion of Ghazan to Islam', *Pembroke Papers* 1 (1990), 159–77
Menander Protector, *The History of Menander the Guardsman*, trans. R. C. Blockley, Liverpool, 1985
Mez, A., *The Renaissance of Islam*, trans. S. Khuda-Bukhsh and D. S. Margoliouth, New York, 1975
Miller, D. A., 'The Logothete of the Drome in the Middle Byzantine Period', *Byzantion* 36 (1966), 438–70
Minorsky, V., 'Tamīm ibn Baḥr's Journey to the Uyghurs', *BSOAS* 12ii (1948), 275–305
Miquel, A., *La Géographie humaine du monde musulman*, Paris, 1973
Moreen, V. B., *In Queen Esther's Garden*, New Haven, 2000
Morgan, D. O., 'Who Ran the Mongol Empire?', *JRAS* (1982), 124–36
The Mongols, Oxford, 1986
'Mongol or Persian: The Government of Il-khanid Iran', *HMEIS* 3 (1996), 62–76
'Reflections on Mongol Communications in the Ilkhanate', in C. Hillenbrand (ed.), *Studies in Honour of C. E. Bosworth*, vol. II, Leiden, 2000, pp. 375–85
'The Mongols in Iran: A Reappraisal', *Iran* 42 (2004), 131–6
'Cassiodorus and Rashīd al-Dīn on Barbarian Rule in Italy and Persia', reprinted in G. Hawting (ed.), *Muslims, Mongols, and Crusaders*, London and New York, 2005, pp. 151–69
Morony, M., *Iraq after the Muslim Conquest*, Princeton, 1984
'Syria under the Persians 610–629', in M. A. al-Bakhīt (ed.), *Proceedings of the Second Symposium on the History of Bilād al-Shām during the Early Islamic Period*, Amman, 1987, vol. I, pp. 87–95
Mufaḍḍaliyyāt, (ed. C. J. Lyall), Leiden, 1924
Mukhtārāt min al-qawānīn al-ʿuthmāniyya, Beirut, 1990
Munajjid, S., '*Qiṭʿa min kitāb mafqūd al-masālik wa al-mamālik li al-muhallabī*', *Majallat maʿhad al-makhṭūṭāt al-ʿarabiyya* 4 (1958), 43–72
Munaymana, H., *Taʾrīkh al-dawla al-buwayhiyya: al-siyāsī wa al-iqtiṣādī wa al-ijtimāʿī wa al-thaqāfī: muqāṭaʿat fāris*, Beirut, 1987
Muqaddasī, Muḥammad ibn Aḥmad, *Aḥsan al-taqāsīm fī maʿrifat al-aqālīm*, Leiden, 1879
Musil, A., *Arabia Deserta*, New York, 1927
Na'aman, N., 'The Distribution of Messages in the Kingdom of Judah in Light of the Lachish Ostraca', *Vetus Testamentum* 53 (2003), 169–80
Nahrawālī, Quṭb al-Dīn, *Kitāb al-iʿlām bi-aʿlām bayt allāh al-ḥaram*, Leipzig, 1857
Naser-i Khusraw's Book of Travels, (trans. W. M. Thackston Jr.), Costa Mesa, 2001
Nawawī, Yaḥyā ibn Sharaf, *Tahdhīb al-asmāʾ*, Göttingen, 1842–7
Nazim, M., *The Life and Times of Sulṭān Maḥmūd of Ghazna*, Cambridge, 1931
'The Pand-Nāmah of Sebuktigīn', *JRAS* (1933), 605–28
Nicol, N. D., 'Early Abbasid Administration in the Central and Eastern Provinces, 132–218 AH/750–833 AD', unpublished PhD dissertation, University of Washington, 1979
Needham, J., *Science and Civilisation in China*, vol. IV, Cambridge, 1971

Niẓām al-Mulk, *Siyāsat Nāma*, Tehran, 1985; trans. H. Darke, *The Book of Government*, London, 1978
Niẓāmī ʿArūḍī, *Chahār maqāla*, trans. E. G. Browne, *The Four Discourses*, London, 1921
Nöldeke, Th., *Geschichte der Perser und Araber zur Zeit der Sasaniden*, Leiden, 1879
Noth, A., and L. I. Conrad, *The Early Arabic Historical Tradition: A Source-Critical Study*, trans. M. Bonner, New Jersey, 1994
Nuwayrī, Shihāb al-Dīn, *Nihāyat al-arab fī funūn al-adab*, Cairo, 1992
Nyberg, H. S., *A Manual of Pahlavi, Part II: Glossary*, Wiesbaden, 1974
Odoric: *Cathay and the Way Thither: Being a Collection of Medieval Notices on China*, vol. II, ed./trans. H. Yule and H. Cordier, London, 1913
Olbricht, P., *Das Postwesen in China unter der Mongolenherrschaft im 13. und 14. Jahrhundert*, Wiesbaden, 1954
Oller, G. H., 'Messengers and Ambassadors in Ancient West Asia', in J. M. Sasson (ed.), *Civilizations of the Near East III*, New York, 1995, 1465–73
Oppenheim, A. L., 'The Eyes of the Lord', *JAOS* 88 (1968), 173–9
Ostler, N., *Empires of the Word: A Language History of the World*, London, 2005
Ostrowski, D., 'The Mongol Origins of Muscovite Political Institutions', *Slavic Review* 49 (1990), 525–42
Parthian Stations: Schoff, W. H., *The Parthian Stations by Isidore of Charax*, London, 1914
Pegolotti, Francesco Balducci, *La pratica della mercatura*, ed. A. Evans, Cambridge, Mass., 1936
Pelliot, P., 'Sur yam ou jam, "relais postale"', *T'oung Pao* 27 (1930), 192–5
Pfeiffer, R. H., *State Letters of Assyria: A Transliteration and Translation of 355 Official Assyrian Letters dating from the Sargonid Period (722–625 BC)*, New Haven, 1935
Photius, *Persica*, trans. J. H. Freese, London, 1920
Pliny, *Natural History*, Cambridge Mass., 1938–62
Polotsky, H. J., 'Aramäisch *prš* und das "Huzvaresch"', *Le Muséon* 45 (1932), 273–83
Poppe, N., *The Mongolian Monuments in HPʿAGS-PA Script*, trans. J. R. Krueger, Wiesbaden, 1957
Popper, W., *Egypt and Syria under the Circassian Sultans: 1384–1468: Systematic Notes to Ibn Taghribirdī's Chronicle of Egypt*, California, 1955–7
Porten, B., *Archives from Elephantine*, Los Angeles, 1968
Preuss, J., *Biblical and Talmudic Medicine*, London, 1993
Procopius, *Buildings*, trans. H. B. Dewing, Cambridge Mass., 1961
History of the Wars of Justinian, trans. H. B. Dewing, Cambridge Mass., 1961–8
Anecdota, trans. H. B. Dewing, Cambridge Mass., 1969
Qābūs Nāma: *A Mirror for Princes: The Qābūs Nāma by Kay Qāʾūs ibn Iskandar*, trans. R. Levy, London, 1951
Qalqashandī, Aḥmad ibn ʿAbdallāh, *Ṣubḥ al-aʿshāʾ fī ṣināʿat al-inshāʾ*, Cairo, 1918–22
Qazwīnī, Ḥamdallāh Mustawfī, *Nuzhat al-qulūb*, ed./trans. G. le Strange, *The Geographical Part of the Nuzhat al-Qulub*, London, 1915–19
Tārīkh-i guzīda, Tehran, 1958–61
Qūchānī, A., '*Pāʾiza*', *Mīrāth-i Farhangī* 17 (1997), 42–5
Qudāma ibn Jaʿfar, [*Kitāb*] *al-Kharāj wa ṣināʿat al-kitāba*, Baghdad, 1981
Rachewiltz, I. de, 'Sino-Mongol Culture Contacts in the 13th Century', unpublished PhD thesis, Australian National University, 1960

'Personnel and Personalities in North China in the Early Mongol Period', *JESHO* 9 (1966), 88–144

Papal Envoys to the Great Khans, London, 1971

Ragheb (= Raghib), Y., 'Lettres de service au maître de poste d'Ašmun', *Archéologie Islamique* 3 (1992), 5–16

'La Transmission des nouvelles en terres d'Islam', in *La Circulation des nouvelles au moyen âge*, (no editor), Rome, 1994, pp. 37–48

Les Messagers volants en terres d'Islam, Paris, 2002

Ramsay, A. W., 'A Roman Postal Service under the Republic', *The Journal of Roman Studies* 10 (1920), 79–86

'The Speed of the Roman Imperial Post', *The Journal of Roman Studies* 15 (1925), 60–74

Rashīd al-Dīn, Faḍlallāh, *Jāmiʿ al-tawārīkh*, vol. II/i, ed. A. A. Alizade, Moscow, 1980; vol. II, ed. E. Blochet, Leiden and London, 1911; trans. J. A. Boyle, *The Successors of Genghis Khan*, New York and London, 1971; vol. III, ed. A. A. Alizade, Baku, 1957

al-Rashid, S. A., *Darb Zubaydah: The Pilgrim Road from Kufa to Mecca*, Riyad, 1980

Renaudot, E., *Ancient Accounts of India and China*, Delhi, 1995 (reprint from London, 1733)

Richards, D. S., 'The Mamluk Barīd: Some Evidence from the Haram Documents', in M. A. al-Bakhit (ed.), *Studies in the History and Archaeology of Jordan III*, Amman, 1987

Robinson, C. F., *ʿAbd al-Malik*, Oxford, 2005

Rostowzew, M., 'Angaria', *Klio* 6 (1906), 249–58

Rubin, Z., 'The Reforms of Khusrô Anūshirvān', in A. Cameron (ed.), *Studies in Late Antiquity and Early Islam III*, Princeton, 1995, pp. 225–97

'Ibn al-Muqaffaʿ and the Account of Sasanian History in the Arabic Codex Sprenger 30', *JSAI* 30 (2005), 52–93

Sabahuddin, S., 'The Postal System during the Muslim Rule in India', *Islamic Culture* 18iii (1944), 269–82

Sabar, Y., *A Jewish Neo-Aramaic Dictionary*, Wiesbaden, 2002

Ṣābiʾ, Hilāl ibn al-Muḥassin, *Kitāb al-wuzarāʾ*, Beirut, 1904

Rusūm dār al-khilāfa, ed. M. Awwad, Baghdad, 1964

Sachau, E., *Routen in Mesopotamien*, Leipzig, 1882

Sadan, J., and A. Silverstein, 'Ornate Manuals or Practical Adab? Some Reflections on a Unique Work by an Anonymous Author of the 10th Century CE', *al-Qanṭara* 25ii (2004), 339–54

Saʿdawi, N., *Niẓām al-barīd fī al-dawla al-islāmiyya*, Cairo, 1953

Ṣafadī, Khalīl ibn Aybak, *Kitāb al-wāfī bi al-wafāyāt*, Wiesbaden, 1931–

Saffār, Muḥammad, *Disorienting Encounters: Travels of a Moroccan Scholar in France in 1845–6*, ed./trans. S. G. Miller, Berkeley, 1992

Samyutta-Nikaya part two, London, 1888

Saunders, J. J., 'The Nomad as Empire-Builder: A Comparison of the Arab and Mongol Conquests', in his *Muslims and Mongols*, ed. G. Rice, Christchurch, NZ, 1977, pp. 36–66

Sauvaget, J., *La Poste aux chevaux dans l'empire des Mamelouks*, Paris, 1941

Schaeder, H. H., *Iranica I: Das Auge des Königs*, Berlin, 1934

Schoeler, G., 'Verfasser und Titel des dem Ǧāḥiẓ zugeschriebenen sog. *Kitāb al-Tāǧ*', *ZDMG* 130 (1980), 217–25

Secret History: U. Onon (trans.), *The Secret History of the Mongols*, London, 2001; and I. de Rachewiltz, *The Secret History of the Mongols*, Leiden, 2004. All references are to Onon's translation unless otherwise stated.

Shaban, M., *The Abbasid Revolution*, Cambridge, 1970

Shahid, I., 'The Arabs in the Peace Treaty of AD 561', *Arabica* 3 (1956), 181–213

ShāhNāma: ed. T. Macan, Calcutta, 1829; trans. A.G. Warner and E. Warner, London, 1912–25

Shaked, S., 'Two Judaeo-Iranian Contributions: 1. Iranian Functions in the Book of Esther', *Irano-Judaica* 1 (1982), 292–303

Shapira, D., 'Judeo-Persian Translations of Old Persian Lexica', in L. Paul (ed.), *Persian Origins*, Wiesbaden, 2003

Sharon, M., 'An Arabic Inscription from the time of Abd al-Malik', *BSOAS* 29 (1966), 369–72

Black Banners from the East, Jerusalem, 1983

Sheldon, R. M., *Intelligence Activities in Ancient Rome*, London, 2004

Sijpesteijn, P. M., 'The Muslim Conquest and the First Fifty Years of Muslim Rule in Egypt', in R. Bagnall (ed.), *Egypt in the Byzantine World*, Cambridge, 2007

Silverstein, A., 'Etymologies and Origins: A Note of Caution', *British Journal of Middle Eastern Studies*, 28i (2001), 92–4

'A New Source on the Early History of the *Barīd*', *al-Abḥāth* 50–1 (2002–3), 121–34

'On Some Aspects of the Abbasid *Barīd*', in J. E. Montgomery (ed.), *Abbasid Studies: Occasional Papers of the School of ʿAbbasid Studies*, Leuven, 2004, 23–32

'Documentary Evidence for the Early History of the *Barīd*', in P. M. Sijpesteijn and L. Sundelin (eds.), *Papyrology and the History of Early Islamic Egypt*, Leiden, 2004, 153–61

'A Neglected Chapter in the History of Caliphal State-Building', *JSAI* 30 (2005), 293–317

Simidchieva, M., '*Siyāsat Nāme* Revisited: The Question of Authenticity', in *Proceedings of the Second European Conference of Iranian Studies*, ed. B. Fragner et al., Rome, 1995, pp. 657–74

Sinnigen, W. G., 'Two Branches of the Late Roman Secret Service', *The American Journal of Philology* 80 (1959), 238–54

'The Roman Secret Service', *The Classical Journal* 57ii (1971), 65–72

Sokoloff, M., *A Dictionary of Jewish Babylonian Aramaic of the Talmudic and Geonic Periods*, Baltimore, 2002

A Dictionary of Jewish Palestinian Aramaic of the Byzantine Period, Baltimore, 2002

Sourdel, D., *Le Vizirat Abbaside de 749 à 936*, Paris, 1959

Sperber, D., 'Angaria in Rabbinic Literature', *L'Antiquité Classique* 38i (1969), 162–8

Sprenger, A., *Die Post- und Reiserouten des Orients*, Leipzig, 1864

Stephens, M., *A History of News: From the Drum to the Satellite*, London, 1997

Subkī, *Kitāb muʿīd al-niʿam wa mubīd al-niqam*, London, 1908

Suetonius, *The Lives of the Caesars I: Julius. Augustus. Tiberius. Gaius. Caligula*, trans. J.C. Rolfe, Cambridge Mass., 1998

Suleman, M., 'The Role of Intelligence in the Successful Defense of Medina in AH 5', *Islamic Quarterly* 28 (1984), 47–52

'Espionage in Pre-Islamic Arabia', *Islamic Quarterly* 32 (1988), 21–33

Ṣūlī, Muḥammad ibn Yaḥyā, *Adab al-kuttāb*, Cairo, 1341 AH
Sun Tzu, *The Art of War*, trans. S. B. Griffith, Oxford, 1963
Sykes, E. C. *Through Persia on a Side-Saddle*, London, 1898
Ṭabarī, Muḥammad ibn Jarīr, *Ta'rīkh al-rusul wa al-mulūk*, Leiden 1879–1901; trans. (various) *The History of al-Ṭabarī*, ed. E. Yarshater, 39 vols., Albany, 1989–98
Tafazzoli, A., *Sasanian Society*, Cambridge Mass., 2000
Tansar: The Letter of Tansar, trans. M. Boyce, Rome, 1968
Tanūkhī, Muḥassin ibn ʿAlī, *Nishwār al-muḥāḍara wa akhbār al-mudhākara*, Beirut, 1972
Tawḥīdī, Abū Ḥayyān, *al-Baṣā'ir wa al-dhakhā'ir*, Damascus, 1964
Thaʿālibī, ʿAbd al-Malik ibn Muḥammad, *Ghurar akhbār mulūk al-furs*, Paris, 1900
Yatīmat al-dahr, Cairo, 1934
Laṭā'if al-maʿārif, trans. C. E. Bosworth, *The Book of Curious and Entertaining Information*, Edinburgh, 1968
Thimār al-qulūb fī al-muḍāf wa al-mansūb, ed. M. A. F. Ibrahim, Cairo, 1985
Theodore of Sykeon, *Vie de Théodore de Sykéon*, ed./trans. A. J. Festugière, Brussels, 1970
Thompson, S., *Motif-Index of Traditional Folk Literature*, Bloomington, 1955
Threadgold, W., *Byzantium and the Army, 284–1081*, Stanford, 1995
Treadwell, L., 'Ibn Ẓāfir al-Azdī's Account of the Murder of Aḥmad ibn Ismāʿīl al-Sāmānī and the Succession of his Son Naṣr', in C. Hillenbrand (ed.), *Studies in Honour of C. E. Bosworth*, vol. II, Leiden, 2000, 397–419
Tübinger Atlas des Vorderen Orients, Wiesbaden, 1977
Ullmann, M., *Zur Geschichte des Wortes Barīd, 'Post'*, Munich, 1997
ʿUmarī, Ibn Faḍlallāh, *al-Taʿrīf bi al-muṣṭalaḥ al-sharīf*, Cairo, 1894
Unvala, J. M., *The Pahlavi Text King Husrav and his Boy*, Paris, 1921
Utas, B., 'The Judeo-Persian Fragment from Dandān Uiliq', *Orientalia Suecana* 17 (1968), 123–36
Van't Dack, E., 'Postes et télécommunications ptolémaïques', *Chronique d'Egypte* 73 (1962), 338–41
Vasiliev, A., 'Harun ibn Yahya and his Description of Constantinople', *Seminarium Kondakaovinium* 5 (1932), 149–63
Vegetius, *Epitoma rei militaris*, Stuttgart, 1885
Wagner, A. (ed.), *Bote und Brief: sprachliche Systeme der Informationsübermittlung im Spannungsfeld von Mündlichkeit und Schriftlichkeit*, Frankfurt am Main, 2003
Waṣṣāf, ʿAbdallāh ibn Faḍlallāh: *Tajziyat al-amṣār wa tajziyat al-aʿṣār*, trans. J. Hammer-Purgstall, *Geschichte Wassafs*, Vienna, 1856
Weber, D., *Corpus inscriptionum iranicarum: Part III Pahlavi Inscriptions, Ostraca, Papyri und Pergamente*, London, 1992
Wensinck, A., *Concordance et indices de la tradition musulmane*, Leiden, 1936–88
Whelan, E., 'Representations of the Khāṣṣakīyah and the Origins of Mamluk Emblems', in P. Soucek (ed.), *Content and Context of Visual Arts in the Islamic World*, New York 1988, 219–43
White, L. jr., *Medieval Technology and Social Change*, New York, 1966
Wiesehöfer, J., *Ancient Persia from 550 BC to 650 AD*, trans. A. Azadi, London, 1996
William of Rubruck, *The Journey of William of Rubruck to the Eastern Parts of the World, 1253–55, as Narrated by Himself, with Two Accounts of the Earlier Journey of John of Pian de Carpine*, trans. W. W. Rockhill, London, 1900

Wittfogel, K., *Oriental Despotism: A Comparative Study of Total Power*, New Haven, 1957
Xenophon, *Cyropaedia*, trans. W. Miller, Cambridge Mass., 1968
Ya'qūbī, Aḥmad ibn Abī Ya'qūb, *Ta'rīkh*, Leiden, 1883
Kitāb al-buldān, Leiden, 1861
Yāqūt ibn 'Abdallāh al-Ḥamawī, *Mu'jam al-buldān*, ed. F. Wustenfeld, Leipzig, 1869
Yarshater, E., 'Were the Sassanians Heirs to the Achaemenids?', in *La Persia nel medioevo*, Rome, 1971, pp. 517–33
Yezdi, Sharafuddin Ali, *The Political and Military Institutes of Tamerlane*, trans. J. Davy, New Delhi, 1972
Yūsuf Khāṣṣ Ḥājib, *The Wisdom of Royal Glory(Kutadgu Bilig): A Turko-Islamic Mirror for Princes*, trans. R. Dankoff, Chicago, 1983
Zachariah of Mitylene, *The Syriac Chronicle Known as that of Zachariah of Mitylene*, ed./trans. E. W. Brooks and F. J. Hamilton, London, 1899
Zamakhsharī, Maḥmūd ibn 'Umar, *al-Fā'iq fī gharīb al-ḥadīth*, Hyderabad, 1906
Zilliacus, L., *From Pillar to Post: The Troubled History of the Mail*, London, 1956
Zubaydī, Muḥammad al-Murtaḍā ibn Muḥammad, *Tāj al-'arūs min jawāhir al-qāmūs*, vol. VII, Kuwait, 1970
Zubayr ibn Bakkār, *Jamharat nasab quraysh*, Beirut, 1962

Index

paykān, 130, 160, 163, 191
Pegolotti, Francesco, 161
perishables, transported via the postal system, 81–2, 134, 164, 181, 187, 191
Persepolis Fortification Tablets (= *PF*), 12, 15, 18, 20, 27
philosophers, use postal metaphors, 137–40
Phocas (Byzantine Emperor, r. 602–10), 35
pigeons, homing, 113–14, 116, 132, 168, 177, 188
pilgrims, 36, 58
pirradaziš (Elamite term for 'express courier'), 18
plague, 182
Pliny, 69
Praetorian Prefect, 36, 40
prisoners, transported by the *Barīd*, 98
private postal systems, 2, 93, 106, 114, 116, 124 (see also: 'Merchants')
Procopius, 33, 34, 35, 38, 39, 41, 117, 191
Ptolemaic Egypt, 103
punishment, for postal delays, 134

Qā'im, al-, 121
qāḍīs, 72, 106, 158
Qajar Iran, 20, 44, 66, 76
Qalqashandī, 133, 166, 173, 175, 180, 181, 182, 183, 184
Qarāmiṭa, 111, 113, 114, 132
Qubilai Khān, 153, 159
Qudāma ibn Ja'far, 93, 94, 99, 102–3, 192
Qur'ān, 48, 138, 140
Qurra ibn Sharīk, 67, 71–2

Rāfi' ibn Harthama, 112
Ragheb, Y., 113
rāhdār, 86
Rashī, 10, 11
Rashīd al-Dīn, 148, 151, 155, 157–8, 159, 161
raṣṣīm (Hebrew term for 'couriers'), 11, 18, 38, 124
rāzbān (Persian term for 'bearer of secrets'), 38
rebellions, reported by the *Barīd*, 79–80
rebels (see also: 'Bandits'):
  transported via postal system, 57, 81
  disrupt postal system, 61, 65, 80–1, 87, 92–3, 107, 177–8, 186
  traced by the *Barīd*, 75
  use pigeon-couriers, 114
ribāṭ, 47, 48, 131
Richards, D. S., 183
risāla mughalghala, 44–5, 47, 55, 84
'Royal Road', 12–13
r.s.l. (Arabic root), 7, 138
Rubruck, William of, 145, 149, 150
runners, 24, 68, 78, 88, 133–4, 160, 163, 169, 183, 188, 192

Sa'adiya Gaon, 18
safīr, 122
Ṣāḥib al-akhbār (or *al-khabar*), 114–15, 127, 128, 130, 136, 138
Ṣāḥib al-Barīd (pl. *aṣḥāb al-barīd*):
  Umayyad, 70, 75, 84
  Abbasid, 62, 65, 67, 79–80, 118, 125, 126, 172
  according to *Siyāsat al-Mulūk*, 97, 101, 103–8
  according to Qudāma, 102
  compared with the *Mushrif*, 116
  Samanid, 125, 127, 128
  Ghaznavid, 125, 128, 129, 130
  according to Niẓām al-Mulk, 137
  used metaphorically, 139
Ṣāḥib Dīwān al-Barīd, 90, 99, 102, 103, 123
Ṣāḥib Dīwān al-Kharāj, 100–1
Ṣāḥib al-ḥaras, 65
Ṣāḥib khabar al-'askar, 82, 114
Ṣāḥib al-Ma'ūna, 101
Ṣāḥib al-Shurṭa, 73
Sa'īd ibn al-'Āṣ, 44, 47
safety along roads, 13–15
Samanids, 125–8
Samaritans, 26, 107, 178
Sauvaget, J., 165, 166, 167, 178
Sebüktigin, 128–9
Secret History of the Mongols, 146, 147, 151
Seljuks, 115, 131, 136–7
Seljuks, lack of a postal system, 136–7, 169
Seven Sleepers, 90
Shahid, I., 49
ShāhNāma, 17–18, 23, 24, 25, 28
Shāh Rukh, 163
Shāpūr II (Sasanid ruler, r. 309–79), 25
Sharaf al-Dawla (Uqaylid *amīr*), 115
Sharaf al-Dawla (Buyid ruler), 134
shu'ūbiyya, 4, 29
signet ring, for the postal system, 28, 74
Sikandar Lodi, 187
sikka, 47, 64, 93–8
Silk Road, 149
Siyāsat al-Mulūk, 87, 97, 99–102, 103–4, 107, 112, 118, 133, 134, 187, 191
slave-soldiers, 89, 99, 113, 169, 172, 184
Solomon, 61
sources, 4–6, 49, 57–8, 71, 91, 144, 145, 154, 155, 166–7, 189
speed of:
  Achaemenid postal system, 13, 191
  Barīd, 66, 81–2, 97, 107, 191, 192
  Buyid couriers, 133, 134, 135, 191, 192
  Cursus Publicus, 31, 191
  Ghaznavid couriers, 130
  homing pigeons, 168
  Mamluk *Barīd*, 176
  merchant postal networks, 119, 193

Cambridge Studies in Islamic Civilization

Other titles in the series

Popular Culture in Medieval Cairo*
Boaz Shoshan

Early Philosophical Shiism
The Ismaili Neoplatonism of Abū Ya'qūb al-Sijistānī
Paul E. Walker

Indian Merchants and Eurasian Trade, 1600–1750*
Stephen Frederic Dale

Palestinian Peasants and Ottoman Officials*
Rural Administration around Sixteenth-century Jerusalem
Amy Singer

Arabic Historical Thought in the Classical Period*
Tarif Khalidi

Mongols and Mamluks*
The Mamluk-Īlkhānid War, 1260–1281
Reuven Amitai-Preiss

Hierarchy and Egalitarianism in Islamic Thought*
Louise Marlow

The Politics of Households in Ottoman Egypt*
The Rise of the Qazdağlis
Jane Hathaway

Commodity and Exchange in the Mongol Empire*
A Cultural History of Islamic Textiles
Thomas T. Allsen

State and Provincial Society in the Ottoman Empire*
Mosul, 1540–1834
Dina Rizk Khoury

The Mamluks in Egyptian Politics and Society
Thomas Philipp and Ulrich Haarmann (eds.)

The Delhi Sultanate*
A Political and Military History
Peter Jackson

European and Islamic Trade in the Early Ottoman State*
The Merchants of Genoa and Turkey
Kate Fleet

Reinterpreting Islamic Historiography
Harun al-Rashid and the Narrative of the ʿAbbāsid Caliphate
Tayeb El-Hibri

The Ottoman City between East and West*
Aleppo, Izmir, and Istanbul
Edhem Eldem, Daniel Goffman and Bruce Masters

A Monetary History of the Ottoman Empire*
Sevket Pamuk

The Politics of Trade in Safavid Iran*
Silk for Silver, 1600–1730
Rudolph P. Matthee

The Idea of Idolatry and the Emergence of Islam*
From Polemic to History
G. R. Hawting

Classical Arabic Biography
The Heirs of the Prophets in the Age of al-Maʾmūn
Michael Cooperson

Empire and Elites after the Muslim Conquest*
The Transformation of Northern Mesopotamia
Chase F. Robinson

Poverty and Charity in Medieval Islam
Mamluk Egypt, 1250–1517
Adam Sabra

Christians and Jews in the Ottoman Arab World*
The Roots of Sectarianism
Bruce Masters

Culture and Conquest in Mongol Eurasia*
Thomas T. Allsen

Revival and Reform in Islam*
The Legacy of Muhammad al-Shawkani
Bernard Haykel

Tolerance and Coercion in Islam*
Interfaith Relations in the Muslim Tradition
Yohanan Friedmann

Guns for the Sultan
Military Power and the Weapons Industry in the Ottoman Empire
Gábor Ágoston

Marriage, Money and Divorce in Medieval Islamic Society
Yossef Rapoport

The Empire of the Qara Khitai in Eurasian History
Between China and the Islamic World
Michal Biran

Domesticity and Power in the Mughal World*
Ruby Lal

Power, Politics and Religion in Timurid Iran
Beatrice Forbes Manz

Postal Systems in the Pre-Modern Islamic World
Adam J. Silverstein

* also available as paperback

Printed in Great Britain
by Amazon

46326403R00131